The illustration
is nothing to you without the application.
You lack half wit. You crush all the particles down
into close conformity, and then walk back and forth on them.

Marianne Moore
To a Steam Roller

Rather than an unsubstantiated account there should be a comprehensive and complete study; rather than exaggerated declarations there should be thoughtful assertions; rather than wild opinions, there should be factual observations. The first law of history is never dare to lie. The second is never fear to tell the truth.

Leo XIII
Saepenumero Considerantes

When then we meet with grave and obvious instances of misrepresentation, and these are repeated from writer to writer, strong suspicion is thrown at once over all such interpretations. . . . These writers are discovered to have taken points for granted, which they had better have examined for themselves, and which turn out to be mistakes.

John Henry Newman
Essays Critical and Historical 2

Were the Popes Against the Jews?

Tracking the Myths, Confronting the Ideologues

Justus George Lawler

WILLIAM B. EERDMANS PUBLISHING COMPANY

GRAND RAPIDS, MICHIGAN / CAMBRIDGE, U.K.

Published 2012 by
Wm. B. Eerdmans Publishing Co.
2140 Oak Industrial Drive N.E., Grand Rapids, Michigan 49505 /
P.O. Box 163, Cambridge CB3 9PU U.K.

Printed in the United States of America

18 17 16 15 14 13 12   7 6 5 4 3 2 1

Library of Congress Cataloging-in-Publication Data

Lawler, Justus George.
Were the Popes against the Jews? : tracking the myths, confronting the ideologues /
Justus George Lawler.
p.   cm.
ISBN 978-0-8028-6629-5 (pbk.: alk. paper)
1. Judaism — Relations — Catholic Church — History.
2. Catholic Church — Relations — Judaism — History.
3. Papacy — History.   4. Antisemitism — History.
5. Christianity and antisemitism — History.
6. Leo XIII, Pope, 1810-1903 — Relations with Jews.
7. Pius X, Pope, 1835-1914 — Relations with Jews.
8. Pius XI, Pope, 1857-1939 — Relations with Jews.
9. Pius XII, Pope, 1876-1958 — Relations with Jews.   I. Title.

BM535.L348   2011
261.2'60903 — dc23

2011022240

www.eerdmans.com

For Ursula Z. Zyzik
Friend and Colleague at SXU
Custodian, Reader, and Lover of Books
Indefatigable Researcher of the History of Ideas

In Memory of Philipp P. Fehl
Friend and Colleague at U of C
Translator at the Nuremberg Trials
Devoted Historian of the Venetian School

Contents

Introduction

To the question in the title of this book, were the popes against the Jews? the answer is, *of course they were.* Their entire tradition was built on the belief that Judaism prepared the way for Jesus and his message, both of which the Jews had rejected. However, a completely different and far more complex answer would have to be given to the more precise question, was the papacy against Judaism and the Jewish people in the manner in which it has been depicted in numerous recent works written by some Catholics, nonbelievers, and Jews? In these books the popes were described as disdainful, contemptuous, and vengeful toward Jews and their beliefs.

Answering that question is the purpose of the present book — which has its own brief history. A year or two after the appearance of the paperback edition of *Popes and Politics: Reform, Resentment, and the Holocaust* (2004), and while aimlessly thumbing through the book, the thought occurred to me that what was now needed was an evaluation of the flood of works that had appeared around the beginning of this century on the church and the papacy in relation to Judaism and the Holocaust. Usually when a writer is speculating on a possible future project, the best way to give it a sense of concrete reality is to give it a name. Since several of these books appeared to be self-serving polemics, I thought the ideal title might be from W. H. Auden, "a low dishonest decade." Unfortunately, that phrase had already become cliché, so it made sense to just give it a simple and direct working title, and a more precise and explanatory subtitle. Thus was conceived *Historians Against History: Inventing Catholic Scapegoats 2000-2010*. The subtitle made clear that this project, if it ever came to fruition, would be a critique of the critics, many of whom were writing in the shadow or under the influence of *The Deputy* by Rolf Hochhuth.

In the event, around 2006 I decided to proceed with the book, and made the criterion for inclusion works that had not been discussed in sufficient detail in *Popes and Politics*. Such titles as the following were on the list, though my remarks on each of them would be expressed in varying degrees of praise or censure. Gerhard Beiser, *The Holy See and Hitler's Germany;* Frank J. Coppa, *The Papacy, the Jews, and the Holocaust;* John Cornwell, *Hitler's Pope: The Secret History of Pius XII;* Beth Griech-Polelle, *Bishop von Galen;* Peter Godman, *Hitler and the Vatican;* Daniel J. Goldhagen, *A Moral Reckoning;* Robert Katz, *The Battle for Rome;* David I. Kertzer, *The Popes Against the Jews;* Dan Kurzman, *A Special Mission: Hitler's Secret Plot to Seize the Vatican and Kidnap Pope Pius XII;* Garry Wills, *Why I Am a Catholic.* There were also a few other titles that had appeared later in the decade, and that could be included as seemed suitable or necessary.

After wrestling with the project for another couple of years, and seeing it balloon to more than 200,000 words, it became obvious that I needed a change in direction. As the editor of several trade publishing imprints, no one knew better than I that big fat books are the bane of the business, even the business of publishing for "intellectually engaged general readers" — ideally the target audience. In the midst of confronting this relatively massive body of work, there emerged from the recesses of my memory, unexpectedly and inexplicably, this fragment of poetry: "this grew. I gave commands." (The recollection of such fragments was not all that unusual, since in addition to being an editor, I had also over the years taught courses in English poetry, and had written several books on it, probably the most notable — or at least the most wide-ranging — being *Celestial Pantomime: Poetic Structures of Transcendence.*) This particular fragment was from Robert Browning, but whereas what he had in mind was cutting short the life of his "last duchess," I had in mind simply a last ditch effort at cutting short an excessively long project — which I proceeded to do.

The decision was not all that difficult since one book, *The Popes Against the Jews,* had already received a critique that was far longer than that for any of the others, and it was also a book that would put to the test my own sense of objectivity, since I had mentioned it favorably in *Popes and Politics.* The obvious reason for this favorable opinion was simply that few people in the twenty-first century would deny that not only the popes but most of the Christian tradition had been "against the Jews," a fact made quite clear by the conventional term used among historians and theologians, *adversus Iudaeos.* That term defined a unique genre of writing and a unique way of thinking about Jews which, from the fifth century and for more than a millennium after, had characterized both Christian theology and popular Christian sentiment.

An additional reason for concentrating on *The Popes Against the Jews* was that Kertzer focused on several popes in a period of nearly a century and a half, with emphasis on the popes from the end of the Napoleonic wars to World War II, while most of the other books focused on the popes immediately before and after World War II, with particular emphasis on Pius XII. (In fact, *The Battle for Rome* by the late Robert Katz was his third book covering the same fifteen months in the reign of that one pope.) Nevertheless, Kertzer's focus was still too broad for the kind of detailed analysis of deeds and texts in which I was engaged.

It was thus in the interests of that analysis — demanding greater precision and exactness — that I decided to omit some of Kertzer's background material and focus on what he himself defined in his subtitle as *The Vatican's Role in the Rise of Modern Anti-Semitism*. This meant taking seriously his own statement that "modern anti-Semitism began just after the collapse of the Papal States," that is, in the early 1860s. That further diminished the problem of excessive length as well as the concomitant problem of generalizations and broad conclusions being substituted for detailed and concise examination of crucial issues. It also reduced the number of those Jew-threatening popes from nine to five.

Fortuitously, this abridged chronological span meant that the book would be useful not only as a study of radically different individual popes, but also as a study of how the church as an institution had coped with unprecedented obstacles in the most crucial phase of its history since the Reformation. During that phase the institution went from confronting modernity head on — during most of the reign of Pius IX from the early 1850s to 1878 — to embracing it, however hesitantly, during the reign of his successor, Leo XIII, who died in 1903. That phenomenon of confrontation and embrace appears to be contradicted by Peter Berger's much quoted observation in *Invitation to Sociology* (1963): "Institutions carry within them a principle of inertia, perhaps founded ultimately on the hard rock of human stupidity." But in fact, since the principle of inertia is not merely one of stasis but of motion as well, it is just as accurate to say that the church in motion under Leo XIII continued in motion under his successors, as the steady forward impetus reflected not stupidity but stability, the stability of the hard rock of Peter.

Although the choice of Kertzer's book was based largely on chronology, there was also the fact that *The Popes Against the Jews* as a work of engaged scholarship was in many ways superior to several of the other possible candidates. Merely in terms of what might be called quantitative analysis, there was the fact that its endnotes and bibliography occupied forty-five pages of dense 8-point type, representing more than 15 percent of the text of the entire work. More significant, it was based on research carried out in several different languages and several different archives, facts of which the author also reminded the reader on several different occasions. The tone of that last clause indicates the gradual evolution from an original highly favorable impression of the book to a growing awareness that these expressions of self-satisfaction on the part of the author often signaled the onset of inaccurate translations, waffled data, and even doctored texts — serious failings that also transformed my original acceptance into accelerating disapproval.

As for the views of others on *The Popes Against the Jews,* it was a bestseller by an author whose previous book, *The Kidnapping of Edgardo Mortara,* was a National Book Award finalist, a rarity for a work on religious issues, much less on combustible ones. The only conceivable predecessor was a very Catholic memoir, *An American Requiem* by James Carroll — who did receive the Award, and who in the event would become a fan of Kertzer. By the latter's own estimation, *The Popes Against the Jews* received "glowing reviews" in the American, Canadian, and British press. *The New York Times* was the most exuberant with an unprecedented three reviews: one in the daily paper, one in the Sunday "Book Review," and another in the weekend "Arts & Ideas" section, the latter written by Carroll.

Even more significant than multiple reviews in the *Times* was the fate of both book *and* author in the larger culture. The book was instrumental in having Kertzer named to the American Academy of Arts and Sciences in 2005; in the same year it was translated into its ninth foreign language, Polish. In 2006, Kertzer was elected president of the Social Science History Association — an election that also hinged on the book. In 2007, Kertzer was featured in the PBS series of four programs, "The Secret Files of the Inquisition," which utilized material from the book. In 2010, he chaired "Pius XI and America: An International Conference" at Brown University to discuss "Latin American church/state politics, Italian fascism, and topics in Vatican diplomacy." The scholars participating in the conference were among the most distinguished church historians and theologians from three continents, and thus may be said to have given a kind of *imprimatur* to Kertzer's views on the papacy as essential to the rise of modern racist anti-Semitism, and, more particularly, to his extremist treatment of Pius XI as an ingrained anti-Semite who had fostered priests that advocated the extermination of all Jews. Lastly, and most important in the present context, whenever issues relative to the church and anti-Semitism came up — which in the twenty-first century may almost be defined as annually, if not monthly — Kertzer's central themes would emerge and he was often quoted as an authoritative voice. Whether that makes him what his own website (www.davidkertzer.com) proclaims ("David Kertzer has become America's foremost expert on the modern history of the Vatican's relations with the Jews") and whether that self-administered accolade is merited can be left to the reader's judgment after reading the ten chapters following this introduction.

In England the book was titled *The Unholy War,* although there and elsewhere in the English-speaking world, it kept the same subtitle mentioned above, *The Vatican's Role in the Rise of Modern Anti-Semitism.* Unfortunately, even regarding that subtitle there is some waffling — a trait that I was beginning to realize surfaced rather frequently — since its thesis is not that the Vatican played *a role* in the rise of modern anti-Semitism, but that it was "crucial" to its rise. What this literally meant for Kertzer, and it is something that has been ignored even by his few critical reviewers, mainly on the religious and political right, can be summarized simply as "no Vatican, no Holocaust" — an ideological position that the present assessment of his book will show is impossible to maintain.

That impossibility is one of the reasons that the first part of the subtitle to this present book is *Tracking the Myths,* since one of those myths — and possibly the central one — is that without the church there would have been no effort at exterminating the Jews of Europe. The term "tracking" emphasizes that the argument of the book is not based on a priori interpretations or religious commitments, but on matters of historical fact that once brought forward any impartial reader can readily follow. The term also makes it clear that this is a work of literary detection by which the reader can follow stage after stage the various stratagems deployed by the author. The goal of such stratagems, in turn, was to support Kertzer's thesis that without Catholicism there would not have been what is commonly designated "modern anti-Semitism" — the latter to be distinguished from traditional Christian anti-Jewishness. Concerning that distinction, Kertzer's final chapter makes it abundantly clear that he has been writing about the church and the uniquely modern form of contempt for Jews known as exterminationist anti-Semitism, since the chapter title explicitly refers to the papacy and the Vatican as the "Antechamber to the Holocaust."

Among the historical facts that contradict the doctored texts, waffled data, and inaccurate translations, mentioned above, I will cite only two instances in this introduction, even though the abridged form drastically minimizes their impact. The first is particularly heinous because it has to do with a real matter of life or death. In 1913, during the reign of Pius X, at what Kertzer himself calls "the most famous ritual murder trial of the twentieth century," the Vatican was asked by various Jewish groups for documents that would exonerate the accused Jew on trial in czarist Ukraine. These documents were willingly provided by the Vatican's secretary of state, but when the historian — on whom Kertzer has been exclusively relying for his step-by-step description of these events — writes that "the Russian Ambassador in Rome did everything possible that the document should arrive in Kiev too late to be submitted as evidence," Kertzer omits that sentence altogether, and without any annotation or validation simply proceeds to say that it was the papal secretary of state who was the responsible party. The intent of that hoax was explicitly to show that the Vatican deliberately refused to save the life of an innocent Jew — and thus to prove to the reader that the popes indeed were "against the Jews."

The second instance, less appalling but still astonishing enough, is in the category of waffled data mentioned above. It occurs in the chapter titled "A Future Pope in Poland," where chronology is manipulated to indict a pope before he was even elected. Every historian of the twentieth-century papacy knows that both the future Pius XI and the future Pius XII spent some time in the Vatican's diplomatic service. What is interesting about this fact is that for both of these popes, it is not during their actual reigns that they displayed the anti-Semitism of which their critics have accused them, but when they were still papal representatives stationed far away from Rome and the Vatican. Kertzer indicts the future Pius XI via correspondence written when he was stationed in Warsaw at the end of World War I, while John Cornwell — shortly to put in a brief appearance here — indicted the future Pius XII via correspondence written when he was stationed in Munich around the same time. (Cornwell raises the ante by also charging Pacelli with anti-black racism.)

These seemingly isolated instances have their counterparts throughout the book, while my techniques for discovering such conjectural calumnies are spelled out in detail in the first chapter. That chapter is also the only one where I write — as I am here in this introduction — mainly in the first person, since those reading techniques are the sort of skills that most editors, analysts, teachers of textual materials, and the like, develop personally over a period of time.[1] Almost instinctively, such professional "readers" learn to de-

---

1. Later in the book, when occasionally treating of present-day events in which I have been personally engaged, the first person will of necessity be used.

tect deviations from the norm, verbal "tics," in a given writer's language and rhetoric that often betray the writer's focus elsewhere — not infrequently on some stratagem or obfuscation that appears to hold the promise of strengthening her or his argument. These traitorous tics can be as rudimentary as the mere misspelling of a word or the kind of grammatical blunders that would usually be automatically avoided or immediately corrected — but which are left standing because the writer is concentrating on a planned ruse. (There are several examples of these tics in my first chapter, each of which betrays some kind of subterfuge on the part of the writer.)

Apart from such deviations, as I was reading the book I was also coming across more and more factual errors, mistranslations, and faulty arguments that cumulatively were beginning to seriously undercut the reliability I had alluded to in the reference earlier to *Popes and Politics*. Although more numerous, these abuses were not as shocking as the ritual murder deception above, nor were they as transparently fraudulent as their parallels in *Hitler's Pope* by John Cornwell — whose aforementioned appearance here provides another example of a writer whose verbal tics signify that manipulated data are in the offing. The occasion of this appearance was Kertzer's request that Cornwell blurb his book — even though compared to Cornwell, and no matter how bad Kertzer's scholarship is, he would still be a Herodotus or a Tacitus when compared with Cornwell. Why then this curious request for a blurb? The answer has to lurk somewhere in that bane of modern society, the domain of celebrity. Cornwell was, after all, the author of the "international best seller" (according to his publisher) or the "recent best seller" (according to Kertzer). But ostensibly what *really* joined the aspirant to success to the authenticated achiever of success was not their common bond as successful chroniclers of papal evils — a negative achievement at best — but their alliance as budding ecumenists. Cornwell nobly affirms of Kertzer: "Painful as his historical narrative may be for Catholics, it is a necessary prelude to a true reconciliation between the Catholic Church and Judaism."

The consequences of this irenic link between blurber and blurbee, between Catholics and Jews, are revelatory, as Cornwell went on to assert: "*Once again* Kertzer has *produced* impressive evidence of the part played by the papacy in the growth of anti-Semitism in the twentieth century" (italics supplied). It was this "once again" tic that pointed to something amiss, since the only previous excursion by Kertzer into what might be called "anti-Semitism" was *The Kidnapping of Edgardo Mortara,* an event that occurred in the nineteenth century and that had little if any connection to twentieth-century anti-Semitism.[2] But it was Cornwell's concentration on making those matters relevant to present-day readers that led to the adoption of the above strange notion of how students of history function in modern societies. The fact, plain even to non-historians, is that the one thing a historian doesn't do is "*produce* evidence" — whether impressive or not. A lawyer in a courtroom or a scientist in a laboratory may produce evidence, but a scholar in an archive or a library discovers or discloses or brings to light whatever he or she is working on. (Here I will engage in some "close reading.")

"Produced" is a word that is related in meaning to such terms as "generated," "manufactured," and "constructed." A less sophisticated and more damning rendition of the meaning of "produced" (as one goes from polysyllabic Latinate to just plain English) is the term "made up" — as a person might casually say, "I made it up." But the most illuminating cognate of "produced" — less in terms of common linguistic roots than of semantic affinities — is with the synonym "fabricated." The English root of the latter is "fabric," a word primarily associated with clothing and cloth, and it is on the basis of that association that the ultimate dismissal of something as sham or fake is to say that it is "made up [of] whole cloth." The latter is something that is totally fabricated, and totally produced.

However, there is one tactic of which Kertzer himself is the preeminent master, and which Cornwell does not even attempt to match. This particular stratagem requires that the author/producer/fabricator also become a reader of minds — a stratagem that is particularly effective when it is the minds of popes that are the subject of the author's charism. Since this is a prerogative usually confined to the writers of novels or plays, the response to this feat might be to declare as John Henry Newman did to his antagonist, Charles Kingsley — who actually was a celebrated novelist: "Why man, you are writing a romance!" But Kertzer nevertheless manages to outdo any of his likely predecessors. After reading a given pope's mind and literally putting words into his mouth, Kertzer then criticizes that same pope for saying the assorted malign things that in fact were conceived by none other than himself, the author of *The Popes Against the Jews*. Again, the parallel with Newman and Kingsley is useful. When the latter said: "I am relieved that you did not mean what you said," Newman retorted: "*Mean* it . . . I never *said* it!"

Neither did Pius IX say the words below that were attributed to him through the happy medium of Kertzer's own fantasies. The following pas-

2. In the twenty-first century, thanks to Miramax the story may soon be at the local cineplex, with Anthony Hopkins in the role of the kidnapping Pope Pius IX.

sage is introduced by a straightforward historical statement, which then elides into a description of events as allegedly perceived by the pope, and ends with the specific words the pope is presumed to be thinking.

> By 1861 all that was left of the Pope's temporal kingdom was Rome and the area immediately around it. Throughout the peninsula, a new secular Kingdom of Italy had been proclaimed. For the Pope the collapse of the Papal States was but another trial sent by God. But the Papal States had fallen to impious forces before — indeed, more than once in the nineteenth century alone — and each time the Church had ultimately triumphed and the forces of darkness were defeated. This time, with God's help, thought the Pope, the same would happen.

Kertzer's divinatory powers were stretched even further in the following paragraph in which the pope is conceiving revenge against his enemies. (The first sentence with its capitalized "the Popes" provides the background for the imagined scenario.)

> But this rearguard action [enforcing ghetto rules], a final desperate attempt to keep *the Jews* in the place that the Popes and canon law had long assigned them, would soon be replaced by a whole new way of viewing *the Jews*. The same forces that had struck against the power of the Church had granted *the Jews* equal rights. In marshaling Catholic public opinion in support of the Vatican and against these forces of secularization, it was tempting, very tempting to make use of this fact. Vilified for centuries, *the Jew* could, if properly conjured up, be used to discredit the forces that had sought to create a modern, secular state. (italics supplied)

What is particularly vicious about this mini-drama is the patent shift from the neutral "the Jews" in the first sentences to the singular epithet "the Jew" in the last — when, presumably, the demented obsession, hinted at in the phrase "it was tempting, very tempting," completely takes over the pope's mind.

Those are just a few of the myths that are tracked and the truths that are confronted in the process of reading this book. As for Peter Berger on institutional inertia, it is the subtext of the last and longest chapters of the book. The eighth chapter concludes with Kertzer's treatment of the Nazi roundup of over a thousand Roman Jews — an event typifying for him the duplicity of Pius XII. Chapter nine is a critique of "liberal" Catholic scholars in general, and opponents of canonizing the allegedly anti-Semitic Pius in particular. The centerpiece of chapter ten is a recently discovered document definitively countering the allegations regarding this pope. The body of the chapter criticizes American church leaders in such areas of sexuality as reproductive rights, gender orientation, the role of women, and the abuse of minors. This leads into Berger's larger theme of institutions ostensibly inspired by noble ideals, but failing to live up to their professed goals: the church and Jewry; the U.S. and slavery; and Israel and Palestinians. The culmination of the chapter is the conflict between the latter which engages, though in different ways, all three institutions, Israel, the U.S., and the church. As for the methodology of the latter, I cite the foreword to a much earlier book, *Nuclear War: The Ethic, the Rhetoric, the Reality* (1965), where I wrote the following — which also remains applicable to *Were the Popes against the Jews?*

> The author of the present work is an editor of books who is also a professor of what are called "the humanities" where he is engaged in the teaching of English poetry. As a consequence, the approach of the book may be broadly termed humanistic, and the method employed is mainly *explication de texte*. The matrix of the whole, as evident particularly in the non-polemical sections, is a viewpoint which is Roman Catholic in inspiration.

This was a book prefaced by Arthur Waskow, still a staunch defender of peacemaking and peacemakers, who among other things said of the book that "it examines the astrologers of counterforce strategy, and finds their belief in the untested axioms of controlled thermonuclear war mere superstition: and like other superstitions, not only unscientific but immoral."

In the index to the book, among the six columns of names, that of the chief astrologer, Herman Kahn, stood out as having the greatest number of citations, in fact, second only to John XXIII. Kahn, who was one of the models for the amalgamation known as "Dr. Strangelove," had written a kind of *summa demonica* of the Cold War, a thousand-page treatise, flatly titled *On Thermonuclear War*. It was even more flatly — if not dismissively — subtitled *Three Lectures and Several Suggestions*. Of the latter, I had asked, "What response other than mockery does such bland insouciance merit?"[3] Kahn then retorted mechanically, but not without a touch of pathos, in a book titled *Unintended War:* "I design buttons and I work very hard at designing

---

3. For a less impersonal encounter with Herman Kahn two decades later, see Justus George Lawler, "Moral Confusion in the Nuclear Age," *The Christian Century*, April 4, 1984.

buttons, both day and night. I got a group of people working about eighty hours a week nowadays designing buttons, and they are all very dedicated, they all think they are doing very good things." To that hardy assertion, this humanist exponent of close reading replies:

> Well, I analyze texts and I work very hard at analyzing texts, both day and night. And I got a group of people, students by the hundreds and aspiring or successful authors by the scores whose texts I analyze and then grade either as passing and publishable or as failing and unprintable. I did that overall, for a period of half a century — the final phase of which resulted in this book.

But the last word must go to Rabbi Arthur Waskow in his preface: "Will the thought, the care, the energy to save both the values and the physical reality of Western civilization yet come from the Church which first bore that civilization? All men know the event would be surprising: but God knows it would be appropriate."

Few are those who would not reply, "Amen."

CHAPTER 1

From Agreement to Discord

When the first reviews of David I. Kertzer's *The Popes Against the Jews: The Vatican's Role in the Rise of Modern Anti-Semitism* appeared in the fall of 2001, the book's enthusiastic reception was not surprising. For more than half a century no historical event had so bewildered the general public, as well as scholars and journalists, as the unforgettable mass murder of six million European Jews. Regardless of the vast number of words devoted to exploring that unique catastrophe, anything new that shed even a small ray of light on it could only be universally welcomed. It merely heightened interest in Kertzer's book that it appeared in the immediate aftermath of a number of other widely read studies that had severely criticized the role of the papacy and the Catholic Church during the wartime period.[1]

At the time of the book's publication, I was finishing *Popes and Politics: Reform, Resentment, and the Holocaust,* which appeared the following year. I had looked at Kertzer's book briefly, and it soon became clear that few historical assertions were less deniable than his opinion that Christian teaching was the soil in which the evil of racist anti-Semitism flourished. But it soon also became clear that a large element of the enthusiasm for the book among Catholics stemmed less from how it validated that opinion than from how it could be enlisted in such causes as reform of the American church and condemnation of the ecclesiastical structures created by various recent popes, particularly Pius XII and John Paul II. Since this reformist theme is a recurrent motif in the chapters that follow, how it was related to Kertzer's book merits a brief examination.

---

1. Since many readers often skip a book's introductory material, there are several paragraphs in what follows that replicate material in the introduction.

Among his early enthusiastic reviewers was Garry Wills in *The New York Times* (September 23, 2001), about whom I said in *Popes and Politics:*

> Garry Wills writes of the author's "sickening task" covering "a stretch of two centuries" while not "giving way to the indignation most readers must feel," and resulting in a "staggeringly thorough job." To all of which anyone would probably say "amen," since the church's role in the horrors of anti-Semitism is a theme on which too much repetition or too many variations — of which Kertzer's book is clearly another — can never be enough.

Wills cited the eminent British historian of the modern church Owen Chadwick to the effect that Pius IX was the only pope who would have canonized the sixteenth-century inquisitor Pedro Arbués. The review ended with Wills's conclusion that "there was only one pope who would have beatified Pius IX — John Paul II." Since Kertzer had mentioned the latter pope only a few times in the entire book, mainly regarding his progress in ecumenical matters and his advocacy of truth telling, his emergence at the end of the review was something of a surprise.

Similarly with Pius XII, whose presence could hardly be overlooked since he put in an appearance by way of a laudatory jacket blurb from the author of *Hitler's Pope,* John Cornwell. The importation of Pius XII into the ambit of the book was also an unexpected development, since Kertzer himself was dismissive of the role of that pope. "The debate over what Pius XII might have done during the Holocaust is a distraction." "With all the attention given to what he did or did not say about the Nazi-led campaign against the Jews — his influence was at best limited." According to Kertzer, Pius's wartime deeds or misdeeds diverted attention from "the more important question, what did the Catholic Church do to help bring on the Holocaust in the first place?" The response in *Popes and Politics* was: "'Much too much' is the obvious answer of history — an answer which has been reaffirmed again and again by the second Vatican Council and by two popes." As I mentioned in the introduction, it was only a few years later, after the appearance of the paperback edition of *Popes and Politics* (2004), that I finally got around to a closer examination of the book and its author.

I began with a brief search for information on Kertzer's own website and on that of his publisher. Both of these supplied the conventional biographical and bibliographical data along with interviews, quotations, links to other comments about the author, and reviews of the book itself. Two quotations — from personal interviews with the author — stood out. The first was the following: "If you're interested in what role the Church played in making the Holocaust possible, it's decades and decades of demonization of Jews." Some readers might have paused at such a sweeping statement being made about "the Church" in general, and some would probably cavil at the word "demonization," but the gist of the observation seemed as unexceptionable as the book's broader thesis mentioned above. However, what was surprising about Kertzer's quotation was its apparent generosity regarding that demonizing church. Most people familiar with the history of Christianity from its dark night of the soul in the Middle Ages and on into the twentieth century would have thought that the author's reference to decades and decades was a generous understatement; certainly this would have been true for those who wholeheartedly embraced the confession attributed to Pope John XXIII: "Across the centuries our brother Abel has lain in the blood which we drew, or shed tears we caused by forgetting Christ's love." But after examining the book itself, it became clear that the author's chronological frame was not intended to exonerate nearly a millennium and a half of Christian abuse of Jews, but rather to emphasize the responsibility of five recent popes for, in Kertzer's words, putting Europe's Jews on "the road to the Holocaust." Those popes were Pius IX, Leo XIII, Pius X, Pius XI, and, to a lesser degree, Benedict XV.[2]

Nevertheless, I wouldn't have decided to analyze *The Popes Against the Jews* had it not been for the doubts raised by the second and much longer quotation I have already mentioned — also from a personal interview with Kertzer and available on his publisher's website. The material there related to the contention that a modern pope on a public occasion had explicitly referred to Jews as dogs that were molesting Christians. Here is the passage from the interview, which is followed by a step-by-step description, tedious but necessary, of the process that raised my suspicions to the point where I decided to undertake a critical examination of a book to which I had originally been sympathetic.

---

2. Thus I will not discuss in detail the first three chapters (out of a total of thirteen), which focus mainly on the horrors of life for Jews in the Papal States from roughly the French Revolution to the revolutions of 1848. As described by Kertzer, and apart from minor disagreements, his account of such things as the personal degradation and horrifying living conditions to which Jews were subjected in the popes' territories, whether in urban ghettos or segregated areas in other cities, are accurate and dismaying enough to evoke the words of John XXIII above.

What bothers me is the misrepresentation of history and an unwillingness to confront the past truthfully. Let me give a small example. A couple of days before the beatification of Pope Pius IX in September 2000, I did a live national Italian radio debate with a monsignor from the Vatican congregation for the promotion of saints. In that debate, in response to the claim that Pius IX was kindly disposed to the Jews, I cited his remarks at an audience in 1871 in which he referred to Rome's Jews as "dogs" who were running barking through the streets, molesting the good people of the city. The next day, at a Vatican press conference, in response to a journalist's question about my remarks, the Vatican official said that no responsible historian would put any credence in what I had said. When the journalist subsequently contacted me about the quote, I referred him to a volume titled "The Speeches of Pio IX" published by the Vatican in 1872, edited by a priest. In addition to giving him the page number where the quote about the dogs was to be found, I pointed out the page of the preface which reported that the Pope himself had read and approved the proofs of the book before publication. If there were any apology I am interested in from the Vatican at the moment, I guess it would be for what was said about me at that press conference. But I'm not holding my breath.

Although readers had no way of knowing what was said about Kertzer at the press conference — because he doesn't tell them — they do get a sense of the complacent mood of the author at his triumph over the obnoxious monsignor. However, even that mood might merely have come from the narrator's gratification at disclosing what he clearly viewed as an important historical fact. But then that concession comes up against the wisecrack about "not holding my breath" — which also didn't quite jibe with the mood conveyed by the offhand "what bothers me." Another seed of suspicion was sowed by the comment about the narrator's truth-seeking goals and those of the unnamed others who implicitly were, if not in search of misrepresentations, then apparently seeking something less than "truth." Nor was that tone entirely dissipated by the narrator's apparent reticence ("a small example") about what he clearly regarded as a large issue.

But it was not just Kertzer's smugness that gave pause. I was left wondering why over a period of what appeared to be at least two, and more likely, three days (the broadcast; the press conference; the journalist's "subsequent contact") hadn't Kertzer, rather than engaging in what even by his own description certainly sound like convoluted exchanges, just shown the disputed passage to the inquiring reporter and/or the insulting Vatican official, and gotten it all over with? Why not just make the misguided monsignor confront the past by exhibiting, perhaps with only a modest flourish, before the dumbfounded prelate's very eyes the infamous statement itself? Instead, Kertzer referred to the volume, provided the title and publication date, mentioned its editorship by a priest, gave the page number of the fateful quotation, and pointed out the page in the preface that indicated the pope's approval of what was in the book — all of which seemed an oddly circuitous way of making a simple point.

It was that last clause about "pointing out the page of the preface" that heightened even these secondary suspicions about what was going on. I couldn't imagine how anyone could do all this without having in hand a copy of the book. It is difficult to believe that Kertzer was fortunately armed with a copy of the page from the preface — but not a copy of the page with the statement about those molestation-prone Jewish "dogs." It should have been the most straightforward thing in the world to just display at the time of this confrontation the incriminating page — and have done with the whole wrangle. Presenting the page with the complete text of the pope's slur would certainly have led to the author's victory in the eyes of everyone involved: the journalist, the monsignor, and the presumably sizeable audience of observers and bystanders, some of whom must have been thinking — as was I when first reading the description of the confrontation — surely somewhere, even in the Eternal City, there was a Xerox machine.

The accusation about a pope calling Jews "dogs" will be scrutinized in detail later, since from it flow a whole series of other bewildering matters that relate to the story that Kertzer has to tell. In the more immediate context, from it also flowed the decision to read carefully *The Popes Against the Jews.* It particularly bothered me that the author of this book, whose central point as far as I understood it was undeniable, would have appeared so devious about so relatively minor a matter. Apart from the cocksureness of his narration, this also raised doubts as to whether he had actually seen the text of the document he kept referring to, or whether he had lifted the information — as proved to be true — from some secondary source. In any case, the whole incident didn't seem quite compatible with his initial concern over misrepresentations of history by those who were "unwilling to confront the past truthfully."

What follows will be the only place in this book where I elaborate anything even remotely autobiographical. But since I have started writing in the first person, and because the preceding discussion takes off from a personal reaction, I will continue in this vein for the next few pages. After nearly half a century of passing judgment on manuscripts for the five publishing imprints of which I had been editor (not to speak of an even longer period of correcting a wide range of undergraduate and graduate student papers), I felt it would be possible to make a reasonably impartial and fair assessment of the book, even though my view of the author was now somewhat colored by the bombast of his encounter with the testy Roman monsignor. Anybody familiar with publishing realizes that a judgment on a manuscript — particularly a controversial one — can't be made on the basis of a given author's personal traits, much less on the compatibility of the author's views with those of an editorial reader.

Over a period of time most editors of general trade books — basically meaning here serious nonfiction — acquire their own techniques for maintaining a sense of objectivity by reining in strong personal biases and opinions. "Technique" is used by design, since what is involved is more an acquired skill in the practical craft of willing one's way to open-mindedness than any kind of ad hoc effort at adopting an alien intellectual position. I don't want to make this process sound too arcane or recherché, because basically it is mainly a matter of respectful and attentive reading — done as speedily as possible.[3] Recent theorists of the art of interpretation, usually following a book that I published, Hans-Georg Gadamer's *Truth and Method*, have maintained that it is impossible to read about any familiar and controversial subject with complete openness. Nevertheless, experience has shown that it is possible to block out prejudices that relate to specific controversial themes — otherwise decisions to publish would all be made on the basis of personally favored positions. In *The Much Too Promised Land* (2008), Aaron David Miller, the Jewish American diplomat who has been involved in decades of negotiations between Israelis and Palestinians, and who won the admiration of both parties, says simply, "try to determine where your biases lie, and overcome them." If you have to do it, you will.

As to the above emphasis on speed, it has nothing to do with time-is-money concerns. Once a decision to read a complete manuscript is reached — usually a matter of simply weighing credentials, book proposal, outline, and so on, and a thumb-through of the first few chapters — the next goal is to get a sense of the book's argument and organization, and most important

---

3. Medieval monks working on texts in a scriptorium followed the principles set forth in one of their prayers: "digne, attente ac devote," that is, do your work "worthily, attentively, and devotedly."

of all, a sense of its author's integrity. The purpose of this quick read is to acquire a "feel" for the work as a rhetorical whole, while concomitantly exposing to the reader anything that might appear slightly unexpected, anything
that didn't harmonize with the larger picture, anything, that is, which would
set off even a faint vibration in what might be thought of as the seismograph
of the mind.

What this comes down to is the practice of a kind of engaged detachment not unlike that described by Linda Stone, an expert in "computer culture," as "continuous partial attention." In the present instance, this means
that quickly grasping the overall drift and structure of the text is the primary
object of attention, while remaining aware of what is taking place on the
borders of one's consciousness is the more or less secondary object — since
it is on those borders that lurk aspects of the text hinting at something amiss.
These hints often take the form of errors in spelling and punctuation, or of
less blatant mistakes having to do with grammar, logic, and chronology. In
themselves these may be insignificant and readily corrected, but they are often a clue to something beneath the surface of the author's presentation that
demands greater attention. The basic assumption behind this entire process
is that any such minor disruptive element in the text of an experienced
writer — and here I return to David I. Kertzer — is a kind of "tic" that betrays preoccupation with some rhetorical or logical stratagem that may reveal more about the author than his explicit statements.

As to the less important but still significant matter of the book's "tone,"
The Popes Against the Jews originally left me with a sense of the author's engaging frankness. This was particularly noteworthy since he also came across
as patently aggressive about making his case — a quality that does not usually appeal to a reader, especially if displayed too early in the book. My initial
more or less empathetic mood was possibly related to the fact that to use the
archives of the papacy to attack the papacy came across as more an exercise
in guilelessness than in vindictiveness. A reader could almost get the impression that the Vatican had a twofold, and oddly ironic, official policy regarding Jews to which it devoted much of its energies: the first aspect of that policy was to defame them, and the second was to meticulously preserve for
posterity all records of the defamation. That this literally preposterous[4] ar-

---

4. Since I will be using "preposterous" literally, it should be pointed out now that the
word etymologically means a phenomenon that is simultaneously both "pre" and "post,"
both "before" and "after" — an impossibility chronologically, ontologically, and just plain
logically. In short, a kind of surd.

rangement appeared to undercut the revolutionary claim that the popes were engaged in a secret conspiracy to make war on Jews — the British edition was called *Unholy War* — only made reading the text more intriguing.

In addition to the seeming ingenuousness of using the popes' archives to attack the popes, there was the comparably naive repetition of terms suggesting that the reader was on the trail of hitherto undiscovered documentary troves that the author had "dug" or "gleaned" or "excavated" from hidden repositories. The latter was not without its enticing resonance of clandestine machinations in dark and mysterious places — particularly when one came across the citation to "Archivio Segreto Vaticano," "the Secret Vatican Archive." This was the sort of thing that evoked bizarre images ranging from nineteenth-century gothic novels to more recent fictional ventures — culminating in *The Da Vinci Code* and *Angels and Demons.* (It also evoked Umberto Eco's axiom that you should check for signs of lunacy whenever you come across any invocation of the Knights Templar.)

Moreover, Kertzer seemed as knowledgeable about the "secular" history of modern Europe as about the history of the popes and the papacy. After a brief description of continuing discrimination against the Jews before the French Revolution, the book proper began with the Congress of Vienna and the restoration of the Papal States, and the "missed opportunity" (the title of the first chapter) on the part of a pope, Pius VII, to maintain the regime of semi-egalitarianism regarding Jews that had been instituted by the Napoleonic reforms. The hero of this period is Cardinal Consalvi, the papal secretary of state, whose efforts for the Jews ultimately proved unavailing, as the old ghetto restrictions were gradually reimposed. The description of those restrictions and of life in the ghettos of the Papal States is so harrowing that it made one wonder whether the mentality that in earlier centuries rationalized setting people on fire for heresy still prevailed in the Vatican of the early nineteenth century. Putting aside explorations into medieval forms of punishment, it nevertheless appeared obvious that by the election of Pius IX, four decades after Consalvi, the pope's domain was the most backward in all of Europe. Only the serfs under the rule of the czar in Eastern Europe or black slaves in the United States lived in comparable squalor.

In fact, as one read further Kertzer's mastery of secular history gradually appeared more impressive than his achievements in the religious arena, particularly those relating to his research in the Vatican archives, which was the publicized raison d'être of his entire enterprise. Concerning the latter, it gradually became more and more difficult to avoid the impression that he seemed almost entirely dependent on the scholarship of Giovanni Miccoli, who in the body of the book is mentioned only once in a single sentence, and that was in a context that Kertzer had spurned — "Pius XII and the Holocaust" — but who appeared to be the source of almost every archival discovery or novel position and perspective in *The Popes Against the Jews*. Kertzer acknowledges standing "on the shoulders" of the Italian historian, but unlike others invoking that imagery, Isaac Newton famously, the acknowledgment was of dependence on the entire previous tradition of scholarship, not on the research of one person.[5]

All of the above material, which relates mainly to the book as a whole, can be here set aside since specific illustrations of this editorial methodology — a quick read combined with oblique attention to textual peculiarities and their consequences — are called for. The first marginal notation in my copy of *The Popes Against the Jews* occurred on the third page of the introduction, and elicited only an inkling of suspicion. It related to the previously mentioned matter of archival research:

> This book rests heavily on these newly available documents from the Inquisition archives, as well as from other Vatican archives that have become open to researchers in recent years. Together with evidence that has been reported in the specialized scholarly literature — mainly in Italy and France — over the past few years, these new sources shed light on a history that until now has remained hidden.

It may appear picayune (perhaps a holdover from correcting too many student papers), but this first passage was bothersome not because it said that what the author was disclosing had been hidden "until now" — though that remark was slightly reminiscent of the bravado in the Jews-as-dogs disclosure — but because it entailed a simple contradiction. I wondered how a history that had been hidden until *now* could be derived from materials — whether archival or published — that stemmed from "the past few years," or from "recent years." This casual contradiction suggested that some wariness might be needed concerning the author's use of chronology — or even of logic.

The second and third balking points also occurred in the introduction.

---

5. Miccoli is mentioned by name in a sentence in the introduction and again in the acknowledgments, where the "standing on the shoulders" reference is introduced. Although he appears as the source of insights and information in more than a dozen endnotes, there is only one page reference after his name in the book's index.

The first was the kind of absolute assertion most scholars avoid unless it can be backed up by a definite source — which this wasn't. "Only in its [history's] light can we understand why, as millions of Jews were being murdered, Pius XII could never bring himself to publicly utter the word 'Jew.'" Apart from the obvious fact that the word "Jew" is English, I had when writing *Popes and Politics* read all the wartime public statements of Pius, and recalled the word *ebreo* appearing more than once, as well as a statement expressing concern for the "huge numbers of refugees, expatriates, emigrants, including those of Jewish descent." But in his first encyclical, *Summi Pontificatus* — a document that will be crucial to the defense of Pius in the ninth chapter of this book — he did give voice to that foreboding and forbidden term. Unfortunately, that won't pass muster with Kertzer since at the time only a few thousand Jews were known to have been murdered. In the Easter message of 1941, the pope referred to the war as "atrocious," and he lamented the condition of the "defenseless, the sick, and the aged," adding that "very dear" to him were Catholics, Protestants, and Jews: "children of the Church of Christ, others with faith in the Divine Savior, or in Our Father Who is in Heaven." Most people when reading this would think it a righteous utterance, particularly given the times and the circumstances.

There was also an article in *The Palestine Post* (April 28, 1944) written by a Jew about a wartime audience with the pope in the autumn of 1941 where Pius XII spoke publicly in praise of the Jews.[6] Historian Michael Burleigh has described "a letter signed by the Pope in October 1940 and sent to Giuseppe Palatucci, Bishop of Campagna in southern Italy, which instructed him to give money 'in aid to interned Jews.'" "A second letter to Bishop

---

6. The language of the statement makes it one of the most significant papal utterances not only of the twentieth century but of the second millennium of the history of the church. I say this fully realizing that *that* is the kind of assertion that sounds so exaggerated it could easily deter any thoughtful reader from continuing. Instead, it is my hope that it will have the opposite effect, since it is only after such a reader has followed the argument of the next nine chapters that the import of Pius XII's affirmation of Jews as such can be appreciated. "As such" is significant, since it will become evident in the body of this book that Jews, when they weren't being viciously persecuted, were tolerated only because they were the "witness people" to the triumph of Christianity, or because they were the protected wards of the papacy, or because of a common Scripture — in short, because of some reason extraneous to their sheer reality as human beings. To that long tradition of humiliation the statement of Pius XII says: "Not so!" For the first time in more than a thousand years (and probably much longer), a pope spoke publicly *of* and *to* Jews as fellow children of God — and this occurred well before the revolutionary reforms of Vatican II. The complete text of Pius XII and its astonishing background are discussed in chapter 10.

Palatucci in November 1940 contained a cheque for 10,000 lira that was to be used for the 'support of Jews interned in your diocese.'"[7] Both letters surfaced in 2002 in a biography of the bishop's nephew, Giovanni Palatucci, who was imprisoned and died in Dachau. On all these references one may consult the indispensable bibliography by William Doino Jr. in *The Pius War* (2004).

My second hesitation, and one less abruptly experienced, was signaled by a penciled line under one term in the body of the text excerpted below, where the author was attempting (as it happened) to refute what he regarded as the conventional view of the role of Pius XII:

> In the literature on Pius XII's failure to speak out during the Holocaust, he is often compared unfavorably to Pius XI, the "good pope," portrayed as a firm foe of anti-Semitism. . . . Thus in John Cornwell's recent bestseller, *Hitler's Pope*, Pius XII's "silence" is linked to his personal antipathy to the Jews along with his larger conservative political agenda which privileged maintaining good relations with the Nazi regime. But what if we find that Pius XII's benevolent predecessor shared the same *stridently* anti-Semitic views? The problem, we would then have to conclude, lies not in the personality or moral qualities of a single pope, but rather in a much more pervasive culture of Vatican anti-Semitism.

The term that I have italicized, "stridently," was jarring not because Kertzer appeared again to be in the process of protecting his academic turf — "the story I tell here for the first time" — and not because he was exempting himself from the misjudgments of most other writers of "the literature" who made Pius XII the villainous bystander of the Holocaust. What elicited more than a quiver on the inner Richter scale was the collision between the judgments in the sentences preceding and following the one with the italicized term. It was difficult to conceive how such passive phenomena as personal antipathy, conservative agenda, and good relations — regardless of what they "related" to — could have been characterized as "stridently" anything. This revelatory tic showed another lapse into cliché thinking — anyone guilty of the abhorred anti-Semitism must be strident — on the part of this experienced and presumably cautious author. It also suggested a possibly excessive concentration on the logically frail ploy being perpetrated in the final sentence about what "we would then have to conclude" — since

---

7. "'Hitler's Pope' Tried to Help Jews," *The Telegraph*, February 16, 2003.

what in fact we would then have to conclude is simply that the predecessor pope was like the successor pope.[8] (As will be seen in chapters 7 and 8, the "first-time" story Kertzer tells about Achille Ratti will not withstand even modest historical scrutiny.)

But the most important clue thus far to something askew was a sequence of rhetorical questions aimed at the reader that were intended to immediately connect the popes to the Holocaust. Few experienced editors or teachers would tolerate a writer repeatedly confronting his audience by directly addressing questions to them, particularly at the beginning of a manuscript. Such a confrontation has an effect similar to that of hearing a person one hardly knows shouting, "Hey, you! what about this?" Even in an era of declining standards, the old maxim about never imposing an obligation on readers until they have confidence in "you" the writer — confidence that is only gained by their progressing satisfactorily further into the text — remains inviolable. So, I couldn't help but wonder whether something was amiss when one paragraph ended calmly with the statement, "I focus in particular on how 'traditional' Catholic forms of dealing with the Jews became transformed into modern anti-Semitism," and the next paragraph began as follows:

> But I cannot resist adding a couple of brief observations here about the Holocaust itself. First, what are we to make of Austria, an overwhelmingly Catholic country that has still not come to terms with the enthusiastic role its people played in the Nazi murder of the Jews? Is there any significance in the fact that Adolf Hitler, a baptized Catholic, spent his early years in Austria, where the Vatican-supported anti-Semitic Christian Social movement was so active? How do we account for the fact that Austrians played a disproportionately large role in the Holocaust? . . . could there be any link between the efficiency of the slaughter of millions of Jews in Poland and the deep anti-Semitism inculcated in the Catholic population there?[9]

8. The shift from singular to plural — "the story *I* tell" . . . "what if *we* find" — is an effective tactical maneuver for implicating the reader in the writer's perspective. Though probably innocent, it nevertheless could be indicative of more formidable rhetorical stratagems that might need to be reckoned with.

9. The mild subterfuge of referring earlier to detailed questions as "brief observations" appeared intended to divert attention from the kinds of questions that might come to the mind of any knowledgeable reader, and which in my initial read I formulated, more or less instinctively — and perhaps a little angrily — as follows: What are we to make of Holland, which had the highest percentage of Jews murdered of any occupied country ex-

The air of catechizing true believers could not but grate on the reader who was being placed in the position of presumably knowing the correct responses; whereas in fact — and merely by having the book in hand — they were anticipating from the author the detailed answers to just such questions in the 350 pages yet to come.

This tone of pedagogical self-satisfaction, first encountered in the Jewish "dogs" narrative, ended up being a kind of basso continuo running through the text. But what was more nettlesome than the repetitive nature of the questions — which could merely be another tic indicating something that needed attention — was that their calm if not bland setting ("adding a couple of brief observations here") could so suddenly erupt into a reference to Austrian "enthusiasm" for murdering Jews and Polish "efficiency" in slaughtering them. The violation of prescriptive rhetorical principles about direct address was only a hint, but it was one that betrayed a tendency to engage in judgmental language about matters that hadn't yet been introduced by the writer, much less resolved by him. Any competent editor or teacher usually insists on the principle that anything that smacks of self-satisfaction, much less of self-righteousness — especially before the writer has gained the confidence of the readers — will antagonize if not completely alienate the very people the writer is seeking to influence.

When I reexamined those sentences in the excerpt above — which I had marked in the introduction — they brought to mind similar comments appearing in the last chapter of the book which, thanks to my quick read, I had just finished. In the final chapter, the author again publicly separated himself from those scholars who allegedly concentrated on Pius XII rather than on his predecessor — a predecessor to whom, he now tells the reader, "we must turn if we want to know how the systematic murder of Europe's Jews could have become possible." Where the first time around there was a sequence of direct questions (although with the implication that "we" all know the answers), now there is a flat-out connection of "the predecessor" to the death camps, with on the part of the writer not merely a tic, but an almost palpable verbal tremor — resulting in the following strange consequences:

cept Poland? What are we to make of the fact that the Dutch archbishop's refusal to be silent about the deportations led initially to a dramatic increase in the persecution of Jewish *Catholics* only? Is there any significance in the fact that atheist Russia and Orthodox Romania followed Catholic Poland in the greatest number of Jews murdered — and that Poland had by far the greatest number of gentiles honored at Yad Vashem? I wasn't at this point concerned about the answers as such, but only about the implications of this author's use of possibly loaded questions.

The role played by the Vatican in the development of the politics of discrimination and harassment that set the stage for the Holocaust are most
clearly on display in those places where the Church's influence was greatest. The case of Germany is complicated by the fact that Catholics composed a minority (albeit a large one). By contrast, in Italy, France, Austria,
and Poland, Catholics formed the great majority of the population, and
the Catholic Church enjoyed a central (although certainly not uncon-
tested) place in society. The case of Italy is . . .

Not for nothing did the ancient creators of the *trivium* link mistakes in
grammar to mistakes in logic and rhetoric. The tic that pointed to something seriously awry here was the bewildering jumble in the first sentence
where the main clause's initiating subject, "the role played by the Vatican,"
has as its only possible corresponding predicate the impossibly ungrammat-
ical, "are most clearly on display." In sum, a startling gaffe. That a seasoned
writer could not only make the mistake but overlook it when correcting at
least a couple of sets of proofs suggested concentration on more pressing
matters — which conventional editorial experience had shown often turned
out to be a planned strategic subterfuge or ruse.

It is a minor item that what preceded the excerpt above was another
privileging of the author's achievement: "The story we tell differs in another
way from that more commonly told," that more common story being about
generalizations by other scholars from an examination of "the Catholic
Church in Germany." This, the author had speedily dismissed: "This is a mistake . . ." — though probably one that didn't need emphasizing again in the
last thirty pages of the book. Nor did it escape notice that in the phrase, "the
story we tell," the plural "we" — which previously was used to indicate a
kind of fellowship between reader and writer — now was deployed more
pretentiously in the sense of the so-called "royal *we*," possibly indicating
more of the self-satisfaction previously glimpsed. By itself that may not be a
scholarly vice, but common sense suggests that it often leads to overreaching
in terms either of rhetoric or of facts.

That "the case of Germany" was "too complicated" and so was disposed
of in a sentence left me wondering whether something more was needed
here about the nation that actually engineered the Holocaust. Did the "minority numbers of Catholics there," by some kind of slanted computation,
diminish the guilt of that nation in order that the author — unlike all those
less perceptive scholars from whom he had separated himself — could concentrate on (in *this* order): Italy, Rome, Vatican, Pius XI? "Yes," was begin-

ning to be my tentative conclusion. The grammatical mistake was so bizarre, it seemed to suggest that the author had left Germany up in the air only in order to hang Italy out to dry.

This is the beginning of the follow-up:

> The case of Italy is of special importance for a number of reasons. First of all, until much later in the century (with John Paul II) the popes were all Italian, as were the large majority of the cardinals who ran the Vatican. Their attitudes were shaped by growing up in Italy, and by participating in a dense network of Catholic organizations there. Once ensconced in Rome, they continued to follow developments in Italian society and politics with special interest. Secondly, because the Vatican and the pope were in Rome, and because both the pope and most of the cardinals of his curia were Italian, the Vatican had more direct influence over popular attitudes in Italy than elsewhere.
>
> *The Protocols of the Elders of Zion* offers a good place to begin in bringing to light the role of Catholic anti-Semitism in the rise of Nazi and fascist anti-Semitism in the 1920s.

Here the reader, in this instance myself, anticipated some kind of dramatic conclusion from the author's survey of Nazi-occupied Europe, culminating in the lengthy paragraph about "the case of Italy." But instead what was encountered in the next sentence was an entirely new topic followed by a baffling non sequitur: "*The Protocols of the Elders of Zion* offers a good place to begin." "Begin what?" one wondered — as the author went into a discussion of the history of the *Protocols,* thus leaving readers groping for an answer to the overarching question that had to be running through their minds: whatever happened to specially important Italy? Instead, one progressed into the following: "The story of the *Protocols* is a convoluted one. Its origins lie in a political pamphlet written by a Frenchman," and so on, as Italy disappeared over the horizon.

Left to evaporate in the ether of history are all those Italian popes, cardinals, and organizations securely ensconced in Rome. By his previous speculation on Austria and Poland — countries related to Christianity, the church, the Holy See, and the pope — as hotbeds of the murder and slaughter of Jews, readers were certainly led to expect that all those references to Italy must entail at least a similar sort of connection. Instead, forgoing any linkage, the author provided in a non-transitional transition the assertion that something here offered "a good place to begin" something entirely new.

At this point, I was beginning to wonder whether among that "recent Italian scholarship" examined by the author for this book were the aphorisms of the Italian American sage, Yogi Berra — who famously observed, "When you come to a fork in the road, take it."

A more pertinent thought at this point was whether all this tergiversation resulted from the collision of triumphalist rhetoric — "we tell for the first time," "this is a mistake" — with elementary logic, and from the attempt to divert readers from the latter by flaunting the former.[10] For that logic, by any standard of reasoning, would have compelled the admission — which the author apparently could not bring himself to make — that the church, "with more direct influence over popular attitudes in Italy than elsewhere," must have been in some way connected or related or at least remotely linked to the universally recognized fact that the ratio of Jews saved in relation to the total number of Italian Jews (more than 38,000 out of 45,000) was dramatically greater in Italy than in any other major nation in Nazi-occupied Europe. And among less-than-major nations, only Denmark had a comparable ratio — due, however, to the universally recognized fact that the Führer did not want to disturb the "aryan" Danes in his "favored protectorate." Adopting Kertzer's language on Austria in the excerpt earlier, the logical question was, "first, what are we to make of Italy, an overwhelmingly Catholic country?" What the author failed to make of that unavoidable question was gradually leading me to believe that he was not particularly opposed to rigging an argument to validate an a priori position. (That criticism can be brought even more severely to the treatment of the influence attributed to something called the "worldwide network" of Catholic publications and the undeniably anti-Semitic Jesuit magazine, *Civiltà cattolica* — both of which will be discussed in the next chapter.[11])

10. I won't labor the point, but will simply note again the air of smugness that not infrequently surfaces in this author's analyses. In another interview available on his website, in response to a question regarding the seriously flawed Vatican document, "We Remember," Kertzer responded: "I agree that the research reported in my book effectively demolishes the thesis of the 1998 Vatican report on the Church's role in the rise of modern anti-Semitism and the Holocaust."

11. Since this is the first mention of the magazine, it is appropriate to note that its virulent hatred of Jews has long been recognized, and in the larger Catholic world has long been discounted as the last gasp of the ultramontanism culminating in Vatican I. The magazine's subsequent refocusing on Jews was a widely discussed commonplace well before Kertzer's book; see, for example, Thomas Sheehan, "Everyone Has to Tell the Truth," *Continuum* (Autumn 1990), where Sheehan in the context of efforts to rehabilitate Martin Heidegger — one of Sheehan's academic specializations — also took on Enrico Rosa, the bigoted editor of

Also on the expanding negative side of the ledger was the repeatedly displayed tone of highly personal animus toward each of the modern popes being analyzed. Kertzer had written of the "demonization" of Jews by the church — as noted earlier, certainly not an unfair description — but one had to wonder whether employing the same contemptuous language for these churchmen did not also place him among the unwashed demonizers. With the exception of Benedict XV,[12] the other popes that Kertzer studies closely — Pius IX, Leo XIII, Pius X, and Pius XI — when they aren't depicted as duplicitous and arrogant anti-Semites (particularly Leo and Pius XI) come across as personally affable although a little simple-minded (particularly Pius IX who was beatified, and Pius X who was canonized). The false note struck by that depiction resonated in the following passage, which at this late stage of my appraisal of the book, I couldn't help but think was a transparently hokey avowal on the part of the author — especially since this seemingly magnanimous admission came two pages after he had introduced his readers to those murderous Austrian and Polish Catholics:

> Yet this is not a book about the battle of good against evil. The Church, whatever else it is, is a human institution, composed of popes, cardinals, bishops, inquisitors, monks, simple parish priests, and loyal (and not so loyal) laity. The story I tell in these pages is the story of these people. The tale includes its share of opportunism and deception, but for the most part it is the story of people who were convinced that they were doing God's own work. If I fail to bring their *worldview* to life, I will have failed to fully accomplish my task. (italics supplied)

Also at this stage, it was becoming fairly clear that this first-person phrase, "the story I tell," usually triggered, or perhaps merely revealed, a dislocation in the author's logical and/or rhetorical skills. The first encounter with the phrase was in the excerpt about "Pius XII's benevolent predecessor [who] shared the same stridently anti-Semitic views" — which proved to be neither strident nor anti-Semitic. Here, too, the "story-I-tell" phrase energized any latent suspicions, as the author first proffered a plaintive benison

---

Civiltà cattolica from 1915 to 1931 as well as chief contributor until his death in 1938 of anti-Semitic diatribes.

12. Benedict XV, who died in 1922, is described as "having the courage to try to chart a new course for papal relations with the Jews"; but he is decried twenty-five pages later for giving the title of "monsignor" to Ernest Jouin, "the best-known exponent of Catholic anti-Semitism in the 1920s."

upon "the Church" (always uppercase) as a human institution — "whatever else it is," in other presumably nonhuman venues — and then concluded with the assertion about confronting the specter of failure in bringing to life the "worldview" of this variegated group. This was all disarmingly noble — until one read further and discovered what it actually meant: "anti-Semitic screeds reflected . . . the worldview of the pope and his secretary of state"; "the Jew as fundamentally evil . . . was very much part of the Vatican's worldview"; "it was inevitable in the context of the Vatican worldview that communism should become associated with Judaism."

It was around this point in the process of evaluating the book that I decided to write a critique. It was getting more and more impossible to ignore the real purpose of the apparently even-handed disclosure that this is not about good and evil, or to overlook the real purpose of the seemingly small "share" of opportunists and deceivers being outweighed ("for the most part") by people who — in another non-persuasive non sequitur — "were convinced they were doing God's own work," but who by all logic, even with those "convictions" could certainly be engaging in "opportunism and deception." It didn't take a "hermeneutic of suspicion," or even a hermeneutic of much of anything but common sense, to deduce that all this was just laying it on too thick. Add to that, a seemingly generous dispensation of membership in the church which, whatever else it is, remains "human," since it is composed of parish priests and laity (modified as "simple" and "loyal") and various hierarchs (unmodified, and therefore presumably complex and treacherous), and one had a mix of negatives so overwhelming that even a sympathetic reader — as I originally was — had to conclude that this author was drastically overreaching, if not intentionally deceiving. Specifically, regarding the ostensibly large-minded and noble-hearted gestures in the excerpt above, it seemed more than obvious that they were merely flank-protecting tactics.[13]

Even with considerable gilding, the fact can't be obscured that *The Popes Against the Jews* really was about good and evil — as the author himself unwittingly acknowledged. In papal statements "there was a bombardment of

---

13. A similar tactic was introduced two paragraphs later. "Here we need to be careful not to view history backwards. While it is clear to us . . . that the Church would have to adapt to the new circumstances [after the capture of Rome in 1870], the popes of the time could be forgiven for not sharing this view." Although the repeated public position of the author is that one must not judge the pre-Holocaust world in the light of post-Holocaust standards, this is the only place in the book where the word "forgive," or any cognate or synonym of that word, is related to the popes.

references to evil Jews," and most of them as we have seen had to do with the "worldview" or "perspective" attributed to such generalized abstractions as "the Vatican," "the Holy See," and "the popes." "So intense was their [Jews'] hatred of Christianity that no evil was too great for them"; "documents aimed at demonstrating the Jews' evil were collected"; "in the eyes of leading churchmen [Jews] had rapidly become evil and insolent masterminds"; "decades after decades, forces close to the Vatican had denounced the Jews as evil conspirators." At the conclusion of the chapter on Austria, the reader's appetite for more of the same was whetted: "Nor were Austria and Galicia the only places where, from a Vatican perspective, this conflict between the good forces of Catholicism and the malevolent forces of Judaism was being played out." And when the Jews were not being described as evil, then the forces of liberalism, secularism, democracy, and the like, were so described. The end result was the same, since for those forces the Jews are the surrogates. "Jews as major beneficiaries of modern times and the new ideas of freedom and equality became in the eyes of the Vatican prelates preeminent symbols of the modernity they abhorred."

As to why the author would so emphatically say in his introduction the opposite of what he says in the body of his book, one might be tempted to speculate that this is merely more "projection" or mirror imaging by the author of the cunning and craftiness he attributes to the popes. But everyone possessed by or at least influenced by the book's "worldview" — readers, reviewers, editors, publishers, and so on — will most likely regard this as a preemptive response aimed at future carpers who might say such things as that the book is a black/white portrayal of the popes, or that the book tars every churchman it analyzes. To this, the author or his representatives and defenders can respond — introducing a fairly conventional escape valve — by saying, in effect, that the book explicitly rejects such simplification; and they can then point to statements like those excerpted above: this is "not about good and evil"; "people doing God's own work"; "if I fail to bring their worldview to life, I will have failed," and so on.

Unfortunately, that defense won't wash. The cover is blown by the repeated use of the same yes/no devisal throughout the book. On the "yes" side, the reader is told: "The Church, despite its hierarchical structure, is not monolithic. In this sense it is misleading to speak of how 'the Church' acted towards the Jews." But on the "no" side the same reader will come across references to "the Church's ritual murder campaign"; "the Church's conduct in the Mortara affair"; "the Church's embrace of modern political anti-Semitism"; and finally, a text that is all-encompassing: "The Church played an important role in promulgating every one of the ideas that are central to modern anti-Semitism." One cannot but conclude that this language is intentionally strategic, as "the Church" becomes interchangeable with "the Vatican" and implicitly with "the pope" — which then allows anti-Semitism to be attributed not just to the first two relatively abstract entities but also — and most important — to the person of each named pope himself.

It was the accumulation of these tactics joined to the flood of errors indicated above that finally led to my decision to examine more closely the entire book. But the tactics and the errors were simply the external indicators of a more profound flaw which appeared to be rooted in some kind of ideological fixation on the papacy, a fixation that is brought to light in the pages that follow. However, it is no condemnation of the author (nor any justification of the Vatican) that this kind of fixation is facilitated by the fact that the Roman curia was famously the most tangled bureaucratic web of any modern polity.[14] Cardinal Newman, who had been enmeshed in that web, wrote that "a thorough routing out of things" was necessary if Rome was ever to become truly functional. As a result, not only was responsibility for a given statement difficult to determine, but sometimes statements were written or edited by unknown or unacknowledged functionaries — and then treated as official. Owen Chadwick in *A History of the Popes 1830-1914* (1998) describes the burlesque bureaucratic fate of an unquestionably official statement of Pope Pius X — and there will be several other similar instances in the next chapter on the Catholic press:

> The chief drafter was the Spanish cardinal Vives y Tutó. But Monsignor [Umberto] Benigni, hammer of the modernists, took a hand and pushed into the wording of the bull about Charles Borromeo quotations on Luther and the Reformers — causing an uproar in Germany. Neither Pius X nor his Secretary of State were pleased at the wording which the drafters had put into the pope's mouth. [Cardinal] Merry del Val said he first heard of the encyclical when it appeared in the *Osservatore romano*.

14. "In fact, the Vatican was a Babel of conflicting views, not to speak of the religious orders also represented there, or the hierarchies in each country, who were in turn susceptible to shifts in clerical and lay opinion. On a number of occasions, Vatican initiatives were retracted at the urging of the national episcopacies concerned. . . . These reminders of the historical reality caution against any loose generalizations about the 'Catholic Church.'" Michael Burleigh, *Sacred Causes: The Clash of Religion and Politics from the Great War to the War on Terror* (2007).

But Kertzer's ideological fixation will not tolerate the notion of bureaucrats meddling in one another's business, of rival factions guarding their turf, of crossed wires, of "red-tapism" (again, a term used by Cardinal Newman), of protective rigmarole — anything of the sort that has characterized every other hierarchical bureaucracy in the world from the present-day Pentagon to pre-Revolution Versailles, and probably all the way back to the court of biblical David. One gets the impression that for Kertzer any statement, however obscure or absurd, which is presumed to originate in anything connected to or even in the vicinity of "the Vatican," must ultimately be attributed to "the Supreme Pontiff." The foundation for this free-wheeling attribution is the ideological conviction, invoked throughout the book like a mantra, that the Vatican press because it was literally "speaking" for the pope was therefore followed by all Catholic publications in the world — an issue to be taken up in the next chapter.

CHAPTER 2

The (Supernatural) Power of the Press

Of the statements I referred to at the end of the preceding chapter as being invariably attributed to the pope, none of them is so directly linked to him as those appearing in *La Civiltà cattolica* and *L'Osservatore romano*. From there it is only a small step for this author to treat every anti-Semitic utterance in "the worldwide network" of the Catholic press — to which he devotes a separate chapter — as somehow sharing in the papal charism, and thus as expressing views or opinions endorsed by the Holy See. This is not because there is a quotation from a papal encyclical, bull, or other official document in the publications making up the "network," but because they follow to the letter the lead of the twice-monthly Jesuit magazine, *La Civiltà cattolica*. As for the Vatican daily newspaper, *L'Osservatore romano*, its unsigned articles were often regarded as having an authoritative character, but they were thought to declare the views of the pope himself only when published on the first page in a different typeface from the rest of the paper.[1]

The entire notion of a papal obsession with Jews and Judaism is extrapolated by Kertzer from the fact that anti-Semitic articles did appear in *Civiltà cattolica*. "The Jesuit journal kicked off its long campaign against the Jews in December 1880. The term 'anti-Semitism' itself had been coined a year earlier, in 1879, by a German Wilhelm Marr." A page later one reads — with some surprise at even this author's hyperbolic claim regarding causality: "*Civiltà cattolica*'s anti-Jewish campaign, coming when it did, proved

---

1. In order to lend a similar credence to *Civiltà cattolica*, the reader is several times informed of such things as that it was "supervised by the popes and their secretaries of state" who personally "reviewed and approved the contents." This claim will be examined presently.

crucial to the rise of modern anti-Semitism." Thus, without the Jesuit magazine the world would not have suffered the blight of this particular horror, and without this particular horror there would not have been a Holocaust. The paragraph that began with the pronouncement about the magazine being "crucial" ended with the magazine giving anti-Semitism "a papal imprimatur." The inevitable conclusion — always skirted though never spelled out in detail — is: no papacy, no six million. The presumable reason this has not been discovered by other researchers is that it has been a closely guarded secret.

A conspiracy is involved and it becomes fundamental to the thesis of Kertzer's book. The popes "in their public statements" would never give voice to their real hatred of Jews.

> But out of the limelight, and with the assistance of their secretaries of state [by definition, a conspiracy requires more than one person] the popes regulated the anti-Semitic campaigns conducted in the Church press — most notably through *L'Osservatore romano* and *La Civiltà cattolica,* over which they exercised control.[2]

The "less notable" way for popes to regulate such campaigns is not revealed, but it is clearly implied that the popes nevertheless exercised their anti-Semitism through other journalistic venues as well. As to Kertzer's thesis, I will examine it in detail shortly, but will briefly point out here how unlikely it was that Pius IX, who had been forced into exile at the beginning of his reign, who lost the Papal States in the middle of it, and finally lost Rome it-

---

2. The operative terms here are "regulated" and "control." The Jesuit biographer of Pius IX, Giacomo Martina, reviewed a history of *La Civiltà cattolica* — *La Segregazione amichevole* (2000), by Ruggero Taradel and Barbara Raggi — in which, among many other issues, the question was raised, "whether the magazine confined itself to expressing the thoughts and directives of the pope or had a line of its own?" Martina said that while the magazine would never be at odds with the pontiff, and sometimes its agreement with him would be in "perfect accord" — offering the example of opposition to Masonry — it would also adopt with more or less emphasis some theses of its own. He then went on to observe how difficult it was to grasp *la mentalità* of Giuseppe Oreglia, Raffaele Ballerini, and Saverio Rondina, the three Jesuit writers who most bitterly and triumphantly attacked the Jews, and who according to Kertzer "kicked off" the campaign that was "crucial to the rise of modern anti-Semitism." Martina concluded by describing the Jesuits of *Civiltà* as differing from their confreres elsewhere, specifically in France and Germany — to which he could certainly have added the entire Anglophone world. (Martina's review of the book appeared in *La Civiltà cattolica* [May 6, 2000], and the book itself is cited by Kertzer.)

self toward the end of it, would have attributed all or even any of these misfortunes primarily if not exclusively to Jews — an attribution that Kertzer will repeatedly make. As for Pius's successor, Leo XIII, he inherited a church on the verge of collapse into chaos, and his preoccupation with staving off the forces of further deterioration led him to address systematically the crucial political, social, cultural, and theological issues of the era. Whether he also had the time and/or the desire to turn away from such overwhelming matters of office, and to conduct organized anti-Semitic campaigns, certainly on the face of it appears unlikely if not farfetched.

But on the other hand — at least it merits mention — there is the verifiable fact that the majority of people who have reviewed *The Popes Against the Jews* or otherwise commented on it publicly have enthusiastically embraced its message, and not all of them can be described as either disgruntled Catholics or embittered Jews. I am not here to compose a new "grammar of assent" as to why people end up believing in this or that religious assumption, theory, principle, doctrine, and the like, but that so many people so wholeheartedly embraced what I was beginning to view as a tissue of weak inferences indicated on the part of the author *either* historically revolutionary research and exceptional rhetorical skills, *or,* on the part of many readers, a responsiveness to repetitive insistence. I would now emphasize particularly the latter, because even in the above comments, mention of *Civiltà cattolica* has occurred half a dozen times, and it actually occurs, according to Amazon's concordance, more than sixty times in the book. Since it is almost entirely from reading the Jesuit magazine that Kertzer created his notion of a secret anti-Semitic papal conspiracy, one can understand the need for such a battery of references.

Ordinarily when a student of any historical period examines the views of its leading protagonists, he or she concentrates on and treats as of the greatest moment their actual writings. When reading *The Popes Against the Jews,* what comes as a considerable surprise is the realization that notwithstanding the earlier emphasis on the importance of "newly opened archives," there are very few citations of the words of any popes, whether from that heralded resource or, even odder, from their published allocutions, bulls, encyclicals, and letters.[3] For Kertzer, that simply proves how crafty those Jew-hating popes were. As to the significance of this, "let me give a small example" — to quote

---

3. The two exceptions that prove the rule — to be examined in detail in the next chapter — are the already encountered "Jews-as-dogs" theme and the putatively anti-Semitic term "synagogue of Satan." They are both from public papal documents.

Kertzer. John Courtney Murray, the theologian who made the most important contribution of any American to the decisions of Vatican II — particularly regarding such issues as freedom of conscience and the relationship between church and state — devoted his life to studying the writings of the popes, most particularly the popes of the same period on which Kertzer concentrates. Murray devoted special attention to Leo XIII, whom most historians would describe as the first pope to address such issues in their modern setting, and whom Kertzer has singled out by name as the pope who "out of the limelight" craftily directed the Jew-hating campaigns.

But where Kertzer began his study with the a priori assertion that no pope would put into writing his anti-Semitism (and then went on to cite magazines and newspapers as speaking for the pope), Murray began his study by a survey of all available papal documents, and came to the following conclusion:

> In the whole Leonine corpus there are some ninety-seven documents which are relevant to the problem of Church and State. Perhaps twenty are of major importance. What follows is an attempt to outline the structure of the doctrine which is evolved in this whole mass of documents, to indicate the themes which are developed, the relative weight of emphasis given to each, their relationships with each other, and their appositeness to the historical problems of the time.[4]

Murray then cited the most relevant documents by name and noted that "citations are usually made from *Acta Sanctae Sedis,* as well as from two other editions of the pope's allocutions, letters, and constitutions" — those two editions together comprising fourteen volumes: in all, a rather large body of writings directly attributable to this pope.

Presumably, it is by examining such texts — along with relevant secondary literature — that a student learns what a particular person believed on a

---

4. Since much of the discussion in *The Popes Against the Jews* is devoted to the historical context of the papacy during the rise of "modern anti-Semitism," it is also fitting to cite Murray on that same period, that is, from 1878 to 1903: "The historical situation is important. Leo XIII did not compose his doctrine in the midst of academic quiet, in the leisure of a library, sealed off from the swirling struggles in the marketplace of the late nineteenth-century world. Rather, he hammered it out as the head of an embattled Church, which was under an attack more radical and total than any that the Church had previously encountered in history" ("Leo XIII on Church and State: The General Structure of the Controversy," *Theological Studies* [March 1953]).

particular issue. But when one seeks to determine how Kertzer learned about the popes' belief in Jewish evildoing and about their embrace of modern racist anti-Semitism, he has foreclosed the possibility that any such texts can be brought forth. This has the happy consequence, at least for him, that there is no need to examine the "whole mass of documents," nor to undertake the burdensome chore of indicating "the themes which are developed, the relative weight of emphasis given to each, their relationships with each other, and their appositeness to the historical problems of the time." Instead, one can read selective issues of the Vatican daily newspaper and the Jesuit fortnightly magazine — which end up being not only intrinsically significant expressions of papal anti-Semitism but also are extrinsically significant since, according to Kertzer, they set the tone and provided the content for "Catholic newspapers throughout the world."

Nor did the roundabout proof of the influence of these two publications entail the kind of argument common to historical deduction or conventional social science research. Instead, there is a barrage of abstractions couched in what grammarians term "third-person indirect discourse" — here resulting in my blizzard of italics. The two publications were "viewed *inside and outside* the Church as communicating the Pope's *true sentiments*"; were "regarded by the network of Catholic newspapers throughout the world as the *most authoritative source*"; were "viewed throughout the Catholic world as offering the *clearest expressions of the Pope's own perspectives.*" Apart from the absolutist language of such phrases as "throughout the world" and "inside and outside the Church," there is the more difficult matter of determining precisely who are — apart from Kertzer himself — these unnamed third parties who "viewed" and "regarded" *Civiltà cattolica* and *Osservatore romano* in these rather grand terms. The nebulous identity of these enthusiastic viewers and regarders proves to be as persuasive for the book's thesis as was the use of such wooly words as "sentiments," "perspective," and "worldview" for what the author then treated as papal certitudes or convictions regarding Jewish evil. The following two sentences offer an elaboration of Kertzer's own "perspective": "The Vatican crusade against the Jews involved not only the two semi-official voices of the Holy See, but a large and growing network of other Catholic newspapers in Italy and beyond." "In the Catholic world, *Civiltà cattolica* came to be regarded as the unofficial voice of the pope himself."

While very few would question the assumption that the Vatican daily, *L'Osservatore romano,* generally represented the views of high church officials, it is less plausible to do the same regarding the Jesuit magazine. But since the latter was viciously anti-Semitic — for which today's Jesuits other than in North America have officially expressed no remorse — Kertzer seems free to indulge in the kinds of generalizations that are ordinarily the bane of experienced scholars: "The most influential Catholic periodical anywhere in the world was *La Civiltà cattolica*." But this, if true, would have made it more influential than the Vatican's own daily newspaper *L'Osservatore romano*, described by Kertzer as "official." It made some sense, then, to later describe the Jesuit magazine as "the unofficial voice of the Pope himself," except that both publications — as evident in the preceding paragraph — were defined as only "semi-official." Certainly the most interesting resolution of the "unofficial," "semi-official," "official" confusion is the judgment of the chief editor *(direttore)* of the magazine itself — one who is not cited by Kertzer but who was certainly in charge of the magazine during the magazine's anti-Semitic campaign. Salvatore Maria Brandi wrote in the magazine in June 1899 that it was neither "official nor authorized by anyone outside the [Jesuit] college of writers who publish their ideas under the ordinary vigilance of Holy Mother Church."[5]

To further validate the pure pedigree of *Civiltà cattolica*, the sentence about its being "the most influential Catholic periodical anywhere in the world" continued by noting that it was "founded at the request of Pope Pius IX and supervised by the popes and their secretaries of state." I will address more extensively the supervision by those two officials in the next chapter, but the role of the Jesuits demands attention here. In the context of the founding of the magazine, Roland Hill, author of the definitive biography, *Lord Acton* (2000), quotes a letter of Acton to his mentor, Monsignor Döllinger, which suggests control by the Jesuits rather than by the pope: "when he [Pius IX] lost his crown on the field of liberty, he became easily convinced that it was to be regained only in the opposite way, and so he went over to the Jesuits who were able to exploit his changed circumstances the

---

5. See John Louis Ciani, *Across a Wide Ocean: Salvatore Maria Brandi, SJ, and the "Civiltà Cattolica": From Americanism to Modernism* (1992).

Brandi was an Italian Jesuit who, after studying and teaching at Woodstock College in the United States for sixteen years, returned to Rome in 1891 to join the staff of the Jesuit magazine, where he would serve as *direttore* from 1906 to 1913. Ciani's work is in effect a study of the disagreements — often quite sharp — between the Vatican and the magazine, particularly regarding political matters in Italy and doctrinal matters in the United States, during the final years of Leo XIII and into the reign of Benedict XV. There is no mention in Ciani's work, which will be cited several times in the pages that follow, of anything related to anti-Semitism on the part of the papacy or the magazine.

more easily for their purposes." Roger Aubert (*Le Pontificat de Pie IX* [1963]) notes that an anonymous statement published at the death of the pope described the editors of *Civiltà cattolica* as constituting "a kind of secret government," another observation that doesn't quite jibe with the close regulation by the Vatican that Kertzer has postulated.

In fact, disagreements between the editors and the pope were apparently more strained during the reign of Leo XIII because his treatment of the "Roman Question" — the pope vis-à-vis the Italian government — became more contentious than it had been during the reign of his predecessor. According to John Louis Ciani, one such conflict occurred toward the end of Leo's reign in 1902, when the Jesuit general received a complaint that the staff of the magazine was divided (four against three) over support for the Christian Democratic Party in Italy. Attacking the idea was Raffaele Ballerini, the then director, and a member of the minority group, in an article titled "False Tendencies of Christian Democracy." The result, according to Ballerini himself, was that the "opposing cliques engaged in a double offensive" of lobbying among interested parties in the Vatican over whether the controversial piece should appear in print — which in the event, it did not. The relevance of these intermural conflicts to the larger issue of papal-regulated anti-Semitism is brought out by Kertzer's characterization of one of Ballerini's screeds against the Jews, which *did* get published, in these terms: "It is hard to imagine a more enthusiastic *Vatican endorsement*" — although it is quite clear that it was the Jesuit *collegio* and not the Vatican that was setting policy. This is not to even hint at the suggestion that there is anything in the anti-Semitism of *Civiltà cattolica* that wouldn't revolt today's reader.

What is omitted from *The Popes Against the Jews* is anything that might indicate the possibility of discord not only between the Jesuits and papal officials, but also between factions among the Jesuit editors, as well as among the advocates of varying currents of opinion swirling around curial officials in general. This brings these issues back to Kertzer's view of papal governance where there are no meddlers, no factions within, and no pressures from without. Rather than the crossed wires and "red-tapism" mentioned in the previous chapter, there is a direct line from what the pope believes to what the editors of *Civiltà cattolica* write. Concerning "pressure from without," a few years later after Leo XIII's death, when the anti-Modernist purge was launched, its crusading supporters known as "Integrists" — the overwhelming majority of whom were also vehement anti-Semites — began to attack the magazine for not being in line with the allegedly authentic views of the pope as found in what they called "the *real* papal press" — which did not include *Civiltà cattolica*.[6]

As for an earlier assertion that the Jesuit magazine was regarded as the "most authoritative" source for "Catholic newspapers throughout the world," Kertzer's description of that world also falls victim to his penchant for exaggeration. The following is from the chapter titled "The Catholic Press." "By the beginning of the twentieth century, Italy had about 500 Catholic periodicals, including 30 dailies." This had been preceded by the observation that "In the last decades of the nineteenth century, daily newspapers, weeklies, bi-weeklies, and monthlies took on an ever-increasing importance." But one can be certain that of the vaunted five hundred, the majority fell into none of those "periodical" categories, but into the category (unmentioned) of "parish bulletins." Certainly the prospect of five hundred Catholic periodicals in Italy alone leaves the reader with the assumption of a comparably sizeable presence elsewhere — though Kertzer will proffer no specific figures. But cumulatively "the network of Catholic newspapers throughout the world" must number, at least by his reckoning, in the thousands — all of which viewed or regarded *Civiltà cattolica* as "the most influential Catholic periodical anywhere" and, in proof of that influence, "quoted its articles constantly."

Unfortunately, although there are pages of vituperative anti-Semitic quotations from *Civiltà cattolica*, there is very little replication of those sentiments elsewhere, and where they are evident, the language is drastically toned down to general terms. Moreover, there is no citation *anywhere* in *The Popes Against the Jews* of an actual quotation from the Jesuit magazine by any member of the worldwide network of the Catholic press. Lastly, out of those five hundred Italian Catholic publications — all of which have been described as subservient to *Civiltà cattolica* — there are only two that are quoted by Kertzer. One of the reasons a reader of his book may find this minuscule figure startling is that there are so many repetitive references to the impact of the Jesuit magazine and so many elaborate descriptions of racist malevolence attributed to it — literally page after page, as we will see in the next chapters — that it is easy to assume there is a slew of church-sponsored publications all over Europe, and even in the New World, that are giving

---

6. The antagonism between the "official" voice of the pope in *Civiltà Cattolica* and the "real" voice in the anti-Modernist press will be examined shortly via the words of the man at the heart of the purge, who is writing contemporaneously in the American *Catholic Encyclopedia*. This is the ubiquitous Umberto Benigni, described in the previous chapter by Owen Chadwick as the "hammer of the modernists" who doctored a papal bull, which then "caused an uproar in Germany."

voice to this seemingly all-pervasive animus. But Kertzer, rather than providing publications and quotations from *Civiltà*'s "network," again mentions only the same two papers, which as we will see are always cited with the implication, or sometimes the actual assertion, that there are many more that could readily be mentioned — but are not. Needless to say, this isn't the way even a serious sociologist would amass statistical evidence to support a given thesis.

After declaring that "the Vatican crusade against the Jews" involved not only the Jesuit magazine but "a large and growing network . . . in Italy and beyond," Kertzer continued: "Many examples could be given, but we cite here only the two that were closest to the Vatican" — as he introduces the diocesan papers in Florence and Milan. I will address the matter of "the beyond," shortly, but for now it suffices to repeat that these are the only Italian Catholic newspapers quoted anywhere in the book, a fact that is obscured because those quotations are scattered over fourteen different pages. (There is, however, mention of an Italian clergy bulletin which cites — an irony that evades Kertzer — a Polish source.) Concerning even those two diocesan papers, after providing several paragraphs of quotations, the treatment ends with intentional ambiguity: "In these articles [from Milan's *L'Osservatore cattolico*], *as in all of the Catholic press* closest to the Vatican, the battle against Jews. . . ." "*Like the rest of the Catholic press*, Florence's *L'Unità cattolica* combined the warning against Jews." But there are no citations providing names and dates where *Civiltà cattolica* is quoted or referenced by any of the 498 other Italian daily newspapers, weeklies, biweeklies, and monthlies — not even to mention parish bulletins — which by Kertzer's own estimate are also part of the worldwide network.

Regarding a series of anti-Semitic articles in *L'Osservatore cattolico,* the reader had earlier been told that "many Catholic papers in Italy, France, Austria, and Germany reprinted extracts from them." But the only validation of the statement is an article in the same *L'Osservatore cattolico* touting that claim. There is no other evidence that newspapers in those four countries reprinted material from the Milanese paper. So then, as though waiving the issue of specifics regarding "all the Catholic press," or "the rest of the Catholic press," Kertzer refocuses attention on the alleged preeminence of those same two papers. It was the editor of *L'Osservatore cattolico,* according to Kertzer, who reported that his "soul filled with joy . . . by the Sovereign's most beautiful expressions of satisfaction" — at a time when the editor "was in the midst of publishing . . . the most gruesome descriptions of how small children were butchered by the Jews." Kertzer then adds that this papal praise was "widely trumpeted in the Catholic press" — which here means trumpeted in the paper edited by the overjoyed editor who is also the only source for the alleged expression of papal satisfaction.

A similar instance of papal "regulation" — and authorial escalation — is proffered regarding *L'Unità cattolica*. When it is first mentioned, it is described as "published by priests with close ties to the Holy See." After it "ran article after article" that tarred "the Jews with the ritual murder charge," the paper is described as "known for reflecting papal perspectives and enjoying close relations with Pius X." But as with those who "regarded" and "viewed" *Civiltà cattolica* as of "worldwide" influence, there is no identification of the "who" it is that knew what the Florentine paper reflected or enjoyed. On the other hand, it was the previously cited *direttore* of the Jesuit magazine itself, Salvatore Brandi, who at the height of the Modernist crisis "contended [that] *L'Unità cattolica*'s methods served neither Catholic nor papal causes." As a result, Brandi had *Civiltà cattolica* terminate all exchanges with the Florentine paper. Addressing specifically the matter of service to pope and church, Brandi then linked *L'Unità cattolica* to *La Riscossa* — the most venomous anti-Semitic, anti-Modernist, and Integrist publication — and described the latter as using "vulgar, bitter language" and committing "gravely offensive abuses."

Equally dubious is Kertzer's foundational assumption that *Civiltà cattolica* was leading the march of mind responsible for modern racist anti-Semitism. The chronology indicates that it is just as likely that those particular Jesuits who wrote the anti-Jewish articles were themselves responding to an already existing surge of racial animus. Giovanni Miccoli, whom Kertzer usually follows assiduously, remarks that "Even *Civiltà cattolica* up to the 1870s only fleetingly mentioned the Jews. The primary artisans of the revolution, in the eyes of the Holy See, remained masonry and the sects."[7] C. J. T. Talar, in a remarkably rich study, also notes that it was not until the 1880s that racist anti-Semitism began to become a mass movement — particularly in France, still chafing at defeat in the Franco-Prussian War — which fused "the anti-Jewish heritage of the Christian tradition, the Judeophobic anti-capitalism of the socialists, and the racist theses of the new anthropological sciences."[8] This three-part confluence is reduced by Kertzer to the

---

7. "Santa Sede, questione ebraica e antisemitismo fra Otto e Novocento," in Corrado Vivanti, ed., *Storia d'Italia, Gli ebrei in Italia,* II (1997).

8. "Anti-Semitism as Ally: Campaigning Against Masonry and Modernism," *Continuum* 2, no. 2 (1993).

monocausal "papacy," as seen through the lens of *Civiltà cattolica* and the al-legedly vast number of publications in its network.

To regard *Civiltà cattolica* as the catalyst of these developments, or the Vatican as instigator or even inspirer of these campaigns, is to mistake effect for cause. Of course, the Jesuit magazine would approve the denunciation of Masonic-Jewish-Sect conspiracies, and some of the denouncers would have received titular honorifics from the Holy See or have had audiences with the pope, though hardly for their advocacy of this or that anti-Semitic plot. Usually they were honored for their vociferous claims to be speaking in de-fense of the Christian tradition and more particularly, during the later years of Pius IX and on and up to the reign of Pius XI, to be speaking for the resto-ration of Rome to papal rule.

What is surprising is that a thesis as historically significant as Kertzer's is supported by so little evidence. But perhaps one should not be surprised since this is also the writer who believed the message of *Hitler's Pope,* and had the author of that "recent bestseller" publicly commend his book. Neither writer had a problem with embracing the notion that the popes in secret for approximately ninety years "conspired," "campaigned," and "led a crusade" against the Jews through the power and influence of a Jesuit magazine that averaged a circulation of around eleven thousand copies an issue. Notwith-standing this tenuous if nonexistent foundation, all readers are expected to believe that because the magazine was "the most influential Catholic periodi-cal anywhere in the world," it therefore was — so the mantra declares — "cru-cial to the rise of modern racist anti-Semitism." The one faintly plausible rea-son for believing any of this is the additional claim that the magazine was leading "the network of Catholic newspapers throughout the world," which "quoted its articles constantly." Unfortunately, verifying the accuracy of that last judgment is going to entail an examination, wearisome but necessary, of the network itself. This examination, coming as it does so early in the book, will be kept as brief as possible.[9]

A beginning can be made with the views of the lowly monsignor, Umberto Benigni, already several times encountered — fudger of papal bulls, premier Integrist — and now appearing as an authority on Italian

---

9. Gerard Manley Hopkins's greatest poem, "The Wreck of the Deutschland," was also very long and very complex and so was referred to as "the dragon in the gate," since it pre-ceded his more accessible other poems. This survey of the worldwide network is this book's dragon. Fortunately for the reader, there is also what PR types now refer to as "incentivization." In what follows, there will be some illuminating references to the greatest pope in the modern era, if not in the history of the papacy, John XXIII.

journalistic efforts via an article for the 1911 American *Catholic Encyclopedia*.[10] As noted earlier, this was also the man who would a decade later publish an Italian translation of the *Protocols of the Elders of Zion*. In the *Catholic Encyclopedia* article he named and described fewer than a hundred publications, a figure that of necessity excludes most of the "500 Catholic periodicals" mentioned earlier by Kertzer. This is what appears in the category, "historical periodicals," relative to the Jesuit magazine and its relations with the pope:

> The oldest and most widely-circulated is the *Civiltà Cattolica,* conducted by priests of the Society of Jesus, forming a community by themselves and directly subject to the General of the Society. This was founded in 1850 under the auspices of Pius IX. Among the founders and early writers Bresciani, Curci, Brunengo, Taparelli, Cornoldi, Liberatore, etc. won distinction.

For Benigni in his *Catholic Encyclopedia* article to treat as merely one among many — not even *primus inter pares* — the publication that was "regarded" or "viewed" as of paramount influence on "the network of Catholic newspapers throughout the world" would seem to suggest at least an element of exaggeration on the part of Kertzer. But since Benigni, a fanatic anti-Modernist, was writing at the height of the crisis, his description should also be read as another version of the kind of criticism *Civiltà* was subjected to by the Integrist editors of *L'Unità cattolica* and *La Riscossa* mentioned above.

Even more intriguing in terms of Benigni himself is the trumpeting of his own journalistic achievements. The publication he founded at the beginning of the Modernist crisis to delate and expose errant clergy and religious scholars, including bishops and cardinals, *Corrispondenza romana* (later for tactical reasons renamed *Corréspondance de Rome*), is described as "an echo of the Vatican." This makes it sound very much like Kertzer's *Civiltà cattolica* — although there is no doubt that during the anti-Modernist crusade Pius X

---

10. Benigni had begun his career in Rome as a professor of church history who would have as a student the future Pope John XXIII. The biographers of the pope, Peter Hebblethwaite and Margaret Hebblethwaite, note that at this date Benigni appeared innocuous, and was influential only on Roncalli's decision to specialize in historical studies. (*John XXIII: Pope of the Century* [2005]).

Throughout *Were the Popes Against the Jews?* Benigni plays a kind of Forrest Gump role, appearing in a variety of unexpected places, circumstances, and guises — none of them particularly benign.

supported Benigni's spy apparatus. In what Benigni categorizes as "political and social reviews," he also makes an interesting distinction: "two tendencies existed, one decidedly liberal, and the other absolutely papal." Then without naming any publications in the former group, he suggests their dissimulation, if not hypocrisy: "The reviews taking this liberal attitude never failed however to profess their allegiance and obedience to authority." He then lauds the anti-Modernist/anti-Semitic publications which, as noted earlier, are equated with "the papal press":

> On the other hand there existed the papal press, which might be characterized by its perfect submission to and advocacy of the prevailing opinions of the Vatican and the episcopate. To this last class belong: the *Riscossa* of Braganse (Mgr Scotton); the *Unità cattolica* (Florence); the *Italia Reale* (Turin); the *Liguria* (Genoa); the *Difesa* (Venice); the *Osservatore romano* (Rome); the *Libertà* (Naples); the *Correspondance de Rome,* and some other small sheets.

To be noted is not only the mention of *L'Osservatore romano* (certainly mandatory in this context), but also and more remarkably, the absence of *Civiltà cattolica,* an absence made more striking by the presence of its alleged Florentine clone, *L'Unità cattolica.* By this reading, "the papal press" does not include the publication repeatedly identified by Kertzer with the voice of the pope. This is not because the others were or weren't anti-Semitic — apart from *L'Osservatore romano,* they definitely were — but because Benigni's target of choice, differing here from that of Kertzer, is the Catholic Modernists, and these are all virulently Integrist publications, including of course Benigni's own *Corréspondance de Rome.* The latter may be said to have been the leader of its own "network," since at least three of the publications mentioned here — the *Riscossa* being the most infamous — were directed by members of the Sodalitium Pianum, Benigni's international spy-and-delate ring mentioned earlier.[11]

---

11. *Riscossa* was controlled by three priest brothers who were constant critics of the administration of Cardinal Andrea Ferrari of Florence ("a seed bed of Modernism"). Ferrari was at that time the spiritual guide of the young Angelo Roncalli who, later as pope, would introduce Ferrari's cause for beatification — brought to fulfillment by John Paul II. The failure of Pius X to rein in *Riscossa* and his shameful treatment of Cardinal Ferrari were raised as objections during the proceedings for the pope's canonization. See Kenneth L. Woodward, *Making Saints* (1990), and Gerald J. O'Brien, S.J., "Anti-Modernism: The Integralist Campaign," *Continuum* (Summer 1965). The latter was the first exposition in the Anglo-

In the category, "historical reviews," Benigni has the following entry, "*Revista storico-critica delle scienze teologiche* (Rome, 1905), recently condemned by the Holy Office." This was the journal briefly edited by Ernesto Buonaiutti, primary author of *Il programma dei modernista*, which was translated into French, German, and English — the latter by George Tyrrell, the leading British Modernist who, like Buonaiutti himself, was also fated to be excommunicated.[12] Buonaiutti had been a classmate of Angelo Roncalli, and it was apparently correspondence between the two of them that led to the now famous file of the Holy Office, "Suspected of Modernism," which would be discovered when he was pope and to which he would append the following: "I, John XXIII, Pope, declare that I was never a Modernist."[13] Later he whimsically told a group of seminarians, "I am the living example that a priest who has been placed under observation by the Holy Office can still be pope."

This brings the survey of what Kertzer called *Civiltà cattolica*'s "large and growing network in Italy and beyond" to the lands of the "beyond," beginning with France. Again, Kertzer provides a few quotations but only a dearth of named sources that could connect the quotations to the Jesuit publication — which remains the central point at issue. It is undeniable that there were many Catholics at all levels of the church and society who embraced the new racist anti-Semitism; there were also many (particularly among the clergy) who also embraced the new theological anti-Modernism. As noted, both "antis" usually went hand in hand. That the tiny number of those who were bilingual found consolation and/or support in *Civiltà cattolica* is probably also not to be questioned. That the latter was the medium for engendering a crucially important and papally regulated anti-Semitism is not only deniable but until some direct connection can be made, it remains merely an oft-repeated assertion that not even pages of Kertzer's generic quotations can bolster.

Moreover, that any of the publications mentioned thus far had anything to do with papal campaigns, whether anti-Semitic or anti-Modernist, would appear to be contradicted by observations like the following from John

---

phone world of the transnational character and extensive influence of Benigni's Sodalitium Pianum, which continued operating with the approval of curial cardinals well into the reign of Benedict XV.

12. See Giacomo Losito, "Ernesto Buonaiuti and the Program of the Modernists," *U.S. Catholic Historian* (Winter 2007). (Readers owe this issue of *U.S. Catholic Historian* to the efforts and wide-ranging expertise of the previously cited C. J. T. Talar.)

13. See Lawrence Elliott, *I Will Be Called John: A Biography of Pope John XXIII* (1973).

Louis Ciani, here writing specifically of the anti-Modernist purge in *Across a Wide Ocean:* "By 1913, not just the *Civiltà,* but also *Etudes* and *Stimmen der Zeit* protested against the methods of the Integrists with the approval of the Jesuit General and to the annoyance of the Pope" (Pius X). The observation is intriguing because it means that in this instance, *Civiltà cattolica* joined hands not with the pope, but with the Jesuit general and the German and French Jesuit publications, both of which were famously renowned for their opposition to anti-Semitism, particularly as it was represented by defenders of the ritual murder charge — a subject to be taken up in chapters 5 and 6.

More specifically related to anti-Semitism in France and to the "crucial" influence of *Civiltà cattolica* on such members of the "worldwide network" as *La Croix* and *L'Univers* is the following observation of J. Derek Holmes in *The Papacy in the Modern World* (1981). He noted that after the condemnation in 1926 of the anti-Semitic Action Française, "the Catholic press in France only slowly and reluctantly followed the lead of the Pope." When Kertzer does supply some excerpts from the French press, the anti-Semitic views are often identical with those of the most militant anti-Catholics.[14] According to Kertzer's thesis, that would, paradoxically, make many of those publications part of the Vatican-inspired worldwide network — while attacking everything the Vatican stood for. Systematically ignored in this barrage of overstatements is the possibility that, given the dramatic upsurge in anti-Semitism from the 1880s on, those publications and their editors, including *Civiltà cattolica,* were responding to a general social-cultural phenomenon of the period. And for that phenomenon the causes, as all the literature attests, are manifold — though it would be a mistake to deny that *Civiltà cattolica*'s own anti-Semitic obsession was also fueled by traditional anti-Jewish theological and biblical texts and their accompanying popular myths and legends.

It was the celebrated thesis of Arthur Hertzberg's *The French Enlightenment and the Jews: The Origins of Modern Anti-Semitism* (1990) that this particular brand of hatred "was fashioned not as a reaction to the Enlighten-

---

14. Owen Chadwick also noted this strange kinship of ideologically opposing views. "A section of the French press, between 1870 and 1914, fastened upon the Jews, a symbol of passion which men felt inarticulately, and which the anti-Semitic press focused for them and thereby infuriated. Anticlericalism in France was first, a feeling in republican bellies; secondly a way of holding together political parties which agreed on little else; and thirdly, a way by which the republican press could form, transmit, articulate and impassion, the feeling in the belly." Chadwick's conclusion — candid, profound, ironic, and witty — is that all this was possible "because, like anti-Semitism, anticlericalism was anti" (*The Secularisation of the European Mind in the Nineteenth Century* [1975])

ment and the Revolution, but within the Enlightenment and the Revolution themselves." Hertzberg went on to say that Denis Diderot and Voltaire had more to do with this upsurge of modern racist anti-Semitism than anything connected to religion. Yet it is the clearly implicit thesis of Kertzer that those two anti-Semitic figures — who were viewed by faithful Catholics as the enemies of everything the church stood for — suddenly a century later were being echoed in all the French Catholic press from *La Croix* to *L'Univers*. Lastly, if one takes as a matter of fact that "out of the limelight, and with the assistance of their secretaries of state the popes regulated the anti-Semitic campaigns in the Church press," then it is no great step to the rather preposterous notion that anti-Semitic Catholics in France or, for that matter, in Austria and elsewhere were allying the Holy See with its archenemy, the proponents of *Écrasez l'infame*.

Regardless of such speculation, there is no doubt of the anti-Semitism of the French Catholic press. However, whether this had anything to do with Rome remains highly dubious. In some cases, as noted above, the assumption of such a link was based on this or that editor having had an audience with the pope.[15] The latter is the source of a quotation now treated as canonical in Garry Wills's *New York Times* review of Kertzer's book and again in his own book, *Why I Am a Catholic*: "The pope wrote in 1899, 'I love *La Croix*. I need a press and I am depending on you.'" Actually, the pope wrote no such thing, and there is good reason for questioning whether he ever said any such thing, since the only source for the tale — as with the diocesan editors in Florence and Milan earlier — is the very editor of *La Croix* who was at that time being reprimanded by the pope.[16]

---

15. *The New York Times* (August 9, 2007) described "a brief meeting between Pope Benedict XVI and a Polish priest accused of making anti-Semitic statements." The *Times* added, "In Poland the Radio Maryja's daily newspaper, *Nasy Dziennik,* printed photographs of the meeting, saying that the pope 'blessed Radio Maryja and its work.'" The Vatican then issued "a one-sentence statement that the meeting consisted of only 'a kiss of the hand, and that it did not imply any change in the well known position of the Holy See and the relations between Catholics and Jews.'"

16. There are several versions of the meeting, but certainly the most deftly told is that by Michael Burleigh. "Again, it is important to note that when Leo XIII received its editor (whose by-line was 'The Monk') he reproved him: 'Dreyfus, Dreyfus, all the time . . . and you might occasionally say some nice things about [president] Loubert.' Whatever the Assumptionists had to say, it was not said with the pope's approval" (*Earthly Powers* [New York: HarperCollins, 2006]). Albert S. Lindemann in *The Jew Accused: Three Anti-Semitic Affairs (Dreyfus, Beilis, Frank) 1894-1915* (1991) observed, "that the Assumptionists [of *La Croix*] played an important role in the [Dreyfus] Affair is highly questionable."

According to Kertzer, *La Croix* and other members of the worldwide network quoted the Roman Jesuit magazine "constantly." But once again it turns out that there are no citations proving this, though there are similar anti-Semitic tirades in both publications. Kertzer himself proffers passages like the following which, however, do not exactly suggest that the Assumptionists and *La Croix* were being controlled from Rome:

> he [the pope] and his secretary of state, Cardinal Rampolla, devoted a great deal of effort trying to rein them [the editors of *La Croix*] in. . . . Father Bailly [the editor of *La Croix*] reported that the pope was worried about the impact that the Church's identification with the anti-Dreyfus movement was having. . . . Reading the correspondence between the papal nuncio in Paris and the secretary of state we know that each had much to lament about *La Croix*.

As for *Civiltà cattolica*'s worldwide influence, it excludes all other continents except Europe, and of Europe excludes all other countries except Italy and France — with a nod to the press in "enthusiastic" Austria, to be considered shortly. Quite understandably, there is no mention of *Le Correspondant*, founded in 1829 on the British model of a free press, and resuscitated in 1855 by the publicly acknowledged liberal Catholic Charles Montalembert to oppose "the fanatic and servile school that everywhere seeks to identify the Church with despotism," by which he meant the ultramontanism of Louis Veuillot's *L'Univers*.[17] Montalembert, who had briefly won the favor of Pius IX by a defense of the Papal States, wrote a lengthy attack on *Civiltà cattolica* the year before his death in 1870, when publication of *Le Correspondant* was briefly interrupted, only to reappear the following year and continue until absorbed half a century later by the French Jesuit *Etudes*. The latter, emerging in the 1880s at the height of the anti-Semitic furor, was a monthly magazine that also wasn't "regulated" by the conspiratorial pope and his secretary of state, since it publicly took positions opposed to those of *Civiltà cattolica* on such anti-Semitic issues as the blood libel and the *Proto-*

17. The quotation is from Roger Aubert, *Le Pontificat de Pie IX*. Intrinsic to French ultramontanism was the anti-Semitism that Kertzer rightly decries, regrettably with a vehemence and insistence that makes it appear as an almost unanimously embraced trait of French Catholicism. In fact, again according to Aubert, the leading prelates — particularly the archbishop of Paris, the soon to be martyred Georges Darboy, and Felix Dupanloup, bishop of Orleans — mistrusted ultramontanism "precisely to the degree that it was represented and personified by *L'Univers* and *La Civiltà cattolica*."

cols of the Elders of Zion, as did also the English Jesuit *The Month.* The position of the latter was due in part to the writings of a great debunker of Catholic superstitionism, Herbert Thurston, another Jesuit who didn't follow the lead of his Italian confreres.

Concerning Austria, we know from the discussion in the previous chapter where it stands in this author's eyes, and apparently in the eyes of the world of the twentieth *and* twenty-first centuries as well.

> First, what are we to make of Austria, an overwhelmingly Catholic country that has still [2001] not come to terms with the enthusiastic role its people played in the Nazi murder of the Jews? Is there any significance in the fact that Adolf Hitler, a baptized Catholic, spent his early years in Austria, where the Vatican supported anti-Semitic Christian Social movement was so active? How do we account for the fact that Austrians played a disproportionately large role in the Holocaust?

As to what "we" are to make of Austria, in the context of the worldwide network of the Catholic press, is that "just two decades before the Holocaust, Catholic publications overflowed with denunciations of the Jews. Emblematic was the prestigious Catholic news weekly *Schönere Zukunft*." But anyone anticipating that even a brief quotation will flow onto the pages of Kertzer's book will have to settle for a descriptive sentence, which leads into another publication — which is as quote-free as the first, but perhaps less "emblematic." That publication in turn leads to the only German publication mentioned in the book — but one evidently not in the network led by *Civiltà cattolica.* Here is the author's diagnosis of the prestigious news weekly, and its sequelae:

> Featuring commentaries on the day's events by bishops and by Catholic professors of theology, week after week it carried attacks on the Jews' pernicious influence on Austrian society. Similarly, the Catholic *Kikiriki* specialized in its portrayals of stock-market Jews, and its pages were filled with venomous caricatures of Orthodox Jews with sidelocks. Indeed, the magazine has been described as a forerunner of Julius Streicher's infamous Nazi weekly *Der Stürmer.*

The only quotation that surfaces in this exposition is the following endnote: "*Der Stürmer*'s motto, *Die Juden sind unser Unglueck* — The Jews Are Our Misfortune — could have been the motto of many Catholic organizations and publications over the fifty years preceding World War II."

For a radically different view of Austria, Vienna, and the press — both Catholic and Jewish — "just two decades before the Holocaust," a more nuanced student of anti-Semitism merits being quoted: "The existing literature makes Vienna — the city of [Karl] Lueger and other formative antisemites — seem an unlikely place to organize against racism."[18] "Many [Austrians] felt distinct from Germans and argued for continued separation: their convictions derived in part from monarchism, pacifism, and anti-Prussian Catholicism and in part from a general desire to keep Hitler out of Austria." John Connelly — who will make a less congenial appearance in chapter 9 — after citing an author who described "Austria as a place of 'violent anti-Semitism' that was 'pursuing the goal of a *Judenfrei* community,'" continued his remedial effort:

> Readers of those words will be surprised to learn that almost a million copies of a weekly combating antisemitism were printed in Vienna in 1934 under the direction of the remarkable Irene Harand, a Catholic who founded the "World League against Racial Hatred and Human Need" in the Austrian capital. Vienna was also a place with a diverse and vibrant Jewish press, where the anti-Nazi circle around [Dietrich von] Hildebrand and [John M.] Oesterreicher could function freely and with official support.[19]

Since Kertzer's narrative is so emphatically negative about all of the above, more of this background should be filled in.

> In September 1933, Irene Harand launched her weekly Gerechtigkeit ["Righteousness," "Justness"] with a call to Austrians to show "the world that there is a German tribe that has a completely different understanding of humanity, truth, and justice than the people who surround Hitler." Al-

---

18. John Connelly, "Catholic Racism and Its Opponents," *Journal of Modern History* 79 (December 2007).

19. Irene Harand was in England when the Nazis moved into Vienna, and ultimately took up residence in the United States. She has been honored as Righteous among the Nations. Both Hildebrand and Oesterreicher managed to evade the Nazis, and arrived in the United States in the same year, 1940, where along with hundreds of other escapees they became major contributors to an invigorated American Catholic culture — which will play a walk-on role in chapter 5. As a matter of record it is to be noted that they both contributed to the present writer's quarterly, *Journal of Arts and Letters,* and that Oesterreicher wrote the introduction to *The Christian Imagination,* which was dedicated to Hildebrand.

fred Missong, a member of [Ernst Karl] Winter's circle, viewed Catholic Austria as a necessary counterbalance to militaristic Prussia. Hildebrand also idealized Austria, and his group projected the "Austrian mission" as involving a "providential collective task of significance for all humanity."

So much for Kertzer's "overwhelmingly Catholic country that has still [2001] not come to terms with the enthusiastic role its people played in the Nazi murder of the Jews."

Kertzer also mentioned a Polish periodical, but it is outside the network since it held views "reaching well beyond anything to which the Vatican would subscribe." In the midst of all this, Kertzer seems to have lost sight of the point at issue. That point was not that there were Catholic anti-Semitic publications — though as we will see, unmentioned is the American *Social Justice*, the most widely circulated and on that ground probably the most influential — but that those publications took both their editorial stance and their content from *Civiltà cattolica*. The now ignored — or possibly forgotten in the accumulation of the data assembled above — original contention was simply that "the network of Catholic newspapers throughout the world quoted its articles constantly."

Other than the reference to *Der Stürmer*, "complicated" Germany goes unmentioned, leaving a gap in the worldwide sweep of *Civiltà cattolica*. This could readily have been filled by the ultramontanist *Der Katholik* of Mainz, the only publication in this survey of which it can be said that it did cite *Civiltà cattolica* — but unfortunately for Kertzer's thesis it cited it on doctrinal *not* on racial matters. The German *Stimmen aus Maria Laach* (later *Stimmen der Zeit*), if it was part of any network it was that of Jesuit centrists like those at *Etudes* and *The Month*. Although the German publication was begun as a response to the widespread criticism of Pius IX's Syllabus of Errors — which Kertzer will discuss in detail — it had nothing in common with its Italian counterpart, even after Otto von Bismarck's *Kulturkampf* and the expulsion of the Jesuits from the First Reich. Equally unaffiliated with the worldwide network was *Hochland*, founded by Carl Muth at the height of the modern racist anti-Semitic upsurge in 1903. It soon circulated ten thousand copies of each issue (a figure comparable to that of *Civiltà cattolica*) and continued to be a vigorous exponent of supranational cultural and religious values — including "Semitic" ones — until it was suppressed by the Nazis in 1941.

The mention of the French, English, and German Jesuit monthlies — all spurning the views of *Civiltà cattolica* — highlights an interesting observation by our author. Kertzer, when discussing an 1872 article on ritual murder in *L'Unità cattolica,* "the Vatican-linked paper in Florence," quoted it as saying that "several popes had cleared the Jews of the charge." Since that undercuts the thesis of the "tremendous influence" of *Civiltà cattolica* in promoting the blood libel, he is obliged to maintain that this kind of "backtracking by a Vatican-linked publication . . . would be unthinkable in the last two decades of the century" — that is, "unthinkable" eight years after the statement was originally published. Clearly, this points to another loose string in the network since in England *The Tablet* twice denounced the ritual murder charge, as Herbert Thurston himself had earlier done in *The Month* — both putatively unthinkable denunciations occurring in the last two decades of the century.[20] While those two publications were obviously not "Vatican-linked" through *Civiltà cattolica,* it would be rather difficult to deny that their official supervisors, the archbishop of Westminster and the provincial of the English Jesuits, did have Vatican "links." Also definitely to be excluded from the network was the *Analecta Bollandiana,* another Jesuit "semi-official" publication whose hagiographical research, even in the nineteenth century, was influential in eliminating from the liturgical calendar assorted and sordid "victims" of Jewish ritual murder.

From all of the above one could at least assume that whatever else the "network" may have been, it certainly wasn't worldwide. It wasn't even European-wide, since by Kertzer's own citations, it appears mainly to have consisted of two Italian diocesan papers, four French newspapers, and a couple of weeklies from Austria. That, of course, raises the question as to precisely why those Jewish-obsessed "regulators" didn't extend their reach to the rest of Europe, or to England and North America, where probably nearly as many Catholic editors and writers read Italian as did those in France and Austria. But there is one interesting possibility, apparently unnoticed by Kertzer, that the calculating anti-Semites in the Vatican actually did promote hatred of Jews in England through *Civiltà cattolica.* Kertzer could certainly have declared the British weekly *Eye Witness* to be a member of the pope's network, since it was founded and edited in the reign of Pius X by Hilaire Belloc, a believer in the Judeo-Masonic conspiracy, an anti-Dreyfusard, an admirer of Drumont's *La France Juive,* and author of its British counterpart,

---

20. Another indication of loose strings in the worldwide network is evident in a remark on the increase in ritual murder charges at the end of the nineteenth century: "*La Croix* would, at that time, almost have excommunicated the English *Tablet*" (W. F. P. Stockley, "Popes and Jewish 'Ritual Murder,'" *The Catholic World,* April 1934).

The Jews. However, the latter work, which Belloc referred to as "my Yid book," might have raised a problem for the thesis regarding the transnational influence of *La Civiltà cattolica*, since the latter's editors were influenced by Belloc rather than the other way around. This is more than a trivial observation, since it might have led the few critical readers of *The Popes Against the Jews* to conclude that not only the British but also the Austrians, French, Italians, etc., were simply responding to the fin-de-siècle explosion of racist anti-Semitism, rather than to the out-of-the-limelight papal regulators manipulating an Italian magazine. Given the inevitability of such a conclusion and its demolition of the larger thesis of the book, any committed author like Kertzer would probably conclude, better to just omit the Anglos altogether — which he did.

That there really was some kind of anti-Semitic "network" — totally unconnected to the pope and his secretary of state — is evident not only from the fact that the editors of *Civiltà cattolica* were reading Belloc, but also that Belloc was showing up in the American weekly *Social Justice*. The latter was founded during the reign of Pius XI — "whose story is told in this book for the first time" — by Charles E. Coughlin, a Catholic priest who publicly professed belief in a slightly more updated conspiracy than Belloc's: the Judeo-Bolshevik one. The omission of Belloc from Kertzer's treatment is a minor matter compared to the omission of Coughlin, who was certainly from the mid-1920s through the Great Depression, and into the period of World War II, the most notorious and the most influential anti-Semite in the English-speaking world — an eminence that owed nothing to *Civiltà cattolica* or the Jesuits or the popes.

Coughlin's own obsession with Jews was largely dependent on an Irish priest, Denis Fahey, whose many books, still in print, are more frequently cited than anything by Coughlin, particularly among such Integrist organizations — the heirs of the anti-Modernists mentioned earlier — as the Society of St. Pius X. Fahey was a member of the Holy Ghost Fathers, a religious institute that had as its belated founder the scion of a rabbinic family who had converted to Catholicism in the nineteenth century.[21] The fact that a French religious congregation with Jewish roots could spawn in Ireland a priest whose conspiracies about the evil Jews were embraced by Coughlin in the United States would seem to offer convincing evidence of a worldwide

---

21. "Belated" because the original Holy Ghost community was combined with another group founded by Francis Libermann, the rabbinic student who had entered the church in 1826.

network linking Catholic anti-Semites. Unfortunately, it was also a network that had nothing to do with the Jesuit magazine in Rome or its out-of-the-limelight overseers.

Despite all the dogged research in Vatican archives, it is not entirely surprising that Kertzer's senior partner, Giovanni Miccoli, hadn't turned anything up on the American priest whose anti-Semitic radio broadcasts reached millions of people. But even though the papers of Pius XI were not accessible when Miccoli-Kertzer were making their numerous discoveries, they did dig up enough material for two complete chapters to be devoted to that pope — to be examined shortly. Moreover, Kertzer, writing in America, would have had a difficult time avoiding Coughlin.[22] If ever there was a Catholic who followed to the letter the "campaign against the Jews" regulated by the pope and his secretary of state, it was "the radio priest." His story has all the ingredients Kertzer had so carefully defined to illustrate the papal war against Jews. Coughlin inveighed against Jewish bankers, regarded Jews as secretly financing the Bolshevik revolution, and, like his fellow priests in France and Italy, Ernest Jouin and Umberto Benigni, also published the *Protocols of the Elders of Zion*. Additionally, he was an ally of the *Protocols'* noisiest, and richest, promoter in America, the automobile magnate, Henry Ford.

The major difference between Coughlin and people like Jouin and Benigni is that the latter never influenced anyone but a small circle of like-minded bigots, whereas Coughlin who had a growing audience in 1926 emerged during the Depression years as a formidable public figure whose nationwide radio broadcasts were estimated to have reached forty million listeners. Moreover, his weekly paper circulated more copies than any Italian or French publications Kertzer devotes page after page to describing — and more copies than the combined circulation of all publications in the *La Croix* chain. Still, *Social Justice* is somehow not viewed as part of "the network of Catholic newspapers throughout the world," and the name of its editor never surfaces in *The Popes Against the Jews*.

Possibly the reason is that unlike Jouin and Benigni, Coughlin received no honors from the papacy.[23] Instead, the opposite was true. He proved to be

22. There were television documentaries devoted to him, and at least five books, two of them published in the 1990s when Kertzer was researching *The Popes Against the Jews*. One of those books, *Charles Coughlin, the Father of Hate Radio,* by Donald Warren, was widely reviewed, including in *The New York Times,* by Richard Bernstein — who a few years later would glowingly praise *The Popes Against the Jews*.

23. "Pius X showered Benigni with honors." "Jouin had already been made a prelate by Benedict XV. . . . Pius XI raised him further appointing him apostolic prothonotary." It is rel-

a thorn in its side, all the while vehemently protesting, as did his European counterparts, that everything he did was out of fidelity to the Holy See. In Coughlin's case this was fidelity specifically to the declarations of Leo XIII and Pius XI; the former being the secret conspirator ("out of the limelight") against the Jews; the latter, the public anti-Semite whose grievous infractions — to be exposed by Kertzer — will be examined in chapter 5. Coughlin's invocation of the popes proved to be of no avail, and in September 1936, one of the two beacons in the network of the Catholic press, *L'Osservatore romano*, criticized Coughlin's bishop, Michael Gallagher, "for claiming that the pope approved of Coughlin's activity," and the paper itself "then denounced Coughlin."[24] A month later, *Time* magazine (October 5, 1936), writing in Timespeak, picked up on the earlier event: "When a news hawk asked whether Father Coughlin would get a 'second rebuke' . . . Bishop Gallagher, angrily pounding his old fist on his desk, snorted: 'The *Osservatore Romano* has no authority over me. . . . There never was a rebuke from the Vatican to Father Coughlin.'"

In that same year Pius XI's co-conspirator against the Jews, the secretary of state, Cardinal Eugenio Pacelli, emerged into the limelight to meet with U.S. officials over the Coughlin matter. Coughlin had also attacked President Franklin D. Roosevelt, publicly calling him a liar, and had antagonized several leading members of the American hierarchy — with the obvious exception of Coughlin's own diocesan, Michael Gallagher. After the Pacelli meeting, according to Coughlin's testimony, the bishop told him, "I got news for you. You're finished." But in fact, nothing happened to Coughlin. It was in 1938, two years later, that Coughlin published the *Protocols of the Elders of Zion*, wrote disdainfully about the pogrom of Crystal Night, and became even more offensive about the power of "Jewish bankers" in *Social Justice*, which at that time had a circulation approaching one million.[25] In the event,

---

atively unimportant that Benigni was showered for his anti-Modernist crusade, and Jouin, for his anti-Masonic crusade; the fact that they were anti-Semites is what links them to the three popes.

24. Martin E. Marty, *Modern American Religion: The Noise of Conflict 1919-1941* (1991).

25. He also attacked Archbishop John J. Mitty of San Francisco, whose public address on the pogrom was the centerpiece of a nationwide radio broadcast. The archbishop expressed "deep and abiding sympathy with the Jewish men and women who are being lashed by the cruelty of fierce persecution." Mitty's address, "Persecution of the Jews in Germany," appeared in *The New York Times* (November 17, 1938). See Maria Mazzenga, "Condemning the Nazis' Kristallnacht," *U.S. Catholic Historian* (Fall 2008) and by the same writer, *American Religious Responses to Kristallnacht* (2009).

it took the election of Pacelli as Pius XII and the pope's appointment of a new archbishop to silence Coughlin. In 1942, this archbishop told Coughlin — again in Coughlin's words: "They want you to quit." According to Coughlin, "they" meant "Rome." He added, "Pius XII was no friend of mine."[26]

In contrast to Kertzer's tidy, no-loose-ends argument — which concluded seamlessly from the anti-Semitism of the Vatican press to a papal war against the Jews — nothing better than the bumbling Coughlin tale exemplifies the exact opposite: the crossed wires, the Babel of conflicting views, the red tape, and the official rigmarole plaguing the slow-moving papal bureaucracy. Perhaps now one is in a position to speculate as to the plausibility of the assertion that, "out of the limelight with the assistance of their secretaries of state, the popes regulated the anti-Semitic campaign conducted in the Church press." It took a change of popes, a change of bishops, and a war before one dissident priest could be "regulated." The ineluctable conclusion from that strange phenomenon has to be that the allegedly monolithic institution whose members move in lockstep to obey the decrees of its rulers — that institution exists primarily in the minds of non-Catholics, whether they are sympathetic or antagonistic to the church as such. Clearly what is needed to remedy such misconceptions is a wide-ranging examination of the relationship between the noble foundational goal of religious institutions and how such a goal is or is not realized as they move through each successive historical epoch. The chapters that follow will contribute each in its own way to such an examination, which will be explicitly formulated at the conclusion of *Were the Popes Against the Jews?*

For the present, it can be said that all the discussion above represents but one of the many weaknesses at the heart of the case that Kertzer makes — a case, according to Owen Chadwick, "that calls for an answer." It is advisable to cite here the most balanced and wide-ranging Anglophone historian of modern Christianity because he best exemplifies the ideal student of the past who has endeavored successfully to narrate events "as they really were." As to the answer itself, it has been first necessary to grapple with Kertzer's methodology and his overarching thesis regarding the "crucial" role of the "Vatican-linked" press in the rise of "modern anti-Semitism." Concerning the fuller response to *The Popes Against the Jews,* it demands resolving the specific issues relative to these presumably anti-Jewish popes: their deriding

---

26. All quotations are from an interview with Coughlin in *American Heritage Magazine* (October 1972).

Jews as "dogs" and the Jewish religion as the "synagogue of Satan" under Pius IX; their approving the blood libel and ritual murder during the reigns of Leo XIII and Pius X; and finally their fostering exterminators of Jewry itself under Pius XI — all those along with related matters will be scrutinized in the chapters that follow, beginning with some background on Kertzer himself and on the broader theme of Catholic anti-Semitism as addressed in the Vatican document "We Remember."

CHAPTER 3

Anti-Semitism vs. Anti-Judaism

As I closed the previous chapter with a comment from Owen Chadwick on the need for a response to *The Popes Against the Jews*, I open this chapter — which will also take up the promised background of the book — with a longer quotation from that same historian on the construction of recent papal myths:

> A people's memory forms legends easily, it deals in crude terms and not in subtleties, and it can have little chance of understanding what happened except in mere outline. . . . In this case legends grew unaided because there was a real failure on the part of many churchmen. . . . So the fables came. It is still believed by many people that Pope Pius XII was a friend of the Nazis, or that he said nothing at all against racial murder during the war, or that he was so frightened for his own skin or his own palace that he was too timid to say anything whatever. (*The Tablet,* March 28, 1998)

Chadwick was referring to the dark legends born of the wartime period. I am referring to tales from the nineteenth century that have taken a similar form; one of them, thanks to Kertzer's book, is the previously mentioned accusation that Pius IX called Jews "dogs." This, along with its companion tale that modern popes called Jews and/or Judaism the "synagogue of Satan," is beginning to take on the shape and ubiquity of those present-day fictions known as "urban myths and legends." Although the alleged papal fabrications are on a more sophisticated plane, they are comparable to the latter in their widespread diffusion and acceptance.[1]

---

1. On the Internet the three terms "Jews," "dogs," "Pope" will generate hundreds of

The ancestors of both were the elaborate secular and religious legends of the medieval period when such tales as Pope Leo's confrontation with Attila the Hun, and Gregory the Great's puns on Angles and Angels, went hand in hand with the stories of Arthur's round table and of Alfred the Great's burnt biscuits. But where the latter in the nineteenth century were eulogized by such artists as Tennyson, Morris, and Rossetti, and in the present era have been identified with Monty Python, "Spamalot," and "Alfred the Cake," the Christian golden legends have given way to scandalous tales of scheming popes and sinister cardinals of which the nineteenth-century Maria Monk literature was the tabloid representative, and *Hitler's Pope, Papal Sin,* and *The Popes Against the Jews* are the present-day expressions.

The story began before the appearance of the last-named book. In the February 7, 1998, *New York Times,* shortly after a Vatican announcement that the secret archives of the Inquisition were being opened to scholars, David I. Kertzer in an op-ed piece wrote: "We can learn much from the newly opened archives. The explanation of what made the Holocaust possible is to be found in no small part in the files of the Inquisition" — a quotation that is treated as highly significant by James Carroll's *Constantine's Sword.* Since the archives had been closed to Kertzer, and he had never seen the files, the fact that he knew this explanation was to be found in them suggested what it is the purpose of this chapter to determine — either scholarly prescience or unscholarly prejudice. That it will turn out to be the latter is not a conclusion of which any sensible reader would say (as did Kertzer earlier), "I'm not holding my breath," since it is becoming rather obvious that there is an ideological anti-papal agenda driving this research.

Three years after his "what made the Holocaust possible" perception, Kertzer in the book's introduction said that even before the Vatican announcement, "I thought someone needed to write a book about the Church and the Jews in modern times, one that would use original archival documents — many never before examined — to tell a story that has remained in important ways unknown." Apart from the self-gratulatory tone of this intuition, there are the unintentional ironies that almost all of Kertzer's archival material is second-hand, being based as we have seen on Giovanni Miccoli, and that the most widely used sources are materials not only in the public domain, but in the most accessible area of that domain, newspapers and

---

thousands of sites, almost all of which are related to Kertzer's book. As of early 2011, the number was 1,600,000, although the exact figures vary from day to day, and obviously many of these reduplicate one another.

magazines. As to the opening of another archive, it presented Kertzer with what he described as "a once-in-a-lifetime opportunity" for writing a book that "rests heavily on these newly available documents from the Inquisition." The language becomes a little more self-revelatory when the documents are described as also "offering the tantalizing prospect of . . ." — almost instinctively this teasing language lures the reader to anticipate something more exciting than what, in fact, is about to be delivered — ". . . new insights into Church history." In the highfalutin language of computer circuitry that sentence is the "microminiaturization" of the structure of the entire book — which originally leads one to a sympathetic response, only to have that response dissipated progressively as the actual results become thinner and thinner. (For that, too, there is an apposite expression, "promising more than proffering.")

The importance of the repetition of terms like "Inquisition" and "Secret Archives" is that they evoke echoes of age-old conspiracies, many of which were revived during the nineteenth-century "no popery" crusades, and ended up in the next century being updated by pop mythopoeists purporting to expose dark and deep historical secrets. Of these fabrications the previously mentioned *Da Vinci Code* and its sequel, *Angels and Demons,* have been the most significant — at least in terms of prevailing cultural values. Nor is it beyond belief that some of this "literature" represents another security blanket to which a declining WASP culture could cling, just as its Catholic counterpart in Europe had earlier clung to tales of ritual murder and the conspiracies of the Elders of Zion. In nineteenth-century North America, it was the waves of immigrants that led to Catholicism and popery becoming the target of choice by superstitious nativist agitators.[2]

Since it would take a book many times longer than the present one to discuss all the myths Kertzer examines, I will concentrate mainly on the four that are most frequently cited by reviewers of books, and by reviewers of reviews of books — thus do legends get replicated. However, these four are merely the pegs or indicators — what the French call *jalons* — which point to other even more disturbing parts of Kertzer's "unknown story." The first of these as mentioned above is that in the latter half of the nineteenth cen-

---

2. The allusion is to Richard Hofstadter's celebrated essay on the paranoid style in American politics that introduced one aspect of that style: "Anti-Catholicism has always been the pornography of the Puritans." Hofstadter also discussed other conspiracy-driven antics by McCarthyites and the John Birch Society, both of which have heirs in twenty-first-century American culture — only now the targets are advocates of "social justice" and enemies of an African American president.

tury Pius IX and his successor, Leo XIII, publicly displayed their anti-Semitism by referring to Jews and Judaism in official documents as the "synagogue of Satan." The second — already mentioned to the point of surfeit — is that Pius IX in a public meeting referred to Jews as dangerous "dogs" who were bothering the Christian citizens of Rome.[3] Third, both Leo XIII and Pius X not only gave credence to the blood libel that Jews killed Christian children for use in religious rituals, but the popes knowingly prevented Jews falsely accused of such crimes from being exonerated. Fourth, the future Pope Pius XI after World War I fostered anti-Semitism and even embraced advocates of the extermination of Jews. In the context of these topics, the broader theme of Kertzer's book — aggressive papal support of the hatred that led to the Holocaust — will be examined. All these frightening accusations, the new papal myths, are believed to be historically established facts by many presumably educated and well-intentioned people, including the writers of those reviews to which Kertzer himself drew attention, as well as the millions of readers in nine languages he also mentioned.

Those who find such credulousness surprising might note that many believers in pop culture myths and legends were also convinced because of "new discoveries" made by the Hubble Telescope — accompanied by photographs and drawings — that the moon is indeed made of green cheese.[4] That this is not an entirely impossible parallel will be shown by the fact that assertions only slightly less absurd have been validated merely by invoking the "never before examined Vatican archives," a place which, according to *The Popes Against the Jews,* is "filled with shocking revelations."

In the years that have elapsed between the publication of the latter book and the present critique, Kertzer has been severely criticized mainly by Catholics who are generally identified with the right, while he has been lauded in the mainstream press — certainly not identified with the right — which has often concentrated on the subject matter *in globo,* rather than on the particulars that constituted the basis of the author's indictment. On his website, he himself had characterized the reviews as "glowing," and most of those appearing in the daily or weekly press were enthusiastic, while those in the

3. The importance of these two texts is not merely that they appear to be contemptuous taunts of a highly personal nature, but that they are the only "anti-Semitic" statements undeniably in the popes' own words, rather than in the words of *Civiltà cattolica* and its journalistic emulators.

4. The tale originally launched as an April Fool's Day joke ended up being taken seriously and was even thought by some to be corroborated by earlier discoveries of the ancestors of Cheddar Man. For aspects of the tale, see www.apod.nasa.gov/apod/ap060401.html.

quarterlies or monthlies were guardedly more critical, though in the overall generally favorable.[5]

Readers and reviewers might have gotten a clearer picture of the author's own historical perspective from his response to the cancellation of a Hillel Foundation symposium on the book at New York University in the aftermath of the World Trade Center attack. In a revelatory retort to the sponsors, Kertzer said, "This is when it is so important for our universities to serve as a place to think about the use of religion to inspire hatred." Given the title of his book, the suggestion that popes were to Jews as terrorists are to Americans was unavoidable — and possibly not unintentional. Another remark over the same incident brought into the twenty-first century more animosities from an older era: "Jews in Rome living under the thumb of the pope lived in fear of offending the popes," presumably just as the Hillel Foundation in New York was knuckling under to local Catholic pressures. This remark was the first indication of a penchant on the part of the author for discovering and disclosing conspiracies.[6]

Kertzer began his book by criticizing the distinction between anti-Judaism and anti-Semitism, particularly as that distinction was made by the papal commission responsible for the document "We Remember," and concluded by observing that the latter "will simply not survive historical scrutiny." He faulted the Vatican document for maintaining — according to his paraphrase — that "the nineteenth century was the key period for understanding the roots of the Holocaust and, in particular, the reason why the

---

5. The reviewers who provide the glowing comments — beginning with the Christians — are a combination of genteel irenicists and kindly reformists. *Eugene Fisher:* "remarkable," "gone through archives," "lively and compelling." *Jack Miles:* "with meticulous documentation tells a sickening story . . . an iron to burn scars in the mind." *John Pawlikowski:* "substantive volume based on sound scholarship . . . serious work that deserves significant attention," "a basically accurate picture." The most fulsome praise was by *Kevin Madigan,* who described Kertzer as a "national treasure" and his book as a "masterpiece." Among the Jewish commentators the following are also representative: *Michael Marrus:* "well documented," "rests solidly upon materials from the Holy See's own archives," "showers us with evidence." *A. James Rudin:* "Those who challenge his disturbing conclusions will have to match Mr. Kertzer's scholarship, research and command of the Italian language." *Robert S. Wistrich:* "a powerful and incisive analysis . . . solid documentation and clear exposition." *Richard Bernstein:* "Important . . . Fascinating . . . [A] riveting piece of historical detective work." Omitted here are several more enthusiastic commentators who will be cited frequently in what follows, and for whose works complete bibliographical references will be supplied.

6. Rachel Donadio, "NYU Hillel Nixes Panel on Jews, Vatican: 'This Is Not the Time to Nurse Old Grievances,' Says Coordinator," *Forward,* October 19, 2001.

Church bore no responsibility for it." (A reader by now initiated into how the author handles language might have instinctively modulated that unnuanced "no" in the last clause.) Kertzer continued by criticizing the document for saying that in that particular century, "there began to spread in *varying degrees* throughout most of Europe an anti-Judaism that was *essentially more* sociological and political than religious." This is a direct quotation from the document that asserts an established historical truism. (The nuanced phrases that I have italicized are intended to point up the contrast with Kertzer's absolutist rhetoric in the previous quotation.)

When the author in his conclusion readopts paraphrase, what had been unnuanced then becomes merely ambivalent:

> The anti-Semitism embraced by the Nazi regime, the report goes on to say, was the product of this new social and political form of anti-Judaism, which was foreign to the Church, and which mixed in new racial ideas that were similarly at odds with Church doctrine.

Though Kertzer is seeking to draw up a severe indictment, his own language twice blurs the issue so that its severity is muted: something that is "foreign" to the church or "at odds" with it is fudging language that can accurately be used to show that both parties in this dispute are right — so far as they go. The churchmen are correct in making the original distinction, since, as we have seen, it is undeniable that there is a sharp difference between the racist anti-Semitism born of the modern era and the theological anti-Semitism born of the Christian Scripture and tradition. The churchmen are wrong in implying that this distinction is exculpatory, since it is undeniable that Christian "anti-Judaism," while not a cause of modern racist anti-Semitism as such, certainly prepared for and sustained the forces of hatred that the latter unleashed. (The obvious parallel is that of slavery, where biblical texts had bolstered the views of slave-owners that people of color were racially inferior and therefore could be subjugated and exploited.)

Thus it soon becomes evident that Kertzer's own repeated assertion — based on those magazines and newspapers examined in the previous chapter — that the pope, the Vatican, and the church (since all are homogenized) constituted the "antechamber to the Holocaust" is a judgment only slightly less embarrassing than are the evasions of "We Remember." However, his language may be justified because he is speaking as a private researcher to his readers, and the commission is speaking "at the express request of His Holiness Pope John Paul II" to "the Catholic Church throughout the world." The following from the commission is the kind of statement that Kertzer rightly criticizes: "But it must be asked whether the Nazi persecution of the Jews was not made easier by the anti-Jewish prejudices imbedded in some Christian minds and hearts." Instead of responding with a simple "yes," or even a brief historical sketch of Christian persecutions, the garbled answer is confined to the immediate period of the Holocaust: "Any response to this question must take into account that we are dealing with the history of a people's attitudes and ways of thinking, subject to multiple influences." Then "We Remember" goes off on truly insoluble matters relative to the Third Reich about widespread fear and greed, about who knew what when, and so on. The tone of the document is less that of a message of concern and repentance from a worldwide religious body than of a PR campaign by a multinational corporation — pharmaceuticals, electronics, whatever — seeking to cover over a scandalous blunder relating to one of its "products." At the very least it must be said that this is not the way a religious body, purporting to speak truth to justice — not to mention proclaiming a gospel of love — apologizes for its dark past in preparation for a brighter future.

Just as the tradition of enslaving people of color was validated by Noah's curse of Ham (or Canaan) in the book of Genesis (9:20-27), so too the tradition of hatred for Jews was validated by the statement about Jesus' blood in the Gospel of Matthew (27:25). If a major historian of slavery, David Brion Davis, in *Inhuman Bondage* (2006) can maintain of the Genesis text that no other passage in the Bible has had such a disastrous influence on human history, then one must maintain that the Gospel passage (along with others like it) is at least a close second. However, it is also to be noted that even in the context of biblical pronouncements, the biological inferiority of both Jews and blacks was sustained by philosophical and scientific exponents of the Enlightenment in France, Germany, and, to a lesser degree, England. Those thinkers, although influenced by the old biblical traditions, also prepared the ground for increased discrimination against people of color as well as for the wave of racist anti-Semitism, discussed in the previous chapter, which swept Europe in the closing decades of the nineteenth century.[7] It should go without saying that the latter is a statement of historical fact that in no way di-

7. The parallel between the history of Jews and the history of blacks is also illuminated by the following from another student of slavery: "It is perhaps important to register that while racial feeling certainly preceded the rise of the slave systems and led to their racial character, the 'proto-racism' of the sixteenth century was quite different from the full-fledged racism that began to emerge in the eighteenth century." Robin Blackburn, "The New World Order," *The Nation*, November 13, 2006.

minishes the undeniable responsibility of the Christian church and/or the popes for over the centuries supporting the forces of hatred that were the major contribution to the inhumane treatment of Jews.

When that Enlightenment strain along with a vulgarized Darwinism was woven into traditional Christian anti-Jewishness, and when the resultant amalgam was joined to social and economic unrest exploited by political leaders, the unpredictable but certainly not inconceivable result was the perversity of twentieth-century Jew hatred. The stage was thus set for Hitler, Nazism, Zyklon B — and the still incomprehensible genocide of the Jews. Nor should it go without notice that it was not practitioners of Judaism the *religion* that were being murdered, it was anyone with the precisely determined degree of Jewish blood — even as ultimately it was a similar racial factor, though without any religious implication, that led to the persecution of the Sinti and Roma.[8]

However, the distinction between racist anti-Semitism and religious anti-Jewishness remains essential. It certainly predates "We Remember," and is made by virtually all scholars in the field, although they may not draw the same conclusions as the vainly pleading churchmen responsible for "We Remember." Guenter Lewy, author of *The Catholic Church and Nazi Germany* (1964), the first book-length study in what may be called the post-Hochhuth era, discussed the many "differences between Hitler's racial anti-Semitism and Christian anti-Judaism." Like most Catholic observers since Vatican II, Lewy also acknowledged the climate of opinion that Christian detestation of Jews created, and thus prepared the way for the wave of anti-Semitism in the late nineteenth century. Still, one of the few glories of "We Remember" is that it is very clear on the shared complicity for this climate among "members of the church" — which includes anyone from the highest levels of the hierarchy, including the pope, to the lowest levels of the laity. On the other hand, had the document stated that it was "the church as such" that was guilty — as many critics, including Kertzer, have contended — there would have been legitimate counter-complaints about how it is impossible for an abstract entity to be complicit in a concrete deed, or about how this would obliterate individual guilt in an amorphous mass of generalized evildoing.

One's initial suspicions concerning the slanted interpretation the author

---

8. In fact, a case can be made that "race" is the determinant factor in condemning arbitrarily selected people *only* because it is their most readily disclosed and most inextinguishable trait. In short, to describe hatred as "racial" is still not to resolve the real issue of the motive for transforming the alien or the different into the untouchable and the condemnable.

of *The Popes Against the Jews* was endorsing were further heightened by the introduction of another and more recent conspiracy. "In the wake of the Second World War, scholars and theologians close to the Church began to look for a way to defend the Church from the charge of having helped lay the groundwork for the Holocaust." The immediate next sentence — unmodulated and unnuanced — tells what happened after those people close to the church had begun their look: "The anti-Semitism/anti-Judaism distinction soon became an article of faith that relieved the Church of *any* responsibility for what happened. Before long, *millions of people* came to assume its historical reality" (italics supplied).

This solemn proclamation with its ex cathedra tone represents the kind of overreaching that too often plays the role of reflection in this book. If "article of faith" is being used in its traditional sense of mandatory Catholic dogma, the statement is nonsense, as is also the absoluteness of the opinion that this relieved "the Church of *any* responsibility."[9] Kertzer manages to get closer to reality when he refers to "millions," since vast numbers of Catholics have been the subject of instruction and catechesis on precisely the point at issue. Though the following statement by the Catholic bishops of the United States is hardly an "article of faith," it does represent what various other episcopal conferences throughout the world have been saying, and it is certainly no warrant for Kertzer's remarks about relieving the church of responsibility:

> But Christian anti-Judaism did lay the groundwork for racial, genocidal antisemitism by stigmatizing not only Judaism but Jews themselves for opprobrium and contempt. So the Nazi theories tragically found fertile soil in which to plant the horror of an unprecedented attempt at genocide. One way to put the "connectedness" between the Christian teaching of anti-Judaism (leading to anti-Jewishness) and Nazi anti-Semitism is that the former is a "necessary cause" to consider in explaining the development and success of the latter in the twentieth century — but not a "sufficient cause." To account for the Holocaust, one must acknowledge the historical role of Christian anti-Judaism. But Christian anti-Judaism alone cannot account for the Holocaust. Semi-scientific racial theories

9. The author is not only canceling (again) his statement about the error of referring en bloc to "the church" doing *x* or *y*, but he is also using with intentional ambiguity a technical religious term, *"article of faith,"* to highlight the chicanery of ecclesiastics. The same stratagem occurs a few pages later when "the *Civiltà cattolica* campaign picked up on anti-Semitic themes, giving them a papal *imprimatur*." The italicized terms here are not generic; they have a specific technical meaning.

and specific historical, ideological, economic, and social realities within Germany must also be taken into account in order to begin grappling with why Nazism succeeded in mobilizing virtually the entire intellectual and technological apparatus of a modern industrial state to its warped purpose of eliminating from human history God's People, the Jews.

The subterfuge that Kertzer thinks he has found in "We Remember" stems from its assertion that uniquely modern anti-Semitism is founded on a notion of race that has always been denounced by Catholic theology. But that this is a fairly conventional view is evident in the quotation from Lewy above and from that below in *Rethinking the Holocaust* (2001) by Yehuda Bauer:

> But the Nazis tried to rule not just Germany but Europe, and ultimately the world, in the name of a new principle, the principle of "race." True, they started from nationalism and acted in the name of the German people. But, moved by their interpretation of the racial doctrine, they distanced themselves progressively from a purely German ideology.

But regardless of how conventional a view this is, no one can argue that it in any way relieves the church of the burden of having strengthened over the centuries the hatred of an all-powerful majority toward a fragile minority.

Kertzer's views also stand in sharp contrast to that of the humanist historian Léon Poliakov, who is mentioned in passing as author of "the classic, *History of Anti-Semitism*," but who is never quoted, and, as we will see in chapter 6, has never been read. It is from the fourth volume of that classic study, *Suicidal Europe: 1870-1933* — which covers most of the period on which Kertzer focuses — that the following is taken:

> It is true that under the long pontificate of Pius IX [1846-78], French and other Catholics did not wage real war against the Jews. Perhaps this moderation can be attributed to the notoriously conservative temperament of the pope, a certain concern for the "People of the Book" that was one of the most venerable traditions of the Holy See. In Italy, the unofficial *Civiltà cattolica* inveighed against the Jews only in the name of Christ. This situation changed under the more modern pontificate of Leo XIII, and it is undoubtedly more than a coincidence. It goes without saying, however, that it took upheavals more radical than a change of popes to induce militant Christians to indulge in anti-Semitic campaigns.

This carefully worded perspective on two popes entails a distinction that is not congenial to Kertzer. For him it is *all* the popes — though a couple to a lesser degree — from the French Revolution to World War II, who were "against the Jews," and thus each of those popes in his own way was creating an "antechamber to the Holocaust." In Kertzer's book, the first hundred pages are set in the historical context of the popes (Pius VII, Leo XII, Pius VIII, and Gregory XVI) who ruled the Papal States in the aftermath of the Revolution. Each of these popes was trying to enforce the pre-Napoleonic religious prohibitions against Jews. Thus it is not surprising that "as late as the 1850s" the last of the popes to rule the Papal States, Pius IX, "was busy trying to evict Jews from most of the towns in the lands he controlled, and forcing them to live in the few cities that had ghettoes to close them in."

Poliakov's quotation refers to the two popes who inherited the broken church described above and who in their separate ways, and certainly in response to changed historical circumstances, confronted head on the newly emerging pan-European phenomenon soon to be known as modern anti-Semitism. Pius IX is the transitional pontiff who lived in both universes and negotiated between religious anti-Jewishness — as exemplified by the coercive policies of the Papal States — and modern political/social/racial anti-Jewishness, as exemplified three decades later by the Dreyfus Affair. It is for this reason that Poliakov can describe Pius IX as not engaged in "real war against the Jews," as embracing "moderation," as respecting the "People of the Book," and so on. "This situation changed under the more modern pontificate of Leo XIII, and it is undoubtedly more than a coincidence." But the "coincidence" was not that Leo's reign was any more or less anti-Jewish than his predecessor's, but that in Kertzer's view he encountered specifically "modern" anti-Semitism, and thus was pope when the wave of racist hatred for Jews swept over Europe toward the end of the century. As to the reality of that "wave," Kerzer himself speaks of "the *ideology* that produced the first modern anti-Semitic political movements in the last two decades of the nineteenth century" (italics supplied).

If we view history in light of the horrifying mystery of the Holocaust half a century later — as we simply must — that racist wave looms over all other events. Because of the overwhelming importance of this period, before taking up in the next chapter Pius IX's references to Jewish dogs and the synagogue of Satan, it is necessary to continue following the course of this uniquely modern form of anti-Semitism as it emerged in the reign of his successor — who also allegedly referred to Jews as the synagogue of Satan.

Freed from the medieval baggage and dead weight of the Papal States, Leo XIII, as we saw briefly in the preceding chapter, was the first pope to attempt an accommodation with the radically new international economic, political, and cultural issues stemming from the French Revolution. Rather than the alleged obsession with Jews previously described, their plight was overshadowed by his preoccupation with an anticlerical regime in France and with the *Kulturkampf* in Germany, at a time when he was also attempting to respond to the rise of socialist movements throughout Europe.

But his most pressing immediate concern, inherited from Pius IX, was how the church should relate to the newly created government that had come into existence after the capture of Rome. No pope for the next five decades entirely accepted the Italian state, much less the loss of the Eternal City. But Leo, unlike Pio Nono, tried to display a conciliatory attitude toward the new regime. In fact, he was so preoccupied with improving relations with the government that this goal became his criterion for assessing the editors of *Civiltà cattolica*. The fundamental issue whereby they were judged, having nothing whatever to do with anti-Semitism, was whether they accepted the pope's policy of compromise with the government of a united Italy. John Louis Ciani in *Across a Wide Ocean* writes:

> In 1879, Valerio Steccanella, then rector (religious superior) of the *Civiltà*, wrote the Jesuit General Beckx, that the Pope was "disgusted" with the review for sharp articles written against Catholic access to the polls. The Pope was also upset by remarks made by Father Giuseppe Oreglia of the *Civiltà* against a new moderate journal, *L'Aurora*, sponsored by Leo XIII.

Such concerns explain the absence of anything significant relating to Jews or Judaism in the writings of Leo XIII, an absence that as we have seen Kertzer relates to the secret conspiracy by the pope to "regulate" campaigns against Jews. The only basis for the conspiracy is that in the 1880s *Civiltà cattolica* began to publish a series of anti-Semitic articles by the aforementioned Giuseppe Oreglia that represented a shift from traditional Christian anti-Judaism (however intrinsically deplorable) to modern racist anti-Semitism (however ultimately destructive). It is the existence of that shift that also explains why Kertzer has no anti-Semitic quotations from the magazine before those by Father Giuseppe Oreglia beginning in 1880. Given Kertzer's tenacity, it is a reasonable assumption that if he could have located any earlier quotations, they would certainly not have been omitted.

The major question to which this shift gives rise is whether *Civiltà cattolica,* as Kertzer persistently insists, was crucial to the rise of modern, racist anti-Semitism or whether, as suggested in the previous chapter, the Jesuit magazine was itself responding to converging tendencies in the larger culture. Certainly one indication that it was the latter is the fact that Father Oreglia, who had been one of the founders of *Civiltà cattolica* in 1850, took more than thirty years to make his discovery of Jewish misdeeds — a subject that over the next decade this veteran writer would fanatically exploit and that would then become part of the public image of the magazine. Oreglia's successors, Raffaele Ballerini and Saverio Rondina — in the preceding chapter singled out by the Jesuit historian Giacomo Martina as confreres whose *mentalità* he could not comprehend — were even more vehement in their rhetoric, almost matching that of the standard bearers in France, the priest editors of *La Croix* and the lay editors of *L'Univers.*

Thus it becomes increasingly difficult to maintain that the Jesuit magazine played a "crucial" role in the emergence of racist anti-Semitism. The chronology confirms what Léon Poliakov had discerned ("it took upheavals more radical than a change of popes") and what is clear from the above — that is, that the Jesuit editors, far from being regulated by Leo XIII, were themselves responding to an already widely diffused ideology of detestation. Hence, too, the quotation from Giovanni Miccoli in the previous chapter: "Even *Civiltà cattolica* up to the 1870s only fleetingly mentioned the Jews. The primary artisans of the revolution, in the eyes of the Holy See, remained masonry and the sects."

Possibly it is only in America during the understandably continuing post-Holocaust era — marked by the desperate search for answers and, consequent on their absence, by the even more desperate search for scapegoats — that someone could launch the notion of a small Italian Jesuit magazine being indispensable in the rise of a continent-wide social and cultural revolution. The very notion is so hard to swallow it suggests some sort of quirky satiric undertaking — a kind of latter-day Yankee in the Papal Court — desperately trying to make, in Mark Twain's own words, "A barrel of soup out of a single bean." But there is more to be added to beef up this thin gruel — of which one could truly say, "only in America." According to Kertzer, all of the follies perpetrated by the Jesuits of *Civiltà cattolica* "had the support of the highest Church authorities, including the popes." By this view, as sketched in the preceding chapter, the magazine was not only sponsored by the Holy See, it was directly supervised by its two highest officials. Kertzer now refines this notion further:

In the Catholic world, *Civiltà cattolica* came to be regarded as the unofficial voice of the Pope himself. . . . Before publication, the proofs of each new issue were sent to the secretary of state for final approval. . . . Five days before each issue came out, the journal director went to the Vatican and, up until Pius XII, in the mid-twentieth century, was often received by the Pope himself, who — along with the secretary of state — reviewed and approved the contents of the upcoming issue.

That from 1850 to approximately 1950, that is, to the middle of the reign of Pius XII, the pope and his secretary of state, less than a week before publication, read and disapproved or approved the contents of each forthcoming issue — *that* is simply not to be believed.[10] Not unlikely, however, is that the *direttore* who had overall supervision of the magazine went to the Vatican to meet with an appointee in the Vatican state secretariat to discuss the contents of future issues. But this twice-a-month personal involvement in the publication of each number of the journal by the two highest officials in the church is as exaggerated as claiming the magazine was crucial to the rise of racist anti-Semitism in Western Europe — even though the first notion has been created in order to validate the second. This theme of direct papal involvement is several times repeated by Kertzer and is enthusiastically endorsed by his glowing reviewers.[11] Not surprisingly, it is based on the touting of the magazine by the magazine itself — a practice similar to that regarding the alleged papal exaltation earlier of the editors of *La Croix* and *L'Osservatore cattolico,* an exaltation that was recorded in detail only in the pages of *La Croix* and *L'Osservatore cattolico.*

To have said, "only in America," was perhaps to be overhasty, since the no-

10. One can imagine the cartoon in *Punch,* perhaps by Robert Doyle, a Catholic artist: the supreme pontiff, Leo XIII, and the secretary of state, Cardinal Mariano Rampolla del Tindaro, hunched over a table strewn with galley sheets, spectacles in place, scissors sharpened, and pens poised to strike. (Pius IX as depicted by *Punch* will presently put in an appearance in the context of the "Jews as dogs" homily by the pope.)

11. Garry Wills in *Why I Am a Catholic* refers to "the Jesuit journal *Civiltà cattolica* whose every article was cleared beforehand by the pope's secretary of state." That is true to the degree that management of the magazine fell within the purview of the office of the secretary of state, which also controlled its budget and paid for its housing and provisioning. Whether "the pope's secretary of state" personally supervised monthly expenditures or the schedules of the Jesuit editors is unlikely. Moreover, for reasons to be set forth shortly, it was precisely during the period from 1870 to 1887, when modern racist anti-Semitism was gestating, that it would have been almost physically impossible for this kind of close Vatican supervision to be exercised.

tion of the pope and his secretary of state's personal involvement in the magazine — although part of its traditional public aura — was "semi-officially" confirmed by the Italian Jesuits in relatively recent years. Kertzer's information about direct hands-on papal supervision of *La Civiltà cattolica* was taken from a book titled *La Civiltà Cattolica,* which appeared under the imprint — as wheels within wheels again spin — of the publishing house La Civiltà Cattolica in the year 2000. Kertzer's own exercise in literalist inference is only a little short of citing the *Chicago Tribune* as journalistically supreme because it proclaims itself, "The World's Greatest Newspaper," or, *The New York Times* as universal in its reportage because it blazons, "All the News That's Fit to Print."

But Kertzer's quoted excerpt above has its own characteristic spin, as these two Vatican dignitaries not only review but also approve "the contents of the upcoming issue," so that in effect everything in the magazine had papal approbation — a claim that was not even made for *L'Osservatore romano.*[12] The suggestion that this approval was the purpose of the alleged examination of proofs is reinforced by another paraphrase of the commemorative volume:

> Three principles determined approval of the text. (1) The articles must conform to the Church's official teaching in matters of faith and morals; (2) on questions involving relations with other states, the position espoused must agree with that adopted by the Holy See; and (3) the timing of publishing the article in question must be opportune.

It is not clear why these criteria are regarded as significant, since numbers 2 and 3 by their very wording can have no bearing on anti-Semitism, racism, or anything else connected to Jews or Judaism, and number 1 would allow everything but heresy and depravity. The enforcement of all three criteria

---

12. Since the surfeit of superlatives accompanying descriptions of both publications is so overwhelming, it might be useful to contrast such descriptions with their most recent manifestation in a statement by the present editor of *L'Osservatore romano,* Gian Maria Vian. In an interview he was asked whether a reader should "interpret the editorial line of the newspaper to be also that of the pope and the secretariat of state?" He responded: "The paper is not official: It is not the expression, in every single part, of the point of view of the Vatican, that is, of the secretariat of state. . . . It's a paper with a very long history and it has always been rightly interpreted as the expression of the thought of the Holy See, without a doubt, but that is not to say that every word that comes out in the paper is exactly the thought of the pope or the secretary of state." If this is said of the green wood of the *Osservatore,* what will be said of the dry wood of *Civiltà*? (see Delia Gallagher, "Vian's Choice," *National Review Online,* June 17, 2009).

would certainly not constitute papal approval, disapproval, or even assessment of the slanders perpetrated by the Jesuit authors in their campaign.

But even assuming that the purpose of the alleged scrutiny was to give the papal stamp of approval to the contents of each issue, and even assuming that this scrutiny was sometimes carried out, even by the pope and/or his secretary of state, few people would find it credible that twice a month the magazine faced the possibility that a given body of text already set in type might be torn apart and either rewritten and reset or otherwise reconstituted at the behest of one or both of those two officials. Such attention to the details of the contents on the part of anyone would have been even more unlikely, if not impossible, during the declining years of Pius IX and the first decade of his successor, Leo XIII. Buried by Kertzer in an endnote is the fact — alluded to earlier — that from 1870, when Rome became the capital of Italy, and up to 1887, nearly two decades in all, the magazine was edited not in Rome but in Florence, thus making the kind of close supervision described above even more unlikely, if not almost impossible.

This is the passage to which the endnote number is attached: "by 1890 the ailing Father Oreglia had passed on his leadership in the Jesuits' crusade against the Jews to colleagues"; this is the endnote itself: "It is worth noting that this new burst of long articles devoted to the denunciation of the Jews came shortly after the journal . . . returned to Rome (1887) and was placed under particular close papal supervision." This would suggest a lack of "particular close papal supervision" from 1870 to the year when the papal campaign was "kicked off" in 1887. Moreover, that latter date doesn't indicate the exercise of close papal control in the subsequent interval, since according to Kertzer the "new" anti-Semitic articles only appeared in 1890, three years later. Thus a conclusion at least as plausible as his is that it was the independent (and over the years, inbred) Jesuit editorial team that made the anti-Semitic decisions — which isn't to suggest that ultimately history should not lay responsibility on the papacy for its lack of supervision. But that is still a far cry from attributing the rise of modern anti-Semitism to conspiracy-prone and Jew-hating popes.

Moreover, the return to Rome had nothing to do with Jews, and everything to do with Leo XIII's real campaign, which was to prevent Jesuit ultramontanists from interfering with his conciliatory plans regarding the Italian state.

In 1885 Giovanni Cornoldi, Director [chief editor] of the *Civiltà*, wrote the Jesuit General that the Pope [Leo XIII] had spoken to him about bringing the journal's offices back to Rome from Florence where they had been since the early 1870's, so that *"I can better manifest to you my will."* Admitting that "this is a delicate point for some of us *who prefer a certain real independence,"* Cornoldi presumed the Pope wanted the *Civiltà* to fight what Leo saw as fanatical extremism, supported by the intransigent Jesuits up to that point.[13]

Both phrases that I have italicized indicate that whereas the separation of the original Jesuit *collegio* from its fellow Jesuits in Rome had been a relatively tolerable situation, its isolation for nearly two decades in Florence not only inhibited Vatican supervision but also — bureaucracies being what they are — conduced to a sense of self-sufficiency and self-righteousness on the part of the editorial team. Other Jesuit editors in England, France, and Germany were part of the "worldwide network of the Catholic press," but only those in Florence were responsible for launching rabid attacks against the Jews, attacks that over the decades could be described as part of the unique "tradition" of that unique publication.

The above history of the relationship of Vatican personnel to events during the period when racist anti-Semitism swept Europe is far more credible than is the following psychological appraisal of Leo XIII — who had been introduced in the chapter titled "The Catholic Press" as the pope who "would transform Church views of the Jews in a dramatic and deadly way." Kertzer's blanket assumption that everything in *Civiltà cattolica* was supervised by the highest officials in the church, "including the popes," is the basis for what was earlier described as the "out of the limelight" conspiracy between pontiff and secretary to regulate their anti-Semitic campaigns. It is an assumption that illuminates the following psychological insights:

> Although Leo XIII was pope while mass anti-Semitic political movements were taking shape in Europe, and he would play a significant role in encouraging them, he made sure to keep a certain distance. He realized that such movements could be dangerous if they spun out of control, and he was also sensitive to the fact that many government leaders whose approval he sought opposed them. Being identified too closely

13. John Louis Ciani, *Across a Wide Ocean* (loc. cit.). Ciani continues with Leo's views on some other members of the worldwide network of the Catholic press. "Not only did Leo speak to Cornoldi about 'fanatical newspapers' of the right, but he also accused the Spanish and French Jesuits of being legitimists ['Carlisti'], and as intransigent as 'Univers' *(sic)* — the latter was a reference to the ultramontaine and anti-Semitic French journal."

with such movements would carry a diplomatic price that the Pope did not want to pay.

How the writer knows all this is not going to be disclosed, although such insights are reminiscent of the mind reading this author will exercise when he is attempting to clinch an otherwise implausible argument — an exercise that will attain the level of tour de force in the next chapter. But it should be noted that when those mass "political movements" — usually identified by historians as the emergence of racist and scientific anti-Semitism — were taking shape, the perfunctory Roman supervision of *Civiltà cattolica* was in abeyance, and the displaced Jesuits in Florence were in the process of becoming a more independent as well as a more inbred *collegio*. That it was over a period of a decade or so that the *Civiltà cattolica* community of Jesuits evolved into a loose cannon is certainly one implication of Father Martina's reference in the previous chapter to the incompatibility of their views regarding Jews with those of other Jesuits in general, and with other Jesuit editors in particular. (Martina mentioned the French *Etudes,* but the German *Stimmen der Zeit* and the English *The Month* would have been equally exemplary.) The first salvo of that cannon was the aforementioned 1880 article by Giuseppe Oreglia infamously "kicking off the papal anti-Semitic campaign."

Léon Poliakov also pointed out that it was nearly ten years after Leo's coronation that "large-scale campaigns against Jews were launched in France." This would suggest to most observers that what influenced such campaigns was not so much the pope or his magazine but the wave of irrational hatred for Jews that swept the continent during those last two fateful decades of the century. According to Poliakov, it may have been to *Civiltà cattolica* that the newspaper *Le Figaro* referred in 1883 when it wrote: "The kind of anti-Semitic movement that exists in certain regions of the earth would be the object of public ridicule in France." But it is improbable that only a short time later, it was the specific influence of *Civiltà cattolica* that led *La Croix* — previously "free of anti-Semitism" according to Poliakov — to take up that banner in 1886. It is more likely that the reason for change in that year was the appearance of the real anti-Semitic catalyst, *La France Juive* by Edouard Drumont, a book that famously went through scores of editions and sold millions of copies, and that can accurately be described as "crucial to the rise of modern anti-Semitism." What refueled that catalyst in the next decade was the Dreyfus Affair, again with Drumont leading the charge in his daily paper, *La Libre Parole.* Poliakov's final response to Kertzer, as it were, is his comment on the priest-editor of *La Croix* who as the century was coming to a close, "wrote to his superior that: 'A great number of semi-non-believers are beginning to find out that in France the only real Frenchmen are Catholics.'" Poliakov observed: "All Catholics did not take this attitude," and added, "however, secular, pseudoscientific, and thoroughly racist anti-Semitism was not without its champions" — thus making the same distinction that Kertzer views as a pretext fabricated by present-day churchmen.

CHAPTER 4

Satanic Synagogues and Jewish Dogs

The Pius IX whom Léon Poliakov viewed as a cause of "moderation" would be called by Cardinal Yves Congar an "homme catastrophique." In fact, he was an affable duffer who had the misfortune to reign too long, who gave too much power to curial "toadies" (Cardinal Newman's term), and who was destined for canonization by John XXIII, a similarly old-fashioned pontiff who didn't reign long enough to fulfill his hopes. He admired Pius's piety and his headstrong and large-hearted ways, the latter best illustrated by the pope's covertly attending the Roman funeral service of his longtime nemesis, the British-born liberal Catholic, Charles Montalembert, introduced in chapter 2 as opposing the Jesuits of *Civiltà cattolica*. The previously cited Giacomo Martina — who along with Roger Aubert and Frank J. Coppa — has done much to transform the monster image of the pope, concluded the last volume of his study by noting that although the long reign of Pius ended on a note of "bitter obstinacy," the devotion fostered by the pope, "warm, firm, and human," had nourished the spirituality of Angelo Roncalli.[1] As for the title of the present chapter, it makes clear that the two most unwarranted

1. Nevertheless, Martina wrote to John Paul II in 1985, when the pope had declared Pius IX "venerable," in order to oppose his advancement to the next stage. Martina was therefore disgruntled at the announcement of the beatification of Pius in 2000. Not entirely unlike the nineteenth-century pontiff, the biographer also adopted a bitter note. When besieged by reporters on the eve of the beatification ceremony, he blurted out, "I must shut up, I must disappear" — "devo stare zitto, devo scomparire"; and he added, "Shut up is the last word we hear" (*La Repubblica*, September 2, 2000). The best summation of the pros and cons of the pope's being raised to the altars is Kenneth Woodward's *Making Saints* (1996), since he interviewed both the postulator, favoring the cause of Pius IX, and the promoter of the faith (formerly, "the devil's advocate"), opposing the cause.

slanders associated with this pope are now going to be run to ground. The second of them, "Jewish dogs," will also open up some rich cultural history relative to animals in medieval and modern religious culture. However necessarily brief, such explorations may serve to supplement and enhance the larger themes, while also providing a short phase of relief from the accelerating fervor of Kertzer's critique of the papacy.

In 1854, six years after his coronation, Pius IX proclaimed the doctrine of the Immaculate Conception of Mary, and ten years later linked that proclamation to the encyclical *Quanta Cura* and its accompanying Syllabus of Errors. The encyclical was widely ignored in the larger world, but the list of errors was gleefully derided in the press as an indication of the gap between the papacy and what the Syllabus itself called "the civilization of the new era." Cardinal Newman in an open letter to the premier Catholic in England, the Duke of Norfolk, sought with characteristically subtle analysis to defuse many of the condemned propositions in the Syllabus, but did not comment on what Kertzer calls its "postscript," which contains the phrase he believes vilifies Jews and their religion, "synagogue of Satan."[2]

Kertzer's own treatment of the Syllabus came near the conclusion to the chapter titled "The End of an Era," which is in effect an inventory of Pio Nono's failures — undeniably many — supplemented by an estimation of his psychological condition. The inventory begins with the period immediately after the pope's election in 1846, when he was hailed as the liberal successor of an autocratic pontiff — a brief period to which we will return. The new pope recognized that "some changes have to be made," but, according to Kertzer, "certainly had no intention of granting equal rights to Jews." The last opinion, however anachronistically worded, is probably accurate, though speaking with certainty about indiscernible intentions entails an exercise in mind reading — a dubious art to which Kertzer in his analysis of Leo XIII earlier had shown himself predisposed. In the event, two and a half years after his election Pius was driven from Rome in the wake of the revolutions of 1848, only to return two years later "a changed man" — an opinion that is probably both true and understandable.

"Despite the image many of his subjects had had of him earlier, Pius IX had *never* been a true reformer, much less a liberal. He had always been deeply traditional, committed to the Church's never-changing verities." How this absolute judgment — the bane of conscientious scholars — was arrived

2. The "postscript" is made up of three paragraphs, later included in the encyclical *Etsi Multa* of November 21, 1873.

at is not disclosed.[3] Nor is it needed, since once again the omniscient clairvoyant takes over: "On his return from exile, he saw the world differently. Forces of evil were arrayed against him, against the Holy Church, and they could be given no quarter or they would sweep away all that was good" — as apparently they did, with the loss of much of the Papal States, so that "by 1861 all that was left of the Pope's temporal kingdom was Rome and the area immediately around it."

It was during this period after his "kingdom" was lost that the pope — with the assistance of Kertzer — posthumously reveals his innermost feelings:

> For the Pope the collapse of the Papal States was but another trial sent by God. But the Papal States had fallen to impious forces before — indeed, more than once in the nineteenth century alone — and each time the Church had ultimately triumphed and the forces of darkness were defeated. This time, with God's help, thought the Pope, the same would happen.

Following this psychological insight, the stage is set for the pope — whom Poliakov viewed as "notoriously conservative" and concerned with the "People of the Book" — to launch his war against the Jews. Following a rather begrudging description of the pope's early reform efforts, and a few lines about renewing ghetto restrictions in Rome and in a neighboring diocese, Kertzer — with a guilelessness that Edmund Morris on Ronald Reagan might have envied — delves deeper into the psyche of Pius. The evil designs lurking there are revealed when the author as well as the reader can overhear the pope reflecting on the ghetto action and witness him succumbing to his inner demons — as summoned forth by Kertzer's divinatory powers, and as previously described in the introduction to this book:

> But this rearguard action [the ghetto restrictions] . . . would soon be replaced by a whole new way of viewing the Jews. The same forces that had struck against the power of the Church had granted the Jews equal rights. In marshaling Catholic public opinion in support of the Vatican and against these forces of secularization, it was tempting, very tempting, to

3. Compare the following by the American authority on the church in modern Italy mentioned above, Frank J. Coppa, who has noted that the future pope in 1845 "had outlined a reformist course for the Papal State" that contained a "fifty-eight-point program" though not surprisingly it did not focus on issues of twenty-first-century concern. "Pio Nono and the Jews: From 'Reform' to 'Reaction,' 1846-1878," *Catholic Historical Review* (October 2003).

make use of this fact. Vilified for centuries, the Jew could, if properly conjured up, be used to discredit the forces that had sought to create a modern, secular state.[4]

In fact, as noted in the introduction, what this scene may actually conjure up in many people's minds is a Monty Python voice saying, "*Nobody* expects the Spanish Inquisition!" But it is now clear why Kertzer has emphasized that "in their public statements, no pope would publicly attack the Jews," and therefore the popes had to weave their plots "out of the limelight" — the latter, a phrase that in the present melodramatic context ("it was tempting, very tempting") cannot but evoke Charlie Chaplin. It would be to further dignify this concocted scenario to remark on the malicious crassness of the shift from the neutral "the Jews" in the first sentence to the contemptuous epithet "the Jew" in the last.

The next paragraph, initiating the proper conjuration, will lead to this whole new way of viewing not only the Jew but Judaism. "Pius IX set the tone in December 1864 when he issued a historic encyclical *Quanta Cura*, and with it distributed a Syllabus of Errors. . . . The Pope embraced a conspiratorial view of the world . . . an outlook that would shape Catholic attitudes for decades to come" — though, to avoid hyperbole, less than three decades, as Owen Chadwick pointed out in *A History of the Popes 1830-1914* when he assessed Leo XIII's *Rerum Novarum* as "breaking the hold of the Syllabus." Nor could the Syllabus shape the attitude of Montalembert, whose 1863 defense of "a free church in a free state" helped precipitate the document — which, however, he accepted but "with secret indignation." Nor did the document shape the world of the young and increasingly censorious Lord Acton, who dismissed both the document as a "folly" and Montalembert as "a foolish man." Nor did it shape the future Cardinal Newman, who declared disbelief in a published assertion that "the recent Encyclical and Syllabus are, beyond question, the Church's infallible utterance."[5] Six years

---

4. One critic of Kertzer's *Amalia's Tale* (2008) says the following of the author: "his attempt to give life to the long-buried past is finally a Frankensteinian effort, the assembly resourceful but the stitching still awkwardly visible. Alongside meticulous research, Mr. Kertzer hazards not only explicit speculation ('Having no clear idea of where to go, she must have asked a woman nearby for directions.') but also a narrative omniscience ('He could not pass these markets without some feeling of dread, for times were not good.')." Jeremy Axelrod, "Milking History," *New York Sun*, June 5, 2008.

5. In his "Letter to the Duke of Norfolk," Newman wrote: "the Syllabus has no dogmatic force; it addresses us, not in its separate portions, but as a whole, and is to be received

after the Syllabus appeared, he wrote that its defenders had "not come into contact with the intellectual mind of the times." This attitude was generally true of the Anglophone world, as represented also by the American archbishop John Ireland, who, around the time of *Rerum Novarum,* wrote: "Propositions reported in the Syllabus as at one time or another 'censured' by Pius IX, represent the excesses, the extravagances of the movements of the age, and not the movements themselves."[6]

As for Kertzer's "decades to come," the implications of even some of the most notorious condemnations in the Syllabus can certainly be viewed as having nurtured the anti-totalitarianism that served predominantly Catholic countries well during the Cold War period. Surely, Poles or Czechs would applaud the condemnation of the following: "The State, as being the origin and source of all rights, is endowed with a certain right not circumscribed by any limits." There was also the condemnation of communism in general, based on the pope's 1846 encyclical, *Qui Pluribus* — from Pius's "good" period. Thus it is not surprising that Michael Burleigh in *Earthly Powers: The Clash of Religion and Politics in Europe from the French Revolution to the Great War* (2006) characterizes the Syllabus as both an expression of "wilful obscurantism" and as a deflation of "the shibboleths of progress."

Nothing reflecting that last perspective surfaces in Kertzer's exposition of this "whole new way of viewing the Jews":

A postscript to the syllabus returned to the theme of the embattled Church. "Venerable Brothers, it is surprising that in our time such a great war is being waged against the Catholic Church." Responsibility for the war lay squarely with a conspiracy of secret sects, the Masons most notable among them. "Anyone who knows the nature, desires and intentions of the sects . . . cannot doubt that the present misfortune must mainly be

---

from the Pope by an act of obedience, not of faith, that obedience being shown by having recourse to the original authoritative documents, (Allocutions and the like,) to which it pointedly refers. Moreover, when we turn to those documents, which *are* authoritative, we find the Syllabus cannot even be called an echo of the Apostolic Voice; for, in matters in which wording is so important, it is not an exact transcript of the words of the Pope, in its account of the errors condemned. Mr. Gladstone indeed wishes to unite the Syllabus to that Encyclical which so moved him in December, 1864, and says that the Errors noted in the Syllabus are all brought under the infallible judgment pronounced on certain errors specified in the Encyclical. This is an untenable assertion (www.newmanreader.org/works/anglicans/volume2/gladstone/index.html).

6. For Acton, see Roland Hill, *Lord Acton* (2000); for Newman, Wilfrid Ward, *The Life of John Henry Cardinal Newman, I* (1912); for Ireland, *The Church and Modern Society* (1903).

imputed to the frauds and machinations of these sects." And then, in a phrase that would later be echoed by Pius IX's successor, Leo XIII, it continued: "It is from them that the *synagogue of Satan,* which gathers its troops against the Church of Christ, takes its strength."

With this phrase, the fateful papal identification of the Jews as the hidden enemies of the Church began to gain ground. "These wicked groups think that they have already become masters of the world." They seek nothing less than "to subject the Church of God to the most cruel servitude . . . and, if possible, to make it disappear completely from the earth."

A decade later, Pius IX returned to the theme that it was the "synagogue of Satan" that lay behind the worldwide conspiracy. In an 1873 encyclical he employed the image to portray the web of forces conspiring to destroy the Church. In this he had ample evangelical precedent, for the term came from the last book of the New Testament, where twice the Jews' places of worship are termed "synagogues of Satan" (Revelation 2,9 and 3.9).[7]

It is the structure of these excerpts that exposes the author's stratagem. The crucial quotation with the italicized phrase, "synagogue of Satan," is preceded by the author's inserted paraphrase about "Pius IX's successor," which intentionally obscures the fact that the antecedent of "them" in the quotation has nothing to do with Jews, but is grammatically the thrice-mentioned "sects" — identified at that time with "Secret Societies," that is, Freemasonry.[8] Moreover, the word "sects" was never traditionally used of Jews, and was only introduced into public discourse in that sense during the first wave of modern racist anti-Semitism late in the 1890s when the "Masonic conspiracy" became the "Judeo-Masonic conspiracy." That is why Kertzer's interpretation in the sentence about "fateful identification" and "hidden enemies" has to precede the next direct quotation, which also never mentions Jews, but merely refers to "groups."

7. (The ellipses and italics are Kertzer's.) Since the phrase is viewed as intrinsically anti-Semitic, it is important that its use by two popes be noted.

8. Pius IX's successor, Leo XIII, was also preoccupied with "sects," as the following from John Courtney Murray indicates: "The sects which Leo XIII identified as the Enemy were the organized adherents of the new political religions whose appearance on the national and international scene was perhaps the most formidable phenomenon of the nineteenth century. And the Sect of sects was, in Leo's view, the Masonic Order." "Leo XIII on Church and State: The General Structure of the Controversy" (loc. cit.), Woodstock Theological Center.

That those who constituted the synagogue of Satan were denominated "sects" is ignored by Kertzer and his source, Giovanni Miccoli, for both of whom just the mention of "synagogue" and "Satan" in the same document by this pope implies "anti-Semitism." It is also significant that the idea of a comprehensive papal condemnation of modern errors had been bruited since the beginning of Pius IX's reign during the pope's "good" period. However, if "sects" meant "Jews" in 1864, when Pius was so publicly maligning them, what did it mean in that earlier period when he saw the world differently?[9] In his first encyclical, *Qui Pluribus* (November 9, 1846), he attacked "those secret sects who have come forth from the darkness to destroy and desolate both the sacred and the civil commonwealth," and he asked the bishops to exhort their people "unceasingly to flee from the sects and the societies of the impious." But if the pope equated "sects" with "Jews," there is no explanation as to why after writing those words about the destruction and desolation brought by them, he went on to introduce reforms for Jews living in the Papal States — since this was also before he was driven from Rome.

In the lengthy excerpt above, the activity of these "sects" was both enormous ("great," "vast") and of relatively recent origin ("last few years," "surprising") so any reader, whether in the nineteenth century or the twenty-first, would certainly find it difficult to interpret this as referring to a religious group more ancient than the pope's own, and in fact a religious group that in relation to Christianity could certainly refer to the latter as a "sect." One would have to make a considerable leap to accept the notion that this tiny religious group could be described — even by a presumably virulent anti-Semite — as "gathering its troops" to engage in "ferocious war" "almost everywhere."

Picking up on the theme of "world mastery" in the next paragraph, Kertzer continues with the last paragraph cited above, beginning with: "A decade later, Pius IX returned to the theme that it was the 'synagogue of Satan' that lay behind the world wide conspiracy." The placement of the sentence is such that the reader now immediately assumes that "synagogue" must mean "Jews" — whereas there is nothing in the entire excerpt that refers to them — and that their role as "hidden enemies" is not something that

9. The reader had earlier been told that in the second year of his reign "popular enthusiasm for the new pope continued to grow"; this enthusiasm was based on the experiences of the previous year, 1846, when "a wave of optimism spread of a kindly new pontiff who was eager to end the abuses of the past."

is merely "beginning to gain ground," but that they are actually behind the entire "worldwide conspiracy." At this point it is merely sufficient for Kertzer to invoke the phrase, with no quotations from the encyclical, as signifying "the web of forces conspiring to destroy the Church." Having made a literal-ist reading of the 1864 utterance, the author is confirmed in his opinion that it is an invidious reference to Judaism by its repetition nine years later. What confirms this circularity — and is proffered as the clinching argument — is the non sequitur that the pope in returning to the theme and employing the image "had ample evangelical precedent, for the term came from the last book of the New Testament, where twice the Jews' places of worship are termed 'synagogues of Satan.'"

Oddly, the endnote reference to that quotation is to the study by Giovanni Miccoli, mentioned above, rather than to anything or anyone — like, say, a Scripture scholar — connected with "the last book of the New Testament." This is equally true of another text cited by Miccoli, a letter Pius wrote to the future martyr, Georges Darboy, archbishop of Paris. Here too the word "sects" is the antecedent to synagogue of Satan. Miccoli then jug-gles these phrases to link them to "stereotipi antiebraici," and getting more conspiratorial than even Kertzer, sees their use as an effort to resuscitate the "ancient conflict between the church and the synagogue."[10] But had Kertzer and/or Miccoli looked at the actual scriptural text, they would have seen that the original phrase "synagogue of Satan" could not even remotely have what today would be called "anti-Semitic" overtones. One commentator refers the phrase to a "heretical sect of pseudo-Jews"; another refers to the community of St. Paul, never regarded favorably by the community writing the last book of the Christian Testament; while a third simply cites Revelation 2:9, and provides this translation: "I know the blasphemy of those who say they are Jews and are not but are a synagogue of Satan."[11]

10. The irony is that Miccoli himself was led to these texts by the third volume of Giacomo Martina's life of the pope, *Pio IX: 1867-1878* (1990), where the chapter titled "Against Masonry, in Europe, in Brazil" begins by noting the pope's preoccupation with such issues as the loss of the temporal power or the progress of liberalism did not lead him to ig-nore Masonry, which is "one of the constants in the thought of Pius IX, expressed in numer-ous documents, encyclicals, letters, allocutions, discourses . . . culminating in the mournful peroration, 'Synagogue of Satan,' in the encyclical *Etsi multa*" — referred to in footnote 2 above. Miccoli does not explain the transformation of a criticism of Masonry to an attack on Jews.

11. Daniel Jonah Goldhagen in *A Moral Reckoning: The Role of the Catholic Church in the Holocaust and Its Unfulfilled Duty of Repair* (2002), though relying entirely on *The Popes Against the Jews,* also fails to glance at the New Testament, and manages to out-Kertzer

This "pre-history" of the term does not explain its future use as a generic epithet of execration, which probably came from the elementary notion of an "assembly of devils." In the context of *odium theologicum*, this had little more to do with anti-Semitism than "whore of Babylon" had to do with anti-Mesopotamianism, or calling one's opponents "thugs" — as Thomas Arnold called Newman's Tractarians — had to do with anti-Hinduism. In the early Middle Ages, Albigensian heretics called the church of Rome "the devil's basilica and synagogue of Satan." Since the Reformation, the term was applied primarily to the Roman curia by Protestants who viewed it as the creation of the devil — or in contemporary cliché, as the court of Hitler's pope. During that same period it was of course applied also to Jews, as in the particularly vicious bull of St. Pius V, *Hebraeorum Gens* (1569), where the witchcraft of Jews lures people to the synagogue of Satan. Cardinal Newman pointed out in *Anglican Difficulties* that the Tractarians had also been called by their critics "the synagogue of Satan." The theologian Ronald Modras cites a collective work by a number of European churchmen attacking the German regime in 1936 in which a Hungarian bishop "identified Nazism with paganism, the synagogue of Satan, and the anti-christ." Since Polish Catholicism is so often indicted for its anti-Semitism, equally noteworthy is the use of the term by the Polish primate, Cardinal August Hlond, who in 1932 denounced "Bolsheviks, atheists, and free thinkers" as the synagogue of Satan.[12]

In sum, the phrase was simply the malediction of choice for people seeking to describe what they regarded as consummate evil. That was certainly how the popes viewed Masonry — "the Sect of sects," as John Courtney Murray said. Of course, there were some Jews among the Masons, particularly in Holland and England, where their presence was a symbol of an "ecumenism," which never was extended to Catholics, as continental Masonry more and more became identified with the new government of united Italy and with the militantly anticlerical party in France. On the other hand, in nineteenth-century America, Masonry went hand in hand with Catholicism as the target of nativist agitators, with the result that gradually Catholics and Masons were joined in an uneasy alliance.

Kertzer by asserting that "'synagogue of Satan' is the name given in the Christian Bible to the Jews' place of worship as the font of modern evil." The last phrase, "font of modern evil," is his contribution — a kind of personal grace note — to the expanding myth.

12. Ronald Modras, *The Catholic Church and Antisemitism: Poland, 1933-1939* (1994). Kertzer will later utilize Modras for a few passages relating to Pius XI, but apparently overlooked this section of the book.

In passing, it is worth noting that all this congealing of animosities led to an interesting conflict in the United States, when in the "fateful year" of 1854 the pope whom Kertzer demonizes as patently autocratic made a special gift to the American people, as many other world leaders had also done, of a block of marble to be used in the construction of the Washington Monument. The gift — about which today's tourists to the nation's capital can still be informed — was rich in symbolism since the block came from the Templum Concordiae, completed in 367 BCE, to commemorate peace between plebeians and patricians in the Roman republic, an institution that the founding fathers had studied closely. Although it was a gesture of admiration for the American nation's dissolution of class distinctions, so fearful were anti-Catholic groups like the burgeoning Know-Nothings, the American Protective Association, and what would later be called the Ku Klux Klan — anti-Semites all — that this "rock of Peter" would taint the monument, they delayed all further construction for a quarter of a century.

On first examining *The Popes Against the Jews,* one might have thought that Kertzer — who has let readers know he is the son of a recipient of a Vatican award for interreligious relations — innocently assumed that the mere conjunction of "synagogue" and "Satan" automatically signaled anti-Semitism. Unfortunately, as the early seventeenth-century moralist Owen Feltham wrote in his *Resolves: Divine, Moral and Political,* "There is an innocential providence as well as the slyness of a vulpine craft," and it is that craftiness that has been displayed above, and that makes it necessary to explore the matter further. At the very least, it provides insights into the rhetorical strategies of an author who has proved to be persuasive to Anglophone readers as well as to readers in more than half a dozen other languages.

The easy acceptance of Kertzer's misreading may also be explained by a telling passage from a nineteenth-century "moralist," Cardinal Newman, which is relevant both to the above discussion as well as to the larger interpretive issue of polemically motivated aberrations being so readily embraced by readers. Newman's text (from which one of the epigraphs of the present book is taken) treats of "dangerous errors" arising from works Newman described as "fertile in facts . . . and recondite in character":

> The relative importance of events, their aspect and meaning, the probability of their having occurred, the value of the particular testimony produced, the force of words, the arrangement of dates, these are but a few out of the many matters, in which, from the nature of the case, the per-

sonal judgment of the reader is almost excluded, and the dictum of the teacher must be received as law. *(Essays Critical and Historical 2)*

But, it must be added, such a dictum results in the rule of law adjudicated in the court of public opinion rather than in the court of history. A pertinent illustration of such a triumph of public opinion is the dramatization by the Pulitzer Prize playwright, Alfred Uhry, of Kertzer's earlier book, *The Kidnapping of Edgardo Mortara,* to be looked at shortly. At the climax of the play, which is titled *God's Child,* Pius IX vehemently inveighs against "the synagogue of Satan" — a dramatic *inventio* worthy of Rolf Hochhuth.[13]

From Kertzer's perspective, the fact that Pius IX referred to Jews as the "synagogue of Satan" long before he referred to them as "dogs" could be taken as another sign of the gradual disintegration of the aging pontiff. At least the first phrase has a vague air of learning — although it also has a briefer history. At one time or another Jews called Samaritans dogs; St. Paul referred to gentiles as dogs; the mishnaic rabbis called Christians dogs; Berbers in scores of swashbuckling novels and films put Christian dogs to the sword. Even Saddam Hussein before his downfall threatened to eradicate all "Jewish dogs" — the latter, a source of innumerable jokes in Israel. The threatened ruling classes for centuries have referred to their social inferiors, the riffraff or the mob, as *canaille* or *canaglia.* Lastly, there is the literary tradition as represented by its most exalted writer, William Shakespeare, who managed to combine the canine canard with the ritual murder libel in the figure of Shylock, insistent on his pound of flesh and crying out: "You call me misbeliever, cut-throat dog." In sum, every denigrator of the "other" — whether fictional or factual — employing this kind of language runs counter to the more ancient and perhaps more all-embracing tradition depicted by Odysseus's and Tobit's loyal hounds, as well as by all the Fidos of folklore.

Nevertheless, even given this checkered history, it is not difficult to understand why the allegation that a pope referred to Jews as dogs would cause an uproar. That it did was attested to by Kertzer himself in the excerpt from the interview that first prompted my examination of his book. Unfortu-

---

13. According to the *Jewish Encyclopedia* (1906), an earlier playwright, H. M. Moos, had taken up the story of the kidnapped boy in *Mortara, or the Pope and His Inquisitors* (1860).

There is a representation of Pius IX by a man who was both a playwright and a diplomat that is useful in providing a different sense of how the pope was regarded by Catholics of the period. It is only a small exaggeration to say that one learns more about the pope and his age from Paul Claudel's *Le Père humilié* than from many historians — certainly, from the historian of the "unholy war" against the Jews.

nately, just as Kertzer refused to show the actual text to his questioners in Rome, he is not going to show it to his readers. In the following "paraphrase" there are only three authentic fragments from the pope's homily:

> One day in August of that year [1871], members of a Catholic women's organization of Rome came for an audience with the Pope. As he addressed them, his mind turned to a topic that clearly had been preying on it, and he abruptly launched into a denunciation of the Jews of the city in ancient times. Pius IX told them, before the time of Jesus, the Jews "had been *children* in the House of God." But, all this had changed, for "owing to their obstinacy and their failure to believe, they have become *dogs*." Speaking just months after Italian forces had freed the Jews of Rome's ghetto, the Pope bemoaned the result. "We have today in Rome unfortunately too many of these dogs, and we hear them barking in all the streets, and going around molesting people everywhere." (italics original)

In this version, the "denunciation" *is* shocking. Here was a pope saying these appalling things in the very year when Jews in the First Reich attained citizenship — and less than seven decades before they would be fated for extermination in the Third Reich.[14]

14. The fate of Kertzer's version merits examination in the context of the discussion that opened this chapter on the creation of papal myths and legends. Just as Kertzer misread the New Testament on the synagogue of Satan, and D. J. Goldhagen misread Kertzer's misreading to further sustain that fabrication, so too another myth is in the process of being created here.

Without going into the commendation of Kertzer's disclosure of the Pius/Jew/dogs theme by Holocaust-denier David Irving and excluding the *literally* thousands of sites on the Internet where the dog story is elaborated, Garry Wills's preoccupation with it is the most creatively credulous. In *Why I Am a Catholic* (2002), Wills cites it first in the context of Pius IX himself. Later he cites it in the context of Leo XIII when, relapsing into chat-mode, he says to his readers: "I ask again, then, why this pope is considered a liberal. Well, I suppose he was — at least by comparison with the Pius who preceded him . . . lashing out at Jewish dogs." Then Wills, introducing John Paul II, refers to him as having "appointed a secret panel to see if he could get away with beatifying Pius IX — the pope who fumed at Jewish 'dogs.'"

Across the ocean in Northern Ireland, Ian Paisley, on the occasion of the beatification, also weighed in on the two papal monsters: "A Pope who kidnaps children and calls Jews dogs is no Saint. Significantly, ultimate responsibility for the beatification of this racist thug reverts to the present Pope." Then taking on the reigning pontiff, he comes up with a new slander — at least to the present writer. "John Paul II himself . . . in the early 1940's was employed as a salesman by the I. G. Farben Chemical Company in Poland. This company sold

As noted above, Kertzer had laid the groundwork for his "synagogue of Satan" insight by entering the pope's mind. But in the above passage psychokinesis is added to psychoanalysis, as the author not only knows what the pope is thinking when his mind "turns" to the matters preying on it, but the author is also present at the scene when he hears the pope "bemoaning" his fate and sees him "abruptly" launching his denunciation. But something more was needed by Kertzer to render even moderately plausible this truncated version. Pius has to be made obsessed by Jews — much as Kertzer himself is by popes. The paragraphs preceding his excerpted text serve that purpose, as he again takes possession of the mind of his protagonist after the occupation of Rome in September 1870:

> Given the siege mentality that now prevailed in the Vatican, the forces of good seemed to face the forces of the devil himself. And from Pius IX's point of view, and that of most other clergy, it was clear enough who had benefitted from the revolutions that had deposed God's emissary on earth: the Jews.

But there is no evidence this was Pius's point of view, much less the point of view of "most other clergy," since obviously to any observer, clerical *or* lay, pope *or* priest, American *or* European, then *or* now, the great beneficiaries would have been the millions of Italian nationalists who finally had a capital for their incipiently unified country.[15]

The next paragraph continues in the same style, as Kertzer introduces an even more unexpected and unaccommodating theme:

> What must Pius have felt when, in 1871, he learned the identities of the key financial advisers at the peace conference of Versailles which followed the

---

cyanide, Zyklon B and malathion — three gases which were used by the Nazis to exterminate millions of Jews and other groups." The gaseous Paisley, in makeover-mode, will appear again in the last chapter of this book as an ally of the Catholic Martin McGuinness, and thus of Pope Pacelli. (For the quotations above, see "The European Institute of Protestant Studies," which can be accessed at: www.ianpaisley.org/article.asp?ArtKey=beatification.)

Lastly, the expositors at *Time* (September 4, 2000), apparently confusing themselves with *The Expository Times*, wrote: "This week the Catholic Church beatifies Pius IX. The flawed 19th century Pontiff, who once referred to Jews as 'dogs,' is an odd candidate for canonization."

15. The magazine *Punch,* introduced earlier — and not exactly a Catholic-friendly venue — managed to get it right. Pio Nono was depicted clutching his keys while Victor Emmanuel II is holding — not brandishing — a sword on which is engraved, "TEMPORAL POWER."

Franco-Prussian War? The French leader, Louis-Adolphe Thiers, had the Jewish banker Alphonse de Rothschild at his side, while accompanying Bismarck was his financial adviser and banker, the Jew Gerson Bleichröder.

The only connection to the pope's homily and the Franco-Prussian War is the year 1871. But why Pius would have "learned" anything about Jews at Versailles goes unexplained, as does also what he "must have felt" about them — not to mention why any of this would have been preying on his mind months later in Rome.[16]

What would probably have been occupying the pope's mind in August 1871 would not be Jewish bankers and financial advisors at Versailles, but the much more recent fate of the archbishop of Paris and several priests. In May of that year, after being imprisoned for months, they had been ruthlessly shot by teenage communards — forerunners of the Red Brigades a century later. The soon to be martyred Archbishop Georges Darboy, mentioned in passing in the previous chapter as sometimes at odds with the Vatican, had been assured by the pope of "his blessing amid all the great misfortunes of his flock" (Owen Chadwick, *A History of the Popes 1830-1914*). If Kertzer's focus on "what Pius must have felt" were going to appear even slightly plausible, Kertzer might better have introduced Karl Marx, who came to the attention of the world, and possibly of the pope, by famously celebrating the assassins of the Paris Commune as "harbingers of a new society." (That they turned out to be harbingers of the Red Army, as experienced by "a future pope in Poland," is the subject of chapter 7.)

At worst, it is Kertzer himself who appears to be trying to stir the muddy waters of anti-Semitism by his incongruous observation that Pius could somehow have been thinking about "Jewish bankers" and "financial advisers" when addressing the Roman women. In fact, this strange focus on Jewish bankers and lenders is the kind of observation that Kertzer will later denounce as a slur exploited in the "*Catholic* anti-Semitic movement." But there is nothing specifically Catholic about Owen Chadwick's comment in *The Secularization of the European Mind in the Nineteenth Century* (1975),

16. This was one of the passages that I marked in the margin during my initial read of the book — actually I marked it with a question mark and two exclamation points — since I couldn't come up with even a faintly plausible notion as to what this was doing here. Kertzer's juxtaposition of a group of Jewish bankers at Versailles and a homily to a group of women in Rome remains one of the more inexplicable riddles relative to the workings of his mind.

that the murder of Archbishop Darboy by the self-proclaimed defenders of freedom and human rights "proved to half of France that the Pope was right. Justice and modern liberty were opposites." Nor is there anything particularly Catholic about the observation that postwar France regarded its defeat as "synonymous with the world of French high finance that had been implicated in all of France's major corruption scandals through men who typically bore German-Jewish names like Rothschild, Reinach, and Fould. Anti-Germanism thus became anti-Semitism."[17]

It is not inconceivable that what Kertzer's (otherwise inexplicable) arbitrary message about Jewish financiers could have been intended to do was draw the reader's attention away from the essential fact that the pope was delivering a short homily on a scriptural passage that the original text — the one Kertzer wouldn't show to his interrogators in Rome and won't now show to his readers — supplies, chapter and verse: "Matthew 15:21-28." That Gospel reference is unavoidably clear in the book that Kertzer cites as his source for the papal remarks. Whether he actually looked at that book, as I mentioned in chapter 1, remains unknown. His endnote reads, "The text of this speech is reproduced in De Franciscis . . . similar remarks are quoted in Miccoli."[18] The nominal "editor," Pasquale De Franciscis, was a priest who had offered his services as amanuensis to the pope, and who took down in shorthand the discourses, which were then corrected by the pope with a view to their publication.

As for Miccoli, he also derived this text from the third volume of Martina's study of Pius IX, and following Martina's lead came up with a number of conventional Christian slurs about Jews — blasphemers, impious, iniquitous, and the like — all rather splenetic, some nasty, but hardly indicative of papal obsessions with Jews. The following is a very brief summary of Martina's own summary of the topics and the tenor of some of the more impassioned discourses that De Franciscis transcribed:

> An indictment of the Risorgimento, specifically its causes, its goals, its leaders; a realistic consideration of its results; and a severe warning to liberal Catholics who constituted a major danger for the church — "a real Trojan horse." Milan and Turin were the centers of heresy and corruption,

17. Wolfgang Schivelbusch, *The Culture of Defeat: On National Trauma, Mourning, and Recovery* (2003). This is a study that has no interest in religion as such, but is concerned with the cultural responses that vanquished societies make to cope with their defeat.

18. The source is *Discorsi del sommo pontifice Pio IX pronunziati in Vaticano ai fedeli di Roma e dell'orbe dal principio della sua prigionia fino al presente* (Rome, 1872).

"vomiting out immoral books and scandalous novels." Those responsible were malcontents seeking "revolution and disruption in order to feed their insatiable wants." The Carbonari and Young Italy were described: "a sect, black in name and deed, dispersed through our fair land . . . another appeared that claimed young people, but in truth was old in evil and iniquity. . . . In the end all carried their turbid and slimy waters to the vast Masonic swamp from which today pestilential miasmas arise."

If the pope's overwhelming preoccupation was concentrated where Kertzer projects it, that last sentence would refer to the "vast Judaic swamp." The subjects cited above are more or less representative of the discourses, but what they, and even more emphatically their language, put on display is the gradual deterioration of the pope's mind, particularly as he approached his last years. But if the rare sympathetic reader were seeking an image for the aging pontiff, it wouldn't be that of an obsessed manager of campaigns against Jews; rather it would more likely be that of a King Lear figure who felt betrayed by those he loved — although, again, to be recommended is a far different dramatic presentation than that of Shakespeare, Paul Claudel's *Le Père humilié*.

But neither of those plays is directly related to the preacher who addressed the Roman women at the beginning of his "imprisonment" and who is both thoughtful, articulate, and temperate. In fact, his language is much more compassionate and obliging than are the Gospel words themselves — an understandable target of feminist exegetes — that the pope alludes to. This is what the pope actually said:

When our faith triumphs over the attacks of our enemies, then certainly we will be free. I recommend to you Women of the Pious Union that you keep the faith and, in accord with it, work ceaselessly with confidence and fervor — as I see that you are doing — and never abandon prayer. Bear in mind the example of the Canaanite (Matt. 15,21-28). The Canaanite was a woman; she was a good woman though of a gentile nation. She begged Jesus Christ for the grace of freeing her daughter from the demon that possessed her. But Jesus Christ would not listen to her and, finally as though indignant, he replied that it is not fitting to take the children's bread and give it to the dogs. The woman said, "Yes, but you have come also to give bread to the dogs, for these same dogs eat the crumbs that fall from the table of their masters." Then Jesus Christ turned and apologized to that good woman and praised her faith, and consoled her with the gift of freeing her daughter. In this way, she ceased being a dog and so, too, with her child. Then the Jews who were the children in the house of God, because of their obstinacy and lack of faith, became the dogs. There are too many of these dogs nowadays in Rome, and we hear how they are barking in all the streets bothering people everywhere. We hope that they will return to being children. Meanwhile, let us imitate the constancy and humility of the Canaanite woman, and do not doubt that if she, who was a gentile, became worthy of the mercy of God, we also shall be worthy, since we are children of God.[19]

The parallel that the pontiff was drawing — though seemingly expressive of a "harsh saying" to the Canaanite woman — is based on the rudimentary Christian teaching that the gospel fulfills the message of the Hebrew prophets. Once the Jews were the children in the house of God — so the gospel and Jesus Christ say — and the gentiles were the dogs. Now the gentiles are the children in the house of God — so St. Paul and the vicar of Christ say — and the Jews are the dogs. But just as the Gospel verses are read as a sign of Jesus' message ultimately being preached to the gentiles, so Pius's statement, "We hope that they will return to being children," is a sign of his desire that Jews will accept the gospel message. This may all appear to be just too "supersessionist," but for better or worse it points up the Christian theological relationship of the "New" Testament to the "Old," even though that latter mildly pejorative modifier is now acknowledged as obsolete.[20]

19. The dog image is a devotional stereotype. In one of the "Tracts for the Times," John Henry Newman cited a prayer of the venerated Anglican bishop and divine, Lancelot Andrewes: "I believe, that though we be neither sons nor servants, but dogs only, yet we have leave to eat of the crumbs that fall from Thy Table." Few would make the case that the bishop was endorsing the notion that he and his fellow British churchmen were dogs. However, what he may unwittingly have been doing was preparing for that reassessment of the role of animals in the economy of salvation that under the rubric "animal theology" has been an almost uniquely Anglican achievement, led by the priest-theologian Andrew Linzey.

Apropos of the "rich cultural history" mentioned earlier, it is to be noted that several art critics have explained the presence of dogs in paintings of the "Last Supper" not as nonce figures inserted into depictions of domestic festivals — as they often appear in paintings of the wedding feast at Cana — but as inspired by Aquinas's Corpus Christi hymn about the "bread of angels" not being given to dogs, a direct reference to the passage from Matthew's and Mark's Gospels. But like Kertzer and his Catholic defenders, there is no awareness of the Gospel roots of the imagery, and like Kertzer such critics persist in this "insight" even though Tintoretto, the painter of more fully conceived "Last Suppers" than any other artist, in at least two of those paintings has a cat.

20. It is not possible here to go into the matter of "supersessionism" or of clichés about

More significantly, there is lurking in the background of the pope's imagery, and having nothing to do with Jews except to rely on their Bible, is a reference to the Republican forces that had occupied the pope's city. Pius's complaint is an echo of King David's when he is inveighing against the forces of his enemy in Jerusalem: "Do not be merciful to any wicked transgressors, who bark like dogs and go all around the city" (Ps. 59:6). The fact that the author of *The Popes Against the Jews* is preoccupied with the Jews does not mean that every seemingly negative expression (including "synagogue of Satan") by anyone connected to the church represents an attack on them. Nor does it mean they were the intended objects of the evil wrath of the pope who, however, could certainly have seen himself as another David surrounded by the enemy in his own city.

As noted, the presumably venomous sentence, "There are many of these dogs nowadays in Rome, and we hear how they bark in the streets, bothering people everywhere," can be recognized as an oblique reference to the Psalms

---

"replacement theology," except to note that Christians who accept those terms and their negative implications — often out of understandable but misdirected guilt for the Christian role in both preparing for and sometimes engaging in the monstrosity of the Holocaust — must if they are true to the meaning of either term reject Jesus and Christianity as the fulfillment of the ancient biblical prophecies. In brief, that means uprooting the foundations of Christian belief, whether Protestant, Orthodox, or Catholic, and rejecting all that the Christian faith has historically stood for. It also explicitly discredits every Jewish convert to Christianity from St. Paul to St. Edith Stein. Lastly, and to broaden this out to the "Free Churches," critics of "supersessionism" might listen to what used to be called "Negro spirituals," hymns native to America that bolstered the faith of slaves and made less unendurable their lives in this Christian nation. Like Israel in Egypt, the slaves longed to be "going home." Stripped of its negative baggage, "supersession," meaning simply "super-added," can be doctrinally legitimized. However, "replacement theology" cannot, since the new covenant does not replace the original covenant with the Jews, which is still in effect and which renders redundant all constraining efforts at conversion but certainly not the acceptance of Christian faith.

For an exemplary and undeniably well-intended expression of such remorse-ridden thinking, see John R. Donahue, "Trouble Ahead? The Future of Jewish-Catholic Relations," *Commonweal,* March 13, 2009. The whole arena of "Jewish-Catholic relations" or "Jewish-Christian dialogue," however intrinsically noble in motivation, is fraught with remorse-ridden denigration of the Christian tradition on the part of those who might be termed "contrasupersessionists." The remorse is understandable, the denigration is not. (The subtext here is: give enough academics a new polysyllabic coinage to wrap their arms and minds around, and they will publicly hug it to death.) Jewish-Catholic relations will put in another and more critical appearance in the last two chapters of this book.

For a less fragile assessment than that of Donahue, see Philip A. Cunningham, "Uncharted Waters: The Future of Catholic-Jewish Relations," *Commonweal,* July 14, 2006.

and a direct reference to the apostles' self-serving insistence, which Jesus ignores, regarding the Canaanite/child/Jew/"dog": "Get rid of her. She keeps crying after us" — is the wording in Mark's Gospel.[21] But a homilist who wanted to avoid mixing his metaphors would realize that dogs don't "cry," and would so amend his text as did Pius: "they bark [*latrare*] in the streets bothering people everywhere." Just as the disciples thought the Canaanite woman bothersome — so the pope thought the Republican partisans and the Jews were also. But to the degree that the focus is on the Jews, then the final implication of the pope's talk is that even as Jesus ended up welcoming the woman, so too would Pius welcome the Jews. The fact that he looked forward to the Jews "returning to being children" signified the approach of the end to the theological hatred for Jews instituted, as noted earlier, by the church fathers who engendered the *adversus Iudaeos* tradition. To get a glimpse of the progress represented by Pius IX's view, one need only compare his use of the Gospel story of the woman and her "possessed" daughter with that of a fourth-century church father, Ephrem the Syrian, who said that the demon that was cast out still lived in the Jews of his own day.[22]

Unfortunately, the pope's homily is also an expression of "supersessionism," a less triumphant term than "replacement theology," but a term which, nevertheless, is at least a far cry — or bark — from saying Jews are literally dogs or devils. Whether this benign understanding of Pio Nono will affect those hundreds of thousands of sites on the Internet exploiting the Jews/dogs theme — that must remain unknown. On the other hand, to replace "replacement theology" with something that sounds less conquistadorial does make sense, and so the relationship of Christianity to Judaism could in the present stage of history stress the "elder-sibling/younger-sibling" family bond. This would also suggest that Christian-Jewish dialogue partners should set aside the entire matter of the nexus between the two *faiths,* and confine their common efforts to collaboration in *works* of charity

21. As noted above, this is a passage that feminist biblical critics have wrestled with. It is also a passage that has attracted artists, most famously, Rembrandt, but most notably Jean Colombe in *Les Très Riches Heures du Duc de Berry.* The latter depicts in one panel the Canaanite woman kneeling before the preoccupied disciples while Jesus turns away from her. In the background on the right can be glimpsed the house where the afflicted child is lying in bed with an attendant nearby. The lower and smaller panel shows the woman, again kneeling, while Jesus and the disciples are all turned attentively facing her. (Thus does art moderate ancient "texts of terror.")

22. "Looking into the Biblical Mirror: *Lectio Divina* in the Writings of Sts. Ephrem and Aphahat," *The Bible Today* (September 2009).

— remembering the scriptural admonition that the one without the other is ineffectual — all the while trusting the common father of history to sort out in the absolutely unknown and unknowable future the permanent nature of the relationship. This *attente-de-Dieu* posture would thus ignore and/or transcend all issues related to primacy, priority, preeminence, and the like — perhaps by regarding them as unresolvable in this world and certainly irrelevant in the next. For this, too, there is a useful principle: "solvitur in excelsis."

Since this entire discussion has been centered on the myth of Jewish dogs, it is worth briefly considering how such a topos can be "validated" by giving it the full academic treatment. The mode of achieving such validation does not differ much from the way that the popular myths and legends encountered earlier were apparently made credible — that is, by endlessly repeating in a variety of ingenious formulations the same newly minted (and often obsessively compulsive) notions. The most inventive work on the Jews/dogs motif has been done not by a theologian or by a historian of religious art, but by a scholar of medieval and early modern Judaism who describes his work as being "not a study of 'anti-Semitism' or 'anti-Judaism.'" "Instead, this book argues that to anchor claims of supersession, Catholics have viewed Jews as metaphoric — and sometimes not so metaphoric — dogs."[23]

The author anchors his claim that Catholics have regarded Jews as real dogs as well as fictionally imagined dogs in an astonishing mélange of statements that almost put one in mind of what the academics described earlier would concoct when they hugged a new polysyllabic coinage to death:

> The dog has for millennia been the focus of impurity, and Catholicism fosters doctrines of physical purity that go hand in hand with those of ritual purity. The purity is that of the "one loaf" spoken of by Paul in Corinthians that is, at once, the Eucharist and the collective Christian Corpus, the body of the faithful. Paul views this "loaf" as physically corruptible, and as John Chrysostom said at the close of the fourth century, the greatest threat to the loaf's purity are the Jews. They are the dogs who wish to steal the bread that belongs exclusively to the children. Eventually, Jews were said to attack the "loaf" through ritual murder and attempts to defile the Host itself; the victim of ritual murder is identified with the Host, as is common in Catholic martyrdom.

23. Kenneth R. Stow, *Jewish Dogs: An Image and Its Interpreters, Continuity in the Catholic-Jewish Encounter* (2006).

To those ends the author, deploying the same kind of manic logic passim, explores a wide range of scholarly works, esoteric and exoteric, as well as some unusual Internet sites to agglomerate such things as

> *Nostra Aetate* and *Dominus Jesus;* Catholic Integrists and Modernists; Chilean refrains about "Jewish dogs stealing bread from the oven"; "Abbot Clement of Cleveland" on the Eucharist, and "Pastor Bob Jones of Nevada" on God's Order Affirmed in Love — GOAL; Jewish leaven spoiling the bread of Christian society, and vice versa regarding Christian leaven; all bread is equated with eucharistic bread; Corpus Christi is equated with the "body politic"; Jewish mothers as lamias; lamias as hyenas; Jewish mothers of Christian children as devourers of their young, etc.

After all that, it is a relatively minor matter that the author also believes midwestern nuns in mid-twentieth century America were teaching their pupils about the reality of ritual murder.

At this juncture, since the blood libel is looming, this author asks:

> To say that the Jewish mother withheld the "bread" and killed the child is also to say that the mother "stole the bread from the oven." Afterwards and certainly later, the bread in the oven, the explicit Eucharist, and the (Christian, Christlike) child were viewed interchangeably as one and the same. Jewish lending at interest was blood letting, and the Jews "guilty of this practice" were "wild and thirsty dogs." This led in the thirteenth and fourteenth centuries to "Jewish prayer, if not all Jewish practice . . . [being] sensed as the yelping of dogs "pra/eying" to devour the host. . . . Eventually, all Jewish sounds, noise, and perhaps even speech might be likened to barking.

That segues into Miccoli-Kertzer, and the homily half a millennium later wherein Pius IX unleashed his canard:

> Having experienced the dismemberment of the papal state and the simultaneous fall of the Roman Ghetto just months before, Pius IX was moved in 1871 to complain that Jews were aurally polluting the city's sacred space. They were "barking" up and down Roman streets. By extension, the smelly Jewish dogs were spreading the infamous "Jewish stench" throughout the city. This thought may have also recalled for Pius the "stinking" and "revolting" rabbinic lore *(foetica et foeda . . . scribarum sapientia)* that

Ramon Martí had deplored in his *Pugio fidei* of about 1278. . . . *Latrare,* I stress, was Pius IX's own word. Yet had he not been preceded in using it, or words like it, by Chrysostom, Agobard, Rupert of Deutz, Henry III, Philip V, Fortunato Coppoli, and Dr. Tiberino, to name but a few?

Alas, would that Pius had been so well read.

Twenty pages later, the pope returns in the same role and to the same place. "It was in a state of disbelief that he referred in 1871 to the now liberated Jews, saying, 'we hear them barking up and down the streets' *(li sentiamo per tutte le vie latrare).* Both Jewishly and politically, the Jews were polluting the Eternal City." The next retrieval of Pius is in the context of a decree against "Jewish noise" at the Third Lateran Council about which the author observes: "We are reminded that noise signified pollution by Pius IX's remark of 1871 decrying the Jews barking throughout the city of Rome, which rendered the city aurally impure, just as Pius thought Jewish meanderings polluted Rome's sanctified urban space." Each reference validates the other in a circular maze from which there is, apparently, no exit.

That play of imagination is also introduced when the author combines the homily to the Roman women with Kertzer's book, *The Kidnapping of Edgar Mortara.* As Stow reads the latter, Pius was "unwilling to give Edgardo back to his parents, regardless of the disastrous political consequence for the papal state, which led to its collapse in 1870." (Almost spontaneously, one thinks, "Better stick with the Middle Ages and Rupert of Deutz.") Not even Kertzer was this imaginative about the occupation of Rome.[24] The combination of the Mortara story and the homily takes the reader as well as the author off the deep end of the deep end where only abyss crying out to abyss can be heard:

> Pius himself, in this scenario, if we may permit ourselves to imagine the fantasies evolving in his brain, was also the Virgin, rescuing the boy Edgardo from the oven into which Edgardo's real father, Salomone, was trying insistently to push him. Thus, Pius had ripped Edgardo, the "bread" incarnate, from the jaws of the hungry Jews. Were these not, after

24. But there is a link to Kertzer made in the context of a rejected contribution by Stow for the *New Catholic Encyclopedia* on "the medieval papacy and the Jews." The reader is told that a draft "was positively vetted only to be rejected afterward as unwanted; this decision possibly reflects reaction to Kertzer, *The Popes Against the Jews.*" Possibly it does, and possibly it doesn't. Not all paranoia is contagious.

all, those very "dogs" about whom Pius himself was to say, they "were barking throughout the city" and polluting it?

Fantastic hyperbole this scenario — perhaps not? . . . Is it not possible, then, that in Pius's mind, the symbols had become confused and rearranged? For Pius, Edgardo was the Jewish dog "domesticated." Yet, as counter-martyr, Edgardo was also the bread itself. Rather than purloining the "bread" as a Jew, therefore, the faithful Edgardo restored it, that is, himself, to its rightful possessor, Christ, in the form of Christ's Vicar on earth, the pope. In this way, Edgardo had succored the needy Christian, his Jewish bite and infection had been warded off. For Pius IX, so it may really have been. Under stress, minds do strange things.

With that last observation the matter of the pope's homily can be laid to rest — while the well-established fact of the pope publicly calling Jews "dogs" becomes a well-established myth.[25]

However, as a release from the verbal mania displayed by Stow and from the horrors of ritual murder awaiting the reader on the horizon, I return very briefly to the observation made at the beginning of this chapter to the effect that the treatment of the pope's homily would also open up some rich history relative to the animals in religious culture. "However necessarily brief, such explorations may serve to supplement and enhance the larger themes, while also providing a short phase of relief from accelerating fervor of Kertzer's critique of the papacy." The point of departure is an achievement of the current guardian of papal primacy.[26] Unlike his Renaissance predecessors, Benedict XVI has emphasized the role of artworks in the preservation and diffusion of the Christian message, even going so far as to suggest that they are among the *praeambula fidei,* the preparatory experiences that attune the mind and spirit to belief in what that message portends. Hence the value of those earlier references to artworks by Tintoretto, by Rembrandt, and by Jean Colombe, all having to do with the gentile woman and her invocation of the *little* dogs — as one version emphasizes — eating the crumbs from the master's table. Those references now find their climax in the *Last Supper* of Pietro Lorenzetti, a painting that Benedict must love and that may

25. See also by the same author, *Popes, Church, and Jews in the Middle Ages: Confrontation and Response* (2007), a collection of previously published pieces, as learned but less zany than the ones excerpted above.

26. This does not negate an earlier observation: The wisest posture would thus be to "ignore and/or transcend all issues related to primacy, priority, preeminence, and the like."

be regarded as conjoining the themes of Aquinas's Corpus Christi hymn, Lancelot Andrewes's prayer, and Andrew Linzey's animal theology.[27]

Three-fourths of the Lorenzetti fresco in the lower church of the basilica of St. Francis in Assisi depicts a canopied room where the supping Jesus and his disciples are seated, while two servants are standing nearby. (One of them appears to be a woman, possibly representing — as might have been suggested by a creative art historian like the late Philipp Fehl, a dedicatee of this book — the Canaanite woman.) The remainder of the picture on the left shows a kitchen where scullions are washing dishes, while at their feet a little dog is licking a platter as a cat looks on. All that is needed to humanize and harmonize further this marvel of what is rightly referred to as "fine art" would be an imaginary caption, paying serious homage to folk art, and emblazoned with the nursery rhymes about "the little dog [that] laughed" and "the dish [that] ran away with the spoon." (For a not-to-be-missed reproduction of the painting, the reader can consult www.commons.wikimedia.org/wiki/File:Assisi-frescoes-last-supper -3931_Lorenzetti_Pietro.jpg.)

Unfortunately, at this juncture, the blood libel is not merely on the distant horizon, it is front and center both in Kertzer's book, where he will soon be seen as introducing Pius IX's own promotion of the ritual murder charge, and in the writings of Kenneth Stow — different from those cited above. Stow was instrumental in the repudiation of ritual murder charges made in the twenty-first century by an Israeli scholar who was writing in Stow's own specialized area of medieval and early modern Judaism. That scholar was Ariel Toaff, son of the chief rabbi of Rome — who had received John Paul II in his visit to the synagogue there — and a professor at Bar-Ilan University, who shocked two continents with the publication of *Pasque di sangue. Ebrei d'Europa e omicidi rituali* (Passovers of Blood: The Jews of Europe and Rit-

---

27. This is being written after a flood of advertisements on TV promoting the film *Agora,* abut the fifth-century prodigy, Hypatia — also the title of a well-regarded feminist journal — brought to many minds her Christian counterpart, St. Catherine of Alexandria, one of the most brilliant fabrications of the early church.

Given the components above, the friendly squabble between Jesus and the Canaanite/ Syro-Phoenician, the references to animals, and the hymns of Aquinas, and it comes as a surprise that the mysterious woman — also a favorite of feminist biblical scholars — had not been raised to the altars by popular acclaim. Rather than the Catherine Wheel and towns and islands named Cartagena and Catalina, there might be more depictions of women with dogs, like the goddess Diana, and more places with names like New Canaan and Phoenix.

ual Murders), a book that in effect stated that the accusation of Jewish ritual murder was not always libelous — an issue that will be before the Holy Office in the next chapter. The book, which is illustrated and heavily annotated, contains an abundance of explications of medieval texts as well as of woodcuts relating to the killing of children.

According to the author, the preoccupation with the latter was rooted in the belief among Jews in Northern Italy that at Passover there should be a commemoration of the hundreds of children who — so the legend maintained — had been killed in order to provide blood to save the life of the Pharaoh. Over the centuries this tale developed into "a veritable obsession with blood" that was shared by "the surrounding Christian-German society." This created a "love-hate relationship between the two groups" that through an evolutionary role-reversal process — Toaff is vague about the details — resulted in Jews at Passover wreaking vengeance on the Pharaoh by seeking Christian blood. This thesis, which ran counter to centuries of Jewish denials of ritual murder, denials that had been confirmed by several popes, engendered shock waves in Italy and Israel.

Kenneth Stow, who is quoted in *Passovers of Blood*, publicly attacked the book as not even acceptable under the broadest terms of conventional academic freedom contracts. Among the many illustrations Toaff supplied is a woodcut described as being "similar, in both design and execution, to the representation of the martyrdom of Simon of Trent in a painting . . . dating back to the first half of the 16th century, a few years after his death." The descriptive text for the woodcut was, "A large group of bearded, big-nosed Jews, with a grim appearance and caricature-like features, crowd around the naked, glorious body of the little martyr, the new Christ, intent on performing their cruel Passover rite on his miserable body." But not only did Toaff embrace "saints" like Simon — who had been dropped from the calendar of the universal church after Vatican II — he did so on the basis of confessions by Jews that had been elicited by torture.

In the event, after considerable public agitation — *Haaretz* published a series of articles on the blood libel — Toaff withdrew the book from publication, and made this ambiguous acknowledgment: "An unprejudiced rereading of the original trial records together with the records of several other trials, viewed within the overall European context [leads] to the reluctant conclusion that . . . the 'Blood Libel' accusation was not always an invention."[28] As we will

---

28. A semi-official translation into English of *Pasque di sangue. Ebrei d'Europa e omicidi rituali* is accessible at www.israelshamir.net/bloodpassover.

see in the next chapter, this kind of negative wording — characteristic of reluctant admissions — will recur when the Holy Office also fudges the issue of whether it is possible to say that in all of history no ritual murder had ever occurred.

As to Pius IX's own promotion of ritual murder, Kertzer observes that the pope gave it "new respectability by moving to put on a firmer footing the cult surrounding a martyred child, Lorenzino of Marostica." The charge was not particularly "unrespectable," but was accepted on the same grounds that led most moderately educated people in Europe at the time to accept the notion of the blood libel. It was an established superstition that appeared to have been confirmed by traditional tales and that had not been dogmatically condemned by the church — although as the next two chapters will evince there is no dearth of papal statements condemning it. In the nineteenth century, acceptance of myths and legends regarding ritual murder was unfortunately not entirely unlike the acceptance in this century of myths and legends about popes and Jewish dogs. People who hear of such things find them alluring, and ultimately that fascination is conveyed to others who then repeat the tales, and so on . . . until, in the present phase of the culture, they become almost endlessly replicated in the heady ether of the Internet.

Again, Kertzer is indebted to a finding of Miccoli about the pope giving new respectability to ritual murder via the Lorenzino tale. One can certainly see from Kertzer's retailing of it why not only the gullible would have found it intriguing. The following severely abridges his vivid narrative, which tends like the original fabrication to be morbidly detailed. "The boy's story was indeed inspiring. Lorenzino was born in 1480 . . . when Lorenzino was just a newborn . . . the ten-day old baby stood up and cried out" to his murder-intent father, "Stop, I am your son." This dialogue, certainly not entirely by accident, evokes the biblical story of Abraham and Isaac — a story fascinating to scores of artists as well as to philosophers like Søren Kierkegaard, and a story that through a quirk of history fed into the ritual murder accusation. There are more grisly details narrated about the victim in the next paragraph, presumably digested by Kertzer from "the Church's official account":

On Good Friday, when Lorenzino went out to play, a bunch of Jews grabbed him, tore off his clothes, and crucified him on a nearby tree, draining him of his blood. When his mutilated body was found . . . [e]ach night a ray of light shone. . . . Pius IX's decree in 1867 affirmed the official status of the cult. Three years later he returned to the matter, declaring the second Sunday after Easter each year to be the sacred holiday devoted to celebrating the little martyr.

But this meant in practice honoring Lorenzino at a local feast, and ultimately keeping the little martyr out of the Roman Martyrology (as for different reasons, he was also kept out of the lengthy lists of ritual murders in the *Jewish Encyclopedia*), and confining that sacred holiday — known as Good Shepherd Sunday in the rest of the Catholic world — to the town of Marostica, whose citizens had requested its celebration. Such celebrations meant business for shopkeepers and other tradesmen, as country folk and villagers converged on a given locale. Nor should it surprise that the people of Marostica would want a saint of their own just like the people of Trent had — the two locales are only about fifty miles apart. Similarly, it shouldn't surprise that not only are the circumstances of the two "martyrdoms" almost identical, but Lorenzino was born only eight years after Simon. None of this had anything to do with giving new respectability to an appalling religious slander; it had to do with the public expression of nineteenth-century rural rivalries, not entirely dissimilar from twenty-first-century urban rivalries — say, the Red Sox and the Yankees.

Unfortunately for the townsfolk, celebrants of the feast of Lorenzino never reached the peak of fervor nor of numbers attained by spectators at the town's nationally known and still celebrated chess match in which a human participant stands for each chess piece on a gigantic outdoor "board." As for the Lorenzino legend, what began as vicious prejudice in the fifteenth century, by the nineteenth and twentieth centuries — a new chapel was built in honor of Lorenzino in 1947 — had become a matter of public pride as more towns vied with each other for a celebrity who among other boons would function as a "tourist attraction."[29] These were not the first nor the last instances of economics being wed to legends, and the two spawning a rewrite of history. Every town in the United States wants a Graceland of its own.

Nor does the Lorenzino tale or that of Simon of Trent constitute the final exemplification of the broader thesis of the present book. As noted in the introduction, and to be elaborated in more detail in the final chapter, it is the

29. Sixty years later, in the twenty-first century, the same motives were at play as an "Italian Saint Stirs Up a Mix of Faith and Commerce," according to *The New York Times* (April 25, 2008). The story was of a new shrine in the town of San Giovanni Rotondo, where Padre Pio, canonized in 2002, had lived for fifty years. The regional "director of tourism" was quoted as saying, "This is an opportunity we have to turn religious tourism into mass tourism."

nature of large institutions with historical roots to be unwieldy and clumsy regarding the treatment of unfortunate deeds and decisions from the past. It is easier to ignore or mute them than to repudiate them. The more cumbersome the institution, the more obtuse the response to tradition-sanctioned mistakes, so that if the latter are repudiated, their repudiation is often attributed to what is designated "providence" but is really "happenstance." If the Holy Office had listened to the Belgian Jesuits writing the *Acta Sanctorum* rather than to the Italian Jesuits writing *La Civiltà cattolica*, there would have been far fewer "victims" of ritual murder, and the study of this phenomenon would not be undertaken by theologians and historians of religion but by specialists in the social sciences investigating deviant behavior.

Lastly, it may be noted that while there is little basis in the Lorenzino tale or in any similar accusations for finding Pius IX guilty of hatred of Jews, that does not exonerate him from the obduracy that characterized his actions in the kidnapping of Edgardo Mortara. But even that unfortunate affair, supported by thousands of ultramontane Catholics, was based on the bad theology of the early church — a person baptized a Christian is subject to Christian, that is, church, law — rather than on evil intent. This remains true, notwithstanding the drama *God's Child*. The support for the pope is comparable to the Cuban-American support for the kidnapping of Elian Gonzalez in 2000. The kidnapping was also based on unfortunate biases; in this case, biases that were neither political nor theological but were founded on the personal feelings of the kidnappers who believed, like Pius IX, that they had the best interests of the boy in mind.

The one instance in the pope's reign of an official statement explicitly attacking Jews goes unmentioned by Kertzer. This was a formal declaration in 1867 at the canonization of Pedro d'Arbuès, the fifteenth-century Spanish inquisitor who had allegedly been killed by Jews — the murder being depicted in several paintings by Murillo, one of which hangs in the Vatican. Next to the Mortara case, the canonization of this "martyr" was the act of the pope that most enraged the broader public. That widespread response had little to do directly with Jews, but resulted from the belief, particularly strong among liberal Catholics, that the pope was really intent on turning the clock back and rehabilitating the Inquisition. Owen Chadwick in *A History of the Popes 1830-1914* writes about the canonization:

> The Pope wanted to say as loudly as he could the axioms of the modern world are wrong; it is right to stop error from being spread; it is right to use force to prevent error. The Syllabus carried more weight in the canon-

ization of d'Arbuès than research into the history of what he did and how he suffered. Where the making of a saint was meant to fly in the face of modern axioms, the drafting could pain contemporaries and those who came after. The Jews were accused of murdering d'Arbuès. Some in the Curia suspected that modern liberal Jewry was responsible for the quarrel that developed over this canonization.

This curial influence led to the following — needlessly and nastily stereotyped — canonization decree: "The divine wisdom has arranged that in these sad days, when Jews help the enemies of the Church with their books and money, this decree of sanctity has been brought to fulfillment." Ten years later Pius IX made Francis de Sales, the gentle exponent of devout humanism, a Doctor of the Church. It would probably be too much to hope that in his last years, the pope may have been trying to correct some of the more inhumane decisions of the curia and of *Civiltà cattolica*.

In the preceding context of the Inquisition, there is one brief remark that fittingly concludes this chapter. It is by *the* authority on early modern Spain, Henry Kamen, in his justly esteemed *The Spanish Inquisition* (1997), and it is particularly pertinent to the kinds of claims made in *The Popes Against the Jews* regarding the worldwide power of the papacy, particularly as displayed in *Civiltà cattolica* and in the latter's influence on what Kertzer touted as the "worldwide network of the Catholic press." Such exorbitant claims are usually the bane of scholarly specialists in a particular historical period or a particular historical entity. Writing of some of these scholars of the Inquisition, Kamen noted that they often "accepted without question the image of an omniscient, omnipotent tribunal whose fingers reached into every corner of the land," whereas what the inquisitors actually controlled, according to Kamen, was merely a "flimsy network." But to this it is necessary to add that regardless of how flimsy a network it may have been, unlike that of the Vatican newspaper, the Inquisition's was dedicated to setting people on fire in the name of the proclaimer of the Beatitudes. Not even the public apologies of the reforming pope, John Paul II, could erase the horrors of that uniquely antireligious phenomenon.

CHAPTER 5

Ritual Murder and the Duplicity of Leo XIII

One of the earlier chapters in Part One of *The Popes Against the Jews* was titled "Ritual Murder Makes a Comeback." The chapter related the story of the mysterious disappearance of a Capuchin friar in Damascus in 1840 who was presumed by many people to have been the victim of Jewish conspirators in search of Christian blood. Ritual murder is also making a comeback in that same part of the world today, as the old blood libel invented by Christians is now being recycled by some conspiratorial Muslims seeking to denigrate Jews in general and Israeli Jews in particular. The defense minister of Syria, Mustafa Tlas, in *The Matzah of Zion* (E.T., 1991), began his exposition with a treatment of the Damascus affair as a ritual murder that had historically occurred. Judith Apter Klinghoffer, an academic researcher at Rutgers, noted that in October 2001, the largest Egyptian newspaper, in the context of Mustafa Tlas's book, went on to say that Palestinian police have "many recorded cases of the bodies of Arab children being found, torn to pieces without a single drop of blood." Nor is it entirely surprising that the vengeful killing of Daniel Pearl, with its televised replication both in the Middle East and in the West, would suggest a ritual murder, this time at the hands of Islamic terrorists.[1]

---

1. The medieval historian Richard Utz in "Remembering Ritual Murder" twice mentions the killing of Daniel Pearl (in Nils Holger Petersen, ed., *Genre and Ritual. The Cultural Heritage of Medieval Rituals* [2005]). As to the Damascus affair and *The Matzah of Zion,* the website of the Anti-Defamation League has a picture of the book's cover depicting the deed. Judith Apter Klinghoffer's essay, "Blood Libel," can be accessed at www.hnn.us/articles/664.html. Ritual murder also briefly appeared to be making a comeback in North America following the murder of several people in Arizona in January 2011, and one politician for unknown reasons invoked the blood libel.

Kertzer's own treatment of the thousand-year-old libel is — at least in terms of established scholarly norms — both unusual and paradoxical: unusual, because in order to implicate modern popes in ritual murder he has to invent a papal conspiracy; paradoxical, because he has to engage in a conspiracy with himself, as he becomes his own "secret sharer" when examining the 1913 trial that is central to his treatment of ritual murder. In what is probably his most exorbitant undertaking, examined in detail in the next chapter, Kertzer rigs the evidence against the papacy by feigning ignorance of indispensable truths that he himself shows he had knowledge of.

As has been mentioned several times, the foundational thesis of *The Popes Against the Jews* is that "out of the limelight, and with the assistance of their secretaries of state, the popes regulated the anti-Semitic campaigns conducted in the Church press." The exact wording of that thesis appears in the introduction to the chapter titled "Ritual Murder and the Popes in the Twentieth Century."

> In their public statements, no pope himself would publicly charge the Jews with ritual murder, nor — in so many words — argue that they were a foreign body destroying Christian society. The popes themselves would not publicly call for revoking the Jews' civil rights, nor for sending them back to the ghettoes. Indeed, in their public pronouncements, the popes generally avoided any specific mention of the Jews at all, permitting the Vatican to deny that the Holy See bore any responsibility for the anti-Semitic movement in Europe. But out of the limelight. . . .

Enunciating this opinion is possibly the author's way of warding off potential criticism of the fact that — unlike Pius IX's public statements regarding Jewish "dogs" and the "synagogue of Satan" — there is nothing in this chapter where an actual declaration of a reigning pope supports ritual murder. In short, the connection indicated in the chapter title is entirely of Kertzer's own making. No word or statement by a pope defending ritual murder figures here.[2] Anyone who feels this sounds like a self-contradiction — the

---

2. There is a statement by the Holy Office maintaining that it is not possible to give an affirmative answer to the question of whether in history ritual murder had never occurred; there is a public validation of the authenticity of papal documents against ritual murder; and there are the recorded words of Pius X regarding an actual ritual murder trial in Kiev: "I pray that the trial end without harm to the poor Jews." These and other related matters will be examined in this and the next chapter.

panda's thumb that is not a thumb — will find that such a presentiment is well-founded.

That in certain areas of the world like the Middle East there are still people who profess to believe that Jews kill male children to use their blood in religious services indicates the lasting power of even the most obscene myths and legends. A century ago that power would have been more manifest in Europe, though less so in the Anglophone world, where ritual murder, invented in twelfth-century England, had been largely discredited among Protestants as well as Catholics since the eighteenth century.[3] It would have been found repugnant even among those Victorians of whom Gertrude Himmelfarb famously wrote: "Men were normally anti-Semitic, unless by some quirk of temperament or ideology they happened to be philo-Semitic." This parlor anti-Semitism prevailed in other countries touched by the Enlightenment, and thus the number of rumors and accusations of ritual murder increased and became more outrageous as one went from the west of Europe to the east.

The fact that such a culture had been created by the teaching that Jews were Christ-killers has been and remains the blight on the entire tradition. But the blood libel itself, for all its horrifying invention and near-millennium existence, was often in the modern era less a cause than a post-factum rationalization of mob action against Jews. Helmut Walser Smith in *The Butcher's Tale: Murder and Anti-Semitism in a German Town* (2002), a case study of a twentieth-century ritual murder, notes that although anti-Jewish riots were often the result of deteriorating economic conditions, the riots themselves were justified by invoking the perverse myths and legends of the Middle Ages. "The people had come to know a series of stories, a collection of murderous tales, which served as an alibi for aggression." Smith also observes that "the vast majority of uprisings [against Jews] occurred in predominantly Protestant towns," and he mentions by name and location more than a score in the two decades after 1881 — precisely the period when

---

3. Chaucer's "The Prioress's Tale" is the most noteworthy literary expression in English. G. K. Chesterton called it "the beautiful legend of the child singing on his way to the crown of martyrdom." "Unfortunately, in the *New Witness*, Chesterton recalled the ritual murders committed by the Jews"; so wrote Léon Poliakov in the fourth volume of his history of anti-Semitism, *Suicidal Europe, 1870-1933*. (Unless otherwise noted all references to Poliakov in this chapter will be to this volume.) It was also Chesterton who, during the upsurge of anti-Semitism at the time of World War I, would invoke ritual murder and threaten Jews with "something that will stun them and terrorize them infinitely more than a mere war." See also Jay P. Corrin, *Catholic Intellectuals and the Challenge of Democracy* (2002).

Pope Leo XIII and his secretary of state were allegedly fostering the charge against the Jews. In that same context, Smith points to the slight impact of the local member of *Civiltà cattolica*'s worldwide network of publications: "The legacy of violence against the Jews was less pronounced in German Catholic towns, even though German Catholics read the *Westpreussisches Volksblatt,* a provincial Catholic newspaper that peddled a mixture of piety and prejudice." So much for the power of the popes to regulate "the anti-Semitic campaigns conducted in the Church press."

Even in the first half of the twentieth century in the United States, where there were several ritual murder accusations — most of them made by recent immigrants from Central and Eastern Europe — economic differences were often the cause. Sometimes ignorance of the meaning of the "ritual" led to accusations based on the alleged disappearance of women, as had also happened occasionally in the medieval period.[4] In the postwar pogrom of 1946 in Kielce, examined by Jan T. Gross in *Fear: Anti-Semitism in Poland after Auschwitz* (2006), the underlying cause according to the author was the guilt felt by Poles who had profited by appropriating Jewish property during the war, while the cause alleged by the perpetrators was that they had been inflamed by rumors of a ritual murder. The bishop of Lublin, Stefan Wyszynski — later to be cardinal primate and a hero of the anti-Soviet resistance — in an interview with a group of Jews was evasive about their request that he make a statement attacking the anti-Semitism of the blood libel; instead, he referred to the ritual murder trial in Kiev in 1913 — the centerpiece of the next chapter — and declared "that the matter of blood was not definitively settled."

Unfortunately for Gross's thesis, he like Kertzer often succumbs to hyperbole, as the fifty or so deaths were viewed in the light of the thousands elsewhere: "The whole area turned into a vast killing field and it was littered with bloody mementos long after. . . . People killed Jews with gusto." The overall horror of this or any pogrom is certainly undeniable, but the details provided here are so sanguinary they thwart understanding — even of Gross's own thesis. The exaggeration regarding vast numbers of people involved is as inaccurate as his assertion that such a massacre "could have happened anywhere in Poland and at any time during this period." Given this penchant for exaggeration, it is not surprising that Kielce is referred to as

---

4. See Alan Dundes, ed., *The Blood Libel Legend: A Casebook in Anti-Semitic Folklore* (1991). The case to be examined in the next chapter, the previously mentioned trial of Mendel Beilis in Kiev, involved the killing of a young woman.

"the bloodiest peacetime pogrom in twentieth-century Europe," even though the pogroms in Kishinev, Odessa, and Kiev had been numerically more appalling.

The sociological ground of the ritual murder accusation is the now relatively well-understood — but not thereby any the less perverse — effort of a dominant group to enhance its identity by radically differentiating itself from a minority or alien group through the social denigration or dehumanization of the latter. When such a dominant group invokes patriotic motives, it is often the result of some alleged national humiliation like the one mentioned in the previous chapter relative to the French defeat in the war with Prussia. That such a response can be engendered in any country is one of the themes of George Orwell in his celebrated 1945 essay on anti-Semitism: "if Britain comes out of the present war greatly weakened . . . the kind of anti-Semitism which flourished among the anti-Dreyfusards in France, and which Chesterton and Belloc tried to import into this country, might get a foothold."[5] Christ-killers were always available as scapegoats for the failings of a nation's rulers or for the onset of natural disasters. Although several popes had denounced the scapegoating of Jews by way of the blood libel, its tangential roots in the gospel nurtured a submerged existence that periodically was sparked to new life when real or imagined disruptions occurred.

Kertzer's chapter, "Ritual Murder and the Popes in the Twentieth Century," began with the statement I cited above about the popes secretly conspiring with their secretaries of state to have Jews accused of various evil practices. According to Kertzer, Leo XIII was using his power, so that "newspapers were filled with the most horrific accounts of Jewish evil in murdering children" — something in which the author has affirmed bishops and flocks were already firm believers, thus raising a question as to why such bigots needed further goading by the pope. But whether in the limelight or out of it, the ability of the pope to manipulate the public by the fragile instrument of *Civiltà cattolica* and its alleged emulators would appear to be so restricted that even to conceive such a campaign as being "crucial" to *anything* would be to court the accusation of paranoia.

---

5. Orwell had in mind the kind of threat Chesterton made in the aftermath of the Great War. "If they attempt to educate London the way they educated Petrograd, they will awaken something that will stun them and terrorize them infinitely more than a mere war" (Poliakov, loc. cit.) The mention of Petrograd referred to the relatively disproportionate large numbers of Jews in the leadership of the new Soviet government of Russia — a phenomenon that will be discussed in chapter 7 in the context of the future Pope Pius XI's period in Poland.

Nevertheless, since the overwhelming power of the pope's word is at the heart of Kertzer's basic argument, it bears further examination. Again, the point of departure is a statement by Léon Poliakov, this time in the context of what would later be called the Holocaust, in which he is describing what appears to be a relatively effective papal campaign — "effective," at least given the circumstances of the time. The statement was titled "The Vatican and the Jewish Question," and originally appeared in *Monde juif* (June 1949), before being translated into several languages the following year. In the United States the article appeared in *Commentary.* In it Poliakov described Pius XII's efforts for the Jews of Rome — the number saved varies, but about five thousand out of six thousand is a noncontroversial approximation — as the "symbolic expression of an activity that spread throughout Europe, stimulating the efforts of Catholic churches in almost every country":

> There is no doubt that secret instructions went out from the Vatican urging the national churches to intervene in favor of the Jews by every possible means. . . . Other communications of this sort were made directly to the civil authorities, as in Hungary and Slovakia. . . . But, more generally, the different ways in which the instructions of the Holy See were followed in the East, in the South, and in the West, may perhaps give us an idea of the limits of the real power that the Vatican was able to exert.[6]

So, the power of the pope was largely "symbolic" and the general indifference to its message shows the "limits of the real power that the Vatican was able to exert." Moreover, Pius XII's "power" — certainly greater than that of Leo XIII and his paper network — also utilized Radio Vaticana and a far more extensive and modern diplomatic corps than the ramshackle collective overseen by Cardinal Rampolla — and yet Pius was ineffectual. This is not to discount the fact that the pope was addressing bishops and flocks terrified of persecution by the Nazis, whereas presumably Leo was seeking to influence through the Catholic press a body of believers already well-

---

6. Joseph L. Lichten, a former director of the Anti-Defamation League, in an article widely publicized by the Catholic League, "A Question of Judgment: Pius XII and the Jews," cites this passage from Poliakov and references it to "a secret instruction to the Catholic bishops of Europe entitled *Opere et caritate (By Work and Love).*" The existence of this secret instruction is then validated by a reference to Paul Duclos, *Le Vatican et la seconde guerre mondiale* (1955), where in fact no basis for the instruction is to be found — nor has it been found elsewhere. By all present indications, the secret instruction is nonexistent.

disposed to embrace his message. How well-disposed they were in fact may be exemplified by the ineffectualness of the *Westpreussisches Volksblatt.*

There are three instances in Kertzer's chapter related to its titular theme of twentieth-century popes and ritual murder. The first appears to be extremely minor if not incidental, and has to do with the significance of two letters over the signature of the secretary of state, Cardinal Rampolla, which by Kertzer's reading approved of a French priest who was clearly obsessed with ritual murder.[7] (It is also an incident that occurred a decade before the "twentieth century" of Kertzer's chapter title.) The second, and obviously more important, has to do with a decree of the Holy Office rejecting the credibility of the opinion that ritual murders had never occurred. The third and most important instance, mentioned several times already, is the trial for ritual murder in Kiev where, according to Kertzer, the papal secretary of state and implicitly the pope himself refused to aid the Jew who was accused of the murder. This treatment entails Kertzer's most clearly demonstrable rigging of arguments and doctoring of texts — at least up to that point in his book.

The chapter begins with a complaint to Cardinal Manning from the chief rabbi of England about a book on ritual murder that its author claimed had the approval of Leo XIII. "Manning replied that he would write to Rome, and told the rabbi, 'You certainly do me justice in thinking that I lend no credence to such horrors.'" The whole matter appears so trivial that the space Kertzer devotes to it seems calculated to inflate a situation that even Giovanni Miccoli — again Kertzer's source — had dismissed in a few sentences.[8] Also, this exchange between rabbi and cardinal might have raised some doubts in the minds of the author and his source about the overall thesis that "out of the limelight" popes promoted the notion of ritual murder, since this correspondence was reproduced within two months in *l'Univers Israélite* (March 1, 1890).

Manning, who had been appointed archbishop of Westminster and created a cardinal by Pius IX — and whose devotion to him led to his becoming the pope's "majority whip" at Vatican I — apparently ignored the infamous statement by that pope about Jewish dogs, though copies of the volume containing it were sent to all the leading prelates in Europe. He must also have

---

7. This incident presumably confirms the notion that "out of the limelight and with the assistance of their secretaries of state, the popes regulated the anti-Semitic campaigns."

8. This is the first mention of Miccoli in the present chapter. Unless otherwise noted all references are to "Santa Sede, questione ebraica e antisemitismo" (cited p. 31, n. 8, above).

ignored the deplorable anti-Semitic reference to the "synagogue of Satan" in the Syllabus of Errors — though even before his appointment as archbishop, he had approved of the Syllabus. Apparently, as archbishop he must also have overlooked the more immediately relevant matter of Pius IX having given "the charge of Jewish ritual murder new respectability" by approving the cultus of Lorenzino of Maristoca — if in fact Manning had ever heard of that little martyr. Nor had the English archbishop been paying much attention to the anti-Semitic "campaigns" carried out during the reign of Leo XIII — although he was one of the two cardinals most instrumental in his election — since he would certainly have known that ritual murder was viewed by the voice of the pope, *Civiltà cattolica*, as one of many "horrors" perpetrated by the despicable Jews.

The reply to Manning from Cardinal Rampolla said that the author of the book in question, *The Mystery of the Blood Among the Jews*, one Henri Desportes, had received "only a form letter, noting the reception of a book sent by its author, but without approval of its content, [a letter] which is always sent before the book is examined, and often even before it has been seen." Manning, who a few years later would be a consultant on the pope's social encyclicals, told the chief rabbi, "Nothing is further from the Pope's nature than wanting to gratuitously wound the sensitivities of the Jewish people." At that point in the narrative, Kertzer gives this directive to his readers:

> Recall that Henri Desportes was the author whom Edouard Drumont had so ardently defended, the priest who had run afoul of his archbishop. Desportes was on his way to becoming one of the main authorities in the Catholic ritual murder campaign in France, and his work would be cited approvingly in Catholic publications throughout Europe well into the twentieth century. Not only did he publish two books on the topic; in 1890 he also founded a monthly titled The Anti-Jewish Alliance (*L'Alliance antijuive*).

While the readers whom Kertzer is addressing might recall that earlier in the book Desportes had been mentioned in a paragraph relating to Drumont, the rest of this information cannot be "recalled" since none of it had been mentioned earlier and all of it relates to events occurring in the future, well after the present matter was over. Presumably the reader is admonished to recall all these future events in order to magnify the role and the person of Desportes — who disappears from the narrative after the present epistolary controversy.

Kertzer continues:

> When one digs through the Vatican archives, a rather different story emerges of the "form letter" that Cardinal Rampolla claimed to have sent Desportes. On July 26, 1889, Father Desportes sent two copies of his newly published book, *The Mystery of the Blood Among the Jews,* to Pope Leo XIII, via Secretary of State Rampolla. In his cover note to the cardinal, Desportes explained the book's thesis, although Rampolla *certainly knew the nature of the book from its title alone.* "This book reveals," Desportes wrote Rampolla, "one of the most monstrous instances of modern fanaticism, and I dare hope that Your eminence, by giving me a word of approval, would want to help me combat this infamy." (italics supplied)

The italicized passage is the first of several where Kertzer shifts the issue from whether Desportes received a "form letter" to the allegation that he received papal approbation of the blood libel. That Rampolla knew about the book "from its title alone" is doubly ironic because Rampolla's letter gets even the title wrong: "I have received the copies of the book that you have published, titled *The Mystery of the Blood,* and, following the wishes expressed . . . presented one of the copies to the Holy Father . . . greatly appreciated your filial offering . . . sends you a heartfelt apostolic benediction."[9] To most people, this probably would sound rather formulaic.

"But if we take a step back" — as Kertzer says — "we" then realize that the basic premise of Kertzer's indictment is completely opposed to his standard practice, which is to judge the past by the standards of the present. In this instance, he fails to employ those standards, since if he did he would conclude that there is no reason for believing any of this involved the secretary of state, much less the pope. Let me also adopt Kertzer's imperative mood; but rather than admonishing the reader to "Recall that . . . ," I suggest to the reader "Assume that. . . ."

Assume that the headquarters of an international organization with

---

9. Miccoli, who did the actual digging in the archives, observes that the secretary of state was not following protocol, since for "special books by persons unknown" the practice was to consult the relevant papal nuncio — in Desportes' case, the nuncio in Paris. But this is based on two quite different cases: in the first, the nuncio in Paris referred a book in order to get a favorable recommendation; in the second, the nuncio in Vienna referred a book in order to get a negative judgment. Neither case sets a precedent regarding a book sent *directly* by the author — nor would Desportes, who had been condemned by his own archbishop, dare to send his book by way of the nuncio.

millions of members, hundreds of branch offices, thousands of managers, and tens of thousands of employees receives a package from an unknown employee addressed to the chief operating officer. The package contains a covering letter, two copies of a book, and another longer letter addressed to the chief executive officer of the organization. How many people would believe that the COO receives this package, opens it, examines the contents, reads the covering letter, and then takes everything to the CEO who, in turn, reads the covering letter as well as the letter addressed to himself, and together the two of them discuss a response which, when mutually agreed upon, the COO dictates, signs, and has posted? The answer to the question about how many people would find this credible — that answer certainly has to be, if not "none," then certainly, "damn few."[10]

Whoever was the aide or assistant to the secretary of state who first opened the packet containing Desportes' materials, after reading that "cover note," almost certainly assigned some other underling to handle the reply — for which there was surely a template for unknown correspondents that probably varied according to their presumed status.[11] That template might be something along the lines of *Risposta A* for a potentially significant personage, *Risposta B* for a relatively unimportant person like Desportes, and *Risposta C* for *una nullità* — a nobody. From the stock wording of the letter to Desportes, it seems safe to assume that not much time was given to the form letter over the secretary of state's signature. It is also likely that the latter didn't have anything to do with the whole matter, since acknowledging receipt of a packet of books is certainly not on the agenda of the second highest official in the Vatican, and most emphatically, of Cardinal Rampolla who, even in Kertzer's account, was preoccupied with negotiations relating to half the governments of Europe.

The "rather different story" that ensued on digging through the archives

---

10. The corporate world imagery and language are not unusual. Rembert G. Weakland, in a memoir of his life as archbishop of Milwaukee, wrote of meetings with curial officials: "I always felt a need to stand tall and not be intimidated, making it clear by my demeanor and responses that I was engaging in a conversation as bishop to bishop and not as a "branch manager to the head office." *A Pilgrim in a Pilgrim Church: Memoirs of a Catholic Archbishop* (2009).

11. Anthony Rhodes in *The Vatican in the Age of the Dictators* (1973) described the Secretariat of State only three decades after the events of this chapter. "During this period, the Vatican possessed a Secretariat of State of a most antediluvian model. . . . This consists of the Cardinal and three Under-Secretaries who deal with all the correspondence. In this, they are assisted by twelve juniors who deal with routine matters."

is based on the assumption that every communication addressed to the secretary of state is personally read by him, discussed with the pope, and then answered in language that presumably represents the considered opinion or viewpoint of either or both of them.[12] As to Desportes' personal letter to Leo XIII, which according to Kertzer "went into greater detail," the reader is provided with two paragraphs of quotations that combine obsequiousness ("devoted son of the Vicar of Jesus Christ") and obscenity ("the synagogue's unknown martyrs," "little innocents"). Continuing to cite this significant communication, Kertzer observes,

> In his last paragraph, Father Desportes told the Pope of his recent banishment at the hands of his archbishop, and portrayed himself as a martyr. "The Jews are powerful and they react hatefully against those who un-

12. As an undergraduate Christian Brother in the late 1940s, I assumed the editorship of a pedagogical quarterly *The Language Teacher,* which I renamed *The Journal of Arts and Letters.* Given the influx of European intellectuals into this country, I did the obvious thing and over the next few years published such writers as Rudolf Allers, A. de Béthune, Dietrich von Hildebrand, Pierre Messiaen, John M. Oesterreicher, Kurt Reinhardt, and H. A. Reinhold. Since I was in "temporary vows" to stave off criticism from any affronted elders, I sent copies of the first issues to the superior general and to the pope, Pius XII, with a view to publishing their answers — if any. The first replied generously, which took care of institutional concerns. The second response headed "Vatican City" was signed, "J. B. Montini. Subst." and went as follows: "At the gracious command of the Holy Father. . . . In your thoughtfulness . . . further re-affirmation of the sentiments of undying attachment of your Institute . . . you and your collaborators . . . stimulating Christian thought. . . . His paternal Apostolic Blessing." I can't imagine that material being vetted by the apostolic delegate in Washington, as Miccoli thinks a requisite before any papal blessing is tendered, and I doubt if anyone in the Vatican looked inside the magazines to read them. But what the letter writer (probably a clerk in the office of the *aiutante* to Montini) did do was translate into more florid terms the original covering letter — a routine that among the lower ranks of Vatican officialdom was probably a convenient and conventional way to dispose of over-the-transom communications. (The fact that there is no reference to the contents of Desportes' letters in the secretary of state's responses is a further indication of how formulaic they were.)

By Kertzer's interpretation of exchanges between Vatican functionaries and Catholics anywhere in the world, it would not be difficult to prove that in the letter above from the secretary of state's *office* — there being at that time no secretary of state with whom the pope could conspire — Pius XII anticipated *Nostra Aetate* by blessing Oesterreicher who shepherded that document through Vatican II, lauded modernist art by blessing de Béthune — already an admirer of Dubuffet — and finally, to the confusion of future scholars, approved radical liturgical reform by blessing Reinhold *and* condemned radical liturgical reform by blessing von Hildebrand. (As for Monsignor Montini, with a little Kertzerian twist, his whole future as Pope Paul VI could be extrapolated from this response.)

mask their villainy. As a result of my act of courage, I had to abandon the place where I was happy, to leave my native town and practically become a beggar.'"

If anything should have raised doubts in Kertzer's mind about anyone in the Vatican taking seriously this self-pitying lament, it is the symbiotic martyrdom of the little innocents and Father Desportes, and the symbiosis of bad archbishop and bad Jews. One also does get the impression that Kertzer not only believes that Leo XIII and/or Rampolla actually read this missive, but also that this kind of fawning would be effective in moving the heartless hearts of Vatican officials — the grounds for the latter apparently being Kertzer's firm faith that so long as anything is anti-Semitic, it will certainly be embraced in the Vatican.

There can be little doubt that the book was never read, but the reason for also assuming that the pope never read the personal letter is that the aide who first opened the packet of materials and read those details about how Desportes' archbishop had done him wrong — that aide would certainly have passed the letter on to the respective Vatican department handling such matters, probably the office for Extraordinary Ecclesiastical Affairs. It is equally certain that *then* the letter would have gotten serious attention, since the archbishop that Desportes was attacking was the primate of Normandy, a prelate of distinction who would be made a cardinal four years after these allegedly significant exchanges were over.

Kertzer then further transforms the original issue regarding the form letter, and remarks: "The secretary of state's later claim, when news of the letter became public, that the Pope had this letter sent without having any idea what the book was about is clearly untrue." But the first thing that is clearly untrue is that "*the pope* had this letter sent"; and the second is that the secretary of state "claimed" anything regarding "what this book was about." The notion of Rampolla expressing anything other than what was in the form letter is entirely of Kertzer's making. This point is to be borne in mind, since Kertzer repeatedly expands the scope and import of the Vatican's brief message so that, finally, it elides into an endorsement of ritual murder — which, of course, has been the purpose of the entire stratagem.

At this juncture in the narrative, the Catholic press puts in another appearance. Kertzer's line of reasoning is, again, that because ritual murder tales were appearing in *Civiltà cattolica* and the rest of the "Vatican-linked" press, then they must have been approved by the pope and the secretary of state. In the immediate context of seeking to prove that Rampolla's letter was really some kind of statement regarding the contents of Desportes' book, Kertzer returns to his basic thesis about the conspiracy between the pope and his secretary of state:

> Both Cardinal Rampolla and Leo XIII knew exactly what kind of book it was, and what its purpose was. There is no question but that they approved of both. It was a book that read very much like the series of twenty-six articles on Jewish ritual murder that *Civiltà cattolica* was in the midst of publishing at the time, a series that was receiving warm praise in the pages of the Vatican daily, *L'Osservatore romano,* as well.

Kertzer provides no date and cites no source for this reference to *L'Osservatore romano* — which weakens his specific argument regarding Desportes. But Miccoli, who devotes only a short paragraph to Desportes — viewing him as one among many proponents of the blood libel — does cite the Vatican daily's "breve articolo" on ritual murder, November 23, 1899. This is ten years after Desportes' letter. But it has little bearing on the Desportes matter that those articles were appearing either at that particular juncture or at some future date. The pathological element — not to say, the scatological element — in the editorial *collegio* of *Civiltà cattolica* has been pointed out earlier and needs no repetition here.

In Kertzer's next paragraph, the import of Rampolla's letter to Manning goes from the pope and the secretary knowing "exactly what kind of book it was" to their claiming "ignorance about what Desportes' books were about" — neither statement having any basis in the texts Miccoli-Kertzer had dug up. Kertzer then pursues these tangential arguments:

> That Desportes believed he had the strong support of the Pope was clear the following year when he wrote Cardinal Rampolla once more, sending two copies of his latest book on ritual murder, *Killed by the Jews.* Father Desportes again asked the cardinal to give a copy to the Pope and to request the Pope's special [*sic*] benediction for his efforts. What was particularly notable about the papal praise that this request received is that the new book seemed particularly well designed to raise warning flags in the Vatican.

But, again, that Desportes "believed he had the strong support of the pope" is irrelevant.[13] Although, if there was anything designed to send warning

---

13. Later Desportes himself will be cited as an authority on his own "new book": "Rome

flags to anyone it would be to the reader of this excerpt who would be put on the alert by the patent tic at the clumsy repetition of "particularly" in the final sentence. Following his remark about warning flags, Kertzer continues: "Cardinal Rampolla received Desportes' letter and book just months after he had written to the archbishop of Westminster claiming ignorance about what Desportes' books were about." Since Rampolla's only claim in the entire brouhaha was that he had written a form letter, this final attempt to shift the grounds to issues of ignorance or knowledge concerning the book can be bypassed. But what cannot be overlooked is the repetition of "about" in this sentence — a tic even clumsier and thus possibly more portending than the repetition of "particularly" earlier.

The reader is thus prepared for an obfuscation that clinches all the preceding ones — as the passage continues immediately with: "Making Desportes' request even more suspect was the fact that the new book carried a prominent preface written by a man who was *supposed* to be anathema to the Vatican, Edouard Drumont" (italics supplied). The first thing to be noted is that the mention of Drumont's name provides all the more strong a reason for concluding that these materials were never in the hands of the secretary of state, much less of the pope. For while there is no doubt that Drumont was "anathema to the Vatican," this would probably not be known to the minor functionary who actually handled the second batch of Desportes' materials. Moreover, in Kertzer's earlier treatment of Drumont, the preeminent French anti-Semite had posed a problem for the thesis of *The Popes Against the Jews,* since Drumont while being raved over by "the Vatican-linked press" was rejected by the Vatican itself, or as Kertzer — speaking unusually *sotto voce* — worded it, "the Pope held Drumont at arm's length." This is certainly not something to be trumpeted, since pages of effort have been expended by Kertzer to prove that there is no difference between "the voice of the pope" and the pope himself.[14]

Hence also the bumbling contrivance above for explaining how the Vatican-linked press wasn't really speaking for the Vatican: "*supposed* to be anathema to. . . ." But since there is no doubt that Drumont *was* anathema, this means that in order to safeguard the notion of the accuracy of the Vati-

---

blessed my book, many bishops and prelates approved of it, and all of the Catholic press defend it."

14. The implications for Kertzer's foundational argument are devastating: it would be as though he suddenly would have to make references to "the supposed condemnation of the Jews as 'dogs'" or "the supposed reference to 'the synagogue of Satan.'"

can press, the pope's own statements have to be rendered inaccurately. The irony of these rhetorical convolutions is that a similar contradiction was embraced by the French episcopate, only now the agents are reversed. According to Kertzer: "Diocesan bulletins throughout France were filled with praises for Drumont"; but the episcopal operators of those bulletins abhorred him. Hence, "Drumont repeatedly lashed out against the bishops." Since Drumont was earlier shown to be the arch-exponent of modern, racist, scientific, political, and so on, anti-Semitism, this would seem to redound to the honor of the entire magisterium — as the college of bishops and its head, the pope, are united in opposition to this new form of anti-Jewishness being expounded by the author of the three-decades best-seller *La France Juive*. However, even more damning for Kertzer's own thesis is the fact that the entire Catholic press is in disagreement with the entire magisterium. This has the disastrous consequence that present-day researchers can learn almost nothing about the papacy and its views, or about national hierarchies and their views by reading the Catholic press — or, more patently, by reading Kertzer's reading of that press. He also devastates his own larger argument that the Catholic press followed the lead of *Civiltà* and *Osservatore* because they were the mouthpieces of the pope and the Vatican.

After a quotation from the "prominent preface" by Drumont, there are two additional paragraphs, this time with detailed excerpts from Desportes' own preface, again touting his newer book, again attacking the primate of Normandy (now less than three years from his red hat), and clearly illustrating what had never been at issue, that is, the fact of either book being about the blood libel. Rather abruptly, and certainly anticlimactically, Kertzer wraps up the whole affair: "How much of the book the secretary of state or the pope, may have read — if any — we do not know."[15] Thus closes an un-

---

15. But it is possible to salvage more from this exercise by Kertzer than relief at its termination. The whole matter of the weight to be attached to such papal letters of "approbation" may have generated a theological *spes hermeneutica*. Their posthumous significance now seems to depend mainly on the interpretation of interested third parties. In an intriguing study appositely titled *(Re)reading, Reception, and Rhetoric: Approaches to Roman Catholic Modernism* (1999), C. J. T. Talar, our authority on the Modernists, makes this observation: "Not until 1936, when a letter of Cardinal Pacelli, acknowledging, in the name of Pius XI, receipt of Lagrange's *L'Evangile de Jésus Christ*, were the last vestiges of suspicion considered to have been removed from the exegete's name." It would be interesting to know the specific wording of that letter, since the only principle, in a case of doubt, appears to be that if a papal communication is formulaic, it is to be regarded as considerably less significant — or even as negligible — than a communication that is detailed and knowledgeable, since the

resolved exchange that constitutes — in ascending order of intrinsic significance and authorial manipulation — the first of the three exemplifications of "ritual murder and the popes in the twentieth century." Undeniably, it has not been an auspicious beginning for the team of Miccoli-Kertzer.

The second example *is* important and, in fact, is potentially disastrous in its consequences. Kertzer begins as follows: "Unease in the English Catholic Church over the Vatican's involvement in the ritual murder campaign continued." The mind reading previously confined to particular individuals has now been extended to an entire church, since this is the first reference to anything regarding the English Catholic Church, much less to its unease, much less to that condition being caused by the Vatican, much less to the latter being involved in a campaign, much less to that campaign being about ritual murder, and so on and on. Up to this point, whatever "involvement" and "unease" had been registered had been confined to an automatic response to an unknown author about an unread book involving one English prelate and one English rabbi. Moreover, that "continuing" unease must have been festering for a decade, since the first occurrence was in 1889 and this one is in 1899.

By separate letters written in that year, Cardinal Herbert Vaughan, the new archbishop of Westminster, along with the Duke of Norfolk and the lord chief justice, wrote to the secretary of state asking that the Holy See "reiterate the repudiations of the ritual murder charge that, they said, popes in earlier centuries had often issued." Knowingly, Kertzer continues: "Cardinal Rampolla immediately took the English letters to the Pope. After conferring, they decided to refer the question to the cardinal inquisitors." The comments about "immediately," "decided," and "conferring" are more of the "insider" insights that embellish this narrative — the letters were received on different dates — and that are intended to drive home the regnant fantasy that it was "with the assistance of their secretaries of state that the popes regulated their anti-Semitic campaigns." In fact, at this point in the narrative

---

latter indicates the personal attention of a high official in the secretariat, if not of the secretary of state himself.

The letter of G. B. Montini that was written to the fledgling Christian Brother was obviously so formulaic as to be of no historical import. However, the letter Montini wrote to Maurice Blondel five years earlier in December 1944 illustrates the mentality of both the pope and his aide. In fact, the letter reflects the admiration of Montini for the philosopher in terms that are so enthusiastic it is surprising that Pius XII didn't feel called upon to tone it down — though it is to be remembered that this was the period of the pope's own ascendant spirit, the time of the two great encyclicals, on the Bible and on the Mystical Body.

Kertzer ignores his source, Miccoli, who noted that Rampolla had warned the Duke of Norfolk that the matter was "highly delicate" because over the centuries all issues relating to the Jews fell within the purview of "the cardinal inquisitors" — a venue that was indifferent to public opinion, occasionally unresponsive to the pope, and in principle, if not in practice, also out of the limelight.[16]

Kertzer continues:

> A glimpse into how the inquisitors handled the request can be gleaned from internal documents recently found in the Holy Office archives. The cardinals, we learn, decided to name a special consultant to help them with the case. The person they chose, Monsignor Rafael Merry del Val, was someone who would soon become famous worldwide, for in just three years he would succeed Rampolla as secretary of state.

The finder was Miccoli, who gleaned one "internal Holy Office note" on the selection of Merry del Val, whose nonexistent worldwide fame is being fabricated here to prepare for his role as premier villain in the actual case of ritual murder that follows the present treatment of the investigation by the Holy Office. The note by the unknown writer was couched arrogantly, and in effect treated Cardinal Vaughan, as Miccoli wrote, "like a pawn in the hands of the Jews." Kertzer continues:[17]

> An internal Holy Office note on the selection of Merry del Val tells us a great deal about the inquisitors' view of the British Catholic request:
> "The Cardinal Archbishop of Westminster has thought to denounce present-day anti-Semitism, especially the matter of ritual murder, to the Holy See. It is easy to understand just how serious the matter is, if one

16. How out of the limelight the case actually was becomes evident from the citation by Miccoli of articles in Henri Drumont's *La Libre Parole* that showed accurate knowledge of the Holy Office's investigation only two months after it had been initiated, while copies of a series of ten anti-Semitic articles from the *La Libre Parole* titled "L'Angleterre juive" were found in the Holy Office files relating to the case. For a change, rather than the guesswork exemplified above, this might have been a significant discovery, since it could indicate material that influenced the final decision — although Miccoli doesn't follow up on that possibility.

17. Apart from the bracketed material in the following excerpt, the strange layout of the original text is exactly as it appears — all double-spaced — in *The Popes Against the Jews*. This means that the lengthy and racist quotation flows without break into the mention of Merry del Val who is thus presented as responsible for the statement itself. This too is preparatory to the creation of del Val as the villain in the ritual murder trial in Kiev.

considers the temerity [*arditezza*] of the powerful Jews of London, who, in their unchallenged rule in Europe have reached the point of such lunacy [*demenza*] that they would pretend to be defended by the Holy See." Why had the cardinals chosen to give the matter to Monsignor Merry del Val for investigation? The Holy Office note provides the answer. Because he has among his ancestors a boy crucified by the Jews and venerated on Church altars. Thus, "he is the man most suited for the task." (bracketed material supplied)

While Coleridgean ancestral voices may explain why the Holy Office selected del Val, it was not necessarily why Leo XIII — who wouldn't have seen the note described above — approved the choice, since in his eyes del Val was *the* authority on matters British. As a young seminarian in Rome he had been part of the Vatican delegation to Queen Victoria's golden jubilee; he was briefly apostolic delegate to Canada; and he had been secretary of the Pontifical Commission on Anglican Orders — about which, more shortly. Additional favorable factors, at least in the minds of the pope and Rampolla, would have been that del Val himself was born in England, where as a boy he went to school, and that he and his family knew two of the petitioners, the Duke of Norfolk and Cardinal Vaughan.

Since the document had mentioned del Val's ancestor, Kertzer inserts at this point in the ritual murder discussion a description of a biography of del Val, published in 1933, three years after the cardinal's death. "Indeed, among the grounds for Merry del Val's fame in the Catholic world was his descent from the same family as Dominguito del Val, a child worshipped[18] in Spain as a martyr and saint" — though since then, by order of Rome, from such devotion demoted. "Dominguito, 'a child of barely seven years old,' we learn, 'was, on Good Friday 1250, crucified on a wall by the Jews out of their hatred for the Catholic religion.'" The biography, for which "the future Pope Pius XII wrote the preface," even has a picture of the seven-year-old martyr: "Indeed, the first illustration . . . shows the hapless boy nailed to the cross" — presumably the cross was attached to the aforementioned wall.

18. The misspelling might be another of those tics pointing to something amiss. Apart from the pomposity of "Indeed," to be repeated shortly, it is to be noted that del Val had no particular fame in 1899 — he was not even an archbishop — though he had some later as cardinal secretary of state under Pius X, when that renown would be transformed to celebrity among anti-Modernists, and notoriety among Modernists. But the tic more likely relates to the foundation being laid, once again, for building the image of del Val, as the real villain in the final instance of "ritual murder and the popes in the twentieth century."

In any case, absent further mention here of del Val, the investigation by the Inquisition proceeded. It took six months before a decision was rendered — presumably due to the press of business unconnected to the British petition — though there was apparently some procrastination by the inquisitors. (There were ten other cases before the tribunal on the day when the ritual murder case was decided.) Kertzer, as he had done with Pio Nono's homily, combines quotation with paraphrase.

On the last day of July the assessor of the Holy Office officially notified Cardinal Rampolla of the decision. "This Supreme [Holy Office] has received repeated petitions, especially from England. . . . These are aimed at obtaining a formal declaration from the Holy See, holding the accusation of so-called Ritual Murder, directed against the Jews from the most remote times, to be false and groundless." After due deliberation, the assessor reported the inquisitors had concluded, with the Pope's approval, that no such declaration of the Jews' innocence could be made.

A note accompanying the decision found [by Miccoli] in the central Inquisition archives but never published, offers a further glimpse into the thinking that lay behind the decision. "Although nothing was found either in the Holy Office or at the Secretariat of State, where careful research was undertaken, bearing on this accusation . . . ritual murder is a historical certainty." . . . The conclusion was thus clear: "Given all this, the Holy See cannot issue the statement that has been requested, which while it may please a few dupes in England, would trigger widespread protests and scandal elsewhere." (ellipses and omissions original)

Concerning the first paragraph, it is worth noting that the Holy Office text said nothing explicit about a formal declaration of Jewish "innocence"; the official statement simply reported that the requested declaration cannot be given ("petitam declarationem dari non posse") because the existence of ritual murder is "historically certain." This kind of negative wording was introduced in the last chapter as characteristic of begrudged apologies. If the inquisitors of *Il Supremo* thought along the *stare-decisis* lines of U.S. Supreme Court justices, everything depended on the specific nature of the "request." Miccoli summarizes what the petitioners had requested in their letters: "to declare unfounded the accusation of ritual murder against the Jews," and/or approval of the judgment that ritual murder was "an ancient, cruel, and completely discredited legend." From that and several other passages in the letters by the petitioners, the inquisitors may have assumed — probably disingenuously — that what was being sought was a declaration that Jews from the most remote times had never engaged in killing Christians. To that proposition even Clement XIV — who had as papal envoy in Poland unequivocally condemned the blood libel — would have said that it is not possible to give an affirmative response.[19] For that reason the wording of the Resolution did not foreclose its reversal in the future. In fact, a little more than a decade later the *Times* of London (May 6, 1912) reported that an official Anglican-Catholic denunciation of ritual murder — "a cruel and utterly baseless libel on Judaism" — had been signed by the Cardinal Archbishop of Westminster and the Archbishops of Canterbury and York.

The point at issue in the second paragraph excerpted above is radically more significant, and not only because of the peculiarly strident language employed, but because it is misleading to refer to "a note *accompanying* the decision." When "the assessor of the Holy Office officially notified Cardinal Rampolla of the decision," there were no accompanying documents whether published or unpublished. The reason for suggesting the opposite is to lend an official aura to the insulting reference to the British petitioners as "a few dupes in England." Miccoli began his own discussion of this obviously offensive "note" by asking at the end of one paragraph "What then were the factors that led the Congregation to decide on [*deliberare*] this reply?" The next paragraph, without any transition, begins as follows: "I have not found the *votum* of Merry del Val who was commissioned to study the question and report his findings to the responsible officials of the Holy Office." Miccoli went on to add

19. At the time of the Kiev ritual murder trial, James George Frazer of *Golden Bough* fame wrote to the *Times* of London: "whilst I discuss hypothetically the possibility of an occasional crime instigated by superstition among the dregs of the Jewish as of the Christian population, I stigmatise such accusations against the Jewish people as a 'monstrous injustice'" (Robert Fraser, "Mere Idle Calumnies," *The Times Literary Supplement*, April 10, 2009).

One historian noted: "Even friends of Jews, people who protested against the masquerade, were not absolutely sure if somewhere Jews did not use blood for ritual purposes." Zosa Szajkowski, "The Impact of the Beilis Case on Central and Western Europe," *Proceedings of the American Academy for Jewish Research* 31 (1963). Another historian, Albert S. Lindemann, in *The Jew Accused: Three Anti-Semitic Affairs: Dreyfus, Beilis, Frank, 1894-1915* (1991) writes: "A few observers, again including Jews, expressed the opinion that even if the charges of ritual murder had no foundation in Jewish law, who could tell what some sort of wayward hasidic sect might conceivably have done."

Perhaps the last word should be left to that aficionado of irony, Ernest Renan, who observed: "It is possible, it is even certain that more than once in fifteen centuries a Christian has been killed by a Jew." (See W. F. P. Stockley, "Popes and Jewish 'Ritual Murder,'" *The Catholic World* [April 1934]).

that such a report is usually printed and sent to the cardinals with a view to its use in their plenary session. "But in this instance, that does not seem to have happened." [Then with no paragraph break or transition, Miccoli continues.] "Nevertheless, there exists a short handwritten text in the folder that contains the documentation relative to the whole case." That "text" is the *note* at issue, which by Miccoli's "contextualization" suggests del Val's authorship — as Kertzer less explicitly also suggests. The degree to which these are factual judgments or judgments influenced by the role of villain del Val will be forced to play at the trial in Kiev by our authors — that cannot be determined, yet.

The present-day significance of all these paraphrases, confusing attributions, and chronological shifts is highlighted by the fact that this reference to "a few dupes in England" has become second only to "Jews as dogs" as the favorite of the glowing reviewers of *The Popes Against the Jews*.[20] Since Kertzer went into needless detail about Merry del Val being the special consultant to the Inquisition, the first issue is whether on its face it is likely that he could have made this remark. The people to which it refers are del Val's family friends, the Duke of Norfolk and the chief justice, as well as Cardinal Vaughan, archbishop of Westminster, under whom del Val as a young priest had hoped to serve. (Had he done so, he might have found himself in America working among recently freed slaves, since that was the assignment that Pius IX — another infamous racist — had given to Vaughan's Mill Hill missionaries.) Since this "short handwritten text" is unsigned, most observers would view this as a strange way for the report of the special consultant — who was "the man most suited for the task" because of his martyred ancestor — to be communicated to the cardinals. Moreover, since del Val had been consecrated to a singularly important titular see — archbishop of Nicaea — two months before the Holy Office decision, there would be every reason for his now more authoritative opinion to have been publicly recognized.

In any case, there has been nothing to show that the note represented the views of the secretary of state, much less of the pope, who approved the final Resolution by the Inquisitors two days after their decision. In fact, other

---

20. Although I will discuss this translation shortly, I want to suggest as a kind of self-administered "thought experiment" the possibility of an alternative reading. The beginning of the original passage is adequately translated by Kertzer: "Given all this, the Holy See cannot issue the statement that has been requested [then one continues with:] which while satisfying a few dreamers in England would result in widespread protests and scandals elsewhere." The issue is whether this translation would engender the prolonged and triumphant fulminations regarding matters Catholic cited below. The original passage is: "la quale, se contenterebbe i pochi illusi d'Inghilterra, solleverebbe proteste e scandali per tutto altrove."

than the Resolution, Leo XIII and Cardinal Rampolla would not have been given the files (or the nine other files on the other decisions being considered at that time). Nor, lastly, would the British petitioners themselves have known anything of this, since what was communicated to them was the gist or drift *(il tenore)* of the Resolution. As to the note itself, there is the matter of language and syntax. Concerning the first, although Kertzer gives no indication of it, the Resolution of the Holy Office is in Latin, whereas the mysterious note is in Italian, and would not have been circulated outside of the plenary session, if there — since it was not part of the printed files. As also noted, the outlandish phrase "a few dupes in England" is Kertzer's wording — and as we will also see, particularly in the treatment of the Kiev trial, Kertzer is not above drastically mistranslating or doctoring crucial texts. As suggested above in the "thought experiment," *illuso* when translated into English as "dupe" has a crude tone that even bigoted churchmen would be unlikely to employ, whether in a never published note or elsewhere.[21] *Illuso* as cognate of "illusory" is better conveyed by "dreamer," "fantasizer," or "wishful thinker," although it should come as no surprise that the most damaging translation will be chosen by Kertzer — and relished by his reviewers. Still, the fact that the two terms most basked in by critics of the papacy, "dogs" and "dupes," are in the real world trivial epithets — that fact may be an indicator of the sensibilities informing such relish.[22]

Concerning syntax, so that the reader knows to whom this slur should be attributed, Kertzer structures his text so that explicit references to

21. *Gonzo* — pre–Hunter Thompson — or *babbeo* or *credulone* are the usual terms for "dupe," which explains why English synonyms are invariably regional colloquialisms or slang. Roget proffers "patsy," "fall guy," "sucker," and the like.

22. Michael R. Marrus, a usually careful reader (though clearly exposing a tic regarding idiomatic epithets), when discussing "the hair-brained claim that Jews killed Christians," maintains that "*Kertzer found* a previously unpublished note accompanying the inquisitors' decision." Marrus also thinks — basing his view on what Kertzer has implied — that the pope also approved the comment about "English dupes." Garry Wills exploits the phrase "English dupes" repeatedly because "internal documents show," "other documents show," and "an internal document noted" that it was attributed to the Holy Office. One can imagine the outrage if the phrase were to be applied to Kertzer, Marrus, and Wills as "dupes in North America."

Popes and their secretaries of state always talk that way about defenders of Jews, but it would be outrageous to talk that way about gullible scholars. Even to take as precedent Cardinal Newman — who referred to three of his Catholic antagonists, one of whom was Vaughan, as "the three tailors of Tooley Street" — would not justify referring to Kertzer, Marrus, and Wills as "the Archdupe Trio."

Leo XIII envelop the outré phrase, resulting in the formula: pope-dupes-pope. The sentence about "the pope's approval" is followed by the note referring to "a few dupes in England"; this in turn is followed immediately by Kertzer's "conclusion": "Perhaps it would have been too much to hope for a change of heart on the part of Leo XIII." To introduce Leo at precisely that juncture is to succumb to even more rigging of the evidence. If on canonical grounds the Supreme Holy Office stood in relation to the pope as the Supreme Court stands in relation to the president, there is no reason to link the pope to the decision — which, as noted, he did accept. Moreover, it is difficult to conceive the pope tolerating, much less endorsing such language as it related to the hereditary earl marshal and scion of the house of Howard, which had been loyal to Rome since the fifteenth century.[23] There is the additional matter of the violation of protocol in writing thus coarsely about the archbishop of Westminster and the lord chief justice.

Furthermore, from Kertzer's perspective, as emphasized in the previous chapter, he forecloses any possibility of disorder and disorganization, of institutional muddle and disarray, or of just plain bureaucratic entrenchment regarding Vatican officials, including those attached to the Holy Office. At no time is the possibility entertained that there are other influential agencies and personalities involved either directly or as necessary auxiliaries in statements or deeds by the papacy. It is unique among complex organizations in that never is any actual influence attributed to, say, embedded cardinals, freewheeling editors, influential foreign diplomats, biased advisers, and the like.[24]

23. It was at the request of the Duke of Norfolk that Leo XIII named John Henry Newman a cardinal. When the learned, liberal, and ill-fated American bishop John Lancaster Spalding told the pope that elevating Newman had "rejoiced all the Catholic world," the pope replied: "Oh well! yes, I thought it would please the Duke of Norfolk, the pupil of Newman. The Duke of Norfolk is the head of the English nobility." This was reported by Baron von Hügel to Alfred Loisy (*Mémoire pour servir à la histoire religieuse de notre temps: 1857-1900*, t. I [1930]).

24. One might look at other comparable events, and draw the obvious conclusion: "In Iraq, the British troops held back while the Arabs went on a rampage, killing and looting the helpless Baghdad Jews. The British would show similar 'restraint' during the anti-Jewish riots that took place in Libya." So, one concludes that Prime Minister Clement Attlee was overseeing anti-Semitic campaigns.

After the war Israeli selective immigration policy "was applied exclusively to North Africans . . . by a growing prejudice among veteran Ashkenazim in Israel against Oriental Jews in general and North Africans in particular." David Ben-Gurion was also overseeing his own brand of anti-Semitic campaign. (See Norman A. Stillman, *The Jews of Arab Lands in Modern Times* [1991]).

In Kertzer's interpretation of events, the decision of the inquisitors meant simply that there had been no "change of heart on the part of Leo XIII."

All this stands in contrast to the more ample vision of personalities and events evidenced by Owen Chadwick — cited several times in these pages, perhaps most significantly for disclosing Umberto Benigni's alterations of the papal bull that resulted in a diplomatic scandal affecting relations with Germany. In that same book, *A History of the Popes 1830-1914,* Chadwick had also disclosed that Gregory XVI did not want the condemnation of de Lamennais that was tendered in the pope's name. "It could only be because [Klemens von] Metternich forced it upon his client state, or because the engine of the Inquisition churned away and could not be stopped even by a pope." However, the churning engine of the Inquisition will not be heard or seen in this illustration of another request to Leo XIII, which also involves del Val as well as some British petitioners — all of whom in the event were rebuffed by Rome, even though the heartless Leo XIII had originally been sympathetic to their interests. In the decision regarding Anglican orders, mentioned briefly above, the pope believed the commission he had appointed would decide favorably, and thus "achieve better relations with the Anglicans." As for his co-conspirator, Cardinal Rampolla "had the same charitable idea and seems to have been persuaded before the event that the evidence pointed to the validity of Anglican orders." Compared to the six months it took to decide the ritual murder issue, that commission labored for two years — only to conclude that the views of Leo XIII and his secretary of state were wrong.

For Kertzer, any connection between the pope and the Jews automatically redounds to the dishonor of the pope. Thus the sentence regarding no "change of heart on the part of Leo XIII" is followed immediately by: "Over the previous two decades he had overseen continuous assaults on the Jews in the Vatican-linked press, and done his best to nourish and to defend a militantly Anti-Semite political party in Austria." This was the party of the anti-Semitic politician Karl Lueger, whose name had been brought up by Kertzer in his introduction when he abruptly said to his readers, "Is there any significance in the fact that Adolf Hitler, a baptized Catholic, spent his early years in Austria, where the Vatican supported anti-Semitic Christian Social movement was then so active? Indeed, Hitler himself admitted to being inspired by its leader, Karl Lueger." But according to Léon Poliakov in *Suicidal Europe, 1870-1933,* the party was opposed by "the upper bourgeoisie and the higher clergy," and supported by Rome because it was "sympathetic to the aspirations of the urban proletariat." Owen Chadwick confirms this when he notes that "the people who voted for it were the lower middle class and artisans" who had been "much encouraged by *Rerum Novarum*." "Indeed," the nurturing of that political party — which had nothing to do with its attitude to Jews — was the work of the celebrated letter writer, Cardinal Rampolla, and for that reason when Rampolla became the almost certain choice to succeed Leo XIII in 1903, the Austrian emperor vetoed his election, and Giuseppe Sarto, patriarch of Venice, became pope, taking the name Pius.

CHAPTER 6

Ritual Murder and the Villainy of Pius X

Kertzer devotes five paragraphs to setting the stage for the new pope. "*Setting* the stage" is the *mot juste*, since once again Kertzer enters the minds of his papal protagonists in order to discern such things as that "Leo XIII enjoyed traveling in a litter," and that Pius X not only recognized "his own lack of experience" but also "saw conspiracies everywhere" — and they both just generally lived in a universe abounding in clichés.

> The contrast between the new pope and his predecessor could scarcely have been greater. The sixty-eight year old Sarto came from a humble family. . . . He was the first pope in centuries to come from peasant stock. . . . While Leo XIII cut an aristocratic figure . . . Pius X was shorter, burly, red-faced, voluble, and affable. . . . Whereas Leo XIII enjoyed traveling in a litter carried on the shoulders of his attendants, Pius X refused to be treated in this way. . . . Yet despite all these differences in background, experience, and temperament, Pius X was no more positively inclined toward the changes identified with the modern world than was Leo XIII. . . . [Although] in the wake of a new wave of pogroms, Pius X sent a letter to the Polish bishops in the Russian empire, reminding them that the Church condemned violence against the Jews. In one of his most important encyclicals, *Pascendi*, in 1907, he condemned modern philosophy, which he denounced as contrary to the ancient faith of the Church. . . . Like his predecessor, Pius X saw conspiracies everywhere, and like him, too, tolerated no disobedience. Recognizing his own lack of experience in diplomacy and in dealing with the world outside the Italian Church, the Pope named Rafael Merry del Val to be his secretary of state, someone who was in many ways his opposite: a man of aristocratic, cosmopolitan background, who spoke several Euro-

pean languages. . . . More significantly, in contrast to the stream of anti-Semitic diatribes published in the papally linked press in the last two decades of Leo XIII's reign, the newspapers closest to the Pope were much less vocal on the Jewish question during Pius X's papacy.

After that final sentence, and with no transition, the next paragraph begins as follows: "And then there is the audience that the Pope had with Theodore Herzl on January 26, 1904. The very fact that he would receive Herzl, who was campaigning for a Jewish homeland in Palestine which the Church strongly opposed was significant." Herzl asked the pope if he would support the Zionist project, and was told, "We won't be able to stop the Jews from going to Jerusalem, but we could never favor it. . . . The Jewish faith was the foundation of our own, but it has been superseded [*superada*] by the teachings of Christ, and we cannot admit that it still enjoys any validity." As noted in chapter 4, while "supersede" and even more its cognate, "supersessionism," have become modish pejoratives, Pius X's declaration of the relation between the two communities has itself been generally superseded by language and imagery related to the reforms of Vatican II. In Kertzer's narrative, Herzl enters the scene in order to signal the "reassertion of a more traditional Catholic view of the Jews." Kertzer then concedes that "there is little doubt but that Pius X had more empathy for the Jews than his predecessor." But that concession is immediately withdrawn: "Yet it would be easy to overstate the significance of these differences."

Before taking up the stated theme of the chapter, "ritual murder," there is introduced into this new plot the ubiquitous Umberto Benigni, the minor Vatican official and anti-Semite we have met several times already, who under Pius X and in response to the anti-Modernist encyclical *Pascendi* became the leader of his own international organization of heresy hunters. Thus in the reign of this new pope, there are to be found, at last, the conspiratorial elements for which Kertzer has been probing, and they are embodied in a man who was more ingenious and cunning than were even his respective masters from Leo XIII to Pius XI — all as conceived by David I. Kertzer. The story of Modernism itself has been often told — as it was briefly sketched in chapter 2 — but there is little doubt that Benigni with the collusion of Merry del Val and the knowledge of the pope was the villain of the piece.[1] Benigni's

---

1. Roger Aubert condemns those who believe in "the legend of the secretary of state who brainwashed a benevolent and pious Pope with intransigence." In Hubert Jedin, ed., *The Church in the Modern World, III* (1993).

detestation of Jews was blatant, but generally confined to pamphleteering until later in his career when his connection to issues of ritual murder took the form of writing its history, *Il delitto rituale* (1922). Also, as noted earlier, during that same period, he published the *Protocols of the Elders of Zion* and publicly espoused fascism.

According to Kertzer, "Pius X showered Benigni with honors [a monsignor] and even more important with influence. In 1906 Benigni was named second-in-command of the Congregation for Extraordinary Ecclesiastical Affairs, giving him the fifth highest office in the entire Secretariat of State." This lasted five years until Cardinal Pietro Gasparri, for two decades a professor at the Institut Catholique in Paris, braved the shower and had Benigni dismissed. Gasparri's young protégé, Eugenio Pacelli, who was working with him on the creation of a unified code of Canon Law, thus ended up occupying that honored fifth highest office. Among Vaticanologists, these appointments have led to a raft of conjectures that make Kertzer's mind-reading hypotheticals appear almost scientific. Before examining the ritual murder case at the center of this chapter, it will be necessary to dispose of this conjectural overload.

Sergio Minerbi, a one-time Israeli diplomat and the author of *The Vatican and Zionism: Conflict in the Holy Land 1895-1925* (1990), observes, though in a later book, that "Eugenio Pacelli entered the Secretatiat of State in 1901 *to work with* Mgr. Umberto Benigni, who was one of the most active anti-Semites in the Church. Eventually, in 1911, Pacelli *replaced* Benigni in the Secretariat of State." One gets an idea of the world in which this kind of speculator dwells not only from the italicized nudges in that sentence, but even more from his making a point to mention that "Cornwell ignores this fact." Minerbi then says: "Nevertheless, I do not consider Pacelli's later papal behavior to be *solely* influenced by the anti-Semitism of his *entourage*" (all italics supplied). The facts are that Pacelli had nothing to do with Benigni, and that, as noted, it was Cardinal Gasparri, Pacelli's mentor, who had Benigni "replaced."

Richard L. Rubenstein concentrates on the evil designs behind the "comprehensive codification" of canon law by Gasparri and Pacelli, which was carried out "in the spirit of Pio Nono." The arbitrary introduction of this particular pope into the discussion is a way of suggesting a sinister fate for the Code of Canon Law which, in fact, Rubenstein regards as a kind of Catholic shari'ah. Coming from Rubenstein, a public devotee of Sun Myung Moon and former president of the latter's Bridgeport University and ombudsman of his *Washington Times*, this by contrast makes Pio Nono look like the spiritual model for Pope John XXIII — who, as noted earlier, was in fact devoted to his nineteenth-century predecessor. Rubenstein also believes that Pacelli's "entire career had been focused on . . . state recognition of the authority of the *Codex* over Catholics." To view the innocuous collating, organizing, and updating of thousands of old decrees and rubrics that constitute the Code of Canon Law as an ominous effort to subject the faithful to papal rule is as persuasive as making Blackstone's *Commentaries* responsible for the end of the British Raj.

It is not entirely unexpected that non-Catholic critics would espouse such notions. What is surprising is that their source is two Catholics, James Carroll and John Cornwell, both of whom certainly knew better. According to *Hitler's Pope*, Pacelli's mission as nuncio in Bavaria was "nothing less than the imposition through the 1917 Code of Canon Law of supreme papal authority." When quoting this in *Constantine's Sword*, Carroll puts it in the context of "absolutist claims" giving "the pope unprecedented power over every aspect of Church life." In both versions one can glimpse a hesitant parallel with the imperial goals described in the *Protocols of the Elders of Zion*. Lastly, Garry Wills in *Why I Am a Catholic* says that Benigni "owed his rise in the church to Leo XIII" — though up to the last years of the pope's reign Benigni was an amateur journalist who had been teaching history in the local seminary. There was about as much of a link between Benigni and Leo XIII as between the typical ambitious employee and the U.S. president — say between Robert Hanssens and Ronald Reagan. It was only after the election of Pius X that Benigni began to exercise real influence as the anti-Modernist spymaster — an influence that nearly derailed the canonization of Pope Sarto. (For Minerbi and Rubenstein, see Carol Rittner and John K. Roth, eds., *Pope Pius XII and the Holocaust* [2001].)

The new ritual murder case, according to Kertzer, "tells us something about how little Vatican views of the Jews changed in these early years of the twentieth century." It will also tell us something about how little the author's views regarding methodology have changed as his book progresses. As indicated earlier, this case is the clearest and the most brazen instance of texts being intentionally manipulated and truncated as well as of facts being distorted or concealed in order to prove that the popes were engaged in unholy war against the Jews. The case was that of a thirty-nine-year-old Russian Jew, Mendel Beilis, on trial in 1913 in czarist Ukraine. The only comparable trial — at least in terms of worldwide impact — was that of Leopold Hilsner at the turn of the century in Polna in Bohemia. Zosa Szajkowski, who is Kertzer's primary source for the Beilis trial, notes: "The difference was that the Russian government directed the anti-Beilis trial, while at Polna it was the people who demanded Hilsner's execution."[2] The indictment of Beilis had for three years roiled two continents and, in the end, the court case would take on the significance of the earlier Dreyfus trial in France. The goal of the Russian government in resuscitating the hoary accusation was believed to be the incitement of nationwide pogroms that would in effect punish the Jews for the political and social reforms forced on the czar after the riots and strikes of the 1905 revolution.

Kertzer's narrative begins by describing the efforts of several Jews to secure the aid of the pope. Paul Nathan, a leading Jewish spokesman in Berlin, and his counterparts in London, Lucien Wolf and Lord Leopold Rothschild, wanted to have the Vatican authenticate the validity of two official papal statements denouncing the blood libel. The documents were written in the thirteenth century by Pope Innocent IV, and in the eighteenth, by Lorenzo Ganganelli, later Pope Clement XIV — whose election was greeted with acclaim by Jews precisely because of his emphatic refutation of the libel. The Jewish petitioners, again through the offices of the Duke of Norfolk, believed the Vatican testimony would be particularly useful because a key defender of ritual murder at the trial was to be a Catholic priest, Justin Pranaitis. "Anyone who has gotten this far in this book should not find it surprising that. . . ."[3] Kertzer describes Pranaitis as "a Roman Catholic priest and professor of theology," but fails to mention that he had a police record as an extortionist and that he had been defrocked. His alleged expertise in Talmudic lore evoked laughter from the few Jews allowed in the courtroom, as he consistently responded to questions about elementary Jewish practices or about common Hebrew terms either incorrectly or with an "I don't know." Maurice Samuel compared one particularly egregious display of ignorance to that of American students seeking to answer the question "Who lived at the Gettysburg address?"[4]

As for the role of the pope, Kertzer says that, "like his predecessor, Pius X

2. Zosa Szajkowski, "The Impact of the Beilis Case on Central and Western Europe" (loc. cit). This work is central to Kertzer's treatment of the trial itself.

3. The quotation continues: ". . . in response to these measures against the Jews neither the Pope nor the Vatican hierarchy uttered a single word of protest."

4. The source for the charge of extortion is *The Decay of Czarism: The Beiliss Trial*, by Alexander B. Tager (1935) — a work that will play a major role in the following discussion. The source for the charge that Pranaitis had been defrocked is Albert S. Lindemann in *The Jew Accused: Three Anti-Semitic Affairs* (loc. cit.). Maurice Samuel in *Blood Accusation: The Strange History of the Beiliss Case* (1966) refers to Pranaitis as "disowned by his superiors." (The spelling of the surname of the accused varies.)

too received a high-level plea for the Vatican to do something to distance it-self from the ritual murder campaign against the Jews." (The "campaign" is presumably a reference to the popes' own out-of-the-limelight activities.) Translated into conventional English, the statement about "distancing" means simply that the papacy was asked to affirm the authenticity of the two historic documents mentioned above by Innocent IV and Lorenzo Ganga-nelli. Kertzer's next sentence, following the reference to a "high-level plea," is the one about "how little Vatican views of the Jews changed." But the con-cerns voiced by the British petitioners had nothing to do with "Vatican views"; their concerns were over international issues relating to the Beilis trial. Those broader issues, examined by Szajkowski, put into perspective the role played by Kertzer's campaigning pope. They have to do with the interests of Jewish activists in England in support of Beilis and the "interests of the Franco-British-Russian Entente directed against Germany." Because of the political alliance among those three powers, Germany became the hub of in-ternational Jewish activities in defense of Beilis, while England and France were officially not involved. Szajkowski continues:

> [The activities were] centralized in the hands of Dr. Paul Nathan who ob-tained from religious leaders and scholars written opinions (Gutachten) in favor of Beilis. To Dr. Nathan's suggestion that Lucien Wolf should try to get pro-Beilis expert opinions in Britain similar to the Gutachten ob-tained by Dr. Nathan in Germany . . . Wolf replied: "All British Ministers refused to sign an appeal in favor of Beilis, and because of this Lord Rothschild was afraid to ask the Lord Mayors [for their] signatures." In another letter, Lucien Wolf writes: "I am sorry to say that Lord Rothschild will not ask the Lord Mayor. He says that as all Cabinet Ministers have re-fused, he does not think it fair to ask people in official positions." (Zosa Szajkowski, loc. cit.)

So where Kertzer keeps circling back to his theme of refractory Vatican offi-cials, it was the French and British officials who in fact were unhelpful, and a Rothschild who was uncooperative — while the assistance of the presum-ably anti-Semitic papacy was both requested and received.

In Kertzer's description of the international atmosphere of the trial, he follows Miccoli in alleging that Wolf, Rothschild, and their associates were haunted by the realization "that little over a decade earlier the previous pope had refused such a request." That the earlier "request" was entirely different — a general statement regarding the historical nonexistence of ritual murder vis-à-vis the validity of two papal documents condemning ritual murder — that goes unmentioned. Miccoli finds in the earlier "experience" the reason why the Jewish petitioners limited themselves "to a mere authentication" of the two documents. There is nothing in the texts that supports either Miccoli or Kertzer. Zosa Szajkowski cites Wolf:

> In investigating the subject I am sorry to say that I find there has been gross exaggeration in all that has hitherto been written and published by Jews in regard to these so-called Bulls. There never were any Bulls, properly so-called and there has only been the Papal Encyclical, that of Innocent IV. . . . The only other Pontifical document of importance to which we can appeal is the Gutachten [report] of Cardinal Ganganelli. . . . I mention this in order to warn you and our German friends against repeating the statement that there have been a number of Papal Bulls denouncing the Blood Accusation, as if the truth were known, we might be subjected to a very prejudicial attack by men like Pranaitis. In our letter to Cardinal Merry del Val we have only asked him to authenticate the Encyclical of Pope Innocent IV and the text of Cardinal Ganganelli's Gutachten if there is any record of it in the Vatican.[5]

In fact, the Jewish spokesmen had tried and failed to get comparable documents on the blood libel from the exarch of the Orthodox Church in Bulgaria and from the patriarch of Constantinople.

Kertzer quotes Lucien Wolf: "I thought, and both Lord Rothschild and Mr. Montefiore agreed with me, that it would be only a waste of time to ask for a further papal declaration on the subject." Wolf meant the words literally both because such a declaration would entail complicated church-wide negotiations, but even more because timing was recognized as crucial since the trial had already begun. When the petition was finally sent to the Duke of Norfolk — who was to forward it to the Vatican — Rothschild noted that "it would be a great advantage if we could have His Eminence's reply at his earliest convenience." But Wolf's statement is taken as the point of departure for Kertzer's most detailed effort in this chapter at the kind of mind reading encountered in Pius IX's fantasizing about "the Jew":

5. Wolf was paraphrasing the article in the *Jewish Encyclopedia* (1901-6) titled "Clement XIV (Lorenzo Ganganelli)," where one reads: "Ganganelli's memorandum was translated into German by A. Berliner, under the heading 'Gutachten, Ganganelli's (Clemens XIV).'"

The Jewish leaders were particularly alarmed by the flood of articles in the Catholic press, telling, in gruesome detail, of past Christian martyrdom at the hands of the Jews. . . . The Jews debated how they could best gain a sympathetic hearing. . . . Leo XIII's rebuff of little over a decade earlier was too vivid for them to have any hope that the Pope would agree to condemn the ritual murder charges himself . . . the cost of a second papal rebuff would be high . . . rather than call on the pope to issue any statement himself, which they regarded as risky. . . . To further increase their chances . . . Wolf and his colleagues decided to address their request to the secretary of state.

There are two pages of this imaginary speculation intermixed with snatches from the correspondence, at the end of which is a single endnote to Szajkowski's article, "The Impact of the Beilis Case on Central and Western Europe" — from which I have been quoting and which says nothing related to the excerpted passage above. In sum, those two pages are more embroidered guesswork. Kertzer's notion that by addressing the request to the secretary of state the petitioners would somehow bypass the pope is both simplistic and self-contradictory, since the book's thesis has been constructed on the motif that, "with the assistance of their secretaries of state, the popes regulated the anti-Semitic campaigns." As noted, Szajkowski's article is Kertzer's only source for factual information on the trial. The one substantive quotation relating directly to the pope — though preceded by the nudge about "regarded as risky" — is the following from another letter by Wolf: "If the memorial were merely to ask for a pronouncement on the Blood Accusation . . . we should get no satisfactory response, but on the question of the authenticity of the Papal Bulls I do not see how in fairness the Pope could refuse to assist us."

That fairness prevailed is clear from the ensuing history. Rothschild's petition, with the covering note from the Duke of Norfolk, was sent to del Val on October 7, and he replied as follows on October 18:

My Lord, in reply to your letter of October 7 th. I am in a position to certify that the type-written copy of Ganganelli's report to the consultors of the Holy Office is substantially accurate. I am able to give you this assurance after inquiries made at the Holy Office where the original document is kept. As to the extract of Innocent IVth's Letter, there can be no doubt of the accuracy . . . which is confirmed by the fact of Ganganelli citing it in his Report.

What does *not* get quoted from Szajkowski is the following excerpt, which describes the impact of the document.

> On October 18, 1913, Cardinal Merry del Val, Secretary for Foreign Affairs of the Vatican, replied affirmatively. This was a sensational blow against Beilis' accusers. The correspondence between Lord Rothschild and Cardinal del Val was published in all newspapers. The Catholic anti-Semitic press tried to explain that Cardinal Ganganelli's statement expressed only his personal opinion. Newspapers wrote ironically that the Jews chose the representative of "the mightiest financial dynasty" to write the letter to the Vatican. However, many newspapers on this occasion ridiculed the blood accusations, e.g., the Catholic Press of England.

Following that passage Szajkowski traces the document to its destiny in Kiev, as Kertzer follows him word for word along the same route.

Szajkowski writes:
On October 22, 1913, Dr. Nathan was already in possession of a copy of the Vatican's reply certified by the Russian Embassy in London.

Kertzer writes:
By October 22, a copy of the secretary of state's letter, certified as authentic by the Russian Embassy in London, was in the hands of Paul Nathan in Berlin.

Szajkowski writes:
He [Nathan] immediately sent the copy by special messenger to Kiev, where the copy was in the hands of Beilis' lawyers on October 27.

Kertzer writes:
He [Nathan] immediately sent it by special courier to Kiev, where it reached Beilis's lawyers on October 27.

Szajkowski writes:
However, the Russian government did not allow the use of the document as evidence in court.

Kertzer writes:
But the Jews were soon disappointed, for the Russian court refused to accept the document.

There is no doubt that the Vatican's reply was of great importance for the defense of Beilis, as Dr. Nathan wrote on October 16, 1913, to L. Wolf. On October 22, 1913, Dr. Nathan was already in possession of a copy of the Vatican's reply certified by the Russian Embassy in London. He immediately sent the copy by special messenger to Kiev, where the document was in the hands of Beilis' lawyers on October 27.[31] However, the Russian Government did not allow the use of the document as evidence in court. Officially it was stated that the document had first to be certified by the Vatican. But the Russian Ambassador in Rome did everything possible that the document should arrive in Kiev too late to be submitted as evidence in favor of Beilis. Still, the document did influence the final stage of the trial; the Czar himself read the Vatican's reply to Rothschild.[32]

How did Lord Rothschild obtain the Vatican's reply? The details are important because they are characteristic of the many difficulties often encountered in an action for the defense of Jewish interests. Both Lucien Wolf in London and Dr. Paul Nathan in Berlin thought of obtaining such a document. Cardinal Ganganelli had made his statement in 1756 in connection with a blood accusation in Jampol (Poland). Scholarly studies on Ganganelli's statement were published by Isidor Loeb, Moritz Stern and Dr. A. Berliner.[33] But the statement remained un-

Allgemeiner Tiroler Anzeiger, Nov. 5, 1913 ("der im Vatikan schutzstehenden jüdischen Haute Finance"); *Neue Mährschles. Presse* (Olmütz), Nov. 11, 1913 ("Israel zwischen Kiev und Rom"); *Tablet* (London), Oct. 24, 1913.

[31] Wolf to Dr. Nathan, Oct. 26, 1913; Dr. Nathan's letters and telegram to Wolf, Oct. 16, 22 and 28, 1913 (Y).

[32] Alexander B. Tager, *The Decay of Czarism*. Philadelphia, 1935, pp. 209–12; Wolf to Dr. Nathan, Nov. 4, 1913:

> The procedure required by the Kiew Court is a very involved one, but Lord Rothschild set to work immediately on Monday morning to get what was wanted. He telegraphed to his agents in Rome to employ an experienced lawyer, obtain the necessary attestations and telegraph to Kiew. At the same time he telegraphed to the Cardinal explaining to him the circumstances which rendered it necessary to trouble him again (Y).

The page from Zosa Szajkowski, "The Impact of the Beilis Case on Central and Western Europe." *Proceedings of the American Academy for Jewish Research* 31 (1963).

Szajkowski writes:
Officially it was stated that the document had first to be certified by the Vatican.[6]

Kertzer writes:
It could only be admitted as evidence if Merry del Val himself sent it directly to the court.

Kertzer has followed his only source step by step, as the cardinal's letter goes from London to Kiev to its rejection by the Russians. The two statements are running on parallel tracks, until an unexpected — and for Kertzer an intolerable — new player enters the scene. Immediately following Szajkowski's excerpt about "Officially it was stated" is the following sentence — which I here underline and which Kertzer entirely omits: "<u>But the Russian Ambassador in Rome did everything possible that the document should arrive in Kiev too late to be submitted as evidence in favor of Beilis</u>." The obvious conclusion from Kertzer's deliberate deletion is that the Russian ambassador has been omitted in order to make room for someone else — who ends up being the villain pre-designated by Kertzer, both in the preceding chapter and in this one, the Cardinal secretary of state, Merry del Val.

But while it is clear that for the sake of his entire thesis Kertzer cannot allow a Russian diplomat to replace the pope's out-of-the-limelight co-conspirator, there must also have been at least a sliver of doubt about the possibility of a too obvious deception being discovered. The fact that the expunged sentence about the Russian ambassador had a footnote at the bottom of the same page — the page that Kertzer was reading and closely paraphrasing — made feigning ignorance appear even more dangerous. The footnote reads, "Alexander B. Tager, *The Decay of Czarism*, Philadelphia, 1931, pp. 209-12." Regarding the number of pages specified (from 209 to 212), they indicate a fairly substantial text — of which Kertzer would have readers believe he was totally unaware, though there is no way short of a sudden attack of amaurosis that the footnote at the bottom of the page from which he has been quoting extensively could have gone unseen. "Indeed" — to enlist Kertzer's favorite self-affirming transition — the book by Tager is the defini-

---

6. My italics make clear (for reasons to be set forth immediately) that Szajkowski meant that the "official" pretext for the rejection of the document was that it required Vatican certification.

tive study of the Beilis trial, a study that changed for the world how it was to be understood, and that is quoted, as we will see, in several books that are cited in Kertzer's own bibliography.

So, not unlike the inept stand-up comedian who has forgotten his punch line, Kertzer simply changes the subject. The paragraph below comes *immediately* after the fabrication mentioning Merry del Val. It is preceded by no additional space and is patently unlike its predecessors in that it has no detailed time frame. In fact, where one anticipates specific dates, the chronology is fudged — as my italics indicate.[7]

> Rothschild had *initially* replied to the secretary of state's letter with a note of thanks, containing his own rosy interpretation of what the cardinal had said. Not only would the cardinal's letter have great weight in the Kiev trial, he wrote, it would also "prove to the world at large that the Holy See at the present moment, as in olden days, utterly repudiates this foul and unjustifiable accusation." When Rothschild *subsequently* learned that the Russian court had rejected the letter, he sent the Secretary of state an urgent telegram. Before the letter could be *used at the trial,* he advised the cardinal, "it is necessary that your Eminence's signature should be legally certified, that is to say, your Eminence will have to telegraph a repetition of your letter to me addressing it to Boldyro the presiding judge of the Kieff District Court of Justice."
>
> But this was going too far. In the Vatican Secret Archives file. . . .[8]

Not only is chronology fudged, but Kertzer deliberately truncates the last clause, "addressing it to Boldyro the presiding judge of the Kieff District Court of Justice." There is no full-stop, no period, at the "end" of the quotation about Boldyro; the sentence does not terminate with the word "Justice" — another damning deletion, to be examined shortly.

First, the chronology; then the deletion. Presumably, the reader, sharing the narrator's sense of righteous ire, will not notice that the central event of this entire history, the verdict, has not been disclosed. The last date mentioned was October 27, when del Val's authentication reached Kiev. But this was the date when the whole watching world knew that closing argu-

---

7. This will lead to an omission far more damaging to Kertzer than was the one about the Russian ambassador — though it is no coincidence that the omitted material will relate explicitly to the latter's role.

8. The remainder of this paragraph will be examined shortly.

ments by the prosecution and the defense over the fate of the accused were concluded. It was the eve of the scheduled verdict, which was in fact rendered on October 28, when a hung jury left Beilis a free man — although there is no mention of this crucial date or of these crucial events in Kertzer's narrative. This is why one gets the context for Rothschild's "urgent telegram" to del Val — without getting its date. But like Szajkowski's clearly evident footnote at the bottom of the page referring to the mysterious Russian ambassador, at the bottom of Rothschild's message that Kertzer is copying down there is an unavoidably evident annotation, "telegramma da Londres, *3 novembre* 1913."

This is why it is literally "preposterous" for Kertzer to say that Rothschild "advised the cardinal" about what he must do "before [pre] the letter could be used at the trial," since the trial as just noted had ended [post] seven days earlier on October 28. Then, still in that impossibly self-contradictory context, Kertzer depicts del Val as icily declining to save a man's life and put an end to the vicious blood libel. This latter stratagem entails the author again entering the cardinal's mind and ascribing to him the presumably angry outburst: "But this was going too far" — the "this" being something as trivial as "addressing it [a telegraph] to Boldyro the presiding judge of the Kieff District Court of Justice." Only a moral monster like del Val — the reader is left to assume — would balk at performing something so simple and with such momentous consequences.

So, there are now two pieces of information proven to have been seen by Kertzer and then intentionally excised from his account: first, the reference to the Russian ambassador who does "everything possible" to block essential evidence getting to the trial on time, and, second, the remainder of Rothschild's wired message to the cardinal — the part that followed the mention of "Boldyro the presiding judge of the Kieff District Court of Justice." In the event, both excisions are intertwined. The rest of the truncated sentence, which Kertzer actually read "in the Vatican Secret Archives file," went as follows and without interruption (including errors in transmission of the telegram):

> . . . the presiding judge of the Kieff District Court of Justice, this message to be certified by the telegraph autoritier [*sic*, presumably "authorities"]. **In order to effect this a representative of the Banca Commerciale Italiana will at my request wait upon your Excellency and explain what is required. I beg your Excellency to grant him an audience** and at the same time to excuse me for asking this very great favour and with mi [*sic*]

highest consideration and esteem I remain your Eminences [*sic*] obedient servant. Rothschild.[9] (boldface added explained infra)

Kertzer could not let that appear because it would undercut his argument that del Val's contempt for Jews made him decline the Rothschild proposal. Even more significant, he could not let it appear because it contains details that are provided only by Tager — a book that Kertzer obviously had examined when he saw the reference to it on the bottom of the page of Szajkowski's article — but which for the sake of his anti-papal thesis he dare not even allude to, since it makes the Russian ambassador and not the Vatican secretary of state responsible for the failure of the document to be entered into the trial proceedings. The presence of the date of Rothschild's "telegramma da Londres" highlights further that subterfuge, since del Val like everybody else — except Kertzer's blindsided reader decades later subjected to the vagaries of "initially" and "subsequently" — knew that the trial had ended a week before this telegram was sent.

Kertzer's next paragraph begins with the exclamation intended to express the fabricated mood of the obstinate prelate who is about to refuse to write the letter that presumably could save a man's life: "But this was going too far." Chronology, for the first time in several pages, is also resurrected by our historian as he continues the charade of never having seen what he simply could not have failed to see in the archives — the rest of the telegram which, in fact, he was holding in his hand. (How otherwise to know at precisely what point he must exercise his manipulative skills by inserting a period immediately after the phrase, "presiding judge of the Kieff District Court of Justice"?)

> But this was going too far. In the Vatican Secret Archives file, handwritten at the bottom of Rothschild's telegram the following note by the Secretary of state, dated November 4, 1913, can be found: "I sincerely regret to have to say that it is quite impossible for me to take initiative of addressing any communication to Kieff. If questioned by a qualified person I am of course ready to confirm statements contained in my letter to you. With highest esteem, Card. Merry del Val." As a result, the Vatican declaration was never officially entered into the Beilis murder trial. But it may have helped anyway. There is evidence that the czar himself read the cardinal's statement, for the czar was watching the trial closely.

9. I am indebted to the staff of the Archivio Segreto Vaticano for all material relating to the Rothschild-del Val correspondence.

That ominous and ambiguously worded statement, deliberately intended to increase the guilt of del Val — "as a result . . . was never officially entered" — is spurious since it is impossible to enter a declaration into a trial that is already over. Moreover, del Val with utmost civility had expressed to Rothschild his willingness to confirm his letter, so that it could be "officially entered," not of course "into the Beilis murder trial," but into whatever record was designated by "a qualified person."[10]

Del Val's willingness will be doubly confirmed in light of that other fact excised by Kertzer about "the Russian Ambassador in Rome." Such an obviously important reference when traced by its footnote — which Kertzer, I repeat, could not avoid seeing on the page from which he had taken all his information regarding the transmission of the Vatican documents — back to its source in Tager's groundbreaking volume provides an even stronger reason why del Val had to find unacceptable what Rothschild was proposing. What Tager disclosed is that the cardinal had already done exactly what the British petitioners had requested — including that he had met with an Italian banking representative, emphasized above in **boldface** in the excerpt from Rothschild's telegram that Kertzer had repressed. Thus there was no point to del Val's once again going through the detailed rigmarole requested by Rothschild, who was spelling out "what is required."

In this treatment of the Kiev trial, it is impossible not to sense a silent dialogue taking place between two texts: the unknown and unread — so Kertzer would have one believe — *The Decay of Czarism* by Alexander B. Tager, and the now too well-known telegram from Rothschild to del Val that Kertzer both unquestionably read and altered. That dialogue becomes vocal when it is apparent that Rothschild at an earlier date had made a similar statement about his Italian banking associate's proposed meeting with del Val. The date of that meeting could only have been some time between the original request to the cardinal for validation of the papal documents (October 7) and del Val's affirmative reply to Rothschild (October 18). Since that is a relatively lengthy period of time, especially considering the urgency expressed in the original request, the possibility that "the Russian Ambassador" impeded the transmission becomes an inevitable conclusion. It was the

---

10. The mystery of why Rothschild made his post-trial request — since the Vatican documents and correspondence had already appeared in the world press — is eclipsed by the larger mystery of how the words "Russian ambassador" are transformed into "Vatican secretary of state." Not all the smoke-blowing about "America's foremost expert on the Vatican's relations with the Jews" can expunge this affront to ethical research or negate the power of ideology to rewrite history.

written proof of such a conclusion that Tager discovered — a discovery that Kertzer could not bring himself to acknowledge, lest his titular thesis, "the popes against the Jews," be compromised. Moreover, in the present instance, he had deliberately manufactured a plot in which the anti-Semitic Vatican co-conspirators refused — "but this was going too far" — to save the life of an innocent man because he was a Jew.

For all the over-touted reliance by Kertzer on various archives, the Russian ambassador actually was exposed by the discovery of a hidden archival document. It was not, however, a document in the Vatican, but one in the even more secretive archives of the Soviet Union. And this document presented its discoverer with a real, not a bogus "once-in-a-lifetime opportunity" to make a genuine contribution to the story of the relations between popes and Jews. As indicated earlier, the oft-mentioned and persistently "overlooked" book, Alexander B. Tager's *The Decay of Czarism: The Beiliss Trial,* remains the seminal and still indispensable study of the case. In its foreword, members of the committee of the Jewish Publication Society of America, which published the book in 1935, described the document and its fate less than a quarter of a century after the trial:

> This document which strikes one with particular horror is a communication from the then Russian Ambassador at the Vatican, Nelidoff, to the then Russian Minister for Foreign Affairs, Sazonoff. As was pointed out above, various Popes had at different times stated that there was no use of human blood in the Jewish ritual. Lord Rothschild had asked the then Cardinal Secretary of state, Merry del Val, to furnish authenticated copies of these statements of the Papacy, which the Cardinal readily agreed to do, but owing to a Russian regulation this document could not be received by the court unless its authenticity was vouched for by a Russian official. And while Nelidoff could not refuse to give the statement of the validity of the documents, he delayed them in order that they might not reach the court until the trial of Beilis was over, thereby becoming useless not only to Beilis but to the Jewish people in their effort to clear themselves of a charge of the use of human blood for ritual purposes. One cannot recall in all history such an entirely conscienceless and shameless act nor such folly as to leave a record of it.

But today's reader can readily recall precisely such an act on the part of Kertzer, even though he was more intent than his Russian predecessor on trying to obliterate the record of it. Tager himself, the discoverer of the letter, included photostats of it in his book and observed: "Nelidoff resorted to a ruse for the purpose of artificially delaying the certification of the signature." This is a quotation that also appears in Maurice Samuel's *Blood Accusation: The Strange History of the Beiliss Case,* generally recognized along with Tager as another definitive study of the trial — though with the emphasis on the day-to-day proceedings in Kiev.

In the document itself, dated November 5, 1913, Nelidoff wrote to the foreign minister that he had undoubtedly read "the long letter [of October 7] that was published in the newspapers from Rothschild to del Val." This was the original request for validation of Innocent IV's statement and Ganganelli's report which, along with copies of the latter, had been released by Rothschild to the press. Nelidoff continued:

> In his very short reply, Cardinal Merry del Val limited himself to the cer-tification of the identity of the copies enclosed in the letter with the origi-nals kept at the Vatican, and to the expression of the hope that his declara-tion "will serve the purpose aimed at by Lord Rothschild." A local banker, a Jew, brought to our Imperial Mission a copy of the Cardinal's reply [to Rothschild] with the request that I certify the authenticity of the un-doubtedly genuine signature of the Cardinal Secretary of state on the copy. I agreed to fulfill this request provided the word "duplicata" was placed on the paper presented to me. When this was done, the copy had to be mailed to Kiev, but it could no longer have any significance, for it would not reach Kiev until after the verdict had been announced in the Beilis case.

The details here and those in the post-trial telegram of Rothschild to del Val (the sentences omitted by Kertzer about the "representative of the Banca Commerciale Italiana" requesting an audience with the cardinal) are so sim-ilar that it is impossible to dismiss this portion of Nelidoff's letter as a fabri-cation. Similarly, the meeting between del Val and Rothschild's Roman banking emissary, as well as the meeting of that emissary and Nelidoff, are undeniable. The latter's meeting with del Val seems unlikely, since it would serve no purpose — the cardinal's signature being "undoubtedly genuine" — except perhaps to elevate Nelidoff's stature in the eyes of his masters in St. Petersburg.[11]

11. Confirming the unlikeliness of a meeting is Nelidoff's detailed "conversation" with the cardinal about the Ganganelli report as a secret document that mysteriously had come to

The intentional deletion of the reference to the Russian ambassador in Kertzer's account raises several issues. The first and most obvious is that if he even acknowledges the existence of the Nelidoff statement, he undermines his foundational thesis that del Val and — it now goes without saying — his co-conspirator, the pope, motivated by their ingrained anti-Semitism, failed to exonerate an unjustly accused Jew. Apart from the fact that Kertzer saw the reference to "the Russian ambassador" and to Tager's book in Szajkowski's article, further proof that Nelidoff was known to Kertzer is the passage he excised from Rothschild's telegram to del Val about the Roman banking agent meeting with the cardinal, instructing him in procedures, and so on. All of the latter followed very closely Nelidoff's own description, so its omission is also prima facie evidence that vindicates del Val and the pope — a notion quite unbearable to the author of a book titled *The Popes Against the Jews.*

What then tends to evoke Joseph Welch on Joseph McCarthy, "have you no sense of decency?" is that the original sentence in Szajkowski about "the Russian Ambassador in Rome" doing everything possible to have Beilis found guilty is replaced by the reference to "Merry del Val himself" working toward that end. There is no issue here regarding dubious testimony; the issue has to do with *manufactured* testimony by Kertzer. In addition to Maurice Samuel's book, there is *The Beilis Transcripts: The Anti-Semitic Trial that Shook the World,* by Ezekiel Leikin (1993); here one may read: "To bolster the prosecution's case at the trial, and to please his superiors, ambassador Nelidoff purposely delayed authenticating the cardinal's signature until the Beilis case was over. In a letter to his superior . . . Nelidoff bragged about his clever ruse." This book is one of the titles that buttresses Kertzer's quite impressive bibliography, and which he refers to in an endnote, guiding his readers to more supporting information: "for details on the Beilis case, see

---

the attention of a Jew in England. According to Nelidoff, del Val — who as noted earlier was by birth and office the Vatican's authority on matters English — speculated on all this in terms of the report perhaps having been stolen from the Vatican, taken to Dublin, and then on to London where it "became known to Rothschild," who would have presumably been otherwise ignorant of it — though he could have read all of its relevant history in the *Jewish Encyclopedia* (under the entries "Blood Accusation" and "Clement XIV" cited above), which had been published to considerable acclaim nearly a decade earlier. To further impress the foreign minister with his good relations with the Vatican, Nelidoff concluded his letter with a dutiful paragraph testifying to its author's access to other top-level officials. What Tager himself emphasized was the following: "Nelidoff also expressed his dissatisfaction with Cardinal Merry del Val's readiness to fulfill the request of Lord Rothschild, as it proved *'the willingness of the Curia when opportunity arises, to please even the Jews'*" (italics original).

. . . Leikin 1993." The presumption of even a layperson when reading this would be that Leikin's book had been consulted by Kertzer, although at this point it is certainly not inconceivable that he may merely have mentioned it to inflate his list of sources, and thus inflate his credentials.

Lastly — and by way of making clear that we are not talking about some obscure items like those "dug up" by Miccoli in various Vatican archives — Léon Poliakov in *Suicidal Europe 1870-1933* also discusses the Beilis trial but concentrates, as a literary historian, on the tricked-up testimony of the Catholic priest, Pranaitis. Nevertheless, Poliakov notes that "The Russian ambassador in Rome distinguished himself by sabotaging the dispatch of copies of pertinent bulls in which past popes condemned the legend of ritual murder." This book is also cited in Kertzer's aforementioned impressive bibliography: *Storia dell'antisemitismo, L'Europa suicida, 1870-1933*. It is also noteworthy that Poliakov began his treatment by observing that his account of the trial was based on the two authors whose works Kertzer somehow managed to avoid: Alexander Tager and Maurice Samuel. Kertzer's seeming obliviousness to all those references can only be rationalized by what moral theologians call *ignorantia affectata,* a state in which a person intent on deception seeks to remain willfully unaware of the truth. What it is called among "historians" must be left to practitioners of that discipline.[12]

---

12. Garry Wills, who showed himself an authority on *ignorantia affectata* in *Papal Sin,* wrote in his *New York Times* review of *The Popes Against the Jews* (September 23, 2001), "Pius X's Secretary of State would not deny the myth, or send information about false uses of it directly to the presiding judge." No one had asked the secretary of state to do either of those things. In *Why I Am a Catholic* (2002), Wills is even more creative when he comes up with matters totally unrelated to the Beilis trial of 1913 — though with a vague connection to the Holy Office decree regarding ritual murder thirteen years earlier. "Cardinal Merry del Val, Pius's Secretary of State, responded that the instances cited had dealt only with the specific guilt of individuals not with the general charge that Jews commit ritual murder." Replace Merry del Val and Pius with "the Holy Office in 1900," and this claim would be only half wrong. The issue of "individuals" vis-à-vis "the general charge" has nothing to do with anything connected to the trial. Wills then continued to invent the irrelevant: "When Norfolk tried, at the very least, to show that individuals had been cleared by Rome, the court in Kiev said it could not accept any such assurance unless it came from Rome itself. Merry del Val would not send such an assurance, informing Norfolk that Rome could not intervene in any other government's procedures." After having transmitted Rothschild's original request of October 7 to Rome, "Norfolk" (as professional historians refer to him) does nothing, says nothing, and has nothing more to do with anything regarding the trial.

Referring to the Beilis trial, Michael R. Marrus in *The New Leader* (September 2001) says that Pius X "remarkably equivocated and lent comfort to the idea of ritual murder." That falsehood takes care of the pope. Turning to del Val, Marrus notes that "the Vatican

But beyond that basic issue, one will also have to conclude that the last sentence in Kertzer's clinching "this-was-going-too-far" paragraph about the czar being "influenced" or the document "helping" because "the czar was following the trial closely" is both a bad guess and a non sequitur. I pointed out earlier the vengeful anti-Semitic motive of the czar in approving the trial in the first place. Concerning the blood libel as such, even more heinous is the fact that, according to Poliakov, the minister of justice with the czar's approval had the presiding judge at the Beilis trial invoke an obsolete regulation whereby there should be two separate issues before the jury: in effect, *first,* whether a ritual murder had been committed, and if so, *second,* whether Beilis committed it. As to the latter, the jury was divided equally and so Beilis was exonerated. As to the former, the verdict was "yes," because of "total loss of blood" — with the blood element being so emphasized — "five glasses," "47 wounds" — that the czarist minister of justice boasted in an interview that the details in the official description of the case left "no doubt about the ritual character of the murder."

So it was the czarists not the papists who safeguarded the blood libel. Maurice Samuel cites Lucien Wolf: "the verdict was engineered by the authorities with the idea of throwing dust in the eyes of foreigners [by acquitting Beilis] while at the same time preserving the Blood Accusation and even giving it a measure of countenance." As repeatedly noted, del Val's letter validating the two earlier papal interventions regarding ritual murder had no impact on the trial. But by reason of the extraordinary publicity given to all the documents — the Rothschild-del Val correspondence, the earlier papal statements and their validation by Rome — a widespread sense of revulsion was generated that did have an impact on the rejection of the blood libel. And this was, in fact, the last public trial for ritual murder in Europe.[13]

---

grudgingly conceded that some earlier popes may have opposed ritual murder in the distant past." Even by reading only Kertzer, that statement is also false.

Marvin Parry and Frederick M. Schweitzer in *Anti-Semitism: Myth and Hate from Antiquity to the Present* (2002) also confuse the Holy Office decree of 1900 with the trial of 1913 — and end up being wrong about both of them: "Similar inaction on the part of the Vatican prevailed at the time of the Beilis trial."

13. The researcher William Doino Jr. notes in *The Pius War* (2004) that Cecil Roth, the Jewish historian of ritual murder, in a private audience with Pius XI had presented to the pope a copy of his (Roth's) recently published (1935) and newly edited translation of the Ganganelli report. After the pope's death, Roth wrote in *The Jewish Chronicle*: "by receiving in this formal fashion the new edition of this document, the pope, in effect, associated himself with the repudiation of the foul libel. . . . And he insisted, during the few moments of

Kertzer's personal guesswork about the czar following the trial closely led to this singularly odd observation:

> When the jury — despite widespread local belief in the Jew's guilt — read its verdict of not guilty, many observers — and not only those committed to the ritual murder charge — suspected that the jurors had been pressured. High government officials, it was thought, sought to spare the Russian government the unfavorable international publicity that a guilty verdict would have brought.

While it is true that the czar was concerned with the trial, had Léon Poliakov's *L'Europa suicida* actually been consulted by Kertzer, his interpretation of that concern might have been less benign. Poliakov, who devoted several pages to the trial, quotes approvingly, "the American ambassador, George Kennan," who observed that "the attitude of the government was influenced in part by the hatred that [Czar] Nicholas bore the Jews, in part by political considerations."[14] It is not surprising that for Kertzer when it comes to a choice between the morality of Pius X and of Nicholas II, of the "holy father" and the "little father," the scales will tip in favor of the latter. This is true, notwithstanding the fact, which Poliakov also points out, that "it was in the field of ritual murder that the regime waged its last stubborn battle against the Jews." Regarding the Beilis case, Poliakov also notes that "as a show trial it bears comparison with the great Moscow trials, although it goes without saying that the staging of the czar was hardly so elaborate as that of the Stalin regime."[15]

---

conversation, how the protection of the Jews had not been confined to a single pope but had been the invariable policy of the papacy."

Possibly even more significant, particularly in the aftermath of the creation of Yad Vashem, is the language in which Roth concluded his article: language that has now become very familiar, but which was much debated at that time among the rabbis as to whom it could be justly applied. Roth wrote of Pius, "May he rest in peace, with all the other righteous ones of the nations of the world." What Kertzer writes about Pius XI will be seen in chapters 7 and 8.

14. This is the uncle of George F. Kennan, the originator of the doctrine of containment of the Soviets. The elder Kennan, who was not an ambassador, had written *Siberia and the Exile System*, two volumes on what would later be called "the gulag archipelago." His article was titled "The Ritual Murder Case in Kiev," *Outlook*, November 8, 1913.

15. Those interested in a less ideologically driven presentation of the Kiev trial than the one invented by Kertzer can read Bernard Malamud's novel based on the Beilis case, *The Fixer*, or watch the John Frankenheimer film with the same title. The most interesting fic-

Following his defense of Russia's "high government officials," Kertzer without any transition hastens to forestall the possibility of high Vatican officials being extended a like reprieve. Having no sense that his deceptions above would ever be disclosed, he attacks another historian, for merely citing an undeniably genuine statement on the trial by Pius X.

> Andrew Canepa, in support of *this interpretation,* cites a letter that the Pope himself sent to his old friend Romanin Jacur, three weeks after Merry del Val sent his famous [*sic*] telegram to Lord Rothschild. In referring to the ongoing trial in Kiev, the Pope assured his friend that "the Holy See will study every means to prevent the fatal consequences of the infamous fanaticism of those populations," and he added, "I pray that the trial end without harm to the poor Jews."[16]

Since there is no way to deny the authenticity of the quotations, Kertzer attempts to debunk them, even though there is nothing in Andrew Canepa's statement that suggests he is commemorating "radical breaks" or announcing "historic turning points." Immediately following the quotation about "the poor Jews," and without bothering about its context or content, Kertzer asks: "But if we take a step back, what exactly does the Beilis case show?" This is a question to which "we" shall return at the end of this discussion, but it will not surprise that the step back will lead to the real story, which is to be found not in any of the preceding history but in the *fons et origo* of papal dissimulation, "the Vatican-linked press."

However, content and context cannot be so facilely dismissed. The purpose of Pius X's writing to Jacur was primarily to congratulate a friend on his recent successful campaign for the Italian senate: "a peaceful and triumphant reelection." It was in that context that the "ongoing trial in Kiev" came up. But Jacur was in fact "an old friend," since the relationship went

---

tional treatment of the subject is *The Bloody Hoax* by Sholem Aleichem (E.T., 1991). In a prince-and-the-pauper scenario, two friends, one Jewish and the other Christian, decide to exchange places — for reasons that the plot makes credible — and the Christian-turned-Jew is accused of ritual murder, forcing him to experience the consequences of the libel his own co-religionists had perpetrated over the centuries.

16. The phrase "this interpretation," which I have italicized, refers to Kertzer's prior assertion: "For those who view Pius X as making a radical break with the Vatican's past attitudes toward the Jews, the Beilis case marked a historic turning point. After decades of papally approved campaigns smearing the Jews with the brush of ritual murder, a pope had stood up and defended them."

back several decades, and had been forged in 1893, when Jacur intervened with a refractory Italian government that was intentionally refusing to give official permission for the future pope to be installed as patriarch of Venice. This show of pettiness on the part of the government was one of the many acts that led the popes to contemplate fleeing Rome, and that were not described under the revelatory rubric, *The Popes' Secret Plot to Capture Rome from the New Italian State.* The latter is the subtitle to the sequel to *The Popes Against the Jews,* a book that Kertzer titled *Prisoner of the Vatican.* (It did not, fortunately or unfortunately for the author or the reader, reap glowing reviews.)

It turns out that the hastily discounted Canepa, to whom Kertzer attributed the notion of a radical break, modestly called his study "a reassessment," and briefly summarized its contents on the first page.[17] The pope "maintained warm personal relations with individual Jews . . . held a positive view of the Jewish character, defended the Jewish people against defamation . . . and was instrumental in halting a twenty-year old anti-Semitic campaign." Where the only people with whom one can sympathize in Kertzer's tale are, quite understandably, maligned Jews, his portrait of all modern popes is so slanted toward demonization that Canepa's study, predating *The Popes Against the Jews* by a decade, at least provides the possibility that maybe one or two of them were occasionally touched by a vaguely humane sentiment. There are also several friends, incidents, and quotations that suggest this particular pope was incapable of being anti-Semitic, and that should be briefly summarized from Canepa's "reassessment," if only as a counterweight to the preponderant opinion expressed by the — now only faintly glimmering — reviewers of Kertzer's book.

At Pius's death, *La Stampa* (a newspaper not "Vatican-linked") reported that when Leo XIII had asked then Bishop Sarto who were the best Christians in the diocese of Mantua, the bishop replied, "To tell the truth, as far as charity is concerned, the best Christians are the Jews." After his election, Pius asked a surprised Jewish member of a delegation from Mantua to bring back the papal blessing to his former diocese: "Have no fear: the packaging is bad but the contents are good" — meaning, it comes from your old bishop, but it is a pope's blessing. At his death, the leading Jewish publication in Italy, *Il Vesillo israelitico* (also not linked to the Vatican), editorialized that "Pius X was the only European leader who had denounced the pogroms in the Russian empire." (Kertzer cites the flagship Jewish journal in this chapter, but

17. "Pius X and the Jews: A Reassessment," *Church History* (September 1992).

apparently did not come across this editorial.) In the canonization proceedings for Pius X, it was his regard for Jews that was singled out as among his saintly traits, although it was his support of Benigni's spy ring — delating a cardinal whom John XXIII would beatify — that was brought up as among his unsaintly ones.

As to Pius X's expression of sympathy for the Jews of Russia, it is so clearly opposed to Kertzer's elaborately contrived thesis that immediately following the quotation from the pope's letter to Leone Romanin Jacur, all the items in Kertzer's revisionist formula are again mixed. Instead of acknowledging the import of Pius X's statement that he was praying that no harm would come to Jews and that the Holy See was seeking to prevent fanaticism toward them, Kertzer simply ignored the words, and proceeded to incorporate the alleged lessons of the Kiev trial into his overarching narrative.

"But if we step back [from Pius X's statement], what exactly does the Beilis case show?" Two possible answers are that the Beilis case shows, first (as we have seen in the above exposition) how biased historians succumb to deceit; and second (as we are about to see) how history books are cooked. The recipe for the latter is familiar: 1, rephrasing the issue; 2, argument *ex silentio;* 3, exposition of the "real" views of the pope; and 4, citations from publications in the worldwide network of the Vatican-linked press where those views are enshrined.

> [No. 1] First of all, the statement released by the Vatican could hardly have been more limited and circumspect. It simply acknowledged the authenticity of two Church texts whose authenticity was never in any serious doubt. [No. 2] Neither the pope nor his secretary of state took advantage of the request to make a general statement repudiating all ritual murder charges against the Jews. [No. 3] More significantly, by not taking this step, the pope allowed the Catholic press . . . communicating the pope's true sentiments, to continue to tar the Jews with the ritual murder charge. [No. 4] *L'Unità cattolica,* in Florence, known for reflecting papal perspective . . . *L'Univers* . . . the French paper closest to the Vatican . . . etcetera.

Kertzer, who doesn't recall his earlier comment that "newspapers closest to the Pope were much less vocal on the Jewish question during Pius X's papacy," and who couldn't find space to quote a half-page homily by Pius IX, now in his triumphant amplitude devotes the next four pages, which conclude this chapter, to quotations from the network journals.

Those pages are preceded by Kertzer's uninterrupted last word — in fact, a full paragraph — on the proper way to understand all of the preceding discussion. He also includes a personal admonition to the reader as to what lessons from all this are to be brought to mind in the perusal process.[18]

> By far the most important documents we have for interpreting the Vatican's position on the Beilis case are the two long articles by Father Paolo Silva that *Civiltà cattolica* devoted to the question. Published in the spring of 1914, in the last months of Pius X's reign, they were read by the Catholic world as putting an end to the polemics in the European press about the Vatican's view of Jewish ritual murder. Recall that the text of the *Civiltà cattolica* articles was sent in advance to the secretary of state for his review. That the journal could have published them without Merry del Val's approval is almost inconceivable.

That is the first paragraph, which is followed by seven more from the Jesuit magazine "interpreting the Vatican's position on the Beilis case."

There is no need to comment further on the above; nor any need to elaborate further on Kertzer's own conspiracy with himself whereby he became his own secret sharer in the omissions, the doctorings, and the truncations exemplified throughout this chapter. Instead, two brief remarks by outside observers are worth considering. Richard Bernstein in his *New York Times* review of *The Popes Against the Jews* noted that "Kertzer was given privileged access to the Vatican archives." This information was imparted to the reviewer by the author. The reviewer, in turn, emulating the author, then proceeded to embellish it.[19] On the other hand, there is no embellishment of the following remark by Archbishop Sergio Pagano, the prefect of the Archivio Segreto Vaticano, who described (www.kattoliko.it) the author of a "book on the relation of the popes and the Jews" who was researching the

---

18. Bringing them to mind is facilitated by the fact that they all entail formularies invoked throughout the book regarding *Civiltà cattolica,* its status as voice of the pope, its supervision by the highest officials, its worldwide influence, and so forth.

19. The reviewer was not entirely at fault, since the hyperbole that distinguishes Kertzer's historical narrative also appears in his presentation of the book. The jacket description, invariably vetted if not written by the author, announces that "John Paul II himself called for a clear-eyed historical investigation into any possible link between the Church and the Holocaust. An important sign of his commitment was the recent decision to allow the distinguished historian, David I. Kertzer, to be one of the first scholars given access to long-sealed Vatican archives."

trial in Kiev, and who cited a document with accusations against Pius X. "In the same folder that he was consulting, there were also various letters of thanks from Jewish personages to Pope Sarto that were systematically ignored, and of which there is not a trace in the book. *È questa la maniera di fare storia?*" Many people after reading the above treatment of the trial in Kiev would probably agree that this is not the way to write history. But even more emphatically they would probably say that ignoring letters of gratitude to a pope is far less grievous an assault on historical scholarship and humanistic values than are the stratagems and ruses in "Ritual Murder and the Popes in the Twentieth Century." Those kinds of activities, which have been illustrated and critiqued in this chapter, will be accelerated and exacerbated in the following chapter on Pius XI who, according to Kertzer, indulged priests who believed that "if the world is to be rid of the Jewish scourge, it will be necessary to exterminate them, down to the last one."

CHAPTER 7

Popes, Poles, and Pogroms

A reader who had followed closely the material in the previous chapter might well have thought that Kertzer's present chapter on "A Future Pope in Poland" augured on the part of the author a shift not only in chronology but also in perspective. But such a reader will quickly learn that this chapter is not going to honor Lorenzo Ganganelli, the papal emissary to Poland who wrote the document denouncing ritual murder that was central to the Beilis trial, and who later became Pope Clement XIV.

However, the invocation of that document does present the opportunity for another observation on the methodology of *The Popes Against the Jews* — an observation that will open up onto a more important conclusion regarding Kertzer's entire project. There is enough good-bad, virtuous-vicious, and boon-bane material relative to the popes and the Jews in the authentic records of history that the vicious distortions embodied in the previous chapter and embraced by Kertzer's ideological supporters begin to look more and more like exercises in rhetorical overkill. For a final example of such mixed messages, the fate of Ganganelli's document, *Non solis accusatoribus credendum,* provides an apposite illustration. On the "boon" side of the ledger is the fact that the document that effectively refuted the claim of ritual murder over the preceding centuries was approved and sanctioned in 1758 by the then reigning pope, Benedict XIV. On the bane side is the fact that some years earlier, he himself had penned an encyclical on the Jews of Poland, *A Quo Primum,* which comprehensively and chillingly detailed all the evils Jews allegedly inflicted on Catholics. One brief conclusion from this juxtaposition of official church documents is that when institutional survival preoccupies church leaders, as it did Benedict, it often eclipses Gospel teachings such as those set forth in the Sermon on the Mount and the Magnificat — teachings that clearly animated Ganganelli. Nor is there any indication that, apart from the Beilis trial, Ganganelli's report to Rome had much impact on the relationship of Polish Catholics to the Jewish community. In fact, Benedict XIV's anti-Jewish polemic, like those of his predecessors, can be said to have prepared the way for racist anti-Semitism, notwithstanding the fact that its author approved the Ganganelli report.

Again, on the boon side, Ganganelli himself, in 1769, succeeded Benedict as pope, taking the name Clement XIV, and according to the *Jewish Encyclopedia* — which also surfaced in the previous chapter — his election "was hailed with particular joy by the Jews."

> [They] trusted that the man who, as councilor of the Holy Office, declared them, in a memorandum issued March 21, 1758, innocent of the slanderous blood accusation, would be no less just and humane toward them on the throne of Catholicism. In this they were not deceived. Two months after his accession Clement XIV. withdrew the Roman Jews from the jurisdiction of the Inquisition and placed them under that of the "Vicariato di Roma."

Clement introduced so many reforms into the Roman ghetto that it took nearly a century for them to be emulated by another pope, Pius IX. Unfortunately, as noted in chapter 4, they were as short-lived as Pio Nono's reign was long.[1] The point of this codicil is twofold: the first element, as mentioned above, is that there is so much genuine history that can be introduced into an assessment of the Vatican's role in the rise of modern anti-Semitism that it ought to (but will inevitably not) make the invention of any more fabrications like those relative to the trial in czarist Russia a fool's errand. The second is that for an institution as ancient and as geographically widespread as the papacy, the pursuit of some unitary unchanging dogmatic teaching — other than that of the most fundamental of creeds, that of "the Apostles" — is also to engage in a fool's errand.

Such an errand was signaled by the assumption that Pius X must have been lying when he said he was praying that the Beilis trial "end without harm to the poor Jews." The errand now nears its goal when "a future pope

---

1. Clement XIV, unfortunately, was also the pope who was forced into suppressing the Society of Jesus and thus aroused the fury of all its members, most vocally those of *Civiltà cattolica,* where he was derided not only as a Jesuit-hater but also as a forerunner of another imaginary heresy, not that of Modernism, but of its elder cousin, "Americanism." See John Louis Ciani, *Across a Wide Ocean: Salvatore Maria Brandi, SJ, and the "Civiltà Cattolica"* (loc. cit.).

in Poland" is described as more anti-Semitic than any of his predecessors. "Indeed," this future pope is at the center of the Holocaust itself, because Kertzer is going to directly link him to the 1943 roundup of Rome's Jews, a tragedy that occurred several years after the pope's death. Having thus placed Achille Ratti in the antechamber to the Holocaust, it is no great intellectual or moral leap for Kertzer to also implicate him in "the death of the overwhelming majority of Poland's three million Jews" — a tragedy that was consummated even more years after his death. How Kertzer makes that leap is by having Ratti foster Polish "exterminators" of Jewry, the fourth of the myths mentioned at the beginning of this exploration of the unholy war waged by the popes against the Jews.

Since Pius XI is fated for demonization, it is important — perhaps if only to avoid the appearance of authorial obsessiveness — that Benedict XV who preceded him as pope be exalted as remarkably noble-minded. In fact, Benedict was in many ways exactly that, working strenuously for peace, putting an end to the anti-Modernist purge, and reversing his predecessor's opposition to Zionist plans in Palestine. The last chapter on Pius X began with Kertzer's abrupt introduction into the narrative of Theodore Herzl, who asked Pius X "if he would support the Zionist project," and was told by the pope, "We won't be able to stop the Jews from going to Jerusalem, but we could never favor it."

That a new outlook animated the Vatican was evident when in 1915, a year after his election, Benedict had an interview with a Jewish journalist, Herman Bernstein, and was asked a similar question. To it the pope replied: "I am in sympathy with the Jewish national aspirations in Palestine. We want liberty and justice, just as the Jews want liberty and justice everywhere."[2] That statement by itself was significant, but there was another made by the new secretary of state, Cardinal Gasparri, that is equally important, as well as more relevant to the events in the previous chapter. In the course of an ordinary conversation between the two men, the new papal secretary of state mentioned to Bernstein:

> Whenever an appeal came to the Vatican from the Jews, especially in recent years, the Popes never failed to speak in their defense. You doubtless recall the statement of the Holy See in the outrageous Beilis affair, in which the Vatican denounced the ritual murder accusation against the Jews.

2. Herman Bernstein, *Celebrities of Our Time: Interviews* (1924).

An even more significant overture to the Jews of Europe and America occurred half a year later on February 9, 1916, when Cardinal Gasparri responded to a request from the American Jewish Committee asking that the pope come to the defense of the Jews in war-torn Poland. This request was made in the context of lengthy and ongoing negotiations — described at length by Kertzer — among the Allied Powers and the Vatican concerning the latter's possible participation in the postwar peace conference already being planned. In the event, the Vatican was excluded, but the secretary of state made another important statement, "that the pope considers all men as brothers and teaches them to love one another. This law must be observed and respected among individuals and nations and must be respected regardless of divergences of religious belief particularly as it relates to the children of Israel."[3] Thus did the conspiring against Jews by the pope and his secretary of state come into the "limelight."

The last phrase regarding the children of Israel touched a chord, and Herman Bernstein, by then the editor of *The American Hebrew* in New York City, described the entire statement in enthusiastic terms. "Among all the Papal Bulls ever issued with regard to Jews throughout the history of the Vatican there is no statement that equals this direct, unmistakable plea for equality for the Jews and against prejudice upon religious grounds." Understandably, some of those views underwent change during the war, so that by its end, the final position of the pontiff was described as anti-Zionist rather than anti-Semitic.[4] It is not known how Herman Bernstein responded to this information, but from a present-day vantage point, it would seem fairly obvious that the pope's views represented a welcome modulation of those of his predecessors.

That, however, was not the opinion of many of Benedict's own subjects who accused him of violating his public promise to maintain absolute neutrality — a promise that would weigh heavily on a successor during what would later become known as World War II. Benedict's critics were from both sides of the divide between the Allies and the Central Powers, and as the war continued both groups of partisan malcontents vented their anger, referring to the pope as "Maledetto XV," the "Boche Pope," or the *"Franzosenpapst."*[5] Alfred Loisy, like many Catholics and ex-Catholics of the era, let his patriotism trump his latent religiosity, and wrote to the comparably

---

3. Dimitri Cavalli, "Who Was Benedict XV?" *Catholic Insight,* July 1, 2006.

4. John F. Pollard, *Benedict XV: The Unknown Pope and the Pursuit of Peace* (2005).

5. J. Derek Holmes, *The Papacy in the Modern World: 1914-1978* (1981).

warmongering, though manifestly pious, Baron von Hügel, a few months after the war had begun: "what is very odd about this situation is that a political pope like Benedict XV should be even more of a failure than a fanatical pope like Pius X," the latter having actually excommunicated Loisy. Léon Bloy, when he realized the pope would not take sides, referred to his "stupefying mediocrity," and said the pope "deceives infallibly." When the war ended, von Hügel called for the abdication of the kaiser *and* the pope.[6]

Such intermural religious diversions do not deter David I. Kertzer. Regrettably for his diminishing credibility, more absolutist rhetoric leads his enthusiastic portrayal of this pope to be couched in self-contradictory terms. "Following Benedict XV's papacy, no pope could return to the intransigence of his predecessors." "By appointing the future Pius XI Apostolic Visitor to Poland, Benedict made what was arguably the most important single decision of his papacy." If Ratti had not been sent to Poland, "the whole twentieth-century history of the Church might have been different." That statement means that Benedict's appointment was responsible for Pius XI becoming penultimate initiator of the Holocaust — the ultimate being the unmentionable Pius XII. As to the observation that after Benedict, "no pope could return to the intransigence of his predecessors," Kertzer is victim of his own penchant for exaggeration, since regarding anti-Semitism these two Piuses not only returned to it, but by Kertzer's lights, pushed it to obscene extremes.[7] Thus, "It is because of who Achille Ratti would soon become that his experience in Poland takes on such enormous importance relating to the rise of fascism and Nazism." As an auxiliary exercise in this mode of historiography, there is also more mind reading on the part of the author. Without

---

6. Carlo Falconi, *The Popes of the Twentieth Century* (1967). See also Darrel Jodock, ed., *Catholicism Contending with Modernity* (2002)

7. Perhaps a mounting wave of bewilderment was overtaking the author as the end of his book appeared to be in sight. Whatever the cause, the muddling becomes extreme. The reader learns that "Benedict XV [was] more favorably disposed to the Jews than his predecessors," and that "Benedict did have the courage to try to chart a new course for papal relations with the Jews." But then one is also told that during his reign "In France, the main champion of the Protocols of the Elders of Zion [was] E. Jouin, 'Prelate of His Holiness,' for Pope Benedict had honored Jouin"; and later "Pope Benedict XV sent Jouin a special brief of recognition." (As noted previously, such recognition usually had to do with vocal support of doctrinal orthodoxy or, more likely, of papal control of Rome.) But undeniably something was putting a strain on the author's powers of discernment, as he also observed that "with the defeat of the *Axis* powers, the future of the Polish territories" remained an issue at the Paris Peace Conference of January 1919. This is the kind of rhetorical tic that is so blatant it may be rightly characterized as "douleureux."

any reference — other than implicitly to his own dramaturgical instincts — readers are told that "Achille Ratti was shocked by the news that the Pope had chosen him for the delicate diplomatic mission to Warsaw."

The overall argument parallels that of the previous chapter on the blood libel, which by any reading could not but conclude that the papacy — at least as distinguished from the Holy Office — had generally responded fairly to the "signs of the time." Not even the maneuver of obscuring that conclusion by five pages of anti-Semitic fulminations from "the press known for enjoying close relations with the pope" proved persuasive. Similarly, the argument undergirding the chapter on Achille Ratti's mission to Poland contains a mass of excerpts from various documents and reports on anti-Semitism, but little of significance that shows a connection between the documents and the allegedly momentous significance of Ratti's visit. Hence the reader is again expected to take as a truth to be memorized, but not investigated, the author's repetitions about "the enormous importance" of the Polish period, which also provides "precious insights," and, two pages later, "priceless insights," and, at the end of the chapter, "a precious resource" on the future pope.

The first mention of Ratti's actual presence in Poland is preceded by a treatment of Polish anti-Semitism in the postwar world during the Soviet-Polish conflict. "When, the following year [1920], the Polish army retreated before an advancing Red Army, both the Polish military and the Church spread the notion that bolshevism was the work of the Jews, an instrument employed in their struggle for world conquest."

> Typical was the letter that the bishops of Poland sent in 1920 to their fellow bishops outside the country. "The real goal of bolshevism is the conquest of the whole world. The race that directs it came to dominate it through their gold and their banks. Today the ancestral imperial impulse that flows through its veins drives it to crush the people under the yoke of its domination." Every Pole knew just which race the Polish bishops were referring to. A new round of pogroms followed.

Although no one questions that there were disproportionately large numbers of Jewish Communists, especially in the upper echelons of the party, Kertzer describes "the Jews' link to the Bolsheviks [as] a theme that ran throughout the Polish anti-Semitic literature of the period."[8] This state-

---

8. In fact, it ran through all the literature of the period, even in countries that might at worst be regarded as only latently anti-Semitic. In *Suicidal Europe* (loc. cit.) Léon Poliakov

ment occurs in the context of almost a page given over to a report commissioned by Ratti "on the relations between the Catholics and Jews of Poland," and written in French by an unidentified man, "most likely a Polish Catholic aristocrat." Kertzer continues as follows in this passage, which is reproduced exactly from the book — indiscriminate punctuation marks, the initial and final quotation marks, bracketed material, and all:

"The Jews of Poland," he informed Monsignor Ratti, "are in contrast with those who live elsewhere in the civilized world, an unproductive element. It is a race of shopkeepers par excellence," he wrote, although he added: "the great majority of the Jewish population is sunk in the depths of poverty." Other than a relatively small number of artisans, he reported, the Jewish race "consists of small merchants, dealers, and usurers — or to be more precise all three simultaneously — who live by exploiting the Christian population." During the recent German occupation, the fact that "the jargon that the Jews speak in Poland [i.e., Yiddish] is but a German dialect" allowed the Jews to profit, and, he argued, the Germans' espionage "was carried out exclusively by the Jews." He attributed the recent pogrom in Lvov, Galicia, to popular anger with the Jews' link to the Bolsheviks, a theme that ran through the Polish anti-Semitic literature of the period. "We must call attention to the Jew's role in the Bolshevik movement. We do not want to claim that every Jew is, ipso facto, a Bolshevik. Far from it. Yet we cannot deny the preponderant role that the Jews play in this movement, both among the Polish communists and among the Russians where — with the exception of Lenin — all the Bolshevik leaders are either Polish Jews or Lithuanian Jews."[9]

In an endnote that relates specifically to what is paraphrased as "the Jews' link to the Bolsheviks" and described by Kertzer as a "theme that ran through the Polish anti-Semitic literature," he acknowledged with a linguistic shift that, "In fact, *a very visible part of the early* Bolshevik leadership in Russia was of Jewish origin"; then, diverting attention from that ambiguous admission, he continued with this neither-here-nor-there observation, "de-

---

cites a series of articles in the *Times* of London that ran for more than a month in November-December 1919, titled "The Jews and Bolshevism."

9. I am citing this text in detail because it can be regarded as one of those precious resources that make Ratti's visit to Poland of such enormous importance. Given the place and the time and the author, the data appearing here do not seem calculated to infect the future pope with anti-Semitism.

rived from the *small minority* of Russian Jews who had left traditional community life and entered national society" (italics supplied). This apologetic curiosity is followed by a quotation from Albert S. Lindemann's *Esau's Tears: Modern Anti-Semitism and the Rise of the Jews* (1997) that "up to half of the top Bolshevik leadership in the years immediately following the war" was of Jewish origin. But that appears to be what the bishops were talking about. They had no interest in early Bolshevik leadership; the statement was made in 1920, when Ratti had been in residence in Warsaw for two years, and when the city was saved by "the miracle of the Vistula" from falling to the Soviet "workers army" organized by Lev Davidovitch Bronstein (i.e., Leon Trotsky) who, historians note, happened to be Jewish.

This is Kertzer's account of the events preceding the episcopal letter of 1920 — an account that is rendered well before Ratti is described as having arrived in Poland:

> The situation, from the Jews' viewpoint, quickly deteriorated, as war erupted that same year [1919] between Poland and the newly created Soviet Union. Polish armies surged deep into Russian territory, and along the way organized pogroms against the Jews. When, the following year, the Polish army retreated before an advancing Red Army, both the Polish military and the Church spread the notion that bolshevism was the work of the Jews, an instrument to be employed in their world conquest.

There is no mention that the advancing Russians also perpetrated their share of pogroms,[10] and that European leaders as far west as Lloyd George in England were terrified at the prospect of "three hundred million people organized into a vast Red Army," until it was driven back from Warsaw in a victory compared at the time to that at Vienna three centuries earlier ("the miracle of the Danube"), when the Poles saved Europe from the advancing Turks. Achille Ratti, who remained in the capital during the Soviet invasion, would later commission for the papal chapel frescoes depicting scenes of the Warsaw victory.

The author, having thus even-handedly set the stage, is about to jumble more chronology — as he had also in the preceding chapter — in a passage

---

10. Herman Bernstein in his audience with Benedict XV said: "I also called his attention to the fact that under the influence of the Russian autocracy, which always sought to incite one portion of the population against another, the Poles conducted an intense anti-Jewish campaign."

certainly foreshadowed by the tic about "the defeat of the Axis powers" in World War I. "It was into this postwar background that the Vatican librarian stepped in June 1918," although this "postwar" period occurred nearly half a year before the war ended and two years before the Red Army invasion. How "the Vatican librarian" managed to step into a background made up of the future events described above also goes unexplained. Nor is it now necessary to labor the fact that during all those events (Poles surging, retreating, Reds advancing, bishops writing, etc.) Ratti was in residence in beleaguered Warsaw, where he had insisted on remaining while most other diplomats fled during the Soviet incursion.[11]

Ratti's first official act was to lead the Polish Bishops' Conference in arguing "strenuously against the formation of a single Catholic political party," which had been supported by a reactionary bishop in Kielce. At this point in the narrative — approximately three months after Ratti's arrival — Kertzer says:

> It was no secret that Ratti was in Warsaw to inform the Pope of the current situation in Poland, and he was deluged by advice from people who sought to influence his outlook. In these conversations and letters, one theme kept coming up: Poland's problems were caused by the Jews.

After this observation there is a treatment of a letter in French from an anti-Semitic Polish nobleman; the letter is quoted for seven lines, after which Kertzer says: "A long, fiercely anti-Semitic analysis of the problems of Poland followed." Just as there had been no recorded response to the earlier letter from "most likely a Polish Catholic aristocrat" there is no recorded response from Ratti to the nobleman.

Although Ratti's mission in Poland was described by Gasparri as "purely ecclesiastical" in helping the Polish bishops "to complete the work of reconstruction," Kertzer focuses, understandably, only on relations with Jews. According to his narrative, other than a few sentences (August 17, 1918) on the bishop of Kielce, the first significant message to Rome from Ratti — pre-

---

11. Of this period, a historian who actually reads Polish has written: "His decision to stand by Poland in its desperate hour, recalled the defiance of Pope Leo I in the face of Attila, became the signature of his nunciature and, in retrospect, his crucial stepping-stone toward the throne of Peter. For the moment, at least, it also won him the gratitude of Poles and allayed their nagging suspicions that the papacy could not be trusted to uphold the interests of their nation." Neal Pease, *Rome's Most Faithful Daughter: The Catholic Church and Independent Poland, 1914-1939* (2009).

ceded by Kertzer's "precious insights" comment — is described in this (complete) paragraph:

> In a letter to Cardinal Gasparri in late October 1918, Ratti reported on the unrest plaguing the country. "There were some days of great excitement, with some threats — soon dissipated or nearly so — by the extremist parties bent on disorder: the socialist-anarchists, the Bolsheviks (veterans of or influenced by the Russian revolution) and the Jews."

The precious insight ends there.

The next paragraph begins. "About a week later, November 2, 1918, the future pope had what, as far as we know, was the only meeting he ever had with Polish Jews."[12] Apart from the effort at providing an extreme context ("*ever* had"), the meeting itself as described by excerpts from Ratti's communications with Rome appears to have been mutually amicable. Ratti greeted the Jewish delegates, and expressed his pleasure that they were visiting on the day when the church "was honoring the birth of Mary, who came from your people." "The rabbi told me that he and his people were grateful and flattered, and it seemed to me and to all the others there that they truly were."

A few weeks later, as unrest and pogroms were reported — leading the archbishop of Warsaw "to call for an end to anti-Jewish violence" — Ratti received a telegram from Cardinal Gasparri (December 22, 1918): "Subject: Look into reported killing of Jews." "Following recent news concerning the killing of Jews, the Holy Father has received petitions. Your Excellency will want to obtain exact information in this regard and to take an interest in their welfare." There are two parallels for this request of Pope Benedict XV; the first is the request of Pope Benedict XIV a century and a half earlier that directed Lorenzo Ganganelli to look into the reported killings of Jews who were allegedly engaged in ritual murder — a directive that Ganganelli followed to the letter. The second request came a year before the message to Ratti by Benedict XV, and it has a bearing on how one might interpret Ratti's reaction to the Gasparri telegram.

12. Since the phrase "as far as we know" has a ring of authority, it should be noted that Michael Burleigh in *Sacred Causes* (loc. cit.) provides several sources that refer to Ratti's having "met large numbers of Jews"; and Russell Hittinger in *The Pius War* (2004) notes the cordiality that prevailed at those meetings "because of Ratti's speaking to the Jewish groups in Hebrew" — a language that Ratti himself often boasted of as having learned from a personal friend, the Chief Rabbi of Rome.

On November 15, 1917, Cardinal Gasparri had sent to another Vatican emissary in Germany, Eugenio Pacelli — also a future pope — this message: "The Israelite community of Switzerland asked the Holy Father to commit himself to the protection of the sites and the Jewish population of Jerusalem. He asks Your Excellency, through us, to influence the German government accordingly in the name of the Holy Father. Card. Gasparri."[13] (By John Cornwell's lights, it was also while in Germany that this other papal nuncio first exposed the rabid anti-Semitism that merited for him the appellation "Hitler's pope.") The coded wire to Pacelli was occasioned by the wartime deterioration of conditions in Palestine where earlier in the year Reuters was reporting that "masses of Jews" had been driven from their homes. This was Pacelli's request to the responsible German authorities:

> The undersigned Apostolic Nuncio [to Bavaria] has the honor to inform Your Excellency that the Israelite Congregations of Switzerland asked the Holy Father to appeal for the protection of the sites and the Jewish population of Jerusalem. His Eminence, the Cardinal Secretary of State has ordered the undersigned to act accordingly and with all care, and to draw this subject to the attention of the Imperial [German] Government. The Undersigned requests that Your Excellency enforce the realization of this goal with every resource at your disposal. *Eugenio Pacelli, Archbishop of Sardes, and Apostolic Nuncio.*[14]

Most people reading this would think it an estimable response by an estimable man to a conventional request, and they would certainly have been surprised to learn that a papal emissary simply didn't do what he was told to do. But that is not a reading that the ideological allies of Kertzer would endorse. In *A Moral Reckoning* (2002), Daniel Jonah Goldhagen, relying on Kertzer *and* Cornwell, opines unwaveringly: "Pius XI and Pius XII were anti-Semites. They were prone, as they themselves gave evidence . . . to almost Nazi-like fantasies and libels about Jews" — an opinion based on their reports from Poland and Germany.

But anyone who reads the texts at issue knows that the future Pius XII in

---

13. Pinchas Lapide, *Three Popes and the Jews* (1967). Since Lapide is frequently contemned as a deluded piophile, if not a papal shill, it should be noted that there is no doubt about the authenticity of the communications, both from and to Rome.

14. The beneficial results of this intervention by Pacelli would take the present discussion too far afield. The following non-Vatican sites should be examined: www.catholicherald .co.uk/articles/a0000485.shtml and www.jewishpress.com/pageroute.do/38422.

Munich was not libeling Jews, any more than was the future Pius XI in War-saw.[15] Regarding the first, I analyze the doctored texts and blatant mistrans-lations by Cornwell in *Historians Against History;* regarding the second, the misquotations and mistranslations will be analyzed presently. Abstracting from Goldhagen's ideological fixation, and merely on the basis of common sense, there are very few people who would embrace the notion that enter-prising men in the relatively early stages of their professional careers — doc-tors, lawyers, and clergy, to take the classic triad — were intentionally going to violate the formal directives of their superiors. While it is obvious that Pacelli did exactly what he was told to do by the secretary of state, his coun-terpart in Poland — at least if one believes the following description — did the exact opposite.

According to Kertzer, Ratti's response to Pope Benedict XV's directive "reveals a great deal." After that comment, and with noticeable abruptness, anti-Semitism — up to this point described in terms of various external factors — takes on a new and personally threatening shape. Intrinsic to that shape is more absolutist language (here italicized), and horrific descrip-tions, here made more shocking by the fact the last thing that the reader had been told about Ratti was his meeting with the grateful rabbi and his people:

> Although Jews in many parts of Poland were being murdered, their homes and synagogues burned to the ground, and the Pope himself had asked him to take an interest in the Jews' welfare, Ratti did *nothing of the sort.* Examination of his activities <u>in the months that followed</u> reveals that, on the contrary, *he did everything he could to impede any Vatican action on be-half of the Jews and prevent any Vatican intervention that would discourage the violence.* The Secretary of state's telegram came in the midst of Ratti's first set of reports to the Vatican on the situation of the Jews of Poland,

15. Lurking in the background of this blurred relationship of pontiff to emissary is the persistent belief that those papal representatives who actively aided Jews during World War II were doing so without any regard for the views of the pope. This is not unlike the opinion that the nearly six thousand people, mostly Jewish, sheltered in religious houses in Rome were do-ing so unknown to the pope. That Pius's understandable preoccupation with impartiality — a preoccupation that by his own words was a cause of distress — prevented him from speak-ing out does not cancel the affirmations of such of his representatives as Angelo Roncalli, Angelo Rotta, and Andrea Cassulo that they were simply following the wishes of "the Holy Father." Either the latter are bought souls traducing themselves out of blind loyalty to the pope, or they are simply telling the truth. There is no other interpretation.

but these reports, *rather than warning about the Jews' persecutors, were aimed at alerting the Vatican to the dangers posed by the Jews themselves.*

Why this future pope in Poland would not only disobey these orders but would also in "the months that followed" take it on himself to do the exact opposite — all that goes unexplained.[16] However, what is more immediately in need of explanation after the assertion about those intervening months, underlined above, is Kertzer's sense of chronology. The December 22, 1918, telegram from Gasparri came "in the midst of Ratti's first set of reports." But the only previous report Kertzer cited was the one about "unrest" (October 24, 1918), and the one a week later about meeting with the Jews and their rabbi (November 2, 1918) — almost two months before the telegram from Rome. There is no way that those *earlier* reports can be used to show anything about the *subsequent* order to look into the killing of Jews. Even more inexplicable is the absence of any statement or annotation that supports the judgment about Ratti doing "nothing of the sort" that had been ordered by the pope and the secretary of state.

As to the "examination of his activities in the months that followed," there are *no* months involved, as Kertzer again — and far more significantly — doctors the record. The complete span of time for which Kertzer provides any documentation goes from the date of the telegram from Rome — which, as noted above, is December 22 — to the date of Ratti's last cited report to Rome (January 15, 1919). It must come as a shock to any readers seeking to make sense out of this chronicle that those "months" are now less than four weeks. But even more shocking is the fact that *all* of the recorded communications between Ratti and Gasparri — which is what Kertzer relies on to determine why Ratti's "experience in Poland takes on such enormous importance" — occurred during a period of less than half a year from the time when "the Vatican librarian stepped into this background in June 1918" and up to his last recorded report, January 1919. To be more precise, the *terminus a quo* is August 17, 1918, the date of the first documented communication between Ratti and Rome. (One can only wonder as to how Rome even knew that he had arrived.) The *terminus ad quem* of this enormously important experience, at least so far as Kertzer's documented treatment goes, is the afore-

16. Neal Pease in *Rome's Most Faithful Daughter* (loc. cit.) severely indicts Polish anti-Semitism, but has the following to say of Archbishop Ratti: "At first astonished and made uneasy by the multitude of Jews he encountered in Polish cities, he adjusted soon enough and in later years drew on the experiences of his nunciature to undergird his relatively enlightened views on the Jewish question."

mentioned January 15, 1919 — generously, in all a period of four months. Of course, there are other documents alluded to or mentioned more or less in passing but they are what might be called "chronology free."[17]

This bears repeating. There is no chronological documentation of anything that relates to the other approximately thirty-two months in Poland, although there is — equitableness to Kertzer demands acknowledging — a seven-word sentence that mentions the date when Ratti left the country at the end of his three-year visitation. So, not only are "the months that followed" Gasparri's request in fact only *three* weeks, but the aggregate of all the reports and communications with Rome during the momentous "three years in Warsaw" covers approximately a seventh of the total time Ratti was actually there. Yet Kertzer has insisted, without of course spelling out the details, that this period — absurdly abridged and abstracted — provides "priceless" and "precious" insights that "allow us, for the first time, to understand the attitude toward the Jews that Ratti brought with him when he became pontiff."[18] Parenthetically, it may be noted that this condensed chronology may explain the language of John Cornwell's firm endorsement of *The Popes Against the Jews:* "Once again Kertzer has produced impressive evidence of the part played by the papacy in the growth of anti-Semitism." The evidence is as impressive as that marshaled by Cornwell to validate his own heralded discovery that Ratti's successor, Pacelli, was really the pawn of the Führer, and thus deserved the appellation "Hitler's pope."[19]

Nor do the kind of insights Kertzer announced surface in the final report of January 15, 1919 — although they may be provided by a report less than a week earlier (January 9, 1919). That report does contain a quotation that appears to support the vaunt, mentioned in the introduction, that "the story I tell here for the first time about Achille Ratti" is more important than the story some other less astute people are telling about Pius XII. (I will not

---

17. "Do the math" is the watchword. Anyone examining the book's bibliographic and explanatory notes on page 322 — which are so meticulously composed as to win an award from the syndics of the *Chicago Manual* or the Modern Language Association — need merely check the dates from notes 14 through 28.

18. Perhaps this chapter should have been titled "Five Months that Shook the World." This chronological farrago also exposes the vacuousness of solemn utterances like "as far as we know [this] was the only meeting he ever had with Polish Jews" — where one may note again the redundancy of the intensifying adverb "ever," and the pomposity of "we."

19. It was Cornwell's claim that he had worked in the Vatican archives for "months on end." Unfortunately, the official archival records showed that he was there "from May 12 to June 2 1997," a period that it would be generous to describe as days on end.

labor the point that whenever Kertzer singles out for praise his "first-time" achievements, he usually bungles the data.) Since the following from the January 9 report contains one of Kertzer's most oft-cited quotations proving the deep-seated anti-Semitism of the future Pius XI, I provide it and its contextualization in full.

> That report came in early January 1919 in the wake of the pogroms and the telegram that Cardinal Gasparri had sent him. For those who see in Achille Ratti the man who, in contrast to his successor Pius XII, would become the "good pope," the ecumenical spirit who would take the interests of Europe's persecuted Jews to heart, the report can only be disheartening.
>
> "For my part, and as a duty that I believe my mission imposes on me, I never stop repeating to these Most Excellent Bishops and Most Reverend priests that the more I have come to admire the goodness and the faith of their people, having gotten to see and know it close up, the more I fear that they may fall into the clutches of the evil influences that are laying a trap for them and threatening them. Unfortunately, if they are not defended by the work of good influences, they will certainly succumb."
>
> After this vague, abstract assessment, Ratti then finally comes to the point. Just who are these enemies of Christianity, of the Church, of the Polish people? "One of the most evil and strongest influences that is felt here, perhaps the strongest and the most evil, is that of the Jews."[20]

This last statement and the revelation, still to come, about the exterminationist priest are the most frequently cited texts used to condemn this future pope. Readers who recall the first mention of Pius XI in the introduction — referred to above — will also recall this rhetorical question by Kertzer: "But what if we find that Pius XII's benevolent predecessor shared the same stridently anti-Semitic views?" While these disheartening sentences hardly represent strident anti-Semitism, neither are they calculated to enhance Ratti's reputation — or at least not as they are translated and paraphrased here.

Although the statement refers to "influences," anyone who has followed the narrative this far will not be surprised that there is no explanation for how Kertzer transforms that word in the first quoted paragraph into "ene-

---

20. This is now a historical fact. "Pius XI himself, who served as a papal diplomat in Poland during World War I, dismissed reports of pogroms there as inventions of Jewish propaganda. He wrote to the Vatican secretary of state: 'One of the most evil and strongest influences that is felt here, perhaps the strongest and the most evil, is that of the Jews.'" Garry Wills, "Before the Holocaust," *The New York Times*, September 23, 2001.

mies" in the next paragraph — much less for how those "influences" have that inimical relationship with "Christianity," "the Church," and "the Polish people." Nor is it clear how something that is "*perhaps* the strongest and most evil" then becomes definitively "*the* most evil." Nevertheless, what Kertzer intends to convey is clear enough, even without this subsequent post-publication revised version: "Achille Ratti, three years before becoming Pope Pius XI, reported to the Vatican secretary of state that 'the most evil' influence in Poland was the Jews."[21] Kertzer's view, by his own assertion, has now become canonical. But like most revisionist history, the original has been transformed if not transfigured in the process of reiteration. Excised are the modifiers, "*one* of the most evil," and, "*perhaps* . . . the most evil."

The relevant texts are not from a document in Kertzer's usual archival source for quotations by Ratti, but from the third volume in a collection titled *Achille Ratti (1918-1921). Acta Nunciaturae Polonae* (Rome, 1995-99), an unquestionably reliable source that contains more than two hundred Ratti documents, of which more than fifty are "reports" to Cardinal Gasparri. Given this large number of documents, the question must arise as to how representative those few sentences above are, since they occur in only one of those reports — in this instance a document of approximately six thousand words. Since that entire volume is a rather large haystack in which to locate this needle, it seems unlikely that anything in those hundreds of other pages is stained by strident anti-Semitism. Relying on what may be called the Zuccotti Factor, it is safe to assume that if anything else even slightly incriminatory had been present, it would certainly have been tracked by Kertzer.[22]

Unfortunately, to maintain his ideological perspective and to make a case Kertzer has to manipulate the language and the structure of the original text — as some exegesis, however wearisome, will show. As to structure, he omits a lengthy passage (ten lines) that occurs between the first reference to evil influences and the second. Since the omitted passage pertains to "influences" on Catholics in Italy, it can possibly be regarded as only in a general way relevant to the situation of Catholics in Poland. However, its omission does make the two references to "evil" appear as not just rhetorically parallel

---

21. This doctored version was presented by Kertzer himself in a letter published in *Commonweal* (November 23, 2001) responding to a critical review of his book by Rabbi Marc Saperstein — a review that will be introduced later in this discussion.

22. Referring to the eleven-volume *Actes et Documents* published by the Holy See and covering the wartime period, Susan Zuccotti in *Under His Very Windows* (2001) states: "Although much that is unfavorable may have been omitted, it is reasonable to assume that all that is favorable was included."

but as identical. It is another juggled translation that will betray the fact that the apparent parallel and identity are nonexistent. The first reference was in the context of Ratti's fear that the people "may fall into the clutches of the evil influences [*cattive influenze*] that are laying a trap for them." This is a translation that is adequate, *at best*, for if one took Leonardo's well-known remark about the appearance of people's countenances in *cattivo tempo*, and said that it referred to how people looked in "evil weather," one's suspicions about Kertzer's devotion to accuracy might be reignited.[23]

Moreover, the second reference about "one of the most evil and strongest influences" is in the original, "una della piu nefaste e della piu forti influenze," which no matter how it is translated, obviously cannot be worded with the identical English term "evil." Unless one were seeking to hoodwink the readers — a precedent established in the blatant deletion of the Russian ambassador from the account of the Beilis trial — the only responsible way to determine the most accurate translation would be to rely on the Latin root, which relates to "fate" or "destiny," and thus requires the deployment of a word that indicates such notions as "unlucky," "unfortunate," "ill-fated," "inauspicious," and the like. That being so, one has to weigh whether the following would sound as threatening as Kertzer's text. "One of the more unfortunate and more powerful influences that is felt here, perhaps the most unfortunate and most powerful, is that of the Jews." Readers can supply their own variations on the theme, but what is undeniable is that to then transform the passage into Kertzer's *Commonweal* rejoinder, "'the most evil' influence in Poland was the Jews," is to perpetrate an even more gross affront to language and logic. (At the end of this chapter, there will be an analysis of an even more outrageous mistranslation of a statement of Leo XIII that accuses Jews of belonging to "the plague-bearing race.")

As to those ten lines that Kertzer omitted, they described conditions in Italy, where *influenze pessime* had prevailed. Ratti then went on to say that these influences — which had nothing whatever to do with Jews and which could scarcely even be described as "bad" — were to be overcome "by holiness [*sanctificazione*] and *azione cattolica* which are especially needed today." As pontiff Ratti would be known as "the pope of Catholic Action," and he

---

23. Further complicating the nonexistent parallels and identities is the fact that the immediate preceding reference to "influences" is not those *"cattive influenze"* Kertzer cites, but *"influenze pessime"* — which in the original context, as will be seen presently, are to be remedied through "Catholic Action." Momentarily disregarding this latter datum, the fact remains that each reference to something "bad" by the pope is cautious and precise, while the translations bulldoze all nuance away. The question recurs: is this the way to write history?

was here responding to Benedict XV's rejuvenation of a movement of social reform, then focused mainly on young people, which had been neglected under Pius X.[24] It is in that latter context of a youth movement that the inadequacy of a univocal translation for terms related to harmful influences becomes obvious, since no one thinks a "bad boy" is identical with an "evil boy." So, at worst or best, in relation to Jews the bishops should promote among their flocks whatever makes them holy.

As to the remaining six thousand words in the document, short of a reference to the disproportionately large number of Jews in university — which Kertzer also notes — there is little indication of any particular preoccupation with them as such. Rather, there is a detailed explanation to his distant readers in Rome of the social, political, and religious life of postwar Poland: countless statistics ranging from the number of students in elementary schools to the size of family farms; discussions of the ravages of the Russian occupation and subsequently of German and Austrian inroads through "a divide and conquer policy"; the fate of peasants and the role of "intelligentsia" — a Russian coinage Ratti finds distasteful; problems related to urbanization, to proliferation of political parties, to the growth of industry and *sindacati,* and so on.

But this larger perspective does raise the issue of the unavoidable tension and then conflict that existed between the two communities in Poland. This is an issue that has been encountered earlier in the different dress of ritual murder and the blood libel relative to the institutional church, and it will be examined more thoroughly in the concluding chapter of the present book. But no historian can ignore the unique situation of Jews in Poland, particularly in contrast to that in other European societies where over the centuries tensions decreased as one moved from east to west — much as accusations of ritual murder had increased as one moved in the opposite direction. Polish Jews were less assimilated than were Jews in England or Germany, and far less than in Italy and France, where there had been Jewish colonies that predated the arrival and the consequent hegemony of Christianized tribes in those areas. Thus it constituted more overreaching for Kertzer to attempt to exploit the opposition of the popes to Zionism as another example of their being "against the Jews," since many French Jews and even more Italian ones had little interest in the Palestinian project, and

24. "Shortly before Italy entered World War I, Benedict XV reorganized what was coming to be called 'Catholic Action' with capitals." Gianfranco Poggi, *Catholic Action in Italy* (1967).

thought of themselves as fully entitled citizens in the countries where they dwelt.[25]

Kertzer does attempt to do justice to the singular place of Jews in Poland. He begins with the observation that "King Casimir the Great, in the fourteenth century, had invited Jews into Poland to serve as intermediaries between the aristocratic rulers and the mass of peasants."[26] He also notes that the Jews "became the traders, the moneylenders, tax collectors, and estate administrators." Moreover, as Kertzer doesn't note, Jews had been exempt — since the eleventh century by church law and since the time of Casimir by royal writ — from the taxes and other duties like military service that were imposed on the native population. All this occurred during a period when feudalism and subsequently occupation by foreign powers reduced the lowest "class" of workers more and more, so that by the eighteenth century they had chattel status. This was not the bold peasantry contemporaneously immortalized in British verse, but it was the period when a Polish prince, Thaddeus Kosciuszko, would devote his life to the freedom of serfs and slaves — victims who differed only in name — in his own country, in the American colonies during the Revolutionary War, and throughout Europe in the aftermath of the French Revolution and the Napoleonic wars.[27] Nor for those serfs was there a "village master who taught his little school" — simply because there were no schools. This was a mass of people reduced to a servitude that grew successively worse, particularly in czarist Poland, until the serfs were finally freed in the early 1860s — at the same time that the Civil War in North America freed the slaves there. And the peasants like the slaves had only one moderately effective social resource, one institution, however loosely organized, to shape their lives and thinking. This was the Christian religion mediated in Poland by the Catholic Church, and in North America by what were called "African" or "Abyssin-

25. "Let there be no misunderstanding or mistake: as a movement or as a political option, Zionism has always represented but a minority of the Jewish people. When Zionism was launched, at the end of the nineteenth century, it was seriously contested by other Jewish movements and trends: bundists, territorialists, autonomists and, of course, all the assimilationists." Claude Klein, "Zionism Revisited," in Raphael Cohen-Almagor, ed., *Israeli Democracy at the Crossroads* (2005).

26. There is a remarkably affecting late nineteenth-century painting, *King Casimir Welcomes the Jews,* by Wojciech Gerson in the Warsaw National Museum.

27. The story of the prince and his dedicated pursuit of freedom for the oppressed — even to severely reprimanding his friends George Washington and Thomas Jefferson for having slaves — is told in Alex Storzynski, *Peasant Prince in the Age of Revolution* (2009).

ian" churches — where the ex-slaves also found relief for body and mind in the chanting of what could be called "supersessionist hymns," but in fact are called "Negro spirituals."

As to Poland alone, one must add the facts that a tenth of its population was Jewish, that most Jews, apart from those in Cracow and Warsaw, lived in their own relatively isolated communities, spoke their own language, and had only commercial relations with their neighbors; add all this in, and one has a mix of factors that gives fairly precise meaning to that overworked term "otherness." Regardless of whether one denigrates such a coinage as post-Freudian or postcolonial jargon, the term conveys very well the sense of alienation experienced by the small minority community and the sense of antagonism felt by the larger host community. Kertzer in the introductory material to this chapter had acknowledged the cause of such tensions, and was very explicit about the privileged state of Jews:

> The Jews' traditional role as middlemen meant that in small towns throughout the country, Jews often owned the only general store, a Jew was the only moneylender in town, and the local livestock dealer was likely to be a Jew. This meant that in hard times, which were all too frequent, it was to a Jew that the Christian peasant had to go to borrow money, often to be turned away; a Jew who came trying to collect on a debt, and a Jew to whom peasants would have to turn to sell their only cows.

He also noted the status of Jews in the Poland that Ratti was visiting:

> Although the proportion of Jews who were economically well off was small, their impact on the modernization of Poland's economy in the early twentieth century was great. Poland entered the twentieth century without a well-developed Christian bourgeoisie. . . . What modern business had developed was largely the product of Jewish enterprise. Poland's modest industrialization was due in good part to Jews, and Jews ran many, perhaps most, of the banks as well. A large presence in Poland's tiny middle class, the Jews were also numerous among the highly educated: by 1920, for example, 40 percent of all Poles with university degrees were Jewish.

The fact that 10 percent of the population had nearly half of the university degrees may explain why in the Ratti report — the one with the rigged treatment of "influences" — there is a brief mention of the fact that the University of Warsaw "has become in large part a Jewish university."

Some readers might regard both excerpts above as an attempt on the part of the author to cover his flanks, since there is much discussion running through the entire book about the stereotypical slurs to which Jews have been subjected because of their facility in banking and other monetary exchanges — which ironically was owed in part to Christian regulations forbidding the receipt of interest on loans. It was even more ironic that Kertzer himself seemed to engage in such stereotypes when discussing Pius IX's homily to the Roman women by bringing up Jewish bankers at the signing of the treaty ending the Franco-Prussian War. But regarding the source of ethnic-religious conflicts in the Poland to which the future pope had been sent, it may be helpful to introduce some statistics — statistics are usually scanted by Kertzer — that do point to a source of underlying tension. These are from an authority whom it would be difficult to impeach, and who is here describing conditions around the time Achille Ratti stepped into the background of Polish-Jewish relations:

> In Poland, the self-definition of minorities was often that of a separate "nationality." Thus, in the Polish census of 1921, 73.76 percent of the overall number of Jews by religion also identified themselves to be Jews by nationality, and in the 1931 census 79.9 percent declared that Yiddish was their mother tongue, while 7.8 percent . . . declared that Hebrew was their first language. That left only a small percentage of Polish Jews who declared Polish to be their mother tongue.

That is from Saul Friedländer's *Nazi Germany and the Jews: The Years of Persecution, 1933-1939* (1997). To his final observation above should be added the fact that such statistics also made it not unlikely that only a relatively small percentage of Jews regarded themselves as Polish. If there are such things as religious texts of terror, there are also such things as religious statistics of terror, and those above meet that definition.

The response to this phenomenon on the part of the native population — indifference, alienation, animosity — seems to generally mystify Kertzer, who underscores its expression by ordinary folk or by churchmen as self-evidently racist. Thus even before the excerpted passage below is cited Kertzer introduces it as painting "a picture of an insidious foreign force eating away at the Polish nation preventing it from realizing its national aspirations." But there is nothing insidious about the ordinary exercise of patriotism in a country that for centuries had not enjoyed self-government and had suffered under what Ratti had referred to in the *Acta Nunciaturae Polonae* document as a "divide and conquer" policy by invaders who were enlisting the minority against the majority. "The foreign occupiers always had to try to protect and to favor the Jews in order to stop and to weaken the Poles." The tension between the two peoples will also be discussed in the last chapter — though it will not be resolved. But it is so difficult to determine what is related to economics, what is related to race, and what is related to mere "otherness," that the entire issue remains unresolved. Most efforts at accuracy and reciprocity entail a kind of medieval *sic et non* treatment whereby each successive positive assertion is balanced by a more negative one.[28]

The remainder of this chapter is laced with quotations from various documents that were received by Ratti, including several scurrilous quotations having to do with Jews and money. What is noteworthy about the documents is that, with one exception, they are all by outsiders denouncing the evil ways of the Jews. As he did with his copious quotations from the newspapers cited at the end of the chapter on ritual murder, Kertzer cites these documents so extensively that the impression is created that they represent the views of Ratti, whereas in fact he is merely the recipient and transmitter of the documents to Rome. Nor should it be overlooked that it is Kertzer who is selecting the passages to be read. When in his lengthy summation of the entire "three-year" visitation — to be examined presently — Ratti comments on these documents, his attempts at evenhandedness cannot be obscured even by Kertzer's slanted glosses.

The most undisguised expression of the latter is his treating as of equal value the reports Ratti sent to Rome and the anti-Semitic documents sent to him by others. It only blurs matters further to read that "these reports, together with the documents that he continued to accumulate, give us a precious insight into his evolving view of the Jews."[29] Ratti wrote the reports — which may give us such insights; it is impossible for insights into his views to be obtained from documents written by others. One of Kertzer's strategies for leading the reader to accept the equal value of "reports" and "documents" is to start using the terms interchangeably, if not indiscriminately, so that once again it is easy for the reader to lose track of Ratti's neutral obser-

---

28. For an effective display of this positive-negative treatment, see Timothy Snyder, "Jews, Poles, & Nazis: The Terrible History," *The New York Review*, June 24, 2010.

29. What his view is "evolving" from or what it is "evolving" into is no more clarified than is the phenomenon of how anything or anyone "evolves" over a period of less than half a year.

vations amid the flood of anti-Semitic texts also being quoted. Thus one reads that "Ratti was presented with a report . . . [that was] fiercely anti-Semitic." "Among his earliest sources of information was a report . . . [saying] the Jews of Poland . . . live by exploiting the Polish people." "Ratti was able to gain insight . . . by another document [about] . . . the campaign of slander by the Polish Socialist Party and the Jews." "Ratti also gathered reports on other recent violence." But the original distinction (reports by Ratti, documents by others) cannot be so easily blurred, since for any official communication with Rome, the term invariably used is *rapporto*.

Nevertheless, the final sentences of the penultimate paragraph[30] in the chapter describing Ratti's experience in Poland will dramatically hammer home Kertzer's effort to make Ratti's own words equally as important as the words of various anti-Semites, named and unnamed, who sent him materials. Until that paragraph is examined, its overture is sounded in the following passage where what Ratti wrote and what was written to him are both referred to as "reports" — as couched in the self-congratulatory rhetoric ("for the first time") that is fast becoming the hallmark of this writer:

> Taken together, the reports on the Polish Jews that Achille Ratti himself wrote to the secretary of state, along with the final report of his mission, and the reports on the Jews that he collected while in Warsaw, provide us with a precious resource. They allow us, for the first time, to understand the attitude toward the Jews that Pius XI brought with him when he became pontiff.[31]

By the most rudimentary logic, it is impossible for the reports that "Ratti himself wrote" to have the same value as the reports that "he collected" from others. In fact, the latter tell us nothing whatever about Ratti's "attitude toward the Jews," though Kertzer's deployment of this sophism does tell us, and not for the first time, something about his attitude toward historiography.

After excerpting anti-Semitic outbursts from a variety of outside sources, Kertzer tells the reader: "On January 15 [1919], Monsignor Ratti was ready to send his report," which was five pages long, and is discussed in three paragraphs by Kertzer. The report is so remarkably neutral and balanced,

---

30. This complicated specification is important because the last paragraph in this chapter contains the most blatant distortion of Ratti's *ipsissima verba* in the entire book.

31. Ronald Modras, previously cited on the synagogue of Satan, draws a conclusion that is at least more accurate than is Kertzer's: "Ratti's papers reveal not his opinions but only those he received." Loc. cit.

that not even the eight pages of vituperative excerpts from the outsiders' documents that Kertzer also supplies — much like those lengthy excerpts from the "Vatican-linked press" that spoke for the popes — can obscure its impartial, even noncommittal tone. Concerning those three paragraphs, the central sentence of the first is: "As for the pogroms and the massacres . . . ,' Ratti wrote, 'I have been looking into them . . . but nothing yet is clear and definitive.'" Concerning the second: "'As for that [pogrom] of Kielce . . . 'The Jews blame the Christians and the Christians blame the Jews.' He awaited, he wrote, further information." The third paragraph notes: "In the area of Lvov Monsignor Ratti reported, the disorders had left 'hundreds of dead and entire areas sacked and burned' . . . it was unclear just who was to blame for the violence." Kertzer's concluding one-sentence paragraph again argues *ex silentio,* and with more absolutist rhetoric: "[Ratti] certainly never did anything to dispute the notion that the murders were the Jews' own fault." Considering the fact that this is the report that was written less than a month after the December 22 telegram from Rome, and that the report was clearly titled "The Anti-Semitic Pogroms," it would be difficult to conclude that Ratti did other than what the Vatican had requested.

Kertzer's paragraph following the one-sentence *ex silentio* conclusion above says nothing about murders or faults, and instead begins with a religious ceremony: "Symptomatically, when the first parliament of the about-to-be independent Polish state opened in February of that year [1919], they began their first session by filing into the grand cathedral of Warsaw to celebrate a solemn mass." What this is symptomatic of is not clarified, but since one cannot have a Mass without clergy this allows the author to introduce specific anti-Semitic priests and, *pari passu,* the fourth of the original papal myths, that is, "a future pope in Poland" supported clerics who wanted to exterminate Jews. The particular priest in question is introduced with the now-established certitudes regarding Ratti:

> The depths of anti-Semitism among the Catholic clergy of Poland at the time could hardly be overstated, yet Monsignor Ratti saw nothing. He had nothing to say, for example about such prominent clerics as Father Józef Kruszyński who, like many of his fellow priests, was a believer in a Jewish world conspiracy. Kruszyński in 1920 explained that "racial purity created what is called an anthropological type."

Since this is almost the last gasp of an expiring thesis, it is not surprising that Kertzer's announcement about seeing and saying nothing takes the reader nowhere, since Kertzer doesn't provide any reason why Ratti could or should have any connection with a priest who is suddenly — and rather clumsily — inserted into the prevailing void, and of whom there is no reason for thinking that Ratti knew anything whatever. That the priest was among a group of prominent clerics "that like many of his fellow priests" believed in a Jewish world conspiracy — whether true or not — also has no bearing on anything related to the nuncio. Finally, to heap the fatuous on the otiose, neither is there any reason to believe that Kertzer himself had ever heard of the prominent cleric until he came across the name in "Nation catholique et racisme culturel," published in the journal *Sens* in 1995.[32]

It is not surprising that an entire chapter that has been constructed on veiled or vague descriptions of Jew-hatred expressed by people with no connection to Achille Ratti except geography and chronology (same country plus same time equals future anti-Semitic pope in Poland) should end with the following from Kertzer, who now utterly forgoes any nexus between Italian prelate and Polish priest. Following the quotation about "an anthropological type," Kertzer continues the excerpt above:

> Three years later, Kruszyński would write: "If the world is to be rid of the Jewish scourge, it would be necessary to exterminate them, down to the last one." Lest such views be thought to be regarded as less than respectable among the Catholic hierarchy in Poland of the time, it is worth recalling that two years later, in 1925, Kruszyński was named head of the Catholic University of Lublin.[33]

The only link between Kruszyński's statement — which is intended to express not only his own opinion but also "the depths of anti-Semitism among the Catholic clergy of Poland" — and the not-seeing-anything, not-saying-anything Monsignor Ratti is that both men were on the same planet.

It is only after three more paragraphs that have nothing to do with anti-

---

32. The article, which either Kertzer did not read or chose to editorially amend, is a summation of a Sorbonne thesis by Paul Zawadzki, *Invention d'une communauté imaginée: construction nationale et antisémitisme en Pologne avant 1939* (1994). Nor does Kertzer mention the full name of the journal — which in this case is pertinent: *Bulletin de l'Amitié Judéo-Chrétienne de France.*

33. Kruszyński had nothing to do with the Polish hierarchy; his title was "Father." The university was founded in 1922. Three years later, after Kruszyński's appointment as rector, it had 448 students. This information about prominent people and events is available at www.kul.lublin.pl/uk/history/after.html.

Semitism, and that relate to such things as Ratti's being "caught in the middle of antagonistic political forces," to his being "upgraded to papal nuncio," and to his involvement in "controversy over upper Silesia" — it is only after those diversionary topics are introduced that there occurs the one short sentence, tacked on at the end of the paragraph following the word "Silesia," which makes clear the chronological obfuscation Kertzer perpetrated above: "In early June 1921, Ratti left Poland." The equally distracting endnote to that observation mutes even further its significance: "Upper Silesia is located at a the point where Germany, Poland, and Czechoslovakia came together." Never is it even suggested — much less made clear — that the statement by the prominent priest about exterminating the Jewish scourge was made after Achille Ratti had left Poland and had, in fact, been reigning as Pope Pius XI for nearly two years.

This concealment of specific dates, a strategy that became a tour de force in the previous chapter regarding the end of the Beilis trial, accounts for the widespread assumption that Ratti knew about Kruszyñski — who, thanks to *The Popes Against the Jews,* is now as renowned as Cardinal Merry del Val and his "famous telegram." It is not surprising that the *Times* of London, in an interview with Kertzer by Richard Morrison (January 18, 2002), would publish the following:

> Pius XI is subject to some of Kertzer's most scathing paragraphs. Before he became Pope he was sent as a papal envoy to Poland. Violent anti-Semitic feelings were being fueled there by prominent Catholic clergy such as the notorious Jozef Kruszynski, who penned the ominous words: "If the world is to be rid of the Jewish scourge, it will be necessary to exterminate them, down to the last one."

Thus this priest, unknown to the larger world, becomes not only prominent but "notorious" for making such a statement, presumably in the environs if not in the very presence of the future pope.[34] One should certainly not be startled that in the next paragraph the interviewer returns us to the now pre-

---

34. The interview also contains its insights into further conspiracies — and further achievements. Morrison asks: "So why did the Vatican authorities open the archives? They must have known of the dark truths waiting to be discovered in those dusty vaults." Kertzer replies: "That's a good question. One theory put to me by an American Catholic priest is that there is now *a faction within the Vatican* that wants all this stuff to come out. They knew the Church itself would never be able to reveal it, but were *quite keen for an outsider like me to find the material*" (italics supplied). "Stuff" is the operative term.

sumably well-established matter of Jewish "influences," and concludes in the triumphant tones that Kertzer himself affects:

> Yet, far from condemning such rabble-rousers, the future Pope seems to have sympathized with them. His report back to Rome includes the words: "One of the most evil and strongest influences felt here is that of the Jews." This is the view of the man who would be Pope during the years when the Nazis came to power.

The final indication of this covenant between exterminationist priest and ableptic prelate — neither of whom had anything to do with one another — is this theatrical (and vicious) fabrication by Kertzer: "As Pope Pius XI, Achille Ratti would die shortly before he could have seen Father Kruszyński's scenario become reality, with the death of the overwhelming majority of Poland's three million Jews." Nothing better exposes the sordidness of that synthetic "scenario" than Kertzer's effort to implicate Pius XI in the Holocaust. Then to intensify the monstrosity of which Ratti is guilty (or to distract the reader from the chronological absurdity Kertzer was perpetrating), there is an endnote stating, "An official census of the Jews of Poland in 1939 counted 3,351,000 Jews. Under 400,000 survived." But for someone with Kertzer's sensibility, the final question must be, why did he stop at "Poland's three million Jews"? The oracular Father Kruszyński wanted "the world to be rid of the Jewish scourge."

What readers are expected to believe — and apparently very many do — is that a future pope who had no connection, neither time nor place, with a particular priest is implicated in that priest's anti-Semitic tirades as well as in the murderous deeds those tirades anticipated. Only two possible explanations of this final conclusion are plausible. From another interview one learned that Kertzer originally wanted to end the book with Ratti's return from Poland,[35] so possibly Kertzer believed he had to draw toward the end of his project with a newsworthy *finale* — the pope directly linked to the slaughter of millions — or he had lost in his various exercises in hyperbole the capacity to recognize the absurdity of his inference: in 1921, a future pope was not only guilty of perversely failing to envision the slaughter of millions of Jews two decades later, but he was also guilty of complicity in that slaughter.[36]

---

35. "Unholy War: An Interview with David Kertzer," by Robert Wilde. www.european history.about.com/library/weekly/aa012502e.htm.

36. There actually was "a future pope in Poland" in that year, 1923, when Father

It is anticlimactic, if not moot, to note as another matter of historic fact that Kertzer is so much more concerned with juggling chronology, geography, *and* mathematics that he cannot recognize in the very terms used, "anthropological type," "Jewish scourge," the words not of popes — who had opposed precisely those conceptualizations — but of nineteenth-century pseudo-Darwinian racists who regarded Jews as "noxious creatures, as carriers of a virus, as a pestilential scourge that could infect the blood of Aryans." All of this resulted in "the appearance of biological metaphors and annihilatory words" to describe the presumably oncoming danger.[37] Such was the power of this image-laden speech that terms like "extirpation" and "elimination" were the common parlance of professional racists in that era. It is hardly surprising, as the appalling ideology moved from the West, that a few years later its freight of bacteriological myths would reach Polish academics like Kruszyński. Again, what all that has to do with Achille Ratti remains undisclosed, save that what "synagogue of Satan" was for Pius IX and Leo XIII, the name Kruszyński is now for Pius XI. But what all this *does* have to do with is Kertzer's lauded scholarship, since in fact this scenario could

---

Kruszyński made his memorably odious but virtually unnoticed statements about the Jewish scourge. Unlike Ratti, however, this future pope wasn't contaminated by the infectious vermin devastating the country, and was merely being initiated into the diplomatic service while brushing up on his French during his stay in Warsaw. While in Poland, he also met with some sympathetic Modernists who had evaded the wrath of Pius X's master spy, Umberto Benigni — at that time busy in London tracking down the exiled founder of the "Popular Party," Don Luigi Sturzo, for Mussolini's Fascists. The study of French had not been undertaken in order to read *La Croix* or *L'Univers*, but did lead to translations of such works as "L'Impossible antisémitisme" by Jacques Maritain, with whom the future pope would become a close friend. Unlike Pius XI, who was linked to the death factories by Kertzer's codded-up Ratti-Kruszyński nexus, this future pope, Paul VI, was linked to the implementation of the declaration regarding Jews and Judaism of Vatican II. See Peter Hebblethwaite, "Polish Intermezzo," in *Paul VI: The First Modern Pope* (1993).

37. Klaus P. Fischer, *The History of an Obsession* (1998). The development of pseudo-Darwinian racism — which had tangential roots in Darwin himself — is described in Richard Weikart's *From Darwin to Hitler: Evolutionary Ethics, Eugenics, and Racism in Germany* (2004), a book that is so "religiously" orthodox that Darwinian evolution itself is almost called into question. Weikart himself is attached to the creationist movement. Historically more reliable is Stefan Kühl's *The Nazi Connection: Eugenics, American Racism, and German National Socialism* (1994). Curiously, one of the first and most vigorous opponents of eugenics was the anti-Semitic G. K. Chesterton. His characteristically witty and insightful *Eugenics and Other Evils: An Argument Against the Scientifically Organized State,* originally published in 1922, was reissued in 2000 (Michael W. Perry, ed.).

only become reality and be linked to Pius XI, or to any other pope, because Kertzer had tampered with his sources — again.

The Sorbonne scholar Paul Zawadzki — who actually read the book with the Kruszyński quotations cited by Kertzer — wrote his study with a view to specifically countering the kind of interpretation that Kertzer exploits. "Let us be precise; 'in order to de-judaize the country' [*désenjuiver le pays*], the priest Kruszyński very clearly did not mean extermination but a planned expulsion, otherwise called a territorial solution." What makes Kertzer's misappropriation of this text all the more damaging is that Zawadzki informs his readers that his work was expressly intended to lead other researchers to not take the tack that Kertzer does, and instead to examine the different types of anti-Semitism in various twentieth-century societies, "while guarding against the reduction of all forms of judeophobia to the National Socialist model." Though that passage is ignored by Kertzer, its basic contention was confirmed by Léon Poliakov when he referred in *Harvest of Hate* to "ostracism and banishment" as having meant, in the writings of fringe social Darwinists, "symbolic murder." Of course, all this must shock any present-day reader, but, even more, it points up the folly of attributing such sentiments to popes who would not have been able to even conceptualize those kinds of fictions.

Concerning the larger issue of church teaching and anti-Semitism, Zawadzki is equally judicious — and ironic. Following the appearance in 1937 of Maritain's "L'imposssible antisémitisme," which guardedly affirmed the incompatibility of Christianity and anti-Semitism, some extremist Polish intellectuals tried to show that anti-Semitism was actually an obligation for Catholics. Zawadzki drily notes:

> reconciling the idea of the non-assimilability of Jews with the idea of a Catholic country compelled several nationalist authors to engage in daunting rhetorical feats. . . . This logomachy is characteristic of numerous nationalist texts of the thirties deploying strained theoretical tactics to reconcile racist practice with universal theological principles.

As to "strained theoretical tactics," they are again exemplified by Kertzer as he provides a wrenched analysis of differences between an abridged version of Ratti's final summation published by the Vatican in 1990, and the original version, edited by Ratti's "most trusted assistant," a Monsignor Pellegrinetti, who had remained behind in Poland. Abandoning entirely the earlier language of "reports" and "documents," Kertzer observes: "Pellegrinetti studied all the letters that Ratti had written to the secretary of state over the previous three years, as well as all the other materials they had collected." After one paragraph describing this final summation, Kertzer begins a new paragraph by describing the "special series of books making the most important documents from the Vatican archives more accessible." This series included the abridged version mentioned above.

But in its transmogrification from Pellegrinetti in 1923 to that book in 1990, "a reader familiar with the original document, found in the Vatican Secret Archives, discovers that something is amiss." What is amiss is that the published version "is interrupted with parenthetical insertions, in italics, providing summaries rather than the actual text" — which in fact sounds much like Kertzer's favored rhetorical mode. His question, "Why was this section on the Jews paraphrased rather than published in its original format?" is something that could have been asked of countless passages that Kertzer introduced to make his own case. The conclusion, never explicitly spelled out, is that present-day Vatican functionaries were doctoring the original report, and thus perpetuating their own version of what had happened in post–World War I Poland. A less invidious conclusion might be that in a general book directed to the general public half a century after the Holocaust, changes that might have been thought desirable or even necessary would be made.

After his question as to why a section in the 1990 book was paraphrased, Kertzer continues as follows:

> In the original document the passage on the features that distinguish the Jews from the Poles includes some not mentioned in the published version: "Not only do they differ visibly from Poles owing to their racial characteristics (shortness of stature, large nose, prominent ears, bags under their eyes, etc.). They differ also because of their religion and the strong consciousness and pretension they have of forming a separate nationality."

So, now that readers know the features not mentioned in the published version, it would have been helpful to learn precisely what features were mentioned. This might at least have indicated whether the Vatican publication was really a scandalously bowdlerized version, or merely one that was trying to present nonprofessional readers more than half a century after the Holocaust with a less vulgarized account of those momentous three years.

Possibly a less serious problem with Kertzer's discussion of these reports is that it is difficult to be certain what precisely represents the views of Ratti, of Pellegrinetti, or even of Ottavio Cavalleri — the Vatican editor who was responsible for parenthetical insertions, italics, and "summaries rather than the actual text." What at least looks like more fudging on Kertzer's part takes the form of launching successive paragraphs as though they were from different sources: "The Russian Czars, Pellegrinetti wrote . . ." "The report painted a picture of the Jews . . ." "With the end of the war and the creation of the new Polish state, Pellegrinetti went on to report . . ." "Here the Ratti report provides a belated response . . ." The next topic sentence — written apparently without any sense of self-consciousness on the part of the author — is: "The report contains the kind of conspiracy theory found repeatedly in the Catholic anti-Semitic Movement." The final paragraph begins, "Pellegrinetti went on to note . . ."

Kertzer is drawing nearer to the end of "A Future Pope in Poland," and it is possible that the onset of the debilitated mood that inserted the Axis Powers into World War I has led to the non sequiturs in the following (complete) paragraph:

> Even the published portions of the Ratti report offer a portrait of Poland's Jews as a danger to society. The report continued: "One finds a sharp contrast between the Jewish capitalists who, unfortunately, have a large part of Poland's wealth in their hands, and the Jewish proletariat among whom the most advanced parties find a following, including Bolshevism, of whom the Jews form the principal force in Poland."

The issue has nothing to do with the stereotypical nature of this portrait, but with how this purely descriptive summation shows them to be "a danger to society." Other than the insertion of the negligible adverb, "unfortunately" — which relates only to the capitalists, thus presumably making the proletarian Bolsheviks quite acceptable — this is an entirely factual observation on the relationship between the two classes of Polish Jews. Whether it is or isn't sociologically accurate is irrelevant to its alleged exemplification of "Jews as a danger to society." The author's assumption seems to be that by this phase of the discussion probably anything emanating from the papacy can be passed off as anti-Semitic.

In the event, the report contains nothing that either ameliorates or further denigrates the future pope, so Kertzer concludes his treatment by noting that "Pellegrinetti received a coded telegram in Warsaw: he had just been named papal nuncio to Serbia.[!] In May he was awarded an archbishopric as well. Pellegrinetti's rise had scarcely been less rapid than Ratti's." Thus, are careerist anti-Semites requited by their Roman masters.

But despite all these efforts at convicting Ratti, one more attempt will be made. Unfortunately, as with his utilization of the work of Zawadski, Kertzer again ends up suborning his own witness. I referred earlier in the context of "evil influences" to a passage that contained the most blatant distortion of a pope's words in the entire book. That passage in the last paragraph of the chapter, "A Future Pope in Poland," begins as follows: "There is even more direct evidence that the Polish experience shaped the view of Europe's Jews that Ratti would hold as pope."[38] That announcement should come as welcome news to Kertzer's readers, who have traversed the blind alleys and evaded the pitfalls of his exposition in the hope of actually weighing "more direct evidence" relating to Ratti's "enormously important" experience — of which, unfortunately, only five months have been documented.

This evidence was gathered from a meeting Benito Mussolini had with Pius XI in February 1932, when "the Pope himself raised the question of the Jews." Although the tone and substance of the meeting would have been set by the pontiff, this kind of language coming in the last paragraph of the penultimate chapter of the book — the antechamber to the antechamber to the Holocaust — makes clear that even at this stage the author ceases to neither toil nor spin. As to the latter, there is the intensifier "himself" in the first sentence, followed by the phrase "the question of the Jews," which like "the Jewish question" was usually employed in articles and books of the period that made a pretense of open-minded concern, while actually perpetuating racial stereotypes.[39]

In a conversation that he had with Benito Mussolini in February 1932, the Pope himself raised the question of the Jews. Lamenting the persecution

38. It may be noted that the most distinguished Anglophone student of Polish history, Norman Davies, in *Heart of Europe: The Past in Poland's Present* (1984), regards the "ringing denunciation of atheism and communism" in the encyclical *Divini Redemptoris* as "inspired by Pius XI's earlier experience in Poland." *Heart of Europe* is the sequel to Davies' two-volume *God's Playground: A History of Poland* (1981).

39. The now definitive study in English is Ritchie Robertson, *The "Jewish Question" in German Literature, 1749-1939: Emancipation and Its Discontents* (1999). Léon Poliakov in *Suicidal Europe, 1870-1933,* wrote: "It is true that as a general rule, the British press and British politicians, accustomed to euphemisms, did not refer to 'the Jewish question,' but to 'the alien question.' . . ." In the United States a similar usage was "the Negro problem" — most notoriously in Norman Podhoretz's "My Negro Problem — and Ours": a feigned effort at collective candor.

faced by the Catholic Church in various parts of the world, he turned his attention to Russia. There, Pius XI told Mussolini, the Church's problems had been caused in part by "Judaism's *antipathy* for Christianity." The Pope went on to say: "When I was in Warsaw I saw that the [Bolshevik] Commissioners . . . were all Jews." *He hastened to add* that the Italian Jews represented an exception. <u>The Pope thought that the Jews in Italy — a few of whom he had met — were basically good. But the mass of the Continent's Jews, the hordes of Jews who lived in central and eastern Europe, were something quite different, a threat to healthy Christian society, a lesson he learned in Poland.</u>[40]

This paragraph is based entirely on a summary of the meeting between the two men by Renato Moro, author more recently of a book critical of Pius XII but also corrective of John Cornwell's myths in *Hitler's Pope*. Kertzer's paraphrase/translation above should be compared with the original passage from Moro's study, which began as follows: "In 1931 Pius XI made an effort to oppose religious persecution involving Jews (and was warmly thanked by Rabbi Da Fano)."[41]

A few months later, when he was speaking with Mussolini in February 1932, he brought up the image of a church surrounded by attacks from Protestants, Communists, and Jews. Moreover, the pope emphasized to the Duce that, in addition to the danger represented by Protestant propaganda, there existed an unfortunate triangulation [*doloroso triangolo*] which was the source of grave concern to the Church, and which was made up of Mexico, a country consumed by Masonry; of Spain, where Masonry and bolshevism worked together; and of Russia, engaged in the politics of de-Christianization. It was regarding the latter that the pope expressed the opinion that behind the anti-Christian persecution going on in Russia, there was "also Judaism's aversion [*l'avversione*] to Christianity"; and he added, "when I was in Warsaw I saw that in the Bolshevik regiments the male or female officers [*il commissario o la commissaria*] were Jews." But then, he specified, "however the Jews in Italy are an excep-

---

40. The ellipsis is Kertzer's, the italics are mine. The word "antipathy" will be discussed presently. "He hastened to add" is not in the original, which reads simply, "*E aggiunse*." The passage that I have underlined is nowhere to be found in Kertzer's source.

41. "Cattolici ed ebrei nell'Italia degli anni venti 1919-1932," *Storia Contemporanei* (December 1988). The excerpt above occurs at the conclusion of a study of more than a hundred pages.

tion to that." And he recalled his friendship with old Massaroni, with Elia Prottes, and his studies with the Chief Rabbi of Milan, Da Fano.

The first thing one notes is that the original passage began and ended with a reference to Rabbi Da Fano, under whom the anti-Semitic Ratti had studied Hebrew, a "lesson" he put to good use when talking to Jews in Poland. And, as seen above, it is not true to say that "the Pope himself raised the question of the Jews." Anyone comparing the two excerpted texts cannot overlook the warping and omissions introduced by Kertzer, including the impossible transformation, highlighted in both excerpts, of *avversione* into *antipatia*.[42] The relatively incidental focus on the Jews is even more evident in Moro's own source regarding the papal audience, since at the actual meeting between the pope and the Duce, it is the treatment of the Russian policy of de-Christianization that led to the mention of Jews, and that occurred only near the end of an audience that had opened with the expression of concern about "Protestant propaganda" briefly mentioned by Moro.[43]

The pope's own concerns, based on a written memorandum for Mussolini, related to such things as military trainees attending Mass, government aid for earthquake damage to church buildings, the delay in appointing nominated bishops, Catholic Action vis-à-vis the Fascist Party, church-state relations, and so on. In the exchange between the two men, the topics touched on ranged from world peace to Japanese incursions in the Far East, disarmament, tariffs, and the state of the world economy. Concerning the latter, if there were any subject that even a person remotely tainted by anti-Semitism in a spontaneous conversation would have expanded on, it would certainly be the relation of the Great Depression to "Jewish bankers." As oft-noted, Kertzer is convinced that each pope he studies was preoccupied with the role of the bankers — although not as obsessively preoccupied as Kertzer

42. This has also now become canonical: "Years later, as Pius XI, Ratti told Italian dictator Benito Mussolini that Jews were causing the Catholic Church serious problems in parts of the world because of 'Judaism's *antipathy* for Christianity.'" A. James Rudin, "How the Popes Systematically Fanned the Flames of Hatred," *Forward*, October 26, 2001. As noted earlier, Rudin also said of Kertzer: "Those who challenge his disturbing conclusions will have to match Mr. Kertzer's scholarship, research and command of the Italian language." The issue here has to do only with "command of the Italian language" in the service of doctoring texts.

43. Angelo Corsetti, "Dalla preconciliazione ai patti del Laterano," *Annuario 1968 della Biblioteca civica di Massa* (1969). This contains Mussolini's own summation of the audience in a transcription prepared for King Victor Emmanuel III.

had shown himself to be when gratuitously naming various bankers in the context of Pius IX's homily to the Roman women, and as he will show himself to be in the context of an interview with an earlier pope, Leo XIII.

Rather than continuing with Kertzer's "direct evidence," entailing his invention of a climactic anti-Semitic papal outburst, I must insert here an excursus on this antecedent incident where the alleged preoccupation of a pope also entailed doctoring an important text — alluded to earlier in the context of Jews and "evil" influences. There is also in this excursus a stratagem similar to the one above whereby "aversion" became "antipathy," although what follows all relates to an event that occurred three decades before the audience with Mussolini — and thus augurs the present chapter's culminating slanderous "mistranslation" whereby Jews will be described as carriers of pandemic blight.

Specifically, this earlier event occurred in August 1892, over halfway into the reign of Leo XIII, when the pope, as part of his overall effort at reconciliation with the modern era, granted a personal interview to a secular newspaper — something totally unprecedented. The resultant article, which appeared on the front page of *Le Figaro,* "caused a sensation," according to Giovanni Miccoli — again, Kertzer's source.[44] Miccoli also noted that the interviewer had expected a condemnation of the Jews, but the pope, who spoke in French throughout the interview, "categorically condemned all war of religion and all war of race," while also maintaining that "the Holy See had always protected the Jews against the violence of the mob."

Kertzer here makes his own contribution by way of another translation/ paraphrase:

In general, he [Leo XIII] kept to a traditional Church outlook, stressing the role of the popes in protecting the Jews and inviting the Jews to accept baptism and convert. However, in warning of a new plague that was affecting modern society, which he termed "the kingdom of money," and insisting on the need to defend against it, the Pope — without naming the Jews — tapped in to one of the main themes of the Catholic anti-Semitic campaign of the time.

44. "Un'intervista di Leone XIII sull'antisemitismo," in *Cristianesimo nella storia. Saggi in onore di Giuseppe Alberigo* (Bologna, 1996). It would be interesting to know what Alberigo, the historian of Vatican II, thought of this contribution to his Festschrift.

(I include this event from the reign of Leo XIII in this chapter because it is here that deviant translations *or* mistranslations, usually related to modern racist anti-Semitism, most abound — as the outrageous ending of this entire chapter will emphatically exemplify.)

With this passage the kinds of linguistic ruses encountered earlier again come into play, as the author shows that his command of French is apparently less intimidating than his alleged command of Italian. The passage from the pope — which in the translation by Miccoli-Kertzer exemplifies his alleged preoccupation with pestilential Jews — is the following brief sentence: "Et voici qu'après tant d'autres fléaux, le règne de l'argent est venu" — meaning simply, *"and thus after so many other calamities, the rule [or reign] of money has come."* The more or less self-evident reason for the statement occurring in this interview with this pope is that the topic "clearly had been preying on his mind" — to cite Kertzer on Pius IX and Jewish dogs. As for Leo XIII, it had been preying on his mind at least since the previous year when he published his revolutionary encyclical, *Rerum Novarum,* subtitled "On Capital and Labor" — both terms rather obviously having to do with money, but neither having anything in particular to do with Jews, save in Kertzer's self-referential speculations.

Miccoli mistranslated the French *règne* as *regno,* meaning "kingdom," rather than "reign" or "rule," and so transformed an abstract category into a personal entity — which his American protégé does also — as they both tap into one of the main themes of the imaginary war against the Jews, i.e., that the popes endorsed modern racist anti-Semitism with all its baggage of Jews as vermin-carrying aliens. The fact is that Leo said nothing about a plague, whether new or old.[45] Kertzer follows Miccoli in transforming the original French plural noun into a singular; but at least Miccoli does use a cognate of *fléaux,* the Italian *flagelli* (E.T., "flails"). But neither in the original French nor in the Italian can the word be Englished as "plague." "Scourges" would be acceptable but clumsy; so, given Leo's specific context, "calamities" (or its synonyms) is the only possible translation — resulting in the italicized passage in the preceding paragraph.

The reason Kertzer persisted in his misreading is that, as seen earlier, this is the language of nineteenth-century popularizers of Darwinian stereotypes, and thus of the specifically racist anti-Jewishness referred to in the subtitle of the book: *The Vatican's Role in the Rise of Modern Anti-Semitism.* It is of the latter that Kertzer has been trying to convict the popes — as we will see again at the end of this chapter, in what I have earlier referred to as

45. Even without Rabbi Rudin's accolades for the linguistic skills of Kertzer, the mere mention of "plague" in the context of the French language should have brought to mind Albert Camus and *La Peste* — along with a still small voice saying: "you can't get away with translating *fléau* as *plague.*"

the author's most shocking rhetorical subterfuge. Concerning the "kingdom of money" — to conclude this excursus — it too was a topos that in his introductory remarks on Pio Nono's homily to the Roman women Kertzer himself had tapped into, and which by his lights the entire text of *Rerum Novarum* would not only be tapping into but could even be identified as *the* source of "the main theme of the Catholic anti-Semitic campaign of the time."

Pius XI, who had in the year before the meeting with Mussolini paid personal homage to Leo XIII's *Rerum Novarum* by writing an encyclical commemorating it, was as little preoccupied with Jews as was his predecessor. Thus the mistranslations above, however slanted, are relatively venial when compared with Pius XI's reference to "Judaism's aversion to Christianity" being transformed into "Judaism's antipathy for Christianity." In fact, what was originally a wide-ranging conversation was reduced to a treatment of the Jews by Moro — entirely understandable given the title of his study — and was further reduced by Kertzer, in a failed effort to make the papal audience with Mussolini "direct evidence that the Polish experience shaped the view of Europe's Jews that Ratti would hold as pope."

"Direct evidence" is hardly how one would characterize the various tactics described above, but even substituting "antipathy" for "aversion" is a mild offense compared with the following concoction — which goes even beyond the mind reading Kertzer had exercised earlier, and which is neither in Mussolini's report to the king nor in Renato Moro's study. These are the last words of the chapter, earlier described as its "culminating slander":

> The Pope thought that the Jews in Italy — a few of whom he had met — were basically good. But the mass of the Continent's Jews, the hordes of Jews who lived in central and eastern Europe, were something quite different, a threat to healthy Christian society, a lesson he learned in Poland.

This assertion is raw, undiluted Kertzer. Like the earlier "satanic synagogues" or "Jewish dogs," these threatening hordes are nonexistent save in the author's imagination. But there is a significant difference in that previously when assaying the mentality of any figure in the Vatican, from pope or secretary of state to the most incidental underling, there was at least some basis in an official document — a letter, a report, a book. Similarly, when Kertzer misinterpreted statements by popes, cardinals, bishops, etc., or completely dismissed their statements in favor of their "real" meaning to be found in various Catholic newspapers, there was at least a semblance of a foundation in something that had actually at one time or another been said by those personages or published in those venues. Now, in order to round out his entire discussion of the overwhelming importance of those "three years" in Poland, and to make them the foundation of Ratti's oncoming anti-Semitic pontificate, words are simply invented by the author to be put in this pope's mouth — far more drastically than when they were put into the mouth of Leo XIII, by changing his concern about the economic innovations that contributed to the "rule of money" into concern about a "plague."

As noted earlier, it was really Kertzer who was tapping into the bacteriological-pestilential fictions of Social Darwinists — explicitly rejected in all papal teaching — about the danger the "mass of the continent's Jews" posed to "healthy Christian society." All of that, the pope told his readers via Kertzer's ventriloquial virtuosity — first tested on Pio Nono — was a lesson he "learned in Poland," though the only comment by the pope that mentioned Jews was the passing observation "when I was in Warsaw I saw that in all the Bolshevik regiments the male or female officers were Jews." Apart from Kertzer's rigging the story of the Beilis trial, it is difficult to imagine the trickery here could be made even more devastating. But Kertzer's earlier speculations suggest an obsession that explains the language of his hatched conclusion to Mussolini's audience with the pope.

When Leo XIII was first introduced Kertzer described him as believing "that healthy Christian society required protection from Jewish depredation." At the beginning of the chapter, "Ritual Murder and the Popes in the Twentieth Century," Kertzer observed: "No pope himself would publicly argue that the Jews were a foreign body destroying Christian society." But now, precisely because no pope would so argue, Kertzer — at the end of what was, even for him, a flagrantly botched treatment — quotes a pope who the reader is expected to believe does publicly say that. But since this is entirely Kertzer's creation, the statement by "the Pope" will be worded even more hyperbolically. It is "the mass of the Continent's Jews" that is the object of concern; and lest that not be derogatory enough, in order to further highlight papal monstrosity, the original exaggeration is inflated to "the hordes of Jews in central and eastern Europe" who are threatening "healthy Christian society." Presumably, papist sympathizers will be able to decrypt this language, since they know that it is the mysterious East that spawns these plague-bearing vermin.

In the mistranslation discussion previously, Kertzer referred to Leo XIII as "tapping into one of the main themes of the Catholic anti-Semitic campaign of the time." Now Kertzer in this manufactured passage has Pius XI tapping into similar racist stereotypes about alien hordes from Central and Eastern Europe, a stereotype, as noted earlier, that was used by anti-Semitic writers contemporaneous with Pope Leo's alleged statement. Léon Poliakov in *Suicidal Europe* cited one of many such authors: "Furthermore, we must not forget that the Jews of Russia, Poland, and almost all the southeast of Europe are not European. They are Asiatic and, in part at least, Mongoloid." So much for the precious resource that this counterfeit direct evidence provides, showing that "the Polish experience shaped the view of Europe's Jews that Ratti would hold as pope."

That experience, the reader was told, was based on "his three years in Warsaw" — of which in fact less than half a year is documented. In that light one might want to reexamine a statement like the following — because this statement will be revivified when Ratti in the next chapter, that is, in the "antechamber to the Holocaust," makes his anguished declaration that "spiritually we are all Semites":

> Although Jews in many parts of Poland were being murdered, their homes and synagogues burned to the ground, and the Pope had asked him to take an interest in the Jews' welfare, Ratti did nothing of the sort. Examination of his activities in the months that followed reveals that, on the contrary, he did everything he could to impede any Vatican action on behalf of the Jews and prevent any Vatican intervention that would discourage the violence.

By this time there is no need to labor the point about the nonexistence of those months that followed. Nor is anything gained by again remarking on the concealment of the essential information that "in early June 1921, Ratti left Poland." But even those maneuvers are trumped in the next paragraph — as my italics indicate: "Ratti departed before his work was finished, for the secretary of state wanted to get a complete, final report of the mission, which had lasted *three eventful years.*"

Finally, there are the following examples of how the warping of historical events — from the pogroms in Poland to the Mussolini report to the Kertzer chapter and up to the year 2010 — is consummated in its final appropriation by professional Holocaust specialists and by professional historians, all of whom are duly exercising their craft. The specialists are first.

> Ratti's experience in Poland was to influence his attitude toward Jews for the rest of his life. In 1932, he told Benito Mussolini, Italy's fascist dictator,

that the Church's problems were partly caused by "Judaism's antipathy for Christianity." The pope did allow that most of Italy's Jews were "basically good," but insisted that the "hordes of Jews" living in Central and Eastern Europe were a threat to healthy Christian society.[46]

There is one intentional mistranslation by Kertzer, "antipathy"; there is one whole-cloth fabrication by Kertzer about threats to "healthy Christian society"; and, lastly, there is one new exercise in creativity by these editors, as the pope "insisted" on describing the pestilential Jewish hordes.

Next, the historians, the first of whom is the previously cited Daniel Jonah Goldhagen, writing in *A Moral Reckoning*. Like the specialists, he indulges even more lavishly in what Harold Bloom would call creative misprisions — as indicated by the italics below:

In 1932 he [Pius XI] *even* confided his *profound* animosity towards Jews, which stayed with him at least through most of his papacy, to Mussolini.[47] The persecution of the Church around the world, Pius XI *volunteered*, was partly the result of "Judaism's antipathy for Christianity" and with the exception of Italian Jews, the Jews of Europe, especially of central and eastern Europe, were a threat to Christian society.

The second historian believes Kertzer's book "persuades as much by a dispassionate exposition of the evidence as by its well articulated argument."

"Ratti deliberately avoided meeting Jewish delegations hoping to enlist Rome's help in the face of popular pogroms then sweeping the country." "Kertzer has credible evidence for suggesting that the lesson Ratti learned in Poland was that the hordes of Jews in central and eastern Europe were a threat to a healthy Christian society." (Richard A. Lebrun at H-Catholic, H-Net Reviews, www.h-net.org/reviews/showrev.php?id=5655)

The last historian, Kevin Madigan — on whom the remainder of this chapter will concentrate — is a medievalist who also writes articles critical of the papacy during the Nazi era, although his focus is more on Pius XII

---

46. Richard L. Rubenstein and John K. Roth, eds., *Approaches to Auschwitz: The Holocaust and Its Legacy* (2003)

47. If ever there were a sentence that would strain a reader's intellectual musculature, it is this tardily appended "to Mussolini." Here disjunctive rhetoric flows from incoherent speculation.

than on his predecessor. One of the more notable of these articles was titled "What the Vatican Knew About the Holocaust, and When" (*Commentary* [October 2001]). This was a detailed and generally accurate survey of various communications received by papal authorities in Rome informing them of the persecution of Jews across Europe. Madigan concluded by saying that the pope "knew enough, but *did not care enough,* to speak more forcefully or to act more courageously than he did." This arbitrary indictment regarding an undetermined *and* undeterminable state of mind — scant concern — cast a long shadow on the motive of the writer, and in the event blurred the article's moral import.[48] It indicated as well that Kertzer's own penchant for reading the minds of others had an emulator in Madigan who, it will turn out, is a passionate admirer of Kertzer's scholarship in general.

Similarly, an earlier Madigan article in a non-Jewish venue, "Judging Pius XII" (*The Christian Century,* March 14, 2001), had made quite clear that for him Pacelli was indeed Hitler's pope. And the book with that thesis had been discussed — very favorably — in a neutral venue by Madigan the previous year (H-Net Reviews, April 2000). Lastly, much of this same narrative and its motivation were even more in evidence in another and far more recent *Commentary* article ("Two Popes, One Holocaust," December 2010), and it is this piece primarily that accounts for Madigan's presence here at the end of this chapter. Unlike the previous discussants, all of whom were vigorously critical of Pius XI, Madigan presents himself in this article as an enthusiastic admirer of that pope, and suggests that he, and not Pius XII, should really be the *candidate for sainthood.* This is his position, even though he — like Goldhagen, Lebrun, Roth, and Rubenstein — is also a supporter, almost wildly so, of the author of *The Popes Against the Jews.* To clarify this paradox, one has to examine the blurb that Madigan wrote for the sequel to *The Popes Against the Jews,* a book published in 2004 and titled *Prisoner of the Vatican.* After praising its author as "a national treasure," Madigan linked the two books by describing the more recent one as "*another* masterpiece."[49] This accolade is surprising because — as readers will recall from my first chapter — the first of these two masterpieces had begun as follows:

---

48. I know nothing of Madigan personally, save that he co-authored a book with Jon Levenson, an author whose *Sinai and Zion: An Entry into the Jewish Bible* I was honored to publish in 1987, and from which I learned much.

49. This is the complete text according to Amazon: "As magically spellbinding as it is enlightening, replete with colorful characters and complex international and ecclesiastical politics and intrigue. Kertzer is a national treasure and his latest book another masterpiece."

The story I tell here for the first time about Achille Ratti in the years just before he became Pope Pius XI in 1922 can be seen in this light. In the literature on Pius XII's failure to speak out during the Holocaust, he is often compared unfavorably to Pius XI, "the good pope," portrayed as a firm foe of anti-Semitism. . . . But what if we find that Pius XII's benevolent predecessor shared the same stridently anti-Semitic views?

But that is precisely what "we" did find when reading Kertzer, so the real question is how does a scholar in a lengthy article systematically undercut the "first time" story told in what he regards as a literary masterpiece, and then proceed to exalt the benevolent predecessor (Pius XI) who was also stridently anti-Semitic. Moreover, if Madigan *is* to be taken seriously, it means that each of the essential themes of Kertzer's "A Future Pope in Poland" is irrelevant. No longer is it possible to believe that "the whole twentieth-century history of the Church might have been different" if Ratti had never been sent to Poland. What was previously asserted as an obvious truism — "Ratti did everything he could to impede any Vatican action on behalf of the Jews" — is now to be rejected. It no longer matters that, according to Kertzer's earlier masterpiece, the future pope in Poland had said that "One of the most evil and strongest influences that is felt here, perhaps the strongest and the most evil, is that of the Jews."

Similarly, those scrupulously annotated "reports and documents" that Kertzer assembled do not really "allow us, for the first time, to understand the attitude toward Jews that Pius XI brought with him when he became pontiff." By Madigan's lights, those "precious" and "priceless" resources and insights that originally proved the anti-Semitism of Ratti have been utterly devalued. But if that is really true, then that lauded "national treasure" of which Madigan wrote contains only fool's gold. It is just not possible to have it both ways: to at once rave about Kertzer's scholarship and literary achievement and, at the same time, to be enthusiastic over the pope whom Kertzer exposed as being at heart another anti-Semite.

Madigan's second *Commentary* article exalting Pius XI had as its occasion — or, better, its pretext — the translation in 2010 of Hubert Wolf's *Pope and Devil: The Vatican's Archives and the Third Reich*, a book that concentrates on the reign of Pius XI in the 1930s when the future Pius XII was his secretary of state. Wolf is one of many church historians examining the newly accessible documents from that period, few of whom are particularly supportive of the kinds of conventional critiques of Pius XII that Madigan himself has launched. But since Wolf is a respected scholar, a clergyman to boot,[50] and his book is relatively timely (and with an eye-catching title), it provided another opportunity for displaying Ratti as the "good pope," and for returning Pacelli to his now well-established role as what might be called the "supreme ponderer" — the anti-Semitic other-worldly man absorbed in celestial sentiments, a role to which Cornwell's fantasies had consigned him. While Wolf says little that has not been said by such scholars as Gerhard Besier, Thomas Brechenmacher, and Peter Godman,[51] the mere fact that the book provided another chance to attack Hitler's pope was a temptation not to be overcome by a committed piophobe — which Madigan has become, and which my reference to the pondering pontiff further illustrates.

This is Madigan in his H-Net review of *Hitler's Pope:*

> Sometimes, as in times of war, this world gets so painful that human hearts turn, as Pius put it, from "the transitory things of earth to those which are heavenly and eternal." As Cornwell, again correctly, points out, this "intensely private interiority" left no room for, or even recognition of, a doctrine of social responsibility. Being Christian, and especially being a saint, for Pius meant, above all, being pious in the intense, private, interior style that Cornwell evokes so accurately.

Apart from the fact that this buys into that bane of all serious historians — the judging of the past in light of present speculation — it has to be pointed out that the quotation from the pope is simply a gloss on Hebrews 13:14: "We have not here a lasting city but look for that which is to come." Moreover, all this theorizing about other-worldly spirituality ignores the historical reality that at the very time being described, this pope wrote a social encyclical on the Mystical Body, and another encyclical embracing the most progressive principles of modern biblical studies. Of course, and it goes without saying, there is also a conventional critique for those activities: how could he have done such things while people were being slaughtered by the thousands! To

50. The title "Father" is never omitted from references to Wolf, and his name is repeated thirteen times. "Father John LaFarge" is also mentioned, but subsequently he becomes plain "LaFarge."

51. Gerhard Besier, *The Holy See and Hitler's Germany* (E.T., 2007); Thomas Brechenmacher, "Pope Pius XI, Eugenio Pacelli, and the Persecution of the Jews in Nazi Germany, 1933-1939: New Sources from the Vatican Archives," *German Historical Institute Bulletin*, (November 2005) (www.uni-potsdam.de/db/geschichte/getdata.php?ID=1275); Peter Godman, *Hitler and the Vatican: Inside the Secret Archives that Reveal the New Story of the Nazis and the Church* (2004).

such criticism, there is only the plain and unadorned response that he must have been convinced that to do other than what he was in fact doing would have resulted in more harm than good. Regardless of how elementary this may sound, particularly when contrasted with the detailed and complex certitudes (chronological, statistical, biographical, geographical, theological, pathological) of strident critics, the only alternative is to believe that this man *was* a moral monster — but of that there is no evidence.

Madigan's review continued by exploiting further the theme of other-worldly spirituality:

> But, in a sense, the blame lies less with any particular individual than with a particular kind of Christian piety then widely popular throughout the world and by which Pius was deeply, if unfortunately, influenced. Cornwell himself states at one point that Pius's failure to "respond to the enormity of the Holocaust" was in part a failure of the "prevailing culture of Catholicism. That failure was implicit in the rifts Catholicism created and sustained — between the sacred and the profane, the spiritual and the secular, the body and the soul."

The notion that this kind of dualism was "created" by Catholicism provides another insight into the perspective of these critics. Nor is one surprised when Madigan concludes by paying homage to his *and* Cornwell's perspicacity: "these pages are among the most profound [Cornwell's insight] and most neglected [Madigan's insight] in the book."

So much for Madigan on Cornwell's *Hitler's Pope.* This is Madigan on Wolf's *Pope and Devil.* As noted several times throughout the previous chapters, obvious flaws and errors (tics) often signal ruses or stratagems by an author who is straining to prove a novel thesis or to make a dubious point. This tic on the first page of "Two Popes: One Holocaust" is almost an embarrassment to the reader — not to mention the author. According to Madigan, who has a penchant for isomorphic pairs, "Ratti served as pope from 1929 to 1939," though his election took place in 1922. That obvious blunder parallels the following more complex sentence where the reader is informed, quite correctly, that Ratti "served as papal nuncio to Poland from 1919 to 1921." What the reader is *not* told is that, while this is chronologically correct, it manages to dispense with the ten months when Ratti was papal apostolic visitor to Poland, the period during which the monstrous misdeeds alleged by Kertzer occurred — all as described in fabricated detail in what Madigan referred to as that "masterpiece," *The Popes Against the Jews.* Also in the area of chronological isomorphism Madigan discovered this almost preternatural pairing: "*On the very day* LaFarge submitted it [the so-called "hidden encyclical"] in *December* 1938, Pius XI tearily explained to a group of Belgian pilgrims . . ." — referring to the pope's anguished cry climaxing with the affirmation that "spiritually, we are all Semites." But in fact there is no connection between the two events, since the "very day" of the *cri de coeur* was in *September,* and had nothing to do with that particular document.

All of these are what might be characterized as gross errors concerning rudimentary facts, so one has to wonder what kind of larger stratagem might have been preoccupying the author. Everybody reading the previous material in this chapter certainly knows by this time that the purpose for introducing Pacelli into the narrative is to twist whatever can be twisted to prove that he was indeed the duplicitous anti-Semite discovered by various people writing in the wake of Rolf Hochhuth's Ur-text. The aforementioned John Cornwell twice referred to the document that he rigged to prove Pacelli's anti-Semitism as "a ticking bomb." Now at the end of the first decade of the twenty-first century, another writer, Father Wolf, is to be enlisted in this same explosive cause by Professor Madigan.

The specific events and language of this enlistment are based on what now constitutes a topos in the story of the Vatican during the early years of Nazi rule. The aforementioned Gerhard Besier, Thomas Brechenmacher, and Peter Godman all analyze this same text — centered mainly on the quoted passage in the excerpt below — in much the same neutral fashion. Not so Madigan, whose treatment is a strange garblement of text and context in order to lead the reader to believe that the future Pius XII as envisioned by Wolf could indeed approximate the cunning figure conjured up by the admired Cornwell.[52] The author of *Pope and Devil* is quoted:

---

52. In the paragraphs preceding the excerpt, Wolf had been describing the different opinions regarding Pius XII's "speaking out or remaining silent" about the Jews. After referring to the pope's 1942 Christmas address, Wolf concluded by saying: "These statements, he [Pius XII] believed, were the outer limits of what he could say without risking the Curia's diplomatic standing *and the ability to continue working to save the Jews.*"

The next paragraph led directly into the excerpt — as the concluding italicized passage indicates:

> But the so-called final solution of the Jewish question was not the first context in which the pope and the Curia were accused of silence. Nor was this criticism first raised after the fact. Rather, as early as the spring of 1933, immediately after Hitler's seizure of power, numerous Jews and non-Jews turned directly to Pius XI, asking him to condemn publicly the persecution of the Jewish people. This meant that the Curia had been more than well

The cardinal secretary of state's reasons for engaging the Roman Curia in this question are particularly interesting: "It is in the tradition of the Holy See to fulfill its universal mission of peace and love for all human beings, regardless of their social status or the religion to which they belong." With this statement, Pacelli had acknowledged in principle the responsibility of the Catholic Church as advocate for and protector of human rights.

The explanation for all those strange chronological and factual blunders put on display above is that Madigan was preoccupied with how to take this straightforward diplomatic quotation, with its expression of love for all human beings regardless of status or religion, and transform it into something that would put on display the malevolence of Pius XII. In the following reconstruction by Madigan, it is the last sentence, which I have underlined, that serves his purpose.

> In the spring of 1933, immediately after Hitler's successful grab for power, Pius XI asked Pacelli to look into the possibilities of Catholic intervention against anti-Semitic excesses. Pacelli complied and actually stated his reasons for doing so, in words that would come back to haunt him, as follows: "it is in the tradition of the Holy See to fulfill its universal mission of peace and love for all human beings, regardless of their social status or the religion to which they belong." <u>With these words, Father Wolf observes, Pacelli had acknowledged the principle, *which he proceeded in the hour of greatest Jewish agony to ignore,* of the responsibility of the Catholic Church as the primary European "advocate for and protector of human rights."</u>

Madigan's effort in this sentence to manipulate language (and punctuation), so that the authoritative "Father Wolf" himself appears to voice the otherwise nonexistent condemnation of the future pope, is a stratagem[53] so base that it evokes the earlier judgment that Pius XII "knew enough, but did not care enough, to speak more forcefully or to act more courageously than he did."

---

informed through a variety of channels of what was going on in the Reich. Only a few days after the audience mentioned above, on April 4, 1933, Pacelli at the pope's behest instructed Orsenigo to look into the possibilities for intervening against "the anti-Semitic excesses." *The cardinal secretary of state's reasons . . . ,*" etc.

53. The blatant rigging of the punctuation is the kind of sophomoric undertaking that inevitably some Harvard grad student is going to post on Twitter.

Before moving on to the two following chapters, the issue must be broached as to why Catholic commentators seem so eager to reconstruct and even doctor texts in order to depict church leaders as the villains of the last century and a half of European anti-Semitism. It is not difficult to understand why a Jewish scholar like Kertzer would undertake such maneuvers, but the Catholics to be encountered in the next two chapters, particularly chapter 9, do not have any such ingrained or deep-seated motive, and yet their misrepresentations and falsifications are often as blatant as those put on display in the previous treatment of popes calling Jews dogs, and supporting and even sponsoring ritual murderers.

CHAPTER 8

Pius XI, Pius XII, and Anti-anti-Semitism

The last chapter of *The Popes Against the Jews* is titled with a phrase to which there have already been several references, "Antechamber to the Holocaust," and which here explicitly refers to the Vatican of Pope Pius XI. The shock value of such a title is alluded to in the previously cited interview with Kertzer by Robert Wilde. He noted that both chapters on Achille Ratti, first as emissary in Poland and then as pope, found [you] Kertzer "more animated, pushing the limits of your evidence and emphasizing your points with a few sharp sentences and literary techniques." Wilde, of course, was not referring to chronological manipulation or mistranslation techniques; he had in mind whether such a push was "a deliberate change of tact [*sic*] from part one?" Kertzer replied: "Yes, it is true that the last segment of the book takes on a less detached tone. . . . I originally planned to have the book end in 1922, when Achille Ratti ascends to the papal throne." He then explained that the reason for the original plan was that the Vatican archives "beginning in 1922 are closed," and that "so much has been written about the 1930s and the war years."[1] But this is a strange answer to the question about pushing "the limits of the evidence" and making a case with "sharp sentences and literary techniques," unless the latter were intended to camouflage the fact that the material relative to the 1930s and the "war years" is based primarily on the author's creative imagination.

As for the chapter title, "Antechamber to the Holocaust," it demands examination since it carries on the "pushing of the limits of evidence" that began with the various counterfeit statements regarding exterminationist

---

1. Robert Wilde, "Unholy War: An Interview with David Kertzer," www.europeanhistory .about.com/library/weekly/aa012502e.htm.

priests and hordes of oriental Jews in the previous chapter. Such a "push" is literally experienced as one traces the following trajectory. Earlier in the book, Kertzer had informed his readers that "the physical elimination of the Jews of Europe came at the end of a long road . . . that the Catholic Church did a great deal to build." Readers were also told that "the teachings and actions of the church, including those of the Popes themselves, helped make it [the Holocaust] possible."[2] These relatively mild and generalized images became more concrete and precise when the papacy helped "to set the stage for the later, eliminationist Nazi anti-Semitism"; and they are quite emphatically exact as "the role played by the Vatican . . . set the stage for the Holocaust."

With "Antechamber to the Holocaust," the Vatican is no longer an auxiliary on "the road," or helping "to set the stage," or even directly "setting the stage" for the death factories. The Vatican now functions, figuratively and factually, like such holding centers as Drancy outside Paris, known as "l'antichambre d'Auschwitz." The malevolence of this regarding "specially important Italy" is that there were no concentration camps in Italy until September 1940, three months after Italy entered the war, and that even those camps in the south — utterly less punitive than their German counterparts — were closed before the war ended. Among the camps was Ferramonti di Tarsia, where nearly four thousand Jews had been interned and, unlike their brethren in the north, managed to survive, not infrequently with the assistance of the pope — as the narrative of "Refugee" will show. Of the camps in the German-controlled area, Fossoli — from which more than three thousand Jews were sent to their deaths — was termed "anticamera di Auschwitz," a name now bestowed on the Vatican by this historian.

The condemnation of the Friends of Israel is the setting for the further attribution of anti-Semitism to Pius XI. In the language of the time, the Amici Israel was a "pious association" that had as its goal to work and pray for the mass conversion of Jews. Going beyond that specific goal was a broader program that sought to end the heritage of New Testament–based

---

2. The previously cited Marc Saperstein notes, "Missing is any indication of how Kertzer understands historical causality. Many things 'helped make [the Holocaust] possible.'" After listing a dozen, ranging from the Versailles Treaty and IBM cards, to American isolationism and gas chambers, Saperstein asks: "How does one rank the importance of such factors, in comparison with the teachings of the church? Is Kertzer's claim really that the Nazis would never have risen to power in Germany, and never been able to put their genocidal program into effect, without the material in his book — no *Civiltà Cattolica*, no Holocaust?" (Marc Saperstein, "An Indictment Half Right," *Commonweal*, September 28, 2001).

accusations against Jews. In the two years since its foundation in 1926, the association had enlisted thousands of supporters including several cardinals — among whom was the author of the "famous telegram," Merry del Val. Del Val, a traditionalist to the end, had been more or less shelved during the reign of Benedict XV, but regained considerable influence in the early years of Pius XI. The immediate occasion of the condemnation was a pamphlet in Latin, "Pax super Israel," which set forth the program and reformist goals of the association. Singled out for criticism was the designation of Jews as the deicide people; the vehemence of Patristic *adversus Iudaeos* texts; the blood libel along with feast days honoring the "victims" of ritual murder; and the Good Friday prayer regarding Jewish "faithlessness" — the latter, a reference to the petition in the liturgy that in vernacular translations prayed for "the perfidious Jews." Since the prayer was reckoned to be almost as traditional as the Gospel teaching that Jews were Christ-killers, del Val led the charge against the Amici Israel which, in the event, was condemned by the Holy Office in March 1928.

Kertzer begins his treatment by again entering the minds of the protagonists:

> The friends of Israel did not last long. The inquisitors were horrified by the heretical doctrines contained in "Pax super Israel," and officially condemned it. Nor did the Holy Office stop there. On March 25, 1928, it issued a decree dissolving the organization, and ordered that "no one in the future write or publish books or booklets that in any way favor these erroneous initiatives." Concerned about the impression that such a draconian move would create outside the Catholic world, the cardinals added a caveat concerning "hatred against the people whom God once chose, that hatred that today is commonly known by the name of 'anti-Semitism.'"

The authoritative tone and psychological illuminations have their now well-established aura of erudite certitude, even though all the author knows about the Friends of Israel is what he retrieved from "Miccoli's excellent analysis of this case." Needless to say, there is no indication of anyone anywhere being "horrified" by teachings that could no more be characterized as "heretical" than they could be characterized as "doctrines." In addition to those embellishments, there is also the last sentence intended to indicate that the Holy Office shared Kertzer's idiosyncratic view that this condemnation was in need of public relations adjustment in order to placate unnamed non-Catholics, and hence the "caveat" — of which only the fragment concluding the excerpt above will be cited by the author.[3]

Unlike the truncated draconian order itself, Kertzer provides his now customary excerpts from *Civiltà cattolica,* preceded by his, also anticipated, description of their author — who here gets the full monty:

> It was left to *Civiltà cattolica* to explain the message that the Vatican intended to impart. In an article whose title, "The Jewish Danger and the 'Friends of Israel,'" signaled its message, the journal supplied what was widely interpreted in the Catholic world as the definitive Church interpretation of the organization's dissolution. Enrico Rosa, author of the article, not only was the longtime director of the journal but was known in the Catholic world as particularly attuned to the Pope's wishes. As Rosa's obituary in the Jesuit journal put it, a decade later, "it is no exaggeration to say that Father Enrico Rosa remained for thirty years at the head of Italian Catholic journalism as interpreter and intrepid champion of the directive of the Holy See."[4]

So attuned to the wishes of the pope is the journal, and so estimable an interpreter of the Holy See is its editor, that there are more than two pages of quotations and paraphrases based on Rosa's fulminations: "struggle against Jewish danger," "bitter enemies and persecutors," "Judaic propaganda," "hegemony in public lives," "bold and powerful," "in industry, in the large banks," "in the occult sects," and so on. (Not that it is of overwhelming import, but it may be noted for the record that there is no mention of the fact that the article also condemned the *Protocols of the Elders of Zion*.) Overlooked in the litanies of Rosa *or* Kertzer is the actual text of the Holy Office decree condemning anti-Semitism that clearly marked another step, however "supersessionist," in the gradual evolution of the institutional church regarding Judaism and Jews.

---

3. The Holy Office may have been more prescient than it would ever know. The founders of the association ended up embracing a millenarianism regarding Jews and Judaism that was similar to that of extreme chiliastic cults in the United States today, invoking the "end time," the "remnant," and the "rapture," regarding Jews and the state of Israel. See Theo Salemink, "Katholische Identität und des Bild der Judischen 'Anderen,'" *Zeitschrift für Theologie und Kulturgeschichte* (January 2006).

4. The nervous tic of repeating "the Catholic world" so late in his book probably betrays the author's own recognition that this *orbis terrarum* did not extend much beyond the city of Rome.

The church frequently prays for the Jewish people who were guardians of divine promises fulfilled in Jesus Christ. . . . Moved by the spirit of charity the Apostolic See has protected this people against injustices, and even as it condemns every kind of hatred and jealousy among nations, it also absolutely condemns [*maxime damnat*] the hatred for this people, formerly God's chosen, which is now commonly known as "anti-Semitism."[5]

When this is contrasted with other statements Kertzer has cited as originating with the Holy Office, its tone and content will strike many as remarkably open-minded for that particular moment in the nearly two-millennium story of Christianity and Judaism.

Several Catholic critics do not share that view, and believe that if this is another step in an evolutionary development, it is still so glacial as to be insignificant. Two of the more noteworthy of those critics are the previously cited Ronald Modras, a theologian and one-time student of Joseph Ratzinger, and Martin Rhonheimer, an Opus Dei priest of Jewish ancestry who teaches in Rome.[6] The Friends of Israel came up in Rhonheimer's lengthy article, which is explicitly on the failure of the church to acknowledge its duties and responsibilities regarding the Holocaust. Along with the Holy Office passage above, another failure according to Rhonheimer was the encyclical *Mit Brennender Sorge*, which "came far too late to be of any help to Jews." Elsewhere he also notes that "The Christian view at that time was that the only solution to 'the Jewish question' was conversion to Christianity."

Looking back from the vantage point of the twenty-first century, it is impossible to deny the element of truth in those judgments. The problem arises over "the Christian view at that time," since it is equally impossible to

5. Peter Godman in *Hitler and the Vatican: Inside the Secret Archives That Reveal the New Story of the Nazis and the Church* (2004) has published many of the documents that ultimately resulted in the condemnation of Nazism in the encyclical *Mit Brennender Sorge*. He notes that it was the Holy Office that specifically wanted the following to be included among the *condemned* propositions in a projected syllabus of errors to accompany the encyclical: "Any mixture of blood with a foreign and inferior race, in particular a mixture of the Aryan with the Semitic race, is, by reason of that mixture alone, a most heinous crime against nature and marks a grave fault in the conscience."

6. Modras was cited earlier in the treatment of "synagogue of Satan." Rhonheimer's article, "The Holocaust: What Was Not Said," appeared in *First Things* (November 2003). What is unusual about this particular venue — known for its wariness of deviation from rigid orthodoxy — is that it also published severe critiques of *The Popes Against the Jews*, the book that is the source of what purports to be factual data in the Rhonheimer piece.

determine how people *then* were even able to conceive of something like a "future" encyclical — much less to criticize it for coming "far too late." The writer draws the following conclusion: "Had the Church really wanted to mount effective opposition to the fate that awaited the Jews, it would have had to condemn — from the very start — not only racism but anti-Semitism in any form." How or why the church could do anything about an entirely unknown fate goes unexplained — but does convey the notion of history adopted by the writer. What is also noteworthy in Rhonheimer's lengthy critique is its nearly complete reliance for specific instances of failures on Kertzer's exposition — though Kertzer himself is mentioned only once — and its embrace of Kertzer's anachronistic standards of judgment.[7] Thus it is no surprise that regarding statements like that of the Holy Office above, Rhonheimer is as disdainful as his model. "That people today can read them as condemnations of anti-Semitism in any form" is for him an indication of "the distance we have traveled since the Second Vatican Council, and especially during the pontificate of Pope John Paul II." That the distance is indeed great is owed to that pope — who, however, did also specifically cite the Holy Office statement as indicative of a further stage in the development of Catholic doctrine regarding Jews and Judaism.

More disingenuous is Rhonheimer's observation that the condemnation of the Friends of Israel "was in full accord, as we now know, with the view of the Jews formed by Monsignor Achille Ratti . . . during his years as papal emissary and Nuncio in Poland." Since the only view of the Jews, Poland, and Ratti that this writer and presumably the readers of *First Things* "now know" is that of Kertzer, this all too familiar certitude ("full accord") remains questionable. Abstracting from the misplaced emphasis on Polish matters, Ratti's view was similar to that of most cultivated Europeans of the day. Within Catholic circles it is probable that his opinions were less rigid than those held by a majority of the Catholic clergy and laity, of whom Jacques Maritain — writing in the year that Ratti left Poland — can be regarded as unfortunately all too representative.[8]

---

7. To be recalled here in this context of anachronisms is Kertzer's preemptive assertion, discussed in the introductory chapter: "Here we need to be careful not to view history backwards."

8. After more than fifteen years of marriage to his Jewish wife Raissa, Maritain addressed "the Jewish question" in this kind of unfortunate language and imagery.

The mass of the Jewish people remains separated and apart by reason of the very decree of providence that made of them throughout history the witness to Golgotha. . . . [Jews] are at the origin of the great revolutionary movements. . . . I won't stress the enormous

Rhonheimer then joins Kertzer in his reading of Pius XI's moving declaration that "spiritually we are all Semites," and declares: "Sympathy for the
increasing distress and misery of the Jews certainly seems the best explanation for the words of Pius XI to Belgian pilgrims in September 1938." That it
only *seems* that way raises the question of what other than sympathy could
have motivated these words, which are then further diminished by the alleged fact that they are "constantly cited for apologetic purposes." But, again,
it is to be noted that among those who constantly cite them is John Paul II,
the pope who also cited the Holy Office's words against anti-Semitism and
who, by acknowledging such additional steps away from traditional anti-
Jewishness, brought the church even beyond the revolutionary achievement
of the Second Vatican Council to the fraternal reconciliation represented by
his visit to the synagogue of Rome and to the Western Wall in Jerusalem.

Before returning to Pius XI's seemingly sympathetic outburst, this *radical* development in the twentieth century of doctrine and practice, impelled
by the emergence of modern racist anti-Semitism, can be recognized as one
of the most dramatic responses to the signs of the times in the history of
Christianity. It appears almost excruciatingly slow only to those who have
actually lived through it. John Paul II, who certainly is not to be numbered
among those apologists that think the church is "beyond reproach," utilized
both the 1928 Holy Office statement and that of Pius XI ten years later — still
to be examined here — as indicators of the development of the pre-conciliar
view, just as he also utilized Pius XII's acceptance of the Good Friday prayer's
vernacular translation as "without faith" or "unfaithful," rather than as

---

role played by Jews and Zionists in the political evolution of the world during the war.
There is the obvious necessity of a struggle for the safety of the public against the Judeo-
Masonic secret societies and international banking; hence, there is the necessity for a certain number of general measures of preservation which were — to tell the truth — more
easily arranged when society was officially Christian." "It is thus [through novenas and
masses] that the Church moved by charity, and despite a kind of *horreur sacré* with which
it protects itself against the perfidy of the Synagogue, and which prevents it from kneeling
when it prays for the Jews on Good Friday — it is thus that the Church continues and re-
peats among us the great cry "Father forgive them" of the crucified Jesus. . . . As much as
they [Catholic writers] must denounce and fight the depraved Jews who along with apostate Christians lead the anti-Christian Revolution, so also they must not close the portals
of the kingdom of heaven to those souls of good will, to those true Israelites — of whom
Our Lord spoke — in whom "there is no guile." (*La Vie spirituelle*, July 4, 1921)

It was only after the rise of Nazism culminating in the Holocaust that Maritain would — like
many others — reject this stereotypical Catholic view.

"treacherous" or any other synonym of "perfidious."[9] John Paul II also utilized Pius XII's 1955 restoration of the genuflection, reversing an anti-Jewish custom of eight centuries' duration — ardently endorsed by Maritain above — during that prayer as another sign of the revolution in Catholic doctrine and practice. Lastly, there is the pre-conciliar — though post-Holocaust — statement of John XXIII striking virtually all previous reformative nuances regarding "faithlessness" from the Good Friday liturgy, and introducing the relatively straightforward, "Let us pray for the Jews . . . who are not excluded from God's mercy." But even under the greatest reforming pope of the last millennium — admittedly shaped by Vatican II — the simplified version is still worded negatively.

Not surprisingly, Rhonheimer's understanding of Pius XI's outburst that "spiritually we are all Semites" is colored entirely by Kertzer's interpretation, an interpretation that is sharply at variance with the original story of the pope. That story, which first appeared in Belgian newspapers on September 14 and 15, 1938, more than a week after the papal audience, was written by a Monsignor Picard, the leader of a group of young Catholic Action pilgrims from Belgium. The story was picked up by *La Croix* on September 17, by *The Tablet* on September 24, and by several other papers well before the original version of Monsignor Picard appeared in *Documentation Catholique*, no. 39 (December 5, 1938), titled "À PROPOS DE L'ANTISÉMITISME, *Pèlerinage de la Radio catholique belge*."[10]

The introductory paragraph by the editors explained that it was being published to provide an accurate version of "a declaration of His Holiness" that had appeared in "various organs of the French and Belgian press." It then continued with Picard's statement:

> On September 6, 1938, His Holiness received in private audience the president, the vice-president, and the secretary of Radio catholique belge; then, in public audience, the 120 pilgrims who came in order to present to the Pope of Catholic Action the respects of our association. . . . Before the

---

9. Jules Isaac had emphasized to Pius XII in a private audience in 1949 that the rescinding of the rubric forbidding genuflection and the saying of "let us pray" and "amen" was more significant than correcting the translations of *perfidis*. Six years later — as we will see — the age-old genuflection and accompanying prayers were restored, making the petitions for the Jews comparable to the other petitions in the Good Friday liturgy. This transformation will be discussed further in the following chapter.

10. Since there has been considerable controversy about the event, the following reproduces most of the *Documentation Catholique* version.

start of the public audience, the Holy Father charged those whom he had just received in private audience to repeat to everybody what he had confided to them in particular ["redire à tous ce qu'il leur avait confié en particulier"].[11]

It is in order to respond to this desire of the Holy Father that we make public the declarations that he made to us in his private office.

Audience privée

His Holiness deigned to converse at length with us. At first, the feeling we have is one of confusion at taking up the time of the Head of the Church. But it is clear that the pope attaches great importance to our apostolate. . . . But what has moved us even more is the kindness with which His Holiness, after having spoken of our work, confides to us the cares which currently preoccupy his fatherly heart. Thus we have been able to reconstruct immediately after the audience, almost word for word, the speech of His Holiness. The text that we present has, therefore, no official or formal standing.

We would not have made it public if the Holy Father himself had not requested it. Needless to say, we have taken extreme care not to write a single syllable that has not been truly pronounced by His Holiness. . . .

Then, we present to His Holiness the missal offered by the pilgrimage of Radio Catholique. . . .[12]

After thanking them for the precious gift, the pope told them that the missal can cast light even on current events. And His Holiness began to leaf through the missal. He stops at the following words from the Canon — of which the Latin, says the pope, is so transparent, so suggestive! Then he reads the words culminating in the invocation of the sacrifice of our patriarch Abraham while his voice grew progressively more emotional.

---

11. At this point the editors of *Documentation Catholique* added their only footnote — which is mildly provocative in its absolutes (here italicized), and which would open the floodgates of speculation decades later. "*L'Osservatore Romano* (9, 9, 38), giving an account of this audience, relates *no word* of the Pope on the Jewish question and makes *no allusion at all* to the Semite problem ["ne fait point allusion au problème sémite"]."

12. In Kertzer's version of events, the audience with the pope occurred when past misdeeds were, in his old age, returning to torment him. Doing what he does best, Kertzer explains what is going on in the mind of the pontiff. "With the Germans preparing for war, and with the Church itself under attack there, he was having deep misgivings about his previous dealings with the Nazi regime." This is a fairly explicit response to the viewpoint of Kevin Madigan at the end of the preceding chapter.

Then after citing the sacrifice of Abel, the sacrifice of Abraham, the sacrifice of Melchisedech, he adds, "In three strokes, in three lines, in three steps, [this is] the whole religious history of mankind." He continues:

"Sacrifice of Abel: the Adamic epoch. Sacrifice of Abraham: the epoch of the religion and of the prodigious history of Israel. Sacrifice of Melchisedech: announcing the epoch of the Christian religion.

"Magnificent texts. Each time that we read these lines We are seized by an irresistible emotion. 'Sacrificium Patriarchae Nostri Abrahmae.' Note that Abraham is called our Patriarch, our Ancestor.

"Anti-Semitism is not compatible with the sublime thought and reality which are expressed in these texts. It is a hostile movement, a movement to which we are not able, we Christians, to belong."

[Monsignor Picard interrupts:]

Here the Pope is not able to restrain his emotion. He did not want to succumb to this emotion. But he was not able to succeed. And it is while weeping that he cited the passages from Saint Paul bringing to light our spiritual descent from Abraham. . . . "The promise is realized in Christ and by Christ in us who are the members of his mystical Body. By Christ and in Christ, we are the spiritual descendants of Abraham."[13]

At this point in the ninth paragraph, after that agonized outpouring of feeling, the pope apparently regained his emotional balance, and concluded: "No, it is not possible for Christians to participate in anti-Semitism." Then, in what appears to be an afterthought, he added, "We recognize for anyone the right to defend oneself, to take the means to defend oneself against whatever threatens one's legitimate interests. But anti-Semitism is inadmissible. Spiritually we are all Semites." Kertzer says of that final statement: "This last phrase may be the most famous words uttered by Pius XI."

Since that "phrase" is obviously a sentence, the grammatical tic — by this time in the book, a red flag — announces another stratagem, which follows immediately. "Less often quoted is what the Pope interjected into the middle of these comments." Notwithstanding the quite patent fact that this papal interjection is a single sentence in the ninth and last paragraph, there is the more significant distortion that in this present era when exploitative

13. Marc Saperstein, cited earlier, refers to Kertzer's "broad and unsubstantiated incendiary claims," and, in the context of Pius XI's *cri de coeur*, to his tendency "to judge every statement by church officials in the worst possible light" (*Commonweal*, September 28, 2001).

journalists write facilely about exterminationist priests being approved by future popes, and about another pope who was the tool of Hitler, few "comments" of Pius XI are as frequently quoted as that "interjected" one — a phenomenon that has led to its often overshadowing its larger context, as Kertzer himself is also about to exemplify. Nor should that surprise. A writer who can cite page after page of vituperation from *Civiltà cattolica,* but quotes only four short fragments from Pius's discourse to the Roman women, could hardly be expected to confine himself to a direct quotation from that "less often quoted" interjection.

But Kertzer first introduces another Vatican face-saving *apologia,* not unlike that relating to the Friends of Israel earlier; he then explains its furtive significance; and, finally, he assays the mental state of Pius from childhood on.

> . . . the meaning of the Pope's caveat is clear: Yes, Catholics too are spiritually Semites, for they are spiritually descended from the Chosen People. But the heavy weight of his early years growing up in a Church where Jews were vilified, followed by his experience in Poland, remained with him. Murdering Jews, burning down their homes and stores, humiliating them, these were all unchristian and inhumane. But taking "legitimate" actions to defend the rest of the population from the Jews, this was something he did not oppose.

Thus the sentence Kertzer bypassed, since it is "less often quoted," provides an opportunity to insert into this declaration an inventory of what the pope allegedly learned from his Polish experience — which, thankfully, is not described as being particularly "precious" or as encompassing "three eventful years."

The language of the excerpt above reiterates the description of Ratti's alleged policy of two decades earlier immediately after he had been told by Rome to "take an interest in their [the Jews] welfare." This was when Kertzer launched what can only be called his Big Lie: "Although Jews in Poland were being murdered, their homes and synagogues burned to the ground, and the Pope himself had asked him to take an interest in the Jews' welfare, Ratti did nothing of the sort." That factual deception was propped up — as also sketched in the previous chapter — by the second Big Lie: "Examination of his activities in the months that followed reveals that, on the contrary, he did everything he could to impede any Vatican action on behalf of the Jews." That chronological deception was exposed when it became clear that those "months that followed" were *three weeks* — the period between the papal re-quest and the last report to Rome.[14] Furthermore, Ratti's Polish "experience" was also transmogrified — invoking the classic trope, "piling Pelion on Ossa" — into an event of "enormous importance" by yoking it to the exterminationist "Kruszyñski scenario," which became "reality, with the death of the overwhelming majority of Poland's three million Jews."

Ironically, the famously anti-Semitic *La Croix* published the pope's dec-laration on the first page under the headline "Anti-Semitism is Unaccept-able"; the article in *The Tablet* was titled "The Holy Father and the Jews"; and a Nazi periodical called the pope "Chief Rabbi of the Christian world." But the larger setting of the pope's outburst was not — as Kertzer would have it — Poland two decades earlier. It was Italy the previous day when the new education decree was announced. This decree, among other restric-tions, forbade all Jews — administrators, teachers, and pupils — any access to any schools at any level. It was this public act of cruelty that precipitated Pius's declaration — something that might have crossed Kertzer's mind, since he had written about the pope's failure to complain when the racial laws made "Jews undesirable."

Relative to the papal audience, there is the additional element, men-tioned earlier, which has led to a scrimmage of speculation among present-day commentators, all of whom seem to have abandoned common sense when examining the pope's *cri de couer*. Immediately following Kertzer's as-sertion that the pope's statement meant "he did not oppose" those who took it on themselves to "defend the rest of the population from the Jews," Kertzer adds that Pius's actual words were "never reported in the Vatican's own newspaper." As noted earlier, this information is in the only footnote to the *Documentation Catholique* report, and it has been explicated by a host of commentators who seem unable to actually envision the events described by Monsignor Picard — and therefore get caught up in a search for discrepan-cies, deceptions, even delusions in the pope's experience.

Apart from plain prejudice, one reason for thinking that the entire se-quence of events relating to the pope's declaration may appear unreliable or synthetic is that today's reader is looking at all this in reverse. The fact that the first thing one hears about the event is that the pope wanted his words

14. This is Kertzer's endnote verbatim for the papal request: "Encrypted telegram, Gasparri to Ratti *(22 dicembre 1918)*, ff. 512-513" (italics supplied).

This is Kertzer's endnote verbatim for Ratti's report: "Ratti to Gasparri, Versavia *15 gennaio 1919;* 'Oggetto: La situazione in Polonia. I pogrom antisemiti.' ff. 868-873r" (italics supplied).

written down for posterity tends to put into the mind of the reader the notion that something rehearsed or scripted is going on. As seen earlier, immediately after Monsignor Picard mentioned the nature of the pilgrimage, and that it entailed a private audience for the three administrators and a public audience for the young pilgrims, he stated: "Before the start of the public audience, the Holy Father charged those whom he had just received in private audience to repeat to everybody what he had confided to them in particular." But if one begins with the description of the private audience only — which one commentator thinks actually occurred the day before the public audience — and views all events as flowing from the gift of the missal, then the spontaneity and authenticity of the pope's response become undeniable.[15]

In fact, they are so overwhelming that one has to wonder what he himself must have felt at the end of this startling experience. Over the decades, this declaration has become so familiar, at least to people in the Catholic world, that the language no longer astonishes. But it must have shocked him, almost as much as it did his first listeners. Monsignor Picard says, "Here the Pope is not able to restrain his emotion. He did not want to succumb to this emotion. But he was not able to succeed." Would he not himself have wondered, and even been concerned at such public loss of control on the part of a "sovereign pontiff"? What possessed him to have broken down and said all those things? What would happen when word got out, as it certainly would, that he had actually cried in public? It was probably at some point in this self-examen that the pope must have decided to insist that the text be preserved *ad literam*. What he certainly didn't imagine was that it would invariably be accompanied by a running commentary.

The decision itself was certainly affected by the passion that had come over him when reflecting on the mystery of the fulfillment of the ancient prophecies, going back to the Adamic epoch, in what St. Paul called "the unsearchable riches of Christ." "And it is while weeping that he cited the passages from Saint Paul bringing to light our spiritual descent from Abraham." He wept because the physical descendants of Abraham were being victimized by "a hostile movement which was incompatible with the sublime thought and reality" expressed in these profound texts — however "supersessionist" those texts might subsequently be derided as being.

---

15. "The three directors of Radio Catholique Belge were received Tuesday, September 6, but the pilgrims were admitted in the morning of Wednesday, September 7." Henri Fabre, *L'Église catholique face au fascisme et au nazisme: les outrages à la vérité* (1994).

But all that is lost on polemicists concerned with exploiting imaginary issues like the absence from *L'Osservatore romano* of any mention of Pius's declaration. Among the latter are not only Kertzer and Miccoli, but also Michael Phayer, Susan Zuccotti, and John Cornwell — all of whom, in variant riffs, make Pacelli the villain of the piece, and all of whom, with the exception of Cornwell, may be described as generally conscientious researchers. In this context Cornwell is particularly intriguing, but less because of his conclusion than because of the flagrantly sham learning he puts on display to reach it — the kind of learning that provides an insight into the overall skills he brought to a book whose central thesis he himself would reject — but only after he had personally benefited from it. I begin with the curious fact that he never consulted the *Documentation Catholique* report; instead, his entire discussion of the pope's statement was derived from Pinchas E. Lapide's *The Last Three Popes and the Jews* (1967), a book unlike any of those by the authors above, since it is very favorably disposed to all three popes.

Cornwell initiated his treatment by observing at the end of a discussion on the "hidden encyclical" — mentioned in the previous chapter and to be examined here shortly: "But a more precise clue to Pius XI's mind can be gleaned from a remark [*sic*] the Pontiff made on September 6, 1938." The next paragraph begins: "A group of Belgian pilgrims had presented him with an ancient missal," and it continues for thirty lines describing the events, and concluding that the pope and his secretary of state betrayed "that familiar strain of anti-Jewishness in early twentieth-century Catholicism . . . clearly expressed by Pacelli in his correspondence to Gasparri from Munich in 1917."[16] According to Cornwell, notwithstanding their having a strain of anti-Semitism in common, "a chasm had opened up between Pius XI and Pacelli on the Jewish question." For that reason "the words of the Pontiff did not appear in *L'Osservatore romano* which Pacelli controlled."

Then Cornwell, illustrating again the fact that he never read the Picard material, proceeds with this observation: "The papal comment [*sic*] survives *only* because the exiled Catholic politician Don Luigi Sturzo, head of the banned Partito Popolare, Fascism's keenest opponent, published them [*sic*] in the Belgian newspaper *Cité Nouvelle* a week later" (italics supplied). There is no point to laboring the fact that it is simply impossible to refer to the

---

16. The latter is a reference to Cornwell's "ticking bomb" found in a document — long known to such scholars as Emma Fattorini in Italy and Frank J. Coppa in the United States — that by his risibly rigged translation exposed Nuncio Pacelli as an anti-Semite; from there it is but a step to the rewards of Hitler's pope.

pope's lengthy outpouring as a "remark" or a "comment"; but to say that Sturzo published "them" "a week later" illustrates the guesswork and plagiarism that are the essential elements of Cornwell's methodology. What Lapide wrote in *The Last Three Popes and the Jews* was the following:

> Neither *Osservatore Romano* nor *Civiltà Cattolica* mentioned a single word of this audience. Were it not for the authority of Don Luigi Sturzo, founder of the "Partito Popolare Italiano" and Fascism's oldest and most illustrious opponent, as well as the identical report in the Belgium newspaper *Cité Nouvelle* of September 15, 1938, one might have doubted the papal words or tears.

By this Lapide simply meant that what had appeared in the Belgian paper (placed there by the leader of the Belgian pilgrimage) about Pius XI proved to be creditable because Luigi Sturzo in his major work, *Church and State* (1939), had referred favorably to the Picard report. It certainly doesn't mean that Sturzo filled the gap left by the silence of the *Osservatore* and therefore took it on himself to publish the report by the leaders of the pilgrimage.

Susan Zuccotti (loc. cit.) says that the absence of anything in the Vatican publication suggests "a coverup . . . [that] again indicates dissension within the Vatican on the issue of anti-Semitism." Kertzer's own comment is even more conspiratorial and more quirkily disjointed — and, as usual, is based almost entirely on Miccoli, with a little personal mind reading inserted for good measure:

> With Pius XI ailing, others in the Vatican — presumably the secretary of state, Eugenio Pacelli, who would soon succeed him as pope, above all — held sway, and they did not approve of Pius XI's remarks on behalf of the Jews. Although earlier the pope had brooked no such internal opposition, by this point, just a few months before his death, he was no longer the powerful figure he had previously been.[17]

17. Following the Pius XI incident, Kertzer devotes two pages to another conspiracy, this one relating to the previously mentioned American Jesuit, John LaFarge, and the "hidden encyclical." In an endnote to his treatment, Kertzer enters the mind of just about everybody involved. "It is significant, though, that he [Pius] entrusted the task to Father LaFarge, who had no experience of working at this level of Vatican responsibility and who only happened to be in Rome by chance. It is hard to avoid the impression that the Pope, in taking such an unorthodox approach, was trying to circumvent normal channels, believing that his closest advisors would oppose preparation of such an encyclical." In the text, Kertzer con-

Michael Phayer in *The Catholic Church and the Holocaust: 1930-1965* (2000) is generally less inclined to embrace this kind of clichéd thinking, and thus gets the essentials more nearly correct. "Realizing that since he had spoken to the Belgian group before the beginning of a general audience his statement would not be printed in the official publication *Acta Apostolicae Sedis* or in the Vatican's newspaper, Pius asked that the Belgian Catholics, who were in the communication field, see to its publication." Apart from Phayer, there is a sense of unanimity among these historians — which is not entirely surprising. But what is, if not surprising, then certainly amusing, is that all of the above speculation has been generated by that single footnote added to the text by the editors of *Documentation Catholique* several months after the events it was describing had taken place. Like the good journalists that they were, they worded it so that it would get attention.

Perhaps a little real history will clarify matters. Rather than coverups, confusions about silences, or theories on Pacelli's sway — to say nothing about Luigi Sturzo — this history demands a return to "the beginnings." As noted above, Monsignor Picard had said: "Before the start of the public audience the Holy Father charged *those whom he had just received in private audience* to repeat to everybody what he had confided to them in particular." This means that the pope's statements and experiences were not made known to the public on September 6, 1938, the day on which they occurred, but were made known only at the time when Monsignor Picard and his associates disclosed these matters to the Belgian press on September 14. Nothing about the private audience appeared in *L'Osservatore romano* because whoever wrote the story there knew nothing about the meeting with the three Catholic Action leaders of Radio Catholique Belge. What appeared in the Vatican paper on September 9 was the pope's talk to the pilgrims under the heading "Fatherly praise [*eulogia*] of His Holiness to the pilgrims of Catholic Youth of Belgium." Nor is there any indication that any of these young pilgrims knew anything about the events that had occurred during the private audience. Like the rest of the world, the pilgrims and the *Osservatore* writer would learn about what the pope had said and done only a week later. So, all the invidious speculation above regarding conflicts, dissensions, and the like, stems from the propensity of these critics to treat a pope or a secretary of state — once they have been dehumanized — as cunning plotters or

---

cludes by noting that the pope died "without having released the encyclical," and adds: "His successor, Pius XII, eager to try to repair relations with Hitler, decided it best to avoid any criticism of Nazi anti-Semitism, and so took no action."

onstage improvisers. Nearer to home, one can only wonder whatever happened to the overriding Miccoli-Kertzer thesis that it was the pope *and* his secretary of state working *together* out of the limelight who conspired against the Jews. Could a matter of a few decades shatter that solidarity? Even worse for the larger thesis, one has to wonder how it could come about that the newspaper touted as "the official voice of the pope" wouldn't even publish the actual words of the pope.

The theological significance of Pius XI's declaration to the Belgian Catholic Action officials as well as of the Holy Office's condemnation of "the hatred which is commonly termed anti-Semitism" has also been downplayed by the two previously introduced commentators, Martin Rhonheimer and Ronald Modras. The latter, who had referred to the declaration of the Holy Office as "hardly a momentous step forward in human relations or in the history of the Christian-Jewish encounter" — although it is treated as such a step in the hidden encyclical — now observes: "Even less do Vatican apologists have reason to make much of Pope Pius XI's celebrated 1938 statement." Here Modras joins Rhonheimer, who also had raised the issue of texts "constantly cited for apologetic purposes."

Both opinions are suspect, since a momentous step occurs in a traditionary institution only in response to a major upheaval. As Cardinal Newman said in the fourth chapter of his *Essay on the Development of Christian Doctrine,* "No doctrine is defined till it is violated." Until such an event occurs, if it does, theologians like everyone else respond to the signs of the time. There is a lesson in the fact that probably the most farsighted and progressive religious thinker in prewar Germany, if not in all of Europe, Dietrich Bonhoeffer — who only a short time before his execution finally accepted the arguments of his associates on tyrannicide — never abandoned the traditional theology of Israel as the people that in the economy of salvation bears witness to the death of Jesus. It is only what might be called post-Hochhuth historians and theologians — writing in an ambience of anti-papalism that has been reinforced by books like Cornwell's and Kertzer's — who as noted in chapter 5 succumbed to the lure of the polysyllabic latinity of "supersessionism," and began to rewrite those prayers from the Mass that had so tugged at the heartstrings of Pius XI.[18]

It is also worth noting that because this or that Catholic official is deemed

18. In the next chapter, what may be called for want of even more pretentious terms, "pandemic anti-pioduodecimalism," will lead to provably doctored texts fabricated to belittle not only Pius XII, but Pius XI and Benedict XVI.

inadequately contrite about the church's role in the Holocaust, or because the dissimulating tears of the non-apology of "We Remember" are rightly regarded as shameful — because of either or both beliefs, there is no reason for assuming that out of a misplaced sense of guilt the kind of post-factum revisionism that Rhonheimer and Modras represent should be embraced. The Catholics who subsequently cited the condemnation of anti-Semitism in the pope's *cri de coeur* or in the Holy Office decree were not interested in apologetics, much less were they "Vatican apologists." They were people well aware of what Cardinal Newman had also written in the *Development of Christian Doctrine,* that such development can take place only "as time proceeds and need arises." And both quotations from Newman may be regarded as preparatory to the final chapter, which explores the nature of, and the restrictions on, institutionalized religion.

Cardinal Saliège, one of the few French bishops to speak out vigorously in defense of the Jews, was not interested in apologetics when he told his countrymen, "follow the teachings of Pius XI rather than the edicts of Innocent III," the latter being the medieval pontiff who first formulated stringent anti-Jewish regulations, and who by Hitler's own words was the model for Nazi racist laws. Theologians in wartime France cited the two Vatican statements as indicative of the church's response to new times and new needs. In *Christian Resistance to Anti-Semitism* (1990), Henri de Lubac told the story of his own experience and that of his colleagues in what has come to be rightly called "the Jesuit Resistance." Among other anti-Nazi efforts, they were associated with the militantly pro-Jewish underground publication *Témoignage Chrétien,* which also had specifically emphasized the importance of the 1928 decree of the Holy Office along with Pius XI's impassioned cry a decade later.[19]

Among those colleagues were the future Cardinal Jean Daniélou; Pierre Chaillet, the force behind the creation of *Témoignage Chrétien;* Gaston Fessard, author of its first published cahier, "France, Beware of Losing your

---

19. Henri de Lubac, in an article published a year after his death, was highly critical of the wartime French hierarchy. "La Question des évêques sous l'occupation," *Revue des deux mondes* (February 1992). Five years later, the French episcopate, led by the Jewish Cardinal Lustiger, made a *collective* statement that could have provided a model to be emulated by the authors of "We Remember." "Priests, religious, and laity — some not hesitating to join underground movements — saved the honor of the church, even if discreetly and anonymously. This was also done, in particular through the publication of *Les Cahiers du Témoignage Chrétien,* by denouncing in no uncertain terms the Nazi poison which threatened Christian souls with all *its* neo-pagan, racist, and anti-Semitic virulence, *and by echoing the words of Pius XI: 'Spiritually we are all Semites'"* (italics supplied).

Soul" (November 1941); and Yves de Montcheuil, distributor of subsequent cahiers until he was shot by German soldiers while ministering to young students in the Maquis. Within six months, the average circulation of the cahiers exceeded that of *Civiltà cattolica*. To demean the efforts of these men and their numerous associates as either rationalizing latent anti-Semitism or being papal apologists is to succumb to an anachronistic view of history. It makes little sense to dismiss the two declarations on anti-Semitism as negligible because they didn't anticipate "the second Vatican Council" or because they merely serve to show "just how much of a revolution the Council really was." No one can disagree with that conclusion — except to amend it by adding that without the Holocaust, the Council would never have passed its revolutionary decree on the Jews. "After Auschwitz it is impossible that the council should do nothing" — said Yves Congar in a judgment that, as we will see shortly, was in fact not as firm as it sounded.

Of course, anyone coming to the Holy Office decree would find it distasteful in this present era, stamped ineradicably by the tragedy of the six million, by the understandably inadequate amends of Vatican II, and even by the gradually more progressive deeds of John Paul II. Still, most people, when reading only those Maritain quotations earlier, would probably say that the condemnation by the Holy Office of anti-Semitism certainly had an impact on Catholic theology and Catholic sensibility, and even more of an impact on Maritain himself — particularly since it came only three years after the condemnation of the aggressively anti-Semitic Action Française, of which Maritain had been a loyal member. To all that should be added, if only as a sign of the times, Maritain's previously mentioned "L'Impossible antisémitisme" of 1937 which, however marred by the remnants of his earlier perspective, nevertheless converged with the pope's anguished declaration to the Belgian pilgrims the following year. Finally, as also noted earlier, there was Pius XII's acceptance of new vernacular translations of *perfidis* a decade later, and his reestablishment of the genuflection and prayer for the Jews in 1955. These are not "momentous steps," but at least they *are* steps, and they prepared for the revolution that the war and the Holocaust brought about, and that Maritain himself was actively engaged in implementing, particularly during his postwar period as French ambassador to the Holy See.

One of those efforts at implementation is of special interest since it relates to the wartime relationship of the pope to the Jews, even though the effort itself was focused on postwar concerns. In a personal letter (July 12, 1946) to his friend and admirer, Monsignor G. B. Montini — first encountered when extending a papal benediction to a young Christian Brother —

Maritain suggested that the pope should make a public declaration on anti-Semitism. After referring to "the tireless charity with which the Holy Father tried with all his might to save and protect the persecuted," de Gaulle's ambassador continued:

> for very good reasons, and in the interests of a higher good, and *in order not to make persecution even worse, and not to create insurmountable obstacles in the way of the rescue that he was pursuing, the Holy Father abstained from speaking directly about the Jews.* . . . But now that Nazism has been defeated, and the situation has changed, could it not be permitted, and that is the purpose of this letter, to transmit to the Holy Father the appeal of so many anguished souls and to beg him to make his voice heard? (italics supplied)

This was followed by an explanation as to why at this particular time such a statement was opportune. There was, first, the fact that "the anti-Semitic psychosis has not vanished" and, second, that "many Jews feel deeply within them the attraction of the grace of Christ, and the word of the Pope would surely awaken in them echoes of exceptional importance."[20] It is difficult to write off the excerpt above — which in effect exonerates the pope's "silence" — as wily diplomatic language. That excerpt is as candid as is the frank expression of "supersessionism" in the second reason for the auspiciousness of a papal declaration on anti-Semitism. The meaning of "awakening echoes" is not difficult to discern.

There are two scenarios for the pope's response to Maritain, one in Baum-Marrus and the other in Michael Phayer's *The Catholic Church and the Holocaust.* According to the first version, a few days later, Maritain met with the pope, who told him that in effect he had answered his request at an audience with a group of Jews coming from German concentration camps in November of the previous year. This was reported at the time in *L'Osservatore romano,* and that account is included with the Baum-Marrus article.

---

20. The source is an article by Gregory Baum in *The Ecumenist* (Spring 2002), based on a lecture by Michael R. Marrus, and reproduced under the title, "Maritain Puzzled by Pius XII — in 1946," in the newsletter of the *Association of Contemporary Church Historians* (September 2002). Baum wrote as follows: "On February 12, 2002, Professor Michael Marrus, honored historian at the University of Toronto, gave a lecture at McGill University in Montreal on the Vatican and the Holocaust. He focused his lecture on a letter of July 12, 1946 written by Jacques Maritain to Giovanni Montini, who at that time held a high post at the Vatican's Secretariat of State." (References below to that article are "Baum-Marrus.")

The text of the pope's address in the *Osservatore* referred to "the abyss of discord, and the hatred and the folly of persecution"; it described the wartime period as "an agonizing time" in which the "threat of imminent death" was manifest. It also referred to "the eternal principles of the law, written by God in the heart of every man, which shines forth in the divine revelation of Sinai and which found its perfection in the Sermon on the Mount." For those so disposed, this might also be written off as another expression of supersessionism.[21] More in accord with the "elder brother" vis-à-vis "younger brother" imagery familiar after Vatican II — though since modified by Benedict XVI — was the pope's conclusion:

> You have experienced yourselves the injuries and the wounds of hatred; but in the midst of your agonies, you have also felt the benefit and the sweetness of love, not that love that nourishes itself from terrestrial motives, but rather with a *profound faith in the heavenly father,* whose light shines on all men, whatever their language and their race, and whose grace is open to all those who seek the Lord in a spirit of truth. (italics supplied)

A more detailed forerunner to this declaration was the pope's comparably irenic Easter message five years earlier — cited in *Popes and Politics* and earlier in the present book — when, referring to the "atrocities" of the war and lamenting the conditions of the "defenseless, the sick, and the aged," he concluded by saying that "very dear" to him were all the victims, the Catholics, Protestants, and Jews: "children of the Church of Christ, those with faith in the Divine Savior, or at least in Our Father Who is in Heaven."

The excerpt from the postwar declaration of Pius XII is followed by two

---

21. In *The National Catholic Reporter* (March 3, 2010), an article with the headline "Catholics, Mormons called 'bulwark' against secular society" described Cardinal Francis George of Chicago at "a historic gathering at Brigham Young University," praising the Mormons for, among other things, their defense of marriage as "the union of a man and a woman" — N.B., *not* "many women." Thus do professional supersessionists find common ground with super-supersessionists in order to engage in superannuated social-religious policies. (One would not be surprised if this enterprising entente also led to agreement on the principle that it is an imbalance of the four humors that causes deviations from Catholic-Mormon moral doctrine.)

Amidst an enormous range of literature, a simple (and timely) place to start is with Jay Michaelson and Candace Chellew-Hodge, "Should Gays and Lesbians Argue Scripture?" (www.religiondispatches.org/archive/sexandgender/4031/). A pioneering study is Mary E. Hunt, *Fierce Tenderness: A Feminist Theology of Friendship,* which in 1991 I was honored to publish. In 2006, there is Margaret Farley, *Just Love: A Framework for Christian Sexual Ethics.*

paragraphs of "Reflections" in which Gregory Baum speaking *in propria persona* explained the significance of "Maritain's exchange with the Pope in 1946." Although clearly seeking to give a balanced report, this most fairminded of theologians concluded in essence that the significance of the exchange is that the pope was not thinking the way that Angelo Giuseppe Roncalli would think twelve years later. Baum also expressed disappointment that "Maritain's letter reveals that even he still longed for the eventual conversion of the Jews to the faith in Christ." But this was a longing in the heart of Dietrich Bonhoeffer, mentioned earlier as probably the most progressive theologian of his time, and presumably it was also something longed for by one of the most progressive theologians of *our* time, the Jewish convert Gregory Baum, whose work I published and whose intelligence and candor I have always held in the highest esteem.[22] This is his last sentence, indicating a penchant — not unlike that of Modras and Rhonheimer earlier, or even of Kertzer himself — for anachronistically judging past events through the lens of present knowledge: "If Pius XII, moved by Maritain's plea, had made a public declaration in 1946, he would have created a different image of himself. For such declarations we had to wait for the Vatican Council II (1962-1965) and the pontificate of John Paul II."

The second scenario by historian Michael Phayer (loc. cit.) is shorter, more complex, and not without a conspiratorial tone. Describing the correspondence, he wrote:

> Maritain spoke openly of the Holocaust, pointing out that hundreds of thousands of its victims were innocent children and infants. The Holy See must speak out about this unprecedented rupture of natural law, Maritain urged, in order to show the pope's compassion for the Jewish people. Maritain followed this letter up with a second, which appealed more to reason than to emotion. Discerningly, he spoke of collective responsibility for genocide rather than of collective guilt.

According to Phayer, it was Maritain's belief that because such organizations as the Gestapo and the SS were agents of the community, then every German

---

22. Among the books were *The Credibility of the Church Today* (1968) and *Man Becoming: God in Secular Experience* (1970). Two brief instances also come to mind: first, the title he proposed for a collection of essays that were to be published under the aegis of Archbishop T. D. Roberts, S.J., in the mid-1960s on one of the controversial issues of the day: *Contraception and Holiness;* second, a spontaneous and passionate intervention in the 1980s at a meeting of the Catholic Theological Society of America in defense of gay rights.

who by definition was part of that community also shared in the nation's crimes — for which, proportionately, that citizen must answer. "Collective responsibility rested as well on the shoulders of German Catholics, or, perhaps, especially on them."[23] Then with no explanation of that seemingly self-canceling fragment, "or, perhaps, especially on them," Phayer commingled the two letters and observed:

> What kind of a hearing Montini was able to get for Maritain's thoughts is unknown. It appears, however, that the pontiff rejected them explicitly when he raised the bishops of Berlin, Cologne, and Münster to the cardinalate early in 1946, to indicate to the world his high esteem for the German church.

There are two problems here. The first has to do with the fact that creating these cardinals has nothing that relates "explicitly" — or implicitly or in any other way — to Maritain, the instigating party of the whole discussion. The second has to do with chronology. As noted earlier, Maritain's correspondence was dated July 1946; the consistory creating these cardinals took place in February of that same year. How an event occurring six months earlier can be an "explicit" rejection of a subsequent proposal is a phenomenon that goes unexplained — and that, in fact, cannot be explained. As for the naming of those cardinals to indicate to the world the pope's high esteem for the German church, this is another variant of the cliché that Pius was blindly partial to all things German. Those bishops were made cardinals for their vigorous opposition to Nazism, as Phayer himself acknowledges: "No other German bishop spoke as pointedly [against Nazi policies] as Preysing [of Berlin] and Frings [of Cologne]." As for the bishop of Münster, Count von Galen, his heroism in condemning the Gestapo has been almost universally recognized — although there will be a vigorous negative opinion vented by an American writer, and assessed in the next chapter. Concerning cardinals being made in order to "indicate" esteem for favored countries, at the same consistory the French bishops, elevated with the strong backing of de Gaulle — in fact, vetted by him — were all publicly recognized opponents of the Vichy regime.[24]

23. This is a line of thought that ran counter to the Holy See's view that culpability fell on the individual evildoer rather than on the society — particularly a society that would later be described as composed of "willing executioners." In traditional Catholic theology, as theologian John Jay Hughes has consistently emphasized, guilt is personal.

24. Relative to the above discussion is Michael R. Marrus, "A Plea Unanswered: Jacques

So much for the original context of the above discussion, which was focused on the incremental progress of the papacy under Pius XI regarding
anti-Semitism, and which had been dismissed because it was dressed-up
apologetics or because it merely showed "just how much of a revolution the
Council really was." No one can disagree with that conclusion, except to
amend it by adding that a definitive condemnation of anti-Semitism might
conceivably have emerged some time in the late twentieth century, but without the Holocaust, there would never have been the kind of radical reassessment of Judaism and Christianity that Vatican II achieved. Parenthetically,
regarding the Council itself, and as briefly noted earlier, the achievements it
realized came about through the foresight of churchmen, almost all of
whom were appointees of Pius XII. On the other hand, no one questions
that without the six million — even if there had been a second general council in the Vatican — there would have been no revolution regarding anti-
Semitism. Only a seismic event could have so rapidly reversed nearly two
millennia of canonized texts, theological traditions, and ingrained popular
customs.

Even at the Council, the enlightened Yves Congar — whose views on
Jews shortly after the war were not much different from those of Maritain
before the war — believed that he might endorse "an alternative statement
which would propose dialogue in general but in strong terms, while condemning violence based on race or religion, and alluding to the Armenian

Maritain, Pope Pius XII, and the Holocaust" (in Eli Lederhendler, ed., *Jews, Catholics, and
the Burden of History* [2005]). Marrus writes: "Justus George Lawler, in a work supposedly
dedicated to correcting factual distortions about the role of the Holy See during the Holocaust, mischaracterizes Maritain's appeal, presenting it as a demand, in July and August 1946,
'for a statement on Germany's collective responsibility for the Holocaust.' Whatever his assessment of Germany, it is clear that Maritain was also concerned about the Vatican's own
responsibility — something that is obviously relevant to Lawler's thesis, but which he ignores altogether."

I have no more interest in debating the notion that *Popes and Politics* is "*supposedly*
dedicated to correcting factual distortions" than in discussing what it allegedly ignored. The
book's treatment of the Maritain correspondence concerned the matters set forth above regarding Michael Phayer's views — including his introduction of "collective responsibility"
into the discourse — and his literally preposterous belief that the request was answered by
the pope several months before it had been made. That is the only relevant issue here. I think
Marrus deserves Gregory Baum's earlier accolade, "honored professor," and I respect his
work, which is exemplified — from my admittedly narrow perspective — by his contribution during the post-conciliar period to an important issue of *Continuum* on anti-Semitism
(to be discussed in the next chapter), but I regret his facile endorsement of Kertzer's excesses
and Phayer's guesswork.

massacre as well as to that of the Jews" (*Mon journal du concile* [2002]). The motive for this seeming retreat was entirely ecumenical. Congar was attentive to the expressions of almost unanimous opposition from Catholic, Orthodox, and Protestant churchmen in the Middle East, most of whom had experienced the disruption, and in many instances the decimation, of their flocks by Israeli forces in Palestine — another subject that will be central to the treatment in the final chapter of this book on what may be termed "the burdens and the benefits of institutionalized religion." That this notion of a less than absolute condemnation of anti-Semitism was entertained by one of the most thoughtful and ecumenically oriented thinkers at Vatican II — that should at least give pause to more recent theological writers who out of what I have termed "misplaced guilt" are suggesting, if not agitating and clamoring for, a version of Christianity that dispenses with Christ and the church as the fulfillment of the prophets of Israel. Finally, it should be noted that it was due in no small part to the moderating influence of a pope, Paul VI, that *Nostra Aetate* ended up being passed so overwhelmingly. For an institution that measures its life in terms of centuries, this sequence of reformative acts — beginning with the condemnation of anti-Semitism in 1928 — constituted a momentous step in the history of Christianity.

Kertzer draws to the end of "Antechamber to the Holocaust" by citing the Italian Fascist Roberto Farinacci — whom the British envoy to the Vatican called "Farinazi" — in order to show that the Italian racial laws "differed little from those that the Church itself had employed when it was in power in Italy."[25] At the conclusion of three pages of fascist vilification, and half a dozen pages before the end of the book, the author without any apparent sense of irony asserts: "Needless to say, Farinacci and the other Fascist leaders who cited the Church to justify the new anti-Semitic laws were doing so for their own political reasons, and there is abundant reason to question their sincerity." After this concession, Kertzer summarizes his book:

> Decade after decade, forces close to the Vatican had denounced the Jews as evil conspirators against the public good. Decade after decade saw the

25. For a different reading of these final months of Pius XI and of the Italian government, including Farinacci, one can consult Owen Chadwick's *Britain and the Vatican during the Second World War* (1986). Among the observations to be noted are that the Italian Foreign Office believed Pius XI to be "Roosevelt in a tiara" and the British Foreign Office believed that the pope's policy "on the major issues of principle corresponds very closely with our own." After the death of Pius XI, Farinacci wrote, "Our enemies are a triumvirate, Stalin, de Gaulle, Pius XII."

Vatican-linked press lament the baleful effects of the emancipation of the Jews. For decades, Church authorities had warned of the harm done by giving the Jews equal rights. For decades, the Italian Catholic press had denounced the Jews' disproportionate influence in Italy. After all this, it should be hardly surprising that Mussolini's anti-Jewish campaign met with little resistance from Italian Catholics.

The language and imagery are no more unfamiliar than is the threefold agglomeration of "Vatican-linked press," "Church authorities," and "Italian Catholic press" — of which, readers will recall, only half a dozen specifics were cited in this multi-decade campaign.

Kertzer's final chapter is the one with the comment examined in my introductory remarks about the difference between "complicated" Germany and presumably less complicated Italy. "The case of Italy is of special importance for a number of reasons" — which were that the popes were "ensconced there," were "all Italian," had "more direct influence over popular attitudes in Italy than elsewhere," and so on. It may also be recalled that the author abandoned the course of that reflection to go off on a tangent about the *Protocols of the Elders of Zion.* For him, apparently the conclusion was so obvious that it could be left to the reader's discernment — much like another post hoc ergo observation, "The rise of modern anti-Semitism began just after the collapse of the Papal States."[26] But as suggested earlier, what seemed the far more plausible deduction from all that "more direct influence" is that it was exercised not through decades and decades of journalistic propaganda, but through centuries and centuries of Christian teaching. As to the conclusion above, "After all this, it should be hardly surprising that Mussolini's anti-Jewish campaign met with little resistance from Italian Catholics," one can agree — but not for the reason Kertzer implies. The fact is, they didn't resist it for reasons similar to those of most people who accept governmental decrees relative to persecuted minorities, whether the latter is

26. He could as readily have said that the rise of anti-Semitism began just after the Franco-Prussian War, but that would have suggested it began because of political and social eruptions — as in fact it did — rather than because of papal conspiracies. More "complicated" Germany was similarly on the anti-Semitic track, due to the rise of nationalism, although without any religious stimulation. "At the very time, after 1870, when German nationalism was becoming more and more an ideological and less and less a patriotic phenomenon, German Judaeophobia became transformed into anti-Semitism: what had been a religious and social consideration became a cultural and racial attitude." John Lukacs, "The Roots of the Dilemma," *Continuum* (Summer 1964).

made up of Jews in fascist Italy, blacks in America during the hundred years after the Civil War, or gays in the present-day United States.

Of course, there were active Catholic collaborators in Italy, though apparently far fewer than in other Axis-dominated countries. After the racial laws expelled Jews from jobs in education and other fields, "non-Jewish Italians made the most of the expulsions to improve their own positions." Of course, non-Jews who were unemployed or employed at lower-paying jobs did not abstain from self-advancement. "A large proportion of all the roundups of Jews for deportation were conducted by groups entirely composed of Italians." Of course, fascist authorities involved in the roundups used Italian workers, as did also the Nazi authorities. This was not as it was in the ghettos of the East where Jewish councils — for reasons that cannot be condemned as other than efforts to cope with an unprecedented and unresolvable crisis — lent their support to selective roundups. "Only when it began to be clear that the Germans were going to lose the war did non-Jewish Italians begin to come to the aid of their Jewish neighbors." Of course, typical Italian women and men did not sacrifice themselves for their neighbors until they saw that they could do so without fear of punishment. Similarly, it was only after the Allied armies successfully moved up the peninsula to Rome that the Italian Partisans took mass action against the German occupiers. Only rarely will religion or patriotism motivate people to transcend the instinct for self-preservation and survival. This is why we have what are called "saints" and "heroes."

All of the quotations above are from David I. Kertzer, who is here writing on the past decade's "outpouring of historical scholarship aimed at correcting the inaccuracies that have clouded our understanding of the assault on the Jews of Italy that began with the passage of the racial laws in 1938 and ended with the Holocaust" (*American Historical Review* [April 2006]). As to the Holocaust itself, another clouding inaccuracy he points out as having been corrected during the past decade was that "Italy's greatest institution, the Vatican, was portrayed by some as working *ceaselessly* to protect Italy's Jews" (italics supplied). Although for Voltaire the adjective is the enemy of the noun, for Kertzer the adverb is not the enemy of the verb. Whether he could bring himself to say "the Vatican was portrayed by some as working to protect Italy's Jews" appears dubious; even more dubious is that he would simply write, "the Vatican was working to protect Italy's Jews." But since nobody anywhere works "ceaselessly" at anything, it would have been interesting to know who these portraitists were.

Nevertheless, in the face of this outpouring, there remains that intractable statistic — separating "specially important Italy" from the other occupied countries — which attests to the saving of disproportionately large numbers of "Italy's Jews." This has not yet been adequately explained, although efforts to do so range from the alleged prevalence of sloppy police work to ethnic stereotypes about *dolce far niente* — neither of which is likely to be embraced by Kertzer. As for an explicit religious element in that statistic, there is the designation by fascist officials of Italians who ignored the racial laws as *pietisti*. These were not members of a fringe Protestant sect, nor people who were merely derided as sanctimonious. The slur was intended to convey the notion of elitist religious hypocrisy acted out against the backdrop of contemned popes.[27] "Pope Pius XII has fully espoused the Jewish cause," said Farinacci.

Again I cite the humanist historian Léon Poliakov, who in this instance is not writing as a remote observer but as a witness to the events he describes. Poliakov, who in the summer of 1943 had managed to flee to Nice, where he was aiding other Jewish refugees to escape, quoted a telegram by the Nazi head of the deportation program in Marseilles: "The numerous reports we have received here reveal incontestably that the Italian authorities are continually demonstrating their pro-Jewish attitude quite openly. In many cases Jews who for whatever reason were arrested by the French police had to be released immediately under Italian pressure." Poliakov also noted that when the Italian government was under intense pressure from the Germans to deport Jews, and that when documents reached Rome describing "the horrible massacres carried out by the SS in Poland," the documents were passed on to Mussolini with a note that said that "no Power — not even allied Germany — could make Italy a partner to such crimes" (*Jews under the Italian Occupation* [1954]). Martin Gilbert in *The Righteous* (2003) quotes a letter (January 29, 1943) from Heinrich Himmler to Joachim von Ribbentrop, the Nazi foreign minister, complaining that the continued presence of Jews in the Italian sphere of influence "provided many circles in France and in the rest of Europe with a pretext for playing down the Jewish question, it being argued that not even our Axis partner Italy sees eye to eye with us on the Jewish issue."

---

27. In the moving story of a Jewish family driven out of their home after passage of the Italian racial laws, this incident is recorded in a chapter titled "False Names": "The landlady at Impruneta knew it was wrong to kick out the Neppi Modonas — she stopped at church that morning to pray for guidance — but she was afraid to help, to be labeled a *pietista* and suffer the consequences." Kate Cohen, *The Neppo Modona Diaries: Reading Jewish Survival Through My Italian Family* (1997).

But Kertzer is right, Italians are Italians — and Germans are Germans. It was not to the bishops of Italy, but to the bishops of Germany that the pope wrote, "We leave it to the senior clergy to weigh the circumstances in deciding whether or not to exercise restraint with a view to avoiding greater evil."[28] The senior clergy in Assisi received a different communication. Bishop Giuseppe Nicolini — along with Aldo Brunacci, like Provost Bernhard Lichtenberg in Berlin, an officer of the cathedral — asserted that a letter in his possession contained instructions from the Holy See to help the Jews. Susan Zuccotti in *Under His Very Windows* maintains that — if the letter had existed at all — it couldn't contain "what the bishop implied that it did." But the bishop's aide, Canon Aldo Brunacci, insisted after the war and again as recently as 2004 that the bishop *implied* nothing. Rather, he explicitly "told" Brunacci the contents. Zuccotti remains convinced that the bishop was deceptive and the canon was delusional, since she refers to "the letter he believes he saw" and "telling the truth as he knows it." Her conclusion is that "the explanation for rescue in Assisi cannot be traced to the pope but rather rests with [*N.B.* the slippage from "trace" to "rests"] the courage and imagination of the individuals themselves." But courage and imagination require motivation, and certainly those centuries of the Christian teaching of contempt provided very little of that, while a message from the pope might have helped reinforce the good will of a bishop and his canon. As to views like those of Zuccotti, there is something daunting about a researcher in this century disparaging people in the previous century who put their lives at risk and who are honored among the righteous at Yad Vashem.[29]

The end of this chapter takes literally its title, "Antechamber to the Holocaust," as it provides a summary of the wartime roundup of more than a thousand Jews in Rome, beginning around five in the morning of October 16, 1943. That narrative has been identified with the phrase "under the windows of the pope," and that phrase, in turn, has become a mantra that by its mere utterance condemns Pius XII. The words were those of the German ambassador to the Vatican, Ernst von Weizsäcker, though he originally modified them by "so to speak." The ambiguity that has been attached to his

28. This was written in April 1943 to Konrad von Preysing, the bishop of Berlin, when the pope also expressed his appreciation of Catholics who had helped "so-called non-Aryans" (his term), and praised particularly an officer of the cathedral, the Provost Bernhard Lichtenberg, who at that time had been nearly two years in Berlin's Tegel prison, and who died in November 1943, when being transported to Dachau (*Actes et Documents du Saint Siège* . . . , loc. cit., vol. 2 [1966]).

29. See "The Assisi Network," www1.yadvashem.org/righteous_new/italy/assisi.html.

name is well-deserved. He gave literal significance to the diploid role of the diplomat as the servant of two masters, in the present instance, Germany and the Führer first; religion and the papacy second. His role, like the *razzia* itself, has been described in a host of documents literally going from A to Z, from *Actes et Documents du Saint Siège* cited above, to Zuccotti's *Under His Very Windows*.[30]

The only additional new information that emphasizes, however obliquely, Weizsäcker's support for the Vatican's Jewish refugee program comes from a postwar statement by a key figure in saving the Jews of Rome. This is the Capuchin friar who was born Pierre Peteul, who was named in his religious order, Marie-Benoit, and who during the war was known as *le Père des Juifs*. He is now also honored among the Righteous at Yad Vashem for having helped "thousands of Jews." The public connection to the ambassador was made after the war when on the occasion of receiving a gold medal from the Italian Jewish Union, the friar went out of his way to commend Weizsäcker for his prudence relative to his "knowing that the Catholic institutions of Rome were packed with Jews."[31]

The pope had been quickly informed of the roundup and, clearly shocked by the information, told Maglione to summon the ambassador. The actual meeting provides Kertzer with a final opportunity for exercising his mode of historiography, the now familiar mix of condensed texts and slanted paraphrases, as well as his personal psychic endowment: the reading of the minds of historic *personae*. "If Cardinal Maglione had ever intended this summons to the German ambassador to be a means of protesting the roundup of Rome's Jews to the Nazi high command, he soon changed his mind." But it is only in a post-Hochhuth universe that anyone would think the purpose of the meeting was to register a protest. No one, then or now, can reasonably argue that once the order came "from the highest levels" of the regime, it could be countermanded at the behest of the Vatican. (Though

---

30. These can be supplemented by Owen Chadwick, "Weizsäcker, the Vatican, and the Jews of Rome," *Journal of Ecclesiastical History* 28, no. 2 (1977), and Leonidas E. Hill III, "The Vatican Embassy of Ernst von Weizsäcker," *Journal of Modern History* 39 (1967).

31. For the life and work of Father Marie-Benoit, there is a documented and illustrated narrative — and one that is also very touching — which is based almost entirely on his personal papers, and which can be accessed at www.peremariebenoit.com/1mariebenoit.htm. I am indebted for this lead to Dimitri Cavalli. For the Italian Jewish Union incident, see J. Derek Holmes, *The Papacy in the Modern World: 1914-1978* (1981). For more on Father Marie-Benoit's work and on its treatment by present-day historians, see chapters 2 and 3 of *Popes and Politics*.

there are apparently still people, James Carroll for one in *Constantine's Sword,* who believe that a flaming protest from the pope might have led the Germans to abandon their genocidal program.) Rather, what does appear to be borne out by the facts is that the meeting was an effort on the part of the secretary of state to use the unprecedented, and apparently intentional, affront to the pope as the lever to forestall further persecution of the Jews. Thus the Vatican, which had been reliably informed of plans for the extradition of Rome's eight thousand Jews (the number according to the original German estimate), viewed the *razzia* itself, however intrinsically appalling, as only the first stage in a much more massive undertaking that had to be frustrated. It was fear for the fate of those remaining Jews that was the central concern of the pope, and this explains the secretary of state's emphasis on the days ahead, rather than on the night that had just passed.

This statement by the secretary to the ambassador is the one that for all critics from Cornwell to Zuccotti puts on display the craven attitude of the pope: "The Holy See must not be placed in the position of having to protest. As for the consequences, should the Holy See be forced to do so, we would simply have to trust in divine providence." Owen Chadwick in a characteristically unembellished assessment says of the communication between the secretary and the ambassador that it "tried to do a bit of good in a situation where neither of them could do any good."[32] That the trust of the Holy See proved to be well-founded is evident from the facts that there was no other roundup in Rome, and that by far the majority of Jews survived the Nazi occupation, most of them in properties owned or supervised by the Vatican. All statistics vary, and some for apologetic reasons are exaggerated, but Martin Gilbert's in *The Righteous* are modest enough to appear reliable, or at least noncontroversial: "As a result of the church's rapid rescue efforts, only 1,015 — fewer than one-fifth — of Rome's 5,730 Jews were seized that morning." The bishop of Rome had to take his own advice, and leave it to the local bishop himself as to how to avoid the "greater evil" he had warned his brother bishops about. A less cautiously modulated protest might not only have doomed Rome's remaining Jews, but might well have entailed a complete disruption of the work of the church — another *Kulturkampf,* only this time instigated by mass murderers and affecting not only one country but all of occupied Europe.

While the passages above are Kertzer's only detailed reference to the reign of Pius XII, other historians know better. By a strange adjustment of

32. "Pius XII's Terrifying Dilemma," *The Tablet,* June 30, 2001.

the facts from macro to micro, it came to be the consensus that the "Holy Father" not only had no concern for Jews but he also had very little concern for Catholics, and even less for those in Rome. From John Cornwell to Robert Katz, and from Michael Phayer to Susan Zuccotti, it has been systematically repeated that people were only incidental to the pope's concerns. What really preoccupied him were the historical buildings, the monuments and treasures of the city.[33] Susan Zuccotti in the conclusion to *Under His Very Windows*, after discussing various "factors in the pope's decision to remain silent about the Holocaust" — fear of communism, a role in peace negotiations, reprisals against Catholics, fondness for Germans, and so on — proffers the following as "the primary explanation." "Above all else, Pius XII feared for the integrity of the Vatican itself." In *The Battle for Rome* (2003), Robert Katz, after describing "the repeated and ardent appeals of the Supreme Pontiff on behalf of the Eternal City," concludes by saying that there was "a spate of notes from Vatican diplomats — *none of which mentioned the safety of the people of Rome*" (italics original). That is a topic to be taken up in *Historians Against History*, which will discuss the body of literature that has grown up around the church in the wartime and postwar period up to the present. But in the immediate context, a very brief response to Katz and Zuccotti, both of whom are Jewish, might well focus on the fact that the entire history of the Chosen People during the common era has been concentrated on the destruction of the Second Temple, and that nothing has more preoccupied faithful Jews everywhere — as well as the Israeli government — than the fate of their "eternal city." (To Cornwell and Phayer, one might also point out that it is Christians worldwide who chant of an allegorized Jerusalem as their "happy home.")

As for Pius XII himself, I have cited Martin Gilbert's *The Righteous* several times. I now cite its author once again on this pope: "At the moment, the evidence for the many historical episodes in which he must have been involved, consulted or given advice to his cardinals and senior clergy — each episode of crucial importance in the Jewish story — is still locked away. As a historian whose instinct is to credit people like Pius with a desire to help, even I cannot predict what the archives will hold" (Martin Gilbert, "The Archive Holds the Answers," *Haaretz*, December 14, 2008). However, until that

---

33. John Cornwell is included in this group only because of a shared belief in the pope's motives. Regardless of my criticism of the others, none of them approaches the level of misinformation and disinformation typical of Cornwell. The book can be best described as trash-talk with footnotes.

wished-for event, there is the correction of bad scholarship, of factual errors, and of slanted translations and intentional omissions that must be undertaken if the myths about the modern papacy, and more specifically about Pius XII, are to be exposed. For that task, new archival material, however welcome, is not needed — as this critique of Kertzer has made clear. Moreover, and certainly at least of equal import as archival disclosures — unless, *per impossibile,* such disclosures reveal Pacelli as Hitler's pope — are the kinds of discoveries made by researchers who believed that much post-Hochhuth scholarship was biased. The most important of these discoveries is the narrative by "Refugee" — mentioned in the first chapter, alluded to subsequently, and to be examined in detail in the concluding chapter — which definitively puts the lie to even a scintilla of anti-Jewish prejudice in the public or private comportment of Pius XII. One can certainly join in Gilbert's hope that every Vatican archive will be opened, but to believe that "the archive holds the answers" may be to launch another myth.

As for a last word on David I. Kertzer and his book, an extremely abridged but hardly inaccurate synopsis would go as follows. The besetting theological, ethical, social, political, economic, scientific, liturgical, pastoral, and administrative issues facing in completely different ways each individual pope from 1846 to 1946 were all interwoven with a plot on the part of each of them by which he orchestrated his own campaign to prevent "the emancipation of the Jews," the "equal rights of Jews," and "the Jews' disproportionate influence" — about all of which not a single one of those aged men would publicly or privately utter a word, but about which everybody can learn by reading publications in the "worldwide network of the Catholic press," because they faithfully followed the lead of the Italian Jesuit magazine *Civiltà cattolica* which, in turn, was "viewed throughout the Catholic world as offering the clearest expressions of the popes' own perspectives." *The Popes Against the Jews* was, in short, a remarkable achievement in weaving together, from a multitude of varying strands, a whole-cloth conspiracy against Jews perpetrated by the elders of the Vatican. But the most important consequence of that malign undertaking is that, according to Kertzer, it directly implicated those evil elders in the subsequent murder of six million Jews.

The preceding paragraph recapitulates the complicated and cumbersome thesis of *The Popes Against the Jews,* a work that in subject matter and methodology is reminiscent of an earlier controversial book, *The Catholic Church Against the Twentieth Century* (1947), written by one Avro Manhattan, and taken with high seriousness in its day by readers and reviewers.[34] It figured most notably in a major controversy between Catholic and Protestant spokesmen, Father John Courtney Murray of the Jesuit seminary, Woodstock College, and Dean Walter Russel Bowie of Union Theological Seminary. The debate was initiated by the editors of *American Mercury,* and was described at length by *Time* (September 12, 1949) as "a hammer & tongs Protestant-Catholic debate to bring the points of antagonism between the two faiths 'into the open for public examination.'" Murray's own concern was with Bowie's "central thesis":

> It is contained in the sentence he approvingly quotes from Avro Manhattan's book, *The Catholic Church Against the Twentieth Century,* to the effect that "the Catholic Church is a *ruthless* and *persistent* enemy of our century and of all that individuals and nations are laboring and sweating to attain." The italics are mine [i.e., Murray's], they indicate the breath-taking sweep of the thesis. ("The Catholic Position — A Reply," Woodstock Theological Center Library)

So far as Kertzer's book is concerned, the rest of Murray's argument would be ancillary to what has been set forth in all the previous discussion regarding "the breath-taking sweep of the thesis" — however caustic and incisive Murray was in dissecting it.[35] But what is more directly pertinent to Kertzer himself is the lengthy review (September 19, 1947) of Manhattan's book in *The Palestine Post* — a publication that will play an important role in the disclosure of the "Refugee" document of Pius XII. The title of the review of Manhattan's screed was "The Vatican and Politics," and the reviewer

34. Avro Manhattan's influence was greater than one would expect for a writer whose obsessive *mentalità* can be seen in the following titles: *Latin America and the Vatican* (1946); *The Vatican in World Politics* (1949); *The Dollar and the Vatican* (1956); *Vatican Imperialism in the Twentieth Century* (1965); *Vatican-Moscow Alliance* (1982); *The Vatican Billions* (1983); and *Murder in the Vatican: American, Russian, and Papal Plots* (1985). Regardless of whatever influence he may have exercised, Manhattan was undeniably a crank of the first water. In *Vietnam . . . Why Did We Go?* (1984), he enlisted Pope John XXIII in a plot to save Vietnam for Catholic imperialism with the aid of President John F. Kennedy.

35. After the appearance of the debate, the editors of the *American Mercury* sent Murray more than fifty letters, to which he responded in part. He also told the editors the following: "Controversy is a dreary business and (as several correspondents remarked) largely a profitless one; I had thought to maintain a certain lightness of tone. It was therefore disconcerting to learn that I had been supercilious, sarcastic, arrogant, slippery, disparaging, cavalier, haughty, disdainful, glib, cocksure, tricky, contemptuous, smug (these are some of the epithets with which your correspondents adorn me)." Alas, a fate endemic to polemic.

was Y. H. Rosenkranz, a former military officer who is described as having been only three years earlier among the Allied soldiers moving into Rome after the fleeing Germans.[36]

Rosenkranz began by observing that "if history were judged in a court of Law," the author "in his 461 page indictment would have made a plausible and at times, even an impressive prima facie case" that the church had "abetted the rise of Fascist dictatorships and 'collaborated' with them when they were in power."

> Presenting only his side of the case, as lawyers are liable to do — but as historians may not — learned counsel would recite a long list of his complaints. The Church fought the Third Republic in France in the nineteenth and the Spanish Republic in the twentieth century. It refused to come to terms with any liberal or democratic Italian Government, but in 1929 it found common ground for agreement with the Fascist Government. . . . He would point to the "significant fact" — significant is one of his favorite words — that the "Crusade against Bolshevism" was preached simultaneously in Berlin and Rome. . . . [He] alleges that the German hierarchy's protests were not directed "against Nazism as such. . . . The Church only protested when her spiritual or material interests were at stake." Turning to the alleged anti-Semitism of the Church [he] correctly quotes the examples of Karl Lueger in Vienna and certain high prelates during the Dreyfus Affair.

The reviewer continued, drawing nearer to his own experience: "But the Vatican could call as witnesses the thousands of Jews who survived the Nazi terror in Catholic monasteries, or Jewish ex-servicemen from Palestine who found the remnants of their people there." He then narrated his own rescue of Jews from church buildings in Rome, and concluded that the indictment in *The Catholic Church Against the Twentieth Century* "is reminiscent of the 'Elders of Zion,' except that here the villain is not a Jew but a Catholic." David I. Kertzer's view of the popes' protocol ["out of the limelight"] for conspiring against Jews is also reminiscent of the "Elders of Zion," and here too "the villain is not a Jew but a Catholic."

---

36. Manhattan apparently still has a following in some circles. Writing of *Hitler's Pope* by John Cornwell, "The Reformation Online" noted: "This new blockbuster book by a Roman Catholic writer is just in time for Reformation Day. He corroborates everything that Avro Manhattan said in his books." www.reformation.org/hitler_pope.html.

However, that last opinion has been spurned by growing numbers of church historians and students of religion who, rather than treating Kertzer as a pariah, appear to have publicly found common ground with him and, by that fact, with his views on the papacy as well. To anyone reflecting on the previous eight chapters of analysis of various deceptions and distortions, the embrace of such an author by other scholars must seem hard to believe, if not utterly preposterous. Ignored would have to be such now established facts as that the popes did not refer to Judaism as Satan's synagogue; that Leo XIII did not secretly organize campaigns to foster the blood libel; that Pius X did not refuse to aid Jews accused of ritual murder; that Pius XI's governance and his reign did not constitute an "antechamber to the Holocaust," etc.

Additionally, it is to be noted that this drastically abridged inventory does not even mention the potpourri of mistranslations, of juggled chronology, and finally, of the out-and-out falsehoods in Kertzer's overall account — and most particularly of Achille Ratti, the "future pope in Poland." As noted in the previous chapter, Ratti fostered clergymen who wanted Jews exterminated: Ratti asserted that Jews were the most evil influences in the country; and — probably the most serious falsehood of all — Ratti, after being instructed by the Vatican to "look into the reported killing of Jews," "did nothing of the sort." The treatment of this particular pope is important because it provides one of the strongest arguments why responsible scholars would find little common ground with such an author.

Yet, the exact opposite has proved to be the case. Kertzer has not only been embraced by the community of papal scholars; he has in effect been greeted with the academic equivalent of all-encompassing hugs. The most noteworthy occasion of such accolades was a conference devoted to that same much maligned Pius XI — who had been the beneficiary of the two lengthy chapters constituting the whole of Part Three, the climactic ending of *The Popes Against the Jews*. The conference was mentioned briefly in the introduction to the present book when I was listing the high points Kertzer himself provided of his academic career.

In 2010, he chaired "Pius XI and America: An International Conference" at Brown University to discuss "Latin American church/state politics, Italian fascism, and topics in Vatican diplomacy." The scholars participating in the conference were among the most distinguished church historians and theologians from three continents, and thus may be said to have given a kind of *imprimatur* to Kertzer's views on the papacy as essential to the rise of modern racist anti-Semitism, and more particularly, to his extremist treatment of Pius XI as an ingrained anti-Semite who had fostered priests who advocated the extermination of all Jews.[37]

The ironies relative to the conference beggar description, as the most virulent critic of Pius XI helped, first, to organize it; then, personally tendered the invitations to it; and, finally, oversaw the affair itself (October 29-30, 2011), while presiding over two sessions and the concluding assembly — all to commemorate the "stridently anti-Semitic" pontiff. In the event, the nearly two dozen participants were mainly North Americans (several priests) and Italians (several women), and also included, notably, two scholars (Frank J. Coppa and Emma Fattorini) each of whom, separately, had seen the document which constituted John Cornwell's "ticking bomb" — proving Pope Pacelli was an ingrained anti-Semite — long before Cornwell "discovered" that non-existent trait, and of course well before Kertzer's own embrace of *Hitler's Pope* and its author.

Although less notably, the historical record makes requisite that two other scholars in attendance, Kevin Madigan and Michael Marrus, be mentioned, if only because of their appearance earlier in this book: Madigan was publicly enthusiastic about Kertzer's research skills and other intellectual attainments; Marrus was less enthusiastic about those skills as exercised by the present writer. Lastly, and also in the interests of the record, it may be noted that a relatively disproportionate number of the attendees were also retirees (as is the present writer) — more or less what the poet called "pensioners of Morpheus' train" — and thus less likely to be impressed by their host's research achievements, if they even knew of them; but also less likely to publicly denounce their fraudulence, if they did acquire such knowledge.

But whatever the composition of the group, it has to be presumed that at least the active participants — who may not have read Kertzer's contributions to Italian anthropological surveys, or such books as *The Kidnapping of Edgardo Mortara* and *Amalia's Tale* — certainly took the time to bone up by reading at least the central work in that larger area of ecclesiastical history, *The Popes Against the Jews*. One has to wonder about the reaction of these participants to their host's somewhat discordant point of view on the mod-

---

37. In fact, the conference was co-sponsored by Brown University, where Kertzer is provost, and three European institutions, the John XXIII Foundation for Religious Studies in Bologna, the University of Münster, and the École Française de Rome, and had been preceded by similar such conferences by the three institutions in Milan, Rome, and Münster. Given the fact — vaunted on Kertzer's website — that *The Popes Against the Jews* had been translated into all the major European languages, there can be little doubt that the directors and members of such institutions had no problems with his scholarship and its conclusions.

ern papacy in general, and on the subject of Pius XI in particular.[38] Obviously until the complete proceedings of the meeting are published, it will remain unknown whether any of the participants went so far as even to allude indirectly to the blatant violation by their host of the basic canons of scholarly integrity.

In any case, that anything seriously critical of Kertzer would have emerged is highly unlikely since most participants in such meetings usually feel bound by the protocol of their common membership in one or another professional organization—in the present instance, membership in the governing guilds of religious studies, the social sciences, and modern history. That such a protocol can sometimes outweigh fidelity to the transcendent pursuit of the historical event "as it really was" is one of the explanations for the dismal phenomenon implicitly explored throughout this book: the mute acquiescence by *homo academicus* in the mendacious, the spurious, and the fabricated.[39] (I will reserve for the next chapter the classic denunciation of

38. A brief report on the conference by a member of the John XXIII Foundation, Alberto Guasco, "Pius XI and America," appeared in *Journal of Modern Italian Studies* (volume 16, no. 3). It contains little that is pertinent to this discussion. The only remotely relevant papers are the following. Giuliana Chamedes of Columbia University noted that the encyclicals condemning Communism and Fascism "contained a new and surprising celebration of the rights of the individual in the face of the state." One paper on "Achille Ratti's Experience as Nuncio in Poland" is mentioned, but is not commented on, so its allegedly "enormous importance" goes untested. Kertzer's own paper co-written with a Brown University colleague was on the response in the United States to the Italian racial laws; Guasco's summation is "that the Vatican opposition to the Racial Laws was limited in scope." The previously mentioned Frank J. Coppa's paper was titled, "The 'Crusade' of Pius XI against Anti-Semitism & the 'Silence' of Pius XII"; according to Guasco, the paper showed "that Pius XI's vocal opposition to Nazi and fascist anti-Semitism, from the opening to the close of his pontificate, was consistent, concluding that the pope was always critical of anti-Semitism, which he found to be inadmissible for Catholics." Of the closing paper by the also previously mentioned Emma Fattorini ("Totalitarianism and the Last Years of Pius XI"), Guasco writes that it "argued that the development of Pius XI's spirituality clearly shows how far his own position on totalitarianism had come to diverge from that of his Secretary of State, Eugenio Pacelli, in the last years of his papacy."

39. In the present context, the best illustrations of this farrago of acquiescence are its two poster children, John Cornwell and David I. Kertzer, with their reciprocating books, each of which was almost invariably lauded by reviewers in what Kertzer himself modestly called "glowing" terms. Not infrequently the reviewer might add in the final paragraphs a flank-covering observation whose drift was along the lines of: "Even if X may occasionally overstate his case or exaggerate the flaws he is disclosing, few are those who would question the accumulated evidence he puts on display or the overall accuracy of his portrayal which is backed up by pages of references to the pertinent literature and by an extensive bibliography

the professoriate from one of Victor Klemperer's diaries.) Such acquiescence, if it is called into question at all, is usually rationalized as representing one's commitment to a given intellectual position, or to the fraternal bonds of scholarship in a particular discipline, or simply to the demands of academic advancement. In short, scholars, like politicians, like humankind in general, quickly learn — in the venerated words of a political visionary — "to love the little platoon we belong to in society." That this was axiomatic for the man whose biographer, F. P. Lock, said, "throughout his life, [Edmund] Burke sought to belong and to be accepted" may provide another insight into the embrace of bogus scholarship which is evident in much of the academy, particularly in fields where — what might be called for want of a better designation — "ideological tenets" often govern the discourse, i.e., preeminently in politics and religion. In the next chapter — the context is the scholarship of emerging Catholic academics, matching that of the established Kertzer — it will become evident how such acquiescence can result in more disastrously flawed historical judgments, including approval of the previously mentioned triad: the mendacious, the spurious, and the fabricated. The presumption of both parties, younger or older, is that during the Hitler era the Catholic hierarchy, from the pope down to local bishops and pastors, was so terrified of offending fascist governments and so victimized by its own latent or actual anti-Semitism that it turned a blind eye to crimes which it knew should be vehemently condemned.

---

of works in several languages. It would be nitpicking to concentrate on minor errors here and there when X also clearly puts on display . . ." (here one can fill in the blanks which relate to both wartime popes), "the cowardice of the Vatican," "the indifference of the pope," "the influence of his years as nuncio," "the obsessive fear of communism," etc. If the subject is Pope Pacelli there will be an anti-canonization coda — creatively telling tales of his anti-Semitism, of his other-worldly spirituality, or of his preoccupation with Rome's monuments and treasures, etc.

All this being generally true of the reception of Kertzer — Cornwell shall be scrutinized in *Historians Against History* — how does one explain the material contained in the previous chapters of the present book? They almost amount to a catalogue raisonné of violations and abuses of scholarly standards. Also to be taken into account is the fact that there is nothing particularly recondite or abstruse about the parsing of texts that constitutes the "methodology" of this entire critique of *The Popes Against the Jews*. It doesn't depend on some elaborate theory of interpretation, or access to new and hitherto unknown sources. As stated in the introduction, as well as in the first chapter, it is simply a matter of "close reading" or *explication de texte* harnessed to a hermeneutic of suspicion. The latter, it must also be said, is not rooted in some passion for the journalistic exposé — the *ressentiment* of a thousand fictional detectives as well as of a host of real-life researchers — it is simply rooted in fidelity to truth.

For the present, it suffices to observe that until the proceedings of the Brown conference are published, there will be no way of knowing if Kertzerian history was defended or denounced by any participants. Until then, one will have to rely on whatever snatches of information happen to turn up. Apart from the brief article months later in *Journal of Modern Italian Studies,* there was a speck of information in an article in the local *Providence Journal* which reported Kertzer as saying:

> . . . while the main theme was to be the relationship between the Church in Rome and the United States, the English- and Italian-speaking participants could not avoid making comparisons between Pius XI, who led the church from 1922 to his death in 1939, and his successor, Pius XII, who is still accused by many as having been too "silent" about the Holocaust.[40]

Of course, Kertzer himself could not be among those participants since — as the mantra has it — "the story I tell here for the first time about Achille Ratti" is that "he shared the same stridently anti-Semitic views" as those held by Pius XII. Ambiguously (or perhaps carelessly), the next sentence in the article says, "Throughout his own papacy Pius XI did not mince words and wrote an encyclical about the Nazi ideology of racism and totalitarianism, which he ordered read from church pulpits." Since it is now generally recognized that the encyclical represents the views of Pacelli as modified by the pope — though unfortunately not the far more vigorous attack on racism prepared by the Holy Office — it isn't clear whether this represents Kertzer's opinion or that of the journalist. If the former, it certainly suggests a retreat (tactical/duplicitous?) from the mantra above.

However, there did appear to be an allusion to a possible publication of the conference proceedings in another newspaper, a non-local one, which came out several months later. On July 3, 2011, an Associated Press "exclusive" appeared in a score of papers around the country, "Miracle Claimed for WW II–era Pope," by veteran religious journalist Nicole Winfield. Briefly, the central story was of an Italian woman who claimed along with her doctor that she had been healed of a life-threatening ailment through the intervention of Pius XII. In the event, there was an effort to enter this as a miracle

---

40. Richard C. Dejardin, "Conference at Brown Studies Work of Pope Pius XI" (October 30, 2010). Why the Italian- and English-speaking participants are singled out for their estimable unrestraint is unknown. These *are* history's bromides, and this *is* an international conference.

in his canonization proceedings, but like most things relative to that pope, public controversy immediately ensued. Winfield wrote:

> More recently, his beatification case has become the symbolic battleground in the debate over the future of the Catholic Church. Progressives are opposed to it because to them, Pius represents the church before the modernizing reforms of the Second Vatican Council. Traditionalists and conservatives are in favor of it for precisely the same reasons.[41]

After noting the pros and cons of the debate, and citing some favorable voices from the "Traditionalist" side, Winfield proffered three opposing views, beginning with David I. Kertzer, whose comment on the wartime pope's canonization—at least in terms of the previous discussion about the conference proceedings—was less significant, and less readily comprehended, than was his context (here italicized):

> "To talk about the pope as anything other than a moral coward as far as the murder of Jews of Rome is concerned is difficult for any of us who study what actually happened to take place," said Brown University anthropologist and historian David Kertzer, *author of a forthcoming book on Pius' predecessor, Pope Pius XI.*

What was intriguing about this observation was not the opinion of Pius XII—very old-tiara—but that Kertzer was writing a book on Pius XI. The initial assumption, more or less unavoidable, was that this was probably an edited collection of the papers delivered at the Brown University conference. After a civil inquiry from the present writer, a civil response was proffered: "I have been working on a book on Pius XI, using the newly opened Vatican archives, for several years. I plan to complete the book only next spring," i.e., spring 2012. (Its arrival is now eagerly anticipated.) Since it is likely that such a book will not be a repetition of *The Popes Against the Jews*, its central theme will probably be the Vatican's relationship with the Italian government. One may anticipate a title with the words "Mussolini" and "Pius XI," in it, which in turn may bring to mind Kertzer's final treatment of

---

41. Why those favoring canonization have a dual allegiance and those opposed are singly characterized makes sense to the present *progressive* writer who — mainly as a matter of taxonomy — would describe the opponents as "ideological *liberals*." The controversy over canonization will be fought out on the "symbolic battleground" of the next chapter.

Mussolini's audience with the pope, a treatment that occasioned such glaring distortion of deeds and words by Kertzer and his supporters that it fully merited what Michael Burleigh referred to as "the shoddy underpinnings of this endeavor."

The above was written immediately after receipt of Kertzer's e-mail message of July 5 — as a slew of memos to colleagues and editors will attest. However, the first confirmation of the specifics of the projected book came much later via the Managing Editor at Eerdmans, Linda Bieze, who had seen in "Publishers Lunch" (October 4, 2011) references to works being hawked at the upcoming Frankfurt Book Fair. Among the fifty or so titles was the following: "David Kertzer's THE POPE AND MUSSOLINI, portraying the co-dependent relationship between Pius XI and Mussolini from 1922 to 1939." Shortly after, the book was described more fully by Kertzer's agent, although the language (here italicized) is even more obviously that of Kertzer himself.

Author of National Book Award–finalist, THE KIDNAPPING OF ED-GARDO MORTARA, which Stephen Spielberg and Tony Kushner are adapting into a feature, Brown University professor David Kertzer's THE POPE AND MUSSOLINI, *based on more than five years of research in the Vatican Archives,* portraying *the co-dependent relationship* between Pius XI and Mussolini from 1922 to1939, *revealing for the first time* how each man relied on the other to consolidate his power and pursue his political goals. (http://www.strothmanagency.com/articles/category/agency-deals)

The "more than five years of research in the Vatican Archives" simply meant that the book took five years to write, while the reference to first-time revelations is conventional Kertzerian bombast. But what is hardly conventional is that the context of pontiff and dictator consolidating their pursuit of political goals is a mutual addiction to power resulting from their "co-dependent relationship." Not since Matthew Fox accused the church of being an addictive organization has anyone made a similar claim. Moreover, Kertzer's mind-reading prowess was a trivial endowment compared to this aptitude for diagnosing old documents to reveal new pathologies — and papal pathologies at that. The co-dependence linking *The Pope and Mussolini* suggests as subtitle for the book: *Twelve Steps to an Unholy Alliance.* Moreover, since the book will certainly be as controversial as *The Popes Against the Jews,* it will inevitably lead to a full-scale rejoinder (not unlike the one I am here making to the earlier work). For that rejoinder, I also proffer a title suggestion: *Were Il Duce and Il Papa Joined at the Hip? Tracking the Footsteps, Confronting the Ilium.*

Returning now to the second and third "opposing views" in the "miracle" altercation, Nicole Winfield's article continued:

> "My position has always been to say—and I've said it to Pope Benedict XVI — that this is a matter that should be deferred until at least the generation of Holocaust survivors is no longer with us, so it's not as if rubbing the salt into their wounds," said Rabbi David Rosen, head of interfaith relations at the American Jewish Committee.

The third opponent to canonization cited in the article was John Pawlikowski, who was also one of Kertzer's "glowing" reviewers. First the context, then the comment.

> Last year, 19 Catholic scholars appealed to the academic in Benedict to give researchers more time to study the full archives: "The question isn't 'Did he do anything?' but whether he might have done more sooner," said the Reverend John Pawlikowski, ethics professor at the Catholic Theological Union, who co-wrote the letter.

There is little point to stressing the absurdity of the phenomenon that pious Catholics — priests included — who wholeheartedly embrace the residual medievalism of miracles as essential to sainthood, suddenly are in the business of rejecting the miraculous if it involves someone they don't approve of. To heap the ironic on the absurd, there were also people discussing the ailing woman's fate who said that her condition couldn't actually have improved at all because the deceased pontiff had no healing power. The inexorable conclusion is that even if medical tests by the woman's doctors proved the woman had been healed — as some tests appeared to do — they could not be credible because over half a century ago a pope failed to do something "more sooner" for the Jews. This is not residual medievalism; this is medievalism full-blown, as "theology" trumps empiric science, and the woman who claimed to be healed is assumed to be delusional. Fortunately, what was done to the deluded in the Middle Ages — also usually women — has since become a violation (to word it mildly) of modern civil law.

As for the views of John Pawlikowski, his little platoon of faithful opponents to the canonization of Pius XII will be mustered and ready for the fray in the next chapter. Whether they will be up to scratch in this ecclesiastical donnybrook — the anti-pioduodecimalist war — remains to be seen. What can be said is that the cry, "doctor," "doctor," will resound in this battleground much as it did in the description of the above controversy, only this time the term will not be a noun, but a verb.

CHAPTER 9

Righteous Petitions and Doctored Texts

The Catholic scholars who according to Nicole Winfield "appealed to the academic in Benedict" had sent the pope (and the press) an open letter asking that he postpone all efforts at going forward with the beatification of Pius XII. The writers of this letter, which will initiate a lengthy discussion — albeit one again concerning rigged historical texts — described themselves as active in "Jewish-Catholic relations." Concerning the latter, I had earlier remarked in the context of Pius IX's homily to the women of Rome, and again in chapter 8, that the field of Jewish-Catholic relations or dialogue, however intrinsically noble in motivation, is often tainted by guilt on the part of the Christians, who then tend to denigrate their own tradition in an exercise of what can be termed "contrasupersessionism." As I have said, the guilt is understandable; the denigration is not. I mention this now to obviate any impression that these particular petitioners are to be numbered among the critics of Christian "supersessionism" — although, as will be seen, some of them are seriously flawed critics of the wartime pope and his supporters.[1]

But the underlying issue to be broached in what follows is whether it is possible to really believe that any statement of any pope, no matter how vigorously and repeatedly proclaimed, could in fact have had any deterrent effect on Hitler's vicious plot for the Jews of Europe. It is difficult to con-

---

1. Much of what is described as Jewish-Catholic dialogue has little to do with the kind of serious theological exchange exemplified by Bruce D. Chilton and Jacob Neusner in *Classical Christianity and Rabbinic Judaism* (2004), much less with the study of such an illuminating work as Neusner's guide to the Mishnah, *Making God's Word Work* (2004). Rather, the "dialogue" too often focuses on support of Israeli policy toward Palestinians and support of critics of the wartime church.

ceive of an affirmative answer to that question. So one soon begins to realize that what is really of concern has less to do with the pope's wartime power to terminate violence and mass murder than with the postwar need for some resolution of the enduring mystery of how that murder could ever have occurred in the first place. Such a quest for answers is almost instinctive, as the following more recent instance of widespread violence — though certainly on an almost infinitely less drastic plane — might indicate. Before the war in Iraq, rumor has it that the prospect of petitioning the pope was bruited about by some groups, a few of whose members toyed with the notion of having him take up residence in Baghdad as hostage against the impending American destruction of the city. Decades from now, when the rationale for the invasion will certainly continue to be debated by historians and journalists, and such obvious factors as imperial arrogance, regime change, oil, Saddam-obsession, etc., will have lost their cachet, it is not entirely unlikely that some revisionists will point to the failure of John Paul II to put his life on the line as *a* — if not *the* — major factor in the precipitation of the conflict. What may seem on its face a farcical suggestion assumes an air of probability when one looks at how the tragedy of the Holocaust two decades later found *a* — if not *the* — major implementor in the person of Pius XII.

Also, it is to be noted that among Catholics there are many who are convinced that the wartime pope was grievously derelict in his duty — presumably that is the belief of the petitioners to Benedict XVI — while there appear to be only a few who would affirm that he probably did as much as he believed he could. This is hardly the kind of disagreement that could be characterized as factious fury (Edmund Burke again), though the difference is the more or less predictable one between liberals and conservatives or, as Nicole Winfield termed it, progressives and traditionalists. Curiously, it is among the former — more accurately identified as "ideological liberals" — that has been displayed so vehement an animus toward the pope that it appears to stem from the belief that he made a conscious and deliberate decision *not* to save lives. Only that explains the persistent vigor with which he has been attacked; and only that explains why a few presumably estimable scholars and signatories to the petition to Benedict XVI have intentionally falsified data and doctored important texts in order to convict the church's leadership of failing in its duty. It is not entirely surprising that a Jewish academic like David I. Kertzer would succumb to the temptation to doctor or otherwise subvert texts in order to attack the papacy; it is less clear why Catholic scholars would want to do something similar. The very fact that scholarly work tainted by deceptions and ruses could be proffered as a gesture of solidarity with the six million raises questions as to whether such denunciations of papacy and church are genuinely impelled by Holocaust concerns — or by something else, possibly related to an agenda regarding church governance or church reform. Certainly to use tainted means for a good end so violates rudimentary ethical principles that it raises doubts about the intentions of the violators.[2]

There used to be a maxim everybody memorized in Ethics 101: *bonum ex integra causa, malum ex quocumque defectu:* "An action is good when good in every respect; it is wrong when wrong in any respect." Furthermore, the phenomenon of seemingly impassioned and outraged scholars deploying sham learning to condemn church leaders is to "instrumentalize" the Shoah, in the sense of subverting it to some unrelated and extraneous goal. Similarly, some public displays of passion or anger over this issue raise the question of whether they may not sometimes be manifestations of dramatized concern, that is, the kind of sanctimony that gives rise to what used to be vulgarly called "crocodile tears." The reason for the latter impression is that some of these angry researchers appear to be always on stage, always eager for an opportunity to publicly vent their shock at the failure of the papacy to prevent the fate of the six million.

Such expressions of rage sometimes had so synthetic a character to them that they appeared to be more evocative of "Don't Cry for Me, Argentina," or "Holocaust: The Musical," rather than of, say, the poems of Nelly Sachs or the fragments of verse left behind by the anonymous victims of the Warsaw ghetto. In fact, this synthetic element brings to mind a kind of latter-day replication of what Christopher Lasch in *The Culture of Narcissism* (1991) called "politics as spectacle." A much more recently coined phrase, "the Holocaust industry," describes a more ugly concept and is embodied in an ugly book. Unfortunately, it too had its counterpart around the turn of the century among those who seemed to be forever on the prowl for something new or more monstrous to say about the failure of the church relative to the six million. What can be called "the Pacelli industry" demanded the pursuit of the novel and the shocking, and thus for some writers the attainment of near-celebrity status — of which John Cornwell

---

2. It is not impossible that the ethical principles guiding this petition may be vague or unformulated. Michael Phayer, a signer of the petition, has described the notion that "the ends must never justify the means" as "traditional Catholic teaching" (*Commonweal,* May 9, 2003).

remains the premier example. Lastly, such antipapal recrimination also indicated an acceptance of the notion that if Catholics can condemn the pope for his failure to save Jews during the Holocaust, such a condemnation must be merited.[3]

The resulting carnival of antipapal recrimination celebrated in several books of the period also indicated the curious phenomenon that among some Protestant authors there was put on display an easy dismissal of the historic reality that *their* European ancestors across Western Europe before the Reformation were themselves involved in "Catholic" anti-Jewishness.[4] Thus these censorious gentiles can be regarded as complicit through their forebears in the sins of the church as are contemporary Roman Catholic heirs of that same hegemonic legacy. Curiously, one doesn't hear much about the need for expressions of repentance by Protestants — though it is not unusual for their churches to have depictions of "Catholic" saints from well after the Patristic era: Francis of Assisi, Thomas of Canterbury, Joan of Arc, even Thomas Aquinas. Similarly, statements of regret over anti-Semitic complicity came from official bodies of European Reformed churches well after *Nostra Aetate* (1965). In North America, the Catholic guidelines for the implementation of that document (1975) long preceded official statements from such Protestant bodies as the Presbyterian Church and the United Church of Christ (1987); the Disciples of Christ (1993); the Evangelical Lutheran Church (1994); and the Alliance of Baptists (1995).

The need for rejecting the exploitation of the Holocaust for self-interested goals is evident in the following by the Israeli historian Tom Segev, author of *The Seventh Million* (1991) — that figure referring to Jews in Israel who also subsequently suffered, though in vastly different ways and numbers, from the slaughter of their brethren in Europe. Discussing efforts in Israel to comprehend the tragedy, Segev notes that at Yad Vashem

> speakers may denounce antisemitism and Holocaust deniers, and may affirm that the Holocaust proves the need for a strong Israel. They may

3. I again echo the language of Susan Zuccotti (loc. cit.) whose monocular perspective allows only a one-sided view of fundamental issues regarding the Holocaust. After condemning two Jewish defenders of Pius XII, Joseph Lichten and Pinchas Lapide, for "distortion of the historical record," she observes: "The theory is apparently that, if Jews can praise the pope for his effort during the Holocaust, it must be true."

4. John K. Roth, cited at the end of chapter 7 on the failings of Pius XI, exemplifies this attitude, as does even more emphatically his contribution to the symposium on *Popes and Politics* in *U.S. Catholic Historian* (Spring 2002).

not, however, go beyond the bounds of the national consensus. The prayers said at the ceremony are carefully worded: the murder of the Jews is described in the passive voice: "those who were tortured, murdered, slaughtered." Generally, the prayers do not identify the murderer. They attribute the horrors to "impure hands," "cruel hands," "the hand of the enemy."

Segev also notes that some members of the Knesset insisted on invoking on all possible occasions the Holocaust: "There was a certain element of competition involved here: members often tried to show that they were more patriotic or more religious than their opponents; similarly, they competed over faithfulness to the Holocaust." However, he also observes that "many were Holocaust survivors" — among whom a sense of righteousness or even self-righteousness would certainly be understandable.

But one wonders at the spectacle of a similar such competition among more detached and remote observers that "goes beyond the bounds" and is careless about specific accusations relative to who can denounce (albeit with "good" intentions) the most vociferously; who can outdo the other in public expressions of outrage; who can call for the most severe indictment of several popes. In sum, who can (of course, again *and always* with good intentions) be most passionately exploitative of the deaths of others. This competition — like that in the Knesset — takes place within a community of like-minded people; but in this case, a community of reciprocally supportive "Holocaust professionals"[5] who accept one another's credentials, who meet to exchange

---

5. The very term is itself contradictory, like the notion of a "professional poet" or even a "professional saint." What might be described as both a diary and a how-to manual for such professionals is *Holocaust Politics* (2001) by the ubiquitous John K. Roth. On the jacket of the book he describes his work as follows:

> More than half a century after Nazi Germany's genocidal assault on the Jewish people, the Holocaust grips our attention as never before, raising hotly debated questions. How is the Holocaust best remembered? What are its lessons? Who gets to answer those questions? Who owns the Holocaust? *Those issues provoke disagreements that can be cutthroat or constructive.*
>
> Taking its point of departure from the controversy that swirled around John Roth's aborted appointment as director of the Center for Advanced Holocaust Studies, a senior post at the U.S. Holocaust Museum in Washington, D.C., *Holocaust Politics* shows how contemporary attitudes and priorities compete to determine that all-important difference. (italics supplied)

Among the blurbists are Michael Barenbaum, Michael R. Marrus, and Carol Rittner.

congruent data, who incautiously applaud fellow members' revelations, and who write collegially supportive articles and book reviews. This inevitably evolves into a "guild" that assembles periodically to live, eat, and "breathe together." The latter phrase suggests, at least etymologically, "conspire." And that suggestion would be excessive, were it not that precisely this accusation of conspiracy has been made by these authors about the Vatican and its officials, in what would appear to be another instance of ideological "projection." Of course, there is a need for Holocaust scholarship as an academic discipline, but a subspecialty or a "minor" in this "field" should not be "Anti-Pacelli studies."

As a manifestation of the cohesiveness of this guild, there is the mind-numbing recital — in this dismal literature that is now almost a literary genre — of the same ambiguous examples, statistics, texts, and anecdotes, all inevitably slanted to the same predictable conclusions about papacy and church. As a manifestation of the influence of this guild there is the book, previously cited, *Pope Pius XII and the Holocaust* (2001), a collective work edited by Carol Rittner and John K. Roth, which is almost identical with many other titles previously or subsequently in print, and with contributions or lengthy citations from authors who appear over and over writing in this genre, and who repeat themselves with only slight variations on their single-minded theme. These writers usually include — in addition to the two named editors — Michael Berenbaum, James Carroll, John Cornwell, Eva Fleischner, Michael R. Marrus, John Pawlikowski, Michael Phayer, Richard L. Rubenstein, and Susan Zuccotti, all of whom in both Roth books are treated with extraordinary deference as authoritative voices by the contributors, who seem to have convinced themselves that the overall writings by or about these people must be accurate — though one or two may be termed "controversial" — largely because these writings are highly critical of the pope and his auxiliaries. Again, we have the counterpart to Zuccotti's conspiratorial reversal: "The theory apparently is that, if Jews can praise the Pope for his efforts during the Holocaust, it must be true," and if Catholics can condemn him, it must also be true. I used the phrase "incautiously applaud" since had these contributors not reached an a priori view, they simply could not so ceaselessly and so ardently endorse such books and articles, however much their writers proclaim themselves horrified by the Holocaust — as what sane human being is not. It is this sheer horror that among Holocaust professionals motivates and then rationalizes this endorsement of dissimulations and distortions, which had they occurred in other historical narratives would have been immediately rejected. This also broaches what is perhaps the *ne plus ultra* of the anti-Pacelli campaign, as two contributors to *Pope Pius XII and the Holocaust* introduced the notion that the ultimate failure of Pius XII was his not having shed his blood to disrupt the Nazi slaughter.[6] How this would have aided Jews in the death camps goes unexplained.

As mentioned above, leading the opposition to the beatification of Pius XII was John Pawlikowski, who has been active in the promotion of Jewish-Catholic relations, not least by supporting these kinds of public petitions.[7] A decade ago in *Pope Pius XII and the Holocaust,* he had said:

> In the light of the remaining gaps in research, the process of fully investigating Pius XII's record should not get short-circuited by raising him to the status of "blessed" or "saint." The initial investigative process in this regard can certainly continue, but no action should be taken until the scholarly assessment of his overall record is much more thorough. There is also need to widen the usual parameters of such a scrutiny relative to sanctification with the inclusion of a wide range of scholarly evaluations of his papacy.

On the occasion of the publication of the present petition (February 18, 2010), Pawlikowski told Catholic News Service: "We sent this letter because we feel that too often the issue of Pius XII is portrayed as one of Jewish concern. We wanted to make it clear that some Catholics who have worked on Holocaust issues have serious concerns about advancing the cause of Pius XII at this time." However, "this time" has now been extended to cover more than a decade. In a joint review in *The Christian Century* (February 2, 2000) of Pierre Blet's *Pius XII and the Second World War* and John Cornwell's *Hitler's Pope,* Pawlikowski wrote: "Both the Blet and Cornwell volumes are also part of the current struggle over the possible beatification and canonization of Pius XII. . . . Many of us who have researched Pius's rec-

---

6. One of them remarks with a kind of transparent candor, "As someone who makes a living researching and teaching about Nazi Germany and the Holocaust, I am also aware that my concerns need to be self-critical," and then raises the issue: "What is it to have faith in God if the pope eschews martyrdom, and even discomfort or difficulty for himself and his followers, in favor of accommodation to the forces of evil?" Another asks: "Did the pope and those around him ever consider that he should perhaps be ready to be killed?" "After all some of the early popes had been martyred (by the Romans)."

7. Another petition and signatories were described in "Should Pope Pius XII be canonised?" *The Sunday Times,* October 21, 2008.

ord are strongly opposed to his canonization, beatification, or even elevation to 'venerable' status."

But for many others who take seriously Kenneth Woodward's telling observation in *Making Saints* (1990) that "over the last nine hundred years only three popes have been declared saints," the canonization of Pius XII is of minor import.[8] Moreover, this whole project of interweaving, or rather interlocking, his "cause" and "Holocaust issues" is itself an ahistorical enterprise whether undertaken because of "Jewish concern" or Catholic "serious concerns" — unless, of course, the implicit belief of all the concerned is that something will turn up that proves Pius XII was in fact, as Cornwell opined, "the ideal pope" for Hitler's mass murders. It is unlikely that all these petitioners would embrace such a position, so it remains incomprehensible why there continues to be this amalgamation of the Holocaust and the canonization process.

Moreover, since it is obvious that after ten years Rome has no intention of responding to these petitions, they have taken on an air of "politics as spectacle," of politics devoted to drawing attention as much to the politicians as to the good of the polity; or, in the present instance, to the petitioners rather than to the petition. Few people can really believe that these pleas (no matter how often redesigned — and no matter how often re-signed — often by the same parties) are going to persuade Rome to simply dismantle an apparatus that was first put in place more than half a century ago by Pope Paul VI. Again, to get a picture of just how complex that apparatus is, one need merely read the 200,000-plus words by Kenneth Woodward in *Making Saints*.

Most Catholic opponents of canonization describe themselves as explicitly concerned about Jewish-Catholic relations — the "Jewish" element of the equation, in the practical order usually simply means "Israeli" — so they are particularly sympathetic to judgments like the following:

In an interview with the Israeli newspaper *Ha'aretz*, Isaac Herzog, Israel's social affairs minister, who is responsible for relations with Christian communities, said efforts to turn Pius into a saint were "an ex-

8. Woodward's work is not only a remarkably learned treatment of the history and the procedures of raising to the altars various Christians through the entire history of the church, it is also a model of fair-mindedness in its navigation of controversial pontiffs — none less carefully or brilliantly than those beginning with Pius IX and on into the present century. Nowhere is this fairness displayed more effectively than in his treatment of Pius XII, a treatment highly to be recommended to the supporters of this petition.

ploitation of forgetfulness and lack of awareness." He accused Pius of having kept silent during the war. (www.guardian.co.uk/world/2008/oct/23/israel)

But they are less likely to respond sympathetically to other voices that also appear to be well-placed to clarify the public issue of canonization. Thus when the Israeli ambassador to the Holy See, Mordechay Lewy, was asked whether his country had "a role to play in the canonization of Pius XII," he replied that canonization was "not our concern." "What concerns us is the historical role of Pius XII. This is a real issue which has been, to my mind, deliberately, but still mistakenly, combined with the [other] matter." Ambassador Lewy himself went on to say:

> Historically speaking, I think he was neither a hero nor a villain. It is probably the right thing to think of a more balanced view of him. The problem is that we are looking at him through the filter of a post-conciliar church. He is definitely a protagonist of the pre-conciliar church, and the pre-conciliar church has, as its main assignment, to seek all possible means to salvation for its own flock. (Interview by Michael Paulson, *The Boston Globe*, June 19, 2009)

Who is deliberately combining the "historical role of Pius XII" and the "canonization of Pius XII" is left unmentioned, but certainly the Hochhuth-Cornwell fabrications, which still haunt all subsequent assessments of the pope, come readily to mind — as, of course, must also the signatories of the petition to Benedict XVI. And although it would certainly be impolitic for a diplomat to explicitly say so, those fabrications have had an influence on the people at Yad Vashem and several Israeli politicians who have voiced vigorously and publicly their criticism of Pius XII. The vigor, of course, is their own business, since they are entitled to make their own rules. The publicness is the business of others, specifically of those who are not petitioning anyone in Israel to embrace the cause of the pope, and who must nevertheless hear or read denunciations of him from those quarters.[9]

9. The Anti-Defamation League (November 22, 2010) put out the following release, occasioned by the appearance of *Light of the World: The Pope, the Church, and the Signs of the Times,* the book resulting from an interview the pope had with Peter Seewald, and which was widely covered by the media. "Pope Benedict XVI's unqualified praise for Pope Pius XII's alleged efforts to save Jews during the Holocaust does a great disservice to the families of Holocaust victims, qualified historians and Catholic-Jewish relations. Pope Ben-

The petition to Benedict XVI began as follows:

As faithful, practicing Catholics, consecrated and lay, we urgently write to you concerning the cause of Pope Pius XII. We are educators who have conducted research and are currently carrying into effect more research on Catholicism under National Socialism and the Holocaust.

Since beginnings are everything, as all composers of formal documents realize, even to a sympathetic reader — which perhaps would partially exclude the present writer — this is not auspicious. It isn't so much the use of the recently resuscitated, but still self-validating redundancy, "practicing," that gives one pause as it is the labored tone of "have conducted research and are currently carrying into effect more research." This overwrought structure suggests the old cliché about a camel as a committee-designed equine, a suggestion reinforced by the fact that this research is "on Catholicism under National Socialism and the Holocaust" — which leaves that seemingly superfluous "and the Holocaust" at the tail end of the collective utterance.

The movement to press forward at this time the process of beatification of Pius XII greatly troubles us. Needless to say, the controversy over Pius XII's actions during the Second World War and the Holocaust is long-standing. . . . scholars still have a great deal of research to complete before final conclusions can be drawn about Pius XII's behavior during the Holocaust.

The notion of research being "complete" and of "final conclusions" being drawn is an affront to common sense rather than to rhetorical finesse. In any case, continuing a rhetorical analysis (e.g., "Pius XII's actions," vis-à-vis "Pius XII's behavior") would be both unkind and tedious — so I at least will press forward without pausing over the distinction between "scholars" and "researchers" in the following:

At the moment, scholars eagerly await the opening of papers from Pius XII's pontificate that you, Holy Father, have so graciously arranged to

edict's conclusions that Pius XII, 'was one of the great righteous men and that he saved more Jews than anyone else' amounts to a double standard — ignoring the Vatican's own position calling on Jewish institutions not to come to conclusions about the World War II-era pope until all the evidence is in." Much of the secular press concentrated on the presumed significance of the pope's adjustment of the condom ban in relation to AIDS. (The Anti-Defamation League will surface again later in this chapter.)

be made available. At the same time, as researchers, we also realize that there are numerous archives, both secular and ecclesiastical, that scholars have yet to access or consult, many of which might shed more light on Pope Pius's actions during the Holocaust.

A non-pressed reader might say this appears to suggest that the goal may not be simply to postpone the beatification process but in effect to put an end to it altogether, since even when the Vatican archives will presumably have been exhausted, there is little doubt that those other "archives, both secular and ecclesiastical," will be invoked to further delay the beatification movement.

> Currently, *existing* research *leads* us to the view that Pope Pius XII did not issue a clearly worded statement, unconditionally condemning the whole-sale slaughter and murder of European Jews. At the same time, *some* evidence also *compels* us to see that Pius XII's diplomatic background encouraged him as head of a neutral state, the Vatican, to assist Jews by means that were not made public during the war. It is essential that further research be conducted to resolve both these questions. As scholars of theology and history, we realize how important the historical critical method is to your own research and we implore you to ensure that such a historical investigation takes place before proceeding with the cause of Pope Pius XII. (italics supplied)

It is somewhat confusing that "*some* evidence" *compels* the signatories to accept X about the pope, but that "*existing* research" only *leads* them to accept Y — although that objection may be waived since the gist of the message is clear enough: the beatification process must stop. Moreover, it is difficult to embrace the notion that these scholars really believe those "final conclusions" might lead to overturning all that "existing research" or to corroborating "the view" that Pius XII *did* issue "a clearly worded statement unconditionally condemning the wholesale slaughter of the Jews." So, the real point of all this talk is to block anything that would raise Pacelli to the altars and thus further antagonize interested Jews, as well as any others who are presumably concerned with such matters.[10]

10. Who exactly would be offended remains undisclosed. Presumably it might be the petitioners' Jewish dialogue partners, but they remain unnamed. There will be an important instance later when signatories of this petition find themselves in opposition to the views re-

In fact, most of these signatories are probably aware that it is a near impossibility anything will be discovered that is stronger and more compelling than what is already available in the published *Actes et Documents du Saint Siège relatifs à la Seconde Guerre Mondiale, 1965-81* (ADSS). The latter was completed nearly three decades before the Pius XI archives were opened (partially in 2003, and fully in 2006), and yet no major revelations were made regarding Pacelli, even though the first period covered (1917-30) was that of Cornwell's bogus exposé of Pacelli's anti-Jewish and anti-black racism. Nor does the major study of a slightly longer period by Hubert Wolf, the previously cited *Pope and Devil: The Vatican's Archives and the Third Reich* (2010), put on display the anti-Semitic, pro-German secretary of state who, allegedly among other stratagems, sought to placate Hitler by sanctioning the dissolution of the Center Party.

Furthermore, few people, scholars or otherwise, really think that this is about the pursuit of historical truth, even if the latter is to be disclosed by deploying the formidable *Historisch-kritische methode.* (After all, this was the method, according to Kenneth Woodward, that sometimes was deployed with so much judicial rigor that it could be twisted to show that Pio Nono merited canonization as a church reformer.) Rather, it's about the pursuit of closure: closure on the part of Roman Catholics for nearly two millennia of denigrating Jews and Judaism by Christian believers; and closure on the part of Jews for the incomprehensible horror of the Holocaust.[11] What better way to resolve all this, at least on the part of understandably guilt-ridden Catholics, than to indicate — at first, hesitantly and politely, then firmly and, in the event, insistently, or even perversely — that the wartime head of the church embodied such denigration; and this, not merely because he was reflecting the traditional teachings of his faith (that would not be enough to make him personally guilty of unsaintly "behavior"), but because he was essentially an anti-Semite, as the unmentioned and unmentionable Hochhuth-Cornwell showed to the world. The logic was impeccable; it was also circular. We know he was an anti-Semite because he was silent, and he was silent because . . .

---

garding canonizations expressed publicly by leaders of the Jewish community — in this instance the same head of the Anti-Defamation League who was responsible for the previously mentioned press release criticizing Benedict XVI. For that reason, among others, it is necessary to examine the relevant public views of some of the petitioners themselves.

11. "Jews have asked repeatedly that the Vatican's wartime archives be opened for study. Silvan Shalom, the Israeli Deputy Prime Minister, repeated the request to the Pope directly when the pontiff visited Rome's synagogue last month" (Philip Pullella, *Reuters,* February 17, 2010).

But, in fact, this too will be fudged. He actually was not *essentially* anti-Semitic, he was only, as we shall see, *in essence* anti-Semitic "symbolically" — which is at least, one may suppose, preferable to being the *per accidens* "floating signifier" of anti-Semitism.

The petition contains further observations on the importance of *Nostra Aetate,* as well as a commendation of Benedict's remarks at the synagogue of Rome ("Your actions were moving and courageous"). But to some observers, the present writer for one, it is difficult to understand how four years after the first publication of "Refugee," its existence, if not necessarily its remarkable importance, has not seeped into treatments of Jewish-Christian relations, particularly by people who presumably are on ceaseless alert for new data relative to anything concerning those relations — whether such people dwell in the United States or Israel. Such comportment is close to what is traditionally called *ignorantia affectata,* since it would put an end to all speculation about the "anti-Semitism" of the pope, as well as to the kind of off-the-wall speculation expressed in the petition as follows:

> For many Jews and Catholics, Pius XII takes on a role much larger than his historical papacy. In essence, Pius XII has become a symbol of centuries-old Christian anti-Judaism and anti-Semitism which, for example, the Rev. Edward H. Flannery has documented and spelled out in his work *The Anguish of the Jews: Twenty-Three Centuries of Anti-Semitism.* It is challenging to separate Pope Pius XII from this legacy.[12]

It is impossible to fathom what dictated *any* book being inserted here, but it is doubly impossible to figure out the choice of a book that even with some rewriting and expanding in later editions is a disastrous piece of Christian apologetics. As several of these signatories know, the present writer — independent *ex professo* of any theological organization or academic group — published a symposium on the first edition of *The Anguish of the Jews* in *Continuum* (Autumn 1966), with contributions not from people concerned with "Jewish-Christian relations" but from Jewish scholars who were recognized as distinguished authorities in their various fields of endeavor: Eliezer Berkovits, Arthur Hertzberg, Erich Isaac, Givin I. Langmuir, Jacob Neusner, Howard

---

12. Although I have never met Father Flannery, I have always regarded him as a good man and a good priest — largely because he was a friend of another good man and good priest, George Higgins, who was called "the labor priests' priest," by another good man and good priest, Charles Curran.

Nemerov, Léon Poliakov, and Steven S. Schwarzschild. Two of these, Arthur Hertzberg and Léon Poliakov, are frequently cited in the present book as well as in *Popes and Politics,* and Jacob Neusner enthusiastically reviewed the latter in "Warts on the Body of Christ" (*The Jerusalem Post,* August 30, 2002).

I had written a short review of the Flannery book in *Herder Correspondence* (June 1965), but it was in the Autumn 1966 issue of *Continuum* that my quite severe critique of the book appeared under the title "Antisemitism and Theological Arrogance" (reprinted in *The Range of Commitment* [1969]). Unlike the petition to Benedict XVI, it was far less concerned with looking back at the church in fascist Europe than to looking at the entire appalling history of the relationship between the Jewish and Christian communities — all with a view to the centuries yet to come. In that light, these petitioners' goal with its obsessive preoccupation with Pius XII now appears narrow and insular, if not petty. ("Anti-Semitism and Theological Arrogance" is the annex at the end of this chapter.)

In the passage excerpted above *ignorantia affectata* brushes up against *mauvaise foi,* as the pursuit of archival research into the "historical papacy" — hitherto the rationale of the entire petition — is subordinated to a symbolic entity whose exact nature is undefined and whose very existence ("has become") is only to be disclosed by weighing and assessing the vagaries of popular opinion. Although W. H. Auden in an engaging put-down of self-serving academic squabbles ("Under Which Lyre") has affirmed, "thou shalt not sit with statisticians nor commit a social science," the rest of us must do both if we are going to determine whether any weight is to be given to this freshly coined notion of Pacelli's symbolic role as embodiment of more than twenty-three centuries of evildoing. Even though Kertzer's books are available in a Babel of languages, and Cornwell sold more copies than the combined sales of all the books of all the signatories to this petition, that is still a far cry from making a recent pope symbolize a phenomenon, whether anti-Semitic or not, that occurred more than three centuries before there was such a historical entity as Christianity, much less such a historical entity as the papacy. Moreover, all this hedging and conflating explains the peculiarly disjunctive structure (as well as disjunctive thinking) of the above quoted passage with its arbitrary and mid-sentence invocation of the Reverend Edward H. Flannery and his book. To make use of the hermeneutical language of the preceding chapters, this is the tic that betrays some subterfuge in the offing. Only the most rampant groupthink mentality or the most rampant self-assurance could have permitted the insertion of that clause into this petition.

Similarly, it takes a considerable flight of imagination to conceive what must have been the mood of several signatories to the document when they realized the absurdity of what they were signing on to. These professional scholars are now on record as asserting that because a non-designated number of people ["many"] believe a given pope is the symbol of "Twenty-Three Centuries of Anti-Semitism," then that self-contradictory assertion should be given credence. As noted, how a twentieth-century Christian can symbolize anything related to three centuries before the Christian era is a judgment that goes unexplained — though it at least does provide another reason for rarely signing on to these kinds of collective petitions. Even loyalty to one's group, party, guild, whatever, should have been overridden at the prospect of endorsing this self-contradictory chronology. One must add to this the equally problematic nature of the petition's implicit prerequisite; i.e., that until there is proof of a clearly worded wartime statement unconditionally condemning the wholesale slaughter of Jews, Pius XII will continue to bear the burden, symbolic or otherwise, of the 2,300 years of anti-Semitism to which these signatories have arbitrarily linked him.

The petition to Benedict XVI continued:

> it is challenging to separate Pope Pius XII from this legacy. Proceeding with the cause of Pope Pius XII, without an *exhaustive* study of his actions during the Holocaust, might harm Jewish-Catholic relations in a way that cannot be overcome in the foreseeable future. (italics supplied)

In fact, this forecast, if not implicit threat, was happily prophetic, since two other figures engaged in Jewish-Catholic relations — though possibly not so symbolic — immediately approved the petitioners. A writer in *The Jewish Week* (February 25, 2010) reported that "Holocaust expert Michael Berenbaum said the signers of the letter, mostly veterans of interfaith work 'who grew up in the shadow of the Holocaust,' and of Vatican II, took to heart the Church's increasing openness to ecumenism over recent decades." The reporter continued: "Abraham Foxman, national director of the Anti-Defamation League and a hidden child in Poland during the Holocaust, called the letter a 'very significant, important gesture. The views of Catholics resonate a lot more seriously' in the Vatican than those of outsiders." Concerning Foxman himself, as briefly noted earlier, at the end of this entire discussion, he will make his own "very significant, important gesture" which, however, will directly contradict the resonating views of subscribers to this petition.

Alas, for the author(s) of the letter and its signatories, the brief passage excerpted above raises the fundamental issue of why Jewish-Catholic affairs are not simply the assessment of history "as it really was." What these scholars of theology and history may have been led to embrace — some certainly out of collegiality, some possibly out of sheer desperation at being badgered for their names — is a position that appears to be less concerned with the exercise of those disciplines in the single-minded pursuit of truth than with their exercise in the pursuit of good relations, regardless of how important such relations otherwise may be. Moralists who don't believe one can make a distinction between the *finis operis* (the goal of the letter) and the *finis operantis* (the goal of the letter writers) may be wondering, whatever happened to *fiat justitia, ruat caeli* — do justice, and let the chips fall where they may. That principle is inviolable even if the consequences (the chips) are unexpected and "cannot be overcome in the foreseeable future." The letter itself ended with a brief repetition of concern over the Pacelli beatification, and concluded as follows: "We thank you for hearing us and reflecting upon the urgent concerns of our request."

Admittedly there is some aura attached to criticizing a pope. As history shows, any "here I stand" proclamation is going to get attention, although probably for reasons of varying import. (At Vatican I the bishop of one American diocese made headlines not so much by the negative content of his message as by the mere fact of his location — as the papers blazoned that Little Rock had opposed "big rock.") In what may be viewed as liberal circles, where any declaration of independence is taken for an assertion of individual high principle, considerable group importance may be attached to this protestant cachet of rebellion. That, however, may be merely the mirror image of the esteem garnered in conservative circles by the embrace of ecclesiastical supervision as an assertion of orthodoxy — also with its attendant approbation from the regnant powers that be.[13]

---

13. In this context of the petitioners' preoccupation with the pope's prewar and wartime conduct, it is obvious that I don't share such concern. My negative view of Hochhuth's thesis appeared, at the time it was first aired, in *Continuum* and in *Blackfriars,* although my own memories of the pope were largely negative. The heroes of my earlier years were people silenced by the pope like Yves Congar and Teilhard de Chardin, both of whom I introduced to *Commonweal* readers, first, in the previously mentioned "The Reformers in the Church" (August 15, 1952), and then in "Chardin and Human Knowledge" (April 18, 1958). The context of the first article was the upsurge in anti-Jewish and anti-Negro racism in this country during the early 1950s. The context of the second was the fascination with the convergence of religion and science in the Paris of the late 1950s after the death of Teilhard. Congar's

Nor should one imagine that every signatory to the letter to Benedict XVI agreed with everything in it. Rather, as suggested earlier it is the gist or the general drift that was being endorsed, and about which anyone may have some serious reservations here or there. On a less impersonal note, concerning the signatories themselves, unquestionably all regarded as reputable scholars, I have been associated with more than half of them: in a few instances this was over public disagreements, but in several instances — more reciprocally constructive and gratifying — this was as publisher of their work, both articles and books in venues where I was editor. Similarly, I have had to decline to publish material by a couple of these signatories — although in both cases, on grounds entirely unrelated to scholarship. Also in the interests of this disclosure, I should note that in the present volume I have sharply disagreed with Michael Phayer while, on the other hand, I have compared the research of signatory Frank J. Coppa to that of Roger Aubert and Giacomo Martina — a welcome voice in what is now an international trinity.

Reading the work of a couple of other signatories, some people might get the impression that they were engaged not only in the previously mentioned "Pius wars," but also in that bane of academia, their very own "turf wars." The first signatory to be so engaged is the initiator of the petition, John Pawlikowski. In a severely critical — though by all journalistic norms perfectly acceptable — review of *Popes and Politics,* he made this curious observation relative to professional Holocaust students:

> It is interesting to note that the book carries no endorsements from scholars who have been central to the discussion of the Holocaust. While I admire the three endorsers (Charles E. Curran, Margaret A. Farley and Francis Schussler [*sic*] Fiorenza), none has ever done any serious work in Holocaust studies.

What is mildly vexing (as well as pretentious) about this observation is that it is someone's standing in what I have referred to as the "guild," and not his

---

words to me during this period were the epigraph for *Popes and Politics* where, perhaps intentionally echoing Newman under Pio Nono, he talked about the impossibility of a *chercheur intellectual* being forced to work under the lash — a fate he shared with Teilhard. Notwithstanding my personal regrets about Pius XII, I came to believe that it was his Christian critics who were more often than not misguided, and that their persistent efforts to condemn him were in many instances based on outright deceptions — as will be borne out, unfortunately, in the rest of this chapter.

or her contribution to the life of the mind, that presumably raises one to the lofty eminence of book blurber.[14] But more seriously disturbing was the implicit assumption by the author of the petition that he occupies the high moral ground — and does so without any apparent awareness that it is on just such heights that the heady winds of self-righteousness often prevail. This is merely by way of noting, at least for the present, the air of complacency at being on the side of the angels that much of the language of this petition exudes.

Add to that the phenomenon that some of these petitioners have not only absorbed this atmosphere of self-satisfaction, but appear also to have responded to it by adjusting and modulating — the appropriate buzzword would be "tweaking" — the pertinent data in order to convict various popes of sympathy for racists and racism. In fact, this has been undertaken by one petitioner with a view to demeaning the pope of the prewar period, the pope of the wartime period, and even the pope of the present-day church — who is here in the process of being petitioned. Some of this is possibly a result of embracing the overall conclusion, if not the theatrical rigmarole, of the original Hochhuth attack. That conclusion, which is on the way to becoming a kind of mantra of liberal smugness, can in fact be partially recapitulated in the aggressive tone and even the message of the following: "Pope Pius XII did not issue a clearly worded statement, unconditionally condemning the wholesale slaughter and murder of European Jews." (After so many absolutes — clearly, unconditionally, wholesale — one cannot but wonder what the implicit distinction between "slaughter" and "murder" is intended to convey.)

How, other than by a high degree of personal self-satisfaction, can one explain that the second signatory referred to above, John Connelly, actually doctored a text by the pope whom he is now petitioning, Benedict XVI, in order to make the latter appear as duplicitous as Pius XI and Pius XII — whose texts he also doctored?[15] "Wow!" has to be the instinctive response

14. Concerning this trivializing criticism, maybe the reviewer, a professional ethicist, overlooked the acute moral dilemma his comments could raise for an author. The subtitle of the book in question is "Reform, Resentment, *and* the Holocaust." Thus to make competence in that latter arena the unique criterion might well — since even dabblers in moral theology have to be finicky about such niceties — discriminate against some other aspiring blurbist who specialized in, say, group psychology or ecclesiology, to complain of being deprived of *his* or *her* rights.

15. This is the John Connelly who was introduced in chapter 2 in the context of his detailed and comprehensive 2007 article, "Catholic Racism and Its Opponents." Unfortunately, even in that generally useful article, "race" had become so hypostatized that it tended to take

here. This is an American scholar targeting three of the most important spiritual leaders of the period. It would be banal to compare this to the little tailor's boasting of "seven at one blow": these aspirations appear to be made of sterner stuff. Perhaps more apposite to this lofty quarry — *three* "Holy Fathers"! — would be Wallace Stevens on John James Audubon's exotically plumaged subjects: "No backyard cheepers for that connoisseur."

Connoisseur Connelly's own fowl ploy — and here I turn to the matter of "historical methodology" mentioned at the end of the last chapter — occurred in a *Commonweal* article on Karl Adam, "Reformer and Racialist" (January 18, 2008). There he began by saying that in 2006 Benedict XVI told the Polish bishops at Czestochowa that the church "looks upon the past with serenity, and does not fear for the future." He then — feigning innocence — asked, "Are these not strange words to be spoken by a German to Poles?" The answer is: "of course they are" — which is why they were never uttered at Czestochowa during that supposedly fateful visit in 2006. As I pointed out six months later in "Benedict, German Catholics & the Holocaust" (*Commonweal,* June 20, 2008), what the pope *did* talk about at Mary's shrine — was Mary. Nor were those "strange words" uttered two days later when the pope visited Auschwitz. There he spoke at length and with visible emotion about how his presence at "that place" was "particularly difficult and troubling for a Christian, for a Pope from Germany." The question that any observer of Connelly's verbal charade would have to ask is: what kind of historical methodology is this? It certainly appears to be more than merely stereotypical thinking to take words spoken in Rome to the College of Cardinals and transform them into words spoken in Poland to Poles. When the phenomenon of two other popes getting similar treatment is factored into this violation of truth and justice, it becomes apparent that a new intellectual entity is in the making, an entity based on the assumption that if it is for a noble liberal cause — and what could be more noble than exposing these presumably anti-Jewish popes? — one can say pretty much whatever one wants.

Benedict XVI, of course, is the easiest target of all, since everyone knows of his zealotry as head of the Congregation for the Doctrine of the Faith, as well as of his plans, described several times by Garry Wills as "overthrowing the conciliar church." That is a sufficient basis for anyone to assume that

---

on all the negative qualities of the term as used by those early twentieth-century pop-Darwinian speculators discussed earlier, and particularly in the previous chapter. Increased confusion then resulted from Connelly's own interweaving of the term as it is used in scientific anthropology and as used in everyday discourse.

there was "something wrong with the message" the pope delivered to Poles at Czestochowa — even though it remains a message he didn't deliver in that place *ever*. Nonetheless, Connelly *is* correct in his subsequent insistence when criticized for doctoring the quotation that he "didn't add or subtract its words" — all fifteen of them are right there. Regrettably, they just don't have anything to do with Poland, with the Nazi era, with the Holocaust, or with the other things that apparently preoccupy Connelly, and toward the resolution of which he could possibly make a contribution if he would cleanse his mind of stereotypes and clichés. That would also free him of the burden of arbitrarily inventing additional questions like, "How can the history of the Catholic Church in the past century — a history Benedict knows intimately — inspire serenity among anyone, *especially Poles?*" (italics supplied). In fact, the pope's "wrong message" had a gentle and concerned tone that should have inspired even a vexed historian — now about to replace the horrors of anti-Semitism with the less horrific but nonetheless real evils of anti-Polonism — to correct his strange behavior.[16]

Given these displays of academic presumptuousness, it is not particularly surprising that Connelly was also "tempted to locate anti-Nazi thought among the progressives." To assist him in overcoming that temptation, he might also undertake a reading of Victor Klemperer's diaries where, among other things, Klemperer expressed admiration for Bishop Clemens August Graf von Galen. (The latter is another object of Connelly's disdain, based on fellow signatory Beth A. Griech-Polelle's disastrous book on the bishop — to be analyzed presently.) Concerning "progressives" specifically, Klemperer addressed the matter in terms of postwar justice. "If one day the situation were reversed and the fate of the vanquished lay in my hands, then I would let all the ordinary folk go and even some of the leaders, who might perhaps after all have had honorable intentions and not known what they were doing. But I would have all the intellectuals strung up, and the professors three feet higher than the rest."[17] Since the Jewish Klemperer — a convert of convenience to Protestantism — was a professor himself, it may be adjudged that he knew whereof he spoke. My original treatment of this privileging of progressives in "Benedict, German Catholics & the Holocaust" concluded with this observation — which also paid tribute to Gordon Zahn, one of the founding editors of *Continuum:*

16. A primer for overcoming anti-Polonism is Justus George Lawler, "The Other Warsaw Uprising," *Commonweal*, September 24, 2004.

17. *I Will Bear Witness: 1933-1941, A Diary of the Nazi Years* (E.T., 2000).

Apart from heroic courage — always rare — the overriding factor according to researchers as different as Nechama Tec and Gordon Zahn was a willingness to violate conventional societal patterns: in short, to go beyond the stereotypes. *German Catholics and Hitler's Wars* by Zahn has as subtitle: *A Study in Social Control*. His model for transcending such controls was neither a bishop nor a "progressive," but a peasant, Franz Jäggerstätter.

The first of the other two popes Connelly targeted was Pius XI, who "came out in 1938 against racial intermarriage" — an assertion that flew in the face of the pope's personal intervention with Mussolini in that same year reaffirming established canon law that "the church approves interracial marriages as long as both parties are Catholics."[18] In the following year the new pope, Pius XII, proved to be even more remiss. According to Connelly, he declared that "the church extended 'blessings' to the 'care which aims at a wise orderly evolution of particular forces and tendencies having their origin in the individual character of each race.'" To most people, that certainly sounds racist. Unfortunately, this too has been doctored — as will be shown presently. In this tour de force of distortions, ideological arrogance has been supplemented by the assumption that the scholarly community will not challenge these opinions — as in the event it did not. Witness the theologians and historians, along with assorted other people, commenting appreciatively and at length on Connelly's original article in their contributions to "dotCommonweal," the magazine's blog.

As I was engaged in this exchange with Connelly[19] — who actually introduced the term "libel" into what he had turned into a personal fracas — my mind kept returning to chapter 6, and its analysis of David I. Kertzer's effort to convict a pope and his secretary of state of having refused to save the life of an innocent Jew at the ritual murder trial in Kiev. This effort required on the part of Kertzer that he pretend he did not see material in the document on which he was completely reliant for his description of the events being chronicled. Even more damning was Kertzer's feigning ignorance of

18. That the *Commonweal* exchanges were instructive is clear. Two years later, rather than *coming out* "against racial intermarriage," "the Church *advised* against it." But the duplicity of papists perdures: "Well known to them" is Pius XI's 1928 condemnation of anti-Semitism; but "less well-known" is the *Amici Israel* — which in fact is known *dans le monde entier* (John Connelly, "In Sheep's Clothing," *The New Republic*, February 8, 2011).

19. There was also introduced into the exchange his proficiency in what he called "American English" as opposed to the language he fancied his antagonist spoke.

material on the very page that he was in the process of quoting and paraphrasing. Connelly's "new player," Pius XII, had also been mentioned from the very beginning, and so could not be ignored. The sentence at issue was from the pope's first encyclical, and stated: "The Church hails with joy and follows with her maternal blessing every method of guidance and care which aims at a wise and orderly evolution of particular forces and tendencies having their origin in the individual character of each race, *provided that they are not opposed to the duties incumbent on men from their unity of origin and common destiny*" (italics supplied). But Connelly had deliberately deleted the last clause, and responded to criticism of his excision by going into considerable detail — which immersed him more deeply in the swamp of untruths where he was already floundering, while also reigniting his anti-Polonism:

> The words on "race" I attribute to Pius XII were spoken by him and are not doctored, as anyone who consults the text of *Summi pontificatus* can discern. The sentence's second part does nothing to weaken the surprising call for the church to concern itself with the "orderly evolution of particular forces and tendencies having their origin in the individual character of each race."
>
> *What in the world did that mean?* Unfortunately, to some East European Catholics it meant boycotting Jewish business, an activity that seemed to promote the forces of race while not endangering the unity of mankind — something understood to be spiritual. (italics supplied)

There is no need to elaborate on the plain falsehood that deleting "the sentence's second part" isn't doctoring "the words . . . that were spoken by him" [Pius XII] in the first part. *"Deleting"* is *"doctoring."* But then to assert that the deleted part "does nothing to weaken" the overall assertion raises serious questions about Connelly's state of mind — which can't even be described as a "state," since it is obviously afflicted with some kind of synaptic disconnect. The schizoid character of the ploy is beyond question: why would anyone go to the trouble of deleting from a text the very passage, which one then claims doesn't affect the text's meaning?

It was this self-righteous cry about "what in the world did that mean?" that exposed the same kind of tic that signaled many of Kertzer's falsifications. The fact that Connelly immediately rushed away from the question to introduce the distracting monstrosities of East European Catholics (by which he meant all those lumpen Poles) made his ruse even more patent. As to his affected befuddlement ("what in the world") about meaning, the first response is that the quotation certainly didn't mean that Pope Pius's explicit proviso regarding humanity's "unity of origin and common destiny" could be simply erased away by fiat. Moreover, it would have been impossible for Connelly to misread the encyclical as having *anything whatever to do with Jews,* much less with boycotting them — as I will show presently.

The fact is that Connelly, in his effort at obscuring his obvious error by playing to the liberal grandstand with his feigned confusion (again, "what in the world"), had backed himself into a corner from which there was no honorable exit. And therein may possibly lie a significant difference between the liberals of an earlier generation and those of Connelly's. For the latter, liberalism is an all-justifying ideology, and that is the explanation for the air of smug certitude that its proponents flaunt. For the former, liberalism was an orientation not a fixation, and that is the reason that, rather than unwarranted certitudes ("the second part does *nothing* to weaken"), the reader more often encounters a tentative tone expressive of possibilities and likelihoods — as in the modulated phrase just mentioned, "*more often* encounters."

These differences must be briefly explored before confronting Connelly with Pius XII's actual encyclical, because they are related to the kinds of mistakes that these ideologically driven papal critics make all too often. Of course, there are such things as honest mistakes. No one can write several thousand words, much less tens of thousands, and not make mistakes. There are several embarrassing ones in *Popes and Politics.* Particularly dumb — since I grew up on Henri Bremond's *L'Humanisme dévot* — was having Pius IX *canonize* Francis de Sales, whereas in fact he had made him a Doctor of the Church. Similarly, having Pius IX write the Syllabus of Errors in 1854 was probably just hastiness or a typo for 1864. But in any case, unless one were a professional letter writer to *The Times Literary Supplement,* no one would pause over these kinds of errors. The rule of thumb for differentiating between the honest and the dishonest is that the latter invariably support the writer's argument and thesis. Those are the kind that were made regarding the three popes, and they are the kind exemplified in the following instances — all intended by the narrator to put himself on the lofty moral heights while denigrating his critic as an advocate of fecklessness.

Affecting outrage, Connelly asked, "And what of killing innocent civilians? Like the American bombers high above Germany, conspirators like Helmuth von Möltke or Johann Georg Elser were willing to (and did) kill innocent people when setting bombs to eliminate Hitler." Unfortunately, this particular effort at scaling the heights resulted in vertigo for the climber. There was only one voice that spoke out against bombing "innocent civilians," and that was Pius XII, who criticized both German and Allied bombing raids throughout the war — although the previously introduced papal critic and petition signatory Michael Phayer believes the pope intentionally ignored the German bombing raids on England and Yugoslavia. I address that matter specifically in *Popes and Politics,* and elsewhere.[20] As for von Möltke, Connelly is accusing one of the most noble spirits in the German Resistance, a man who spent months of self-debate seeking to determine the ethics of tyrannicide, and certainly never went about "setting bombs" to achieve that goal. As for Elser, he should be honored as one of the great heroes of the incipient German Resistance since had he succeeded in killing Hitler, the history of humankind would have been *absolutely* different — not different, as Blaise Pascal said, in that the face of the world would have been changed. Rather, *everything* would have been changed. The entire course of Western civilization as we now know it would have been reversed.

Since I had introduced Bishop von Galen into my original critique, contrasting his welcome to the overtures by the Resistance with the rebuff of them by Konrad Adenauer, Connelly makes his own moral point regarding the bishop:

> Note that Adenauer the politician tried to lie low during Nazism and was twice arrested nonetheless, whereas Bishop von Galen publicly challenged the regime and was left in peace. From this *we* learn that other German bishops could have risked more. No one forced them to pray publicly for German victory, or to send birthday greetings to Hitler. (italics supplied)

Yes, "we" in the twenty-first century learned that, but how would those other bishops have learned it? As to Adenauer, his first arrest was for two days in 1934; the second was following a general roundup after the failed Claus von Stauffenberg assassination attempt of a host of possible suspects, many of whom like Adenauer and Bishop von Galen's brother had been linked to the Center Party. Connelly says of possible public opposition to the regime by Adenauer, "It is probably fortunate for German democracy" that he did not take that path. How was it good for democracy that Adenauer — a Holocaust denier *avant la parole* — appointed to the two highest positions in his regime militant Nazi criminals, Hans Globke and Herbert Blankenhorn? But

---

20. "Moral Confusion in the Nuclear Age," *The Christian Century* (April 4, 1984); "Dresden: The Fire Last Time," *Cross Currents* (Summer 2004); "Terror Bombing," *America* (September 4, 2006).

all that is merely a side issue in the lesson Connelly wants to teach. That lesson is that those he earlier called "progressives" — and I have called ideological liberals — are more courageous than ordinary run-of-the-mill people, including run-of-the-mill bishops, and so are ideologically entitled decades later to be condemnatory of the latter. "From this we learn" that if Bishop von Galen was heroic, any other bishop could have also been heroic. But what we really learn from this is that a researcher studying opposition to the Nazis in Germany can rig the argument so such opposition appears not much more terrifying than, say, opposition to the U.S. government during the Vietnam era. It is as though all that was required of the citizenry was to organize a free speech movement.

Connelly's excerpt above ended with this advisory: "Those wanting to find out more about the complex Bishop von Galen should consult Beth A. Griech-Polelle's recent biography *Bishop von Galen: German Catholicism and National Socialism*" — a book actually published in 2002, and about which Connelly is writing in 2008. In fact, I had consulted that book, and it is cited in a lengthy chapter in *Historians Against History* as well as in a lengthy article titled "Hitler's Hammer, the Church's Anvil" (*First Things* [November 2005]). Probably the best thing that can be said about the Griech-Polelle book is that it embodied, far better than anything Connelly himself had written, all the traits designated by the omnibus phrase introduced earlier, "ideological liberal." He, however, would not be expected to have read the even more "recent" eight-thousand-word von Galen article, appearing as it did in a publication that is farther to the right than *Commonweal* is to the left. As mentioned earlier, to maintain *ignorantia affectata* relative to Pius XII's "symbolic" anti-Semitism, it is important that one's mind be closed to the existence of a document like that by "Refugee." Similarly, one's virginal papal animus would be violated by reading a study of von Galen that did not treat him as the villain conjured up by Griech-Polelle — another signatory to the petition to Benedict XVI.

However, this time Connelly's advice is worth following, since Beth A. Griech-Polelle's "recent biography" is such a masterwork of doctoring, mistranslating, expunging, and manipulating texts and sources — not to mention outright factual blunders — that it would be impossible to characterize them in the terms introduced earlier regarding "honest" or "dishonest" mistakes. The first paragraph on the first page of the book begins the manipulation. Writing of the papal encyclical on Nazism, *Mit Brennender Sorge,* the author criticizes it because it "did not endorse Catholic participation in an open rebellion against the government." Any reader with a faint sense of history cannot but wonder, participation in what "open rebellion" *in 1937?* As to matters of tone, notwithstanding the fact that the book is a reworked dissertation, it still manages to put on display the superciliousness and hauteur of a seasoned ideological liberal.

The note of pretentiousness is struck at the beginning of chapter 1, "Von Galen's Early Life," when a religious commonplace instilled in the two young brothers by their parents, "human authority is a reflection of divine rule," is followed immediately by this malicious non sequitur: "Thus the religious *Führerprinzip* coincided with the Nazi's secular *Führerprinzip*." The comment startles less by its pompous anachronism — employing jargon from the pop-Darwinian speculators mentioned earlier — than by its equation of a pious truism with a fascist slogan. In the 1980s, the term would be central to the resuscitated Martin Heidegger controversy over the embrace of Nazism in his 1933 rectorial address — with staged outbursts of "Sieg Heil!" — as well as to its role as leitmotif of his grandiose philosophical enterprise. The best (or worst) that can be said of Griech-Polelle's opinion is that it is unquestionably the first work to relate the career of the caitiff philosopher to that of the courageous prelate. After such an equation, it is patently absurd to speculate as to how this "religious *Führerprinzip*" led one son to become the leading anti-Nazi Catholic bishop and the other son to be imprisoned by the Nazis in Sachsenhausen.

A different kind of "tone" than superciliousness or hauteur is also introduced into this discourse — though it was certainly a tone that would also raise eyebrows, as well as provide an insight into the delicate susceptibilities cultivated by this author.

> "Clau," as the young count was affectionately called, led a lifestyle marked by spartan simplicity and rigorous Catholicism that was going to continue throughout his life. Castle Dinklage had no running water, no heat in the majority of its rooms, and no indoor bathrooms. The family lived, *so to speak*, close to nature. (italics supplied)

Also in the context of religion, child-rearing, and "lifestyle," the reader was told — and it might be borne in mind that this is still the first chapter of the book:

> From Ferdinand [the father], "Clau" learned that owing to original sin there was no such thing as a "Paradise on earth." Living such a strict life with no "amenities" such as heat would certainly have highlighted that view.

All this is in the first chapter — which is not titled "Oprah Writes History."

As for the "doctoring" mentioned above — and a recurrent practice in this entire discussion — it is difficult to say whether the following would satisfy Connelly's selective definition of the term. The text at issue relates to the consecration of von Galen as bishop of Münster, an event that Griech-Polelle summarizes in detail, mentioning the presiding clerics, as well as "columns of SA and SS men marching in procession with the swastika flags flying." "In the evening they participated in a torch-lit procession in front of the bishop's palace." She then adds: "Eyewitness interpretations of the event vary widely."

> The bishop's would-be hagiographers, Heinrich Portmann and Max Bierbaum, emphasize Catholic Münster's support for their new bishop. In contrast, Catholic scholar and philosopher Josef Pieper, who was a resident of Münster, observed, "It is just not true that, in the summer of 1933, when the name 'Galen' was announced as the new Bishop the whole diocese broke out in rejoicing. . . . *Nor is it the case that Galen was* immediately recognized as being a great opponent of the despotic regime. On the contrary the pugnacious pastor of St. Lambert's was regarded, to put it bluntly, as a Nazi." (italics supplied)

The careful framing of the quotation regarding time, "summer of 1933," "immediately recognized," indicates an omission on the part of the author. The following is the excised passage — taken from Joseph Pieper's autobiography *No One Could Have Known* (E.T., 1987) — which follows immediately the ellipsis Griech-Polelle had inserted in the text: [He] "eventually reached the rank of Cardinal, which, as everyone knows signified worldwide recognition of his resistance to the regime of terror. Such resistance, interiorly, so to speak, was equivalent to a willingness to accept bloody martyrdom. It was only the tactical considerations of those holding power that stopped things going that far. *Nor is it the case that Galen was . . .*"

The next doctored passage is slightly more subtle but also more patently vicious, as the author advances her case that the newly appointed bishop's views of the regime were if not sympathetic, then tolerant. Again, it relates to a public ceremony and procession at an annual festival in Münster — also as allegedly described by Pieper:

> His [von Galen's] message would have been much more forceful if he had refrained from appearing with Nazis in uniform marching beside him.

Josef Pieper, upon witnessing the procession, remarked, "*And is it incomprehensible, therefore, that the ordinary man, watching the brownshirts* walking in the procession alongside Bishop von Galen, did not immediately regard them as mercenaries of the Antichrist?" (italics supplied)

Here the doctoring takes the form of excision. Intentionally deleted in her eagerness to indict the bishop is the beginning of the paragraph that supplies the actual context of Pieper's otherwise seemingly derogatory remark in his autobiography:

When American friends of mine have found inconceivable that the Germans ever fell for such criminals, I have often told the story of the "Grand Procession" in Münster . . . which is by statute an event organized by the town as a political community. From time immemorial the chief bürgermeister and the members of the town council have accompanied the Blessed Sacrament through the streets, in close proximity to the bishop. And that is exactly what happened in 1934. *And is it incomprehensible, therefore, that the ordinary man, watching the brownshirts . . . ?*

In addition to explaining her deliberate decontextualizing of the incident, perhaps Griech-Polelle might have explained to *her* American readers why she imagines mere proximity would make one less "forceful" in opposing evil. And, of course, another of her friends, John Connelly, might want to explain why those wanting to learn more about "the complex Bishop von Galen" should consult this particular book. To critics of the above stratagems, Griech-Polelle could certainly respond, as did Connelly, that all the right words are in the right order, and she could then go on to say: "The words I attribute to Josef Pieper were spoken by him and are not doctored, as anyone who consults the text of his book can discern." Lastly, both of those writers might take to heart the words of a serious student of interpretation who is also a complex bishop: "Texts matter, but contexts matter even more" (N. T. Wright, *Jesus and the Victory of God* [1996]).

It was on the occasion of another procession that Bishop von Galen vigorously denounced the disruptive tactics of "the brownshirts" to an audience of twenty thousand Catholics. After describing the incident, Griech-Polelle adds: "Here it is necessary to stop and ask: if the bishop had so successfully thumbed his nose at the Nazis and done so repeatedly, why did he not try to raise his voice concerning the injustices and persecution of other minorities in the Reich?" By this point it is fairly obvious what the strategy is. The bishop is gradually being revealed as an "anti-Semite," a depravity akin to what a conservative commentator, Andrew Napolitano, in *Constitutional Chaos* (2004), has called a "favored crime," that is, one in which merely to be accused is tantamount to being guilty, and therefore, a crime whose gravity automatically exonerates the accuser — as Griech-Polelle has exemplified.

Shifting abruptly from his early years as bishop, she titles the next chapter "Von Galen and Church-State Relations," by which is meant his efforts to create a religious society in Germany. This goal will be shared by an Anglican clergyman, as the chronologically challenged reader is catapulted into the postwar world, and the ideologically challenged author steps into an ecumenical interchurch anti-Semitic conspiracy — entirely of her own making:

> Dr. G. K. A. Bell, Anglican bishop of Chicester [*sic*], met von Galen in October 1945. Bell described how impressed he was with the Catholic bishop, and said that von Galen "believed firmly that Catholics and Protestants would work together. He said to me that it was clearly imperative that all who were at one in their belief in God, in their faithfulness to Christ and in their conviction of the soul's immortality should come forward on behalf of righteousness and peace."

Although by this time, the reader has come to realize that this complex bishop has proven to be utterly incomprehensible to this simple writer, still there is nothing anywhere in the statement made by the Anglican bishop that provides grounds for the following slander: "The notion of an alliance between Catholics and Protestants in order to form a Christian state apparently was *unaltered by the end of World War II and the full revelations of what racist anti-Semitism had wrought.*"

The reason a writer can calmly set forth in print this kind of atrocious lie is the same reason that one can calmly manipulate any texts, from those by observant Catholic philosophers like Pieper to those by popes like Pacelli — and we still haven't looked at John Connelly on the complete text of that racist encyclical, *Summi Pontificatus.* The reason is that the manipulator really believes he or she occupies the higher moral ground; he or she is on the side of justice, he or she represents the prevailing ideological consensus; and thus, he or she can indulge in an occasional overstatement, a bit of exaggeration here or there, a little fiddling with the facts — after all, it's for the good of the liberal cause.

That *mentalità*, as represented by the interpretation of the excerpt above, dictates that Bishop von Galen's obliviousness to "racist anti-

Semitism" puts him in the same category as those contemptible East European Catholics introduced earlier. Thus it is hardly surprising that he is conspiring with a British bishop, who is depicted here as equally indifferent to
the lessons of the war and who, therefore, is obviously another anti-Semite.
And this conspiracy is nothing less than to establish a state made up of like-
minded "Catholics and Protestants." It doesn't matter that the actual text being analyzed says nothing whatever related to Jews or race or anti-Semitism;
and it doesn't matter that it explicitly says that faithful Christians whether
Anglican or Roman Catholic "should come forward on behalf of righteousness and peace."

Even though there is no basis in the above, nevertheless the "he or she"
mentioned above — Connelly or Griech-Polelle — feel perfectly free to read
their own personal obsessions, Jews, race, anti-Semitism — into an encyclical or a *eulogy* where there is not even the faintest hint of any of them. This is
not called eisegesis, it is called paranoia — here pushed to paranormal extremes. Bishop G. K. A. Bell, who had first met von Galen only six months
earlier, had been deeply impressed by the latter's civility, faith, and ecumenical spirit. What provides another insight into the sensibility of this author —
less revolting but more gruesome than her "close to nature" remark earlier
— is that the relatively lengthy quoted statement in the excerpt above was
occasioned by the sudden death of von Galen, and hence my emphasis on
"eulogy" and mention of "paranormal." Entirely apart from the grotesquerie
of using Bishop Bell's statement to slander his newly discovered German
counterpart, one would have thought the presence of this English bishop
might have presented, at the least, a "research problem" for the author of her
dissertation.

The grist for her mill is no longer taken from remote secondary German
sources about the vacillating Catholic prelate selectively deciding what he
wants to condemn in the Nazi regime. Traducing von Galen in the name of
anti-anti-Semitism may have passed muster before her examiners at
Rutgers, her editors at Yale, her supportive blurbists, and her fellow petition
signatories.[21] But the mention of this other bishop — and an Anglophone at

21. Walter Lacquer, although no shill, writes curtly: "This clearly written book about
von Galen is backed by meticulous scholarship." Michael Berenbaum (mentioned earlier
regarding the petition to Benedict XVI), author of a glowing commendation for another
Yale press book, Susan Zuccotti's *Under His Very Windows*, is considerably more fulsome:
"Griech-Polelle debunks the myth of von Galen and writes with authority not only in history but also in theology, understanding well the inner workings of the Church and the
climate in which von Galen worked." This is largely formulaic blurbism, but what can at

that — should certainly have given pause to someone, to a friend, to a guide, to a colleague, to anyone. . . . Apparently not. "Dr. G. K. A. Bell," clearly unknown to the author and a whole stable of mentors and ideological buddies, becomes just another figure to be casually passed off as a villain of the same stripe as the now patently shifty von Galen. Thus, as with the doctoring and deleting earlier, the reader is expected to simply accept the notion that the two of them were equally unconcerned with "what racist anti-Semitism had wrought."

Notwithstanding this display of rampant ignorance concerning George Bell of Chichester, it is to be noted that in the non-ideologically oriented world, he is still recognized — as he was in his lifetime — as one of the great churchmen of the twentieth century. He was a prewar supporter of dissenting German clergy, a fiery antagonist of Winston Churchill's saturation bombing — which led to his blocking Bell's elevation to Primate — a postwar leader in the antinuclear movement, an international ecumenist, and, finally, an admired recipient of the last words of his close friend, Dietrich Bonhoeffer: "This is the end — for me the beginning of life." (For what it may be worth, at least among the piophobe school of historians, Bishop Bell was also the hero of Hochhuth's *other* play, *The Soldiers*.[22])

Since this entire discussion is prelude to John Connelly's interpretation of Pius XII's first encyclical, it may be useful to briefly consider how the author he so highly recommended handles subsequent statements of the pope — handles them, in fact, in a chapter titled "Von Galen and the Pope." The goal now is to defame Pius and, *pari passu*, his subordinate in Münster. In a message to Bishop Konrad von Preysing, a close friend of the pope from his days in Berlin, the latter is described by Griech-Polelle as telling the German bishops, "We emphasize that, because the Church in Germany is dependent upon your public behavior . . . in public declarations you are *duty bound to exercise restraint*" (italics original). Although this is referenced correctly to the second volume of *Actes et documents du Saint Siège relatifs à la Seconde Guerre Mondiale* (ADSS), there one instead reads: "But that the bishops, who have so courageously and flawlessly championed the cause of God and

---

least be distilled from it is that compared to Griech-Polelle, Susan Zuccotti is a veritable Thucydides.

22. Michael Burleigh, after noting in *Sacred Causes* (loc. cit.) that "no Anglican leaders were sympathetic to Nazi views on race," went on to directly address Bishop Bell's concerns. "[He] worked tirelessly through his ecumenical contacts in Sweden and Germany to convince the British government that there was 'another Germany' ready and willing, if not able, to displace Hitler." It was that other Germany that von Galen and Bell were planning.

his Church, will always enjoy Our Support — that is something about which We need not give you and your colleagues assurance."[23] The statements attributed to the pope, not unlike those Connelly assembled earlier, are the exact opposite of what the author has Pius emphatically requiring, that is, that the German hierarchy should publicly protest. Nevertheless, Griech-Polelle for half a page goes on interpreting the sinister implications of the statement — which the pope never made.

I am following the author's somersaulting chronology, so it is necessary here to examine the most renowned sermons of the bishop, delivered in midsummer 1941. Though they are all in one way or another on the persecution of the church, their real subject is abuses by governmental agencies primarily in the Münster area, and of those agencies, the Gestapo is singled out by name repeatedly. But because the sermons did not specifically condemn the persecution of the Jews, according to Griech-Polelle, von Galen was guilty of "single-issue dissent," or as she sometimes calls it, "selective opposition." Presumably a man like Bishop Bell might also be convicted of single-issue dissent because while he condemned the firebombing of German cities, he failed to call for the bombing of the death camps.

Moreover, it is not particularly clear as to how the writings widely described in the literature as the "summer sermons" relate to single-issue dissent — by which Griech-Polelle means von Galen's anti-Semitic indifference to the fate of Jews during the Holocaust. Chronology and geography plus personal witnessing may help disabuse her of that opinion. Concerning the first two categories, the much-doctored autobiography of Josef Pieper is useful. Pieper noted that "In *late fall* of that year [1941] we got the *first* rumors of operations by special detachments *behind* the Russian front. *No one* who had not been there knew anything definite." (The kindergarten italics are intended to make unquestionably evident that the midsummer sermons cannot be demeaned for failing to mention events unknown to their preacher.) Even in early winter there would have been little firm knowledge in the city that was among the most remote from the eastern battleground — a battleground that by spring of the following year would have been completely overrun by *Einsatzgruppen*.

The following chronologically impossible and ideologically condescending statement about the sermons from Peter Godman's *Hitler and the*

---

23. "Dass aber die Bischöfe, die mit solchem Mut und dabei in so untadeliger Form wie Bischof von Galen für die Sache Gottes und der hl. Kirche eintreten, an Uns immer Rükhalt finden werden, das brauchen Wir dir und deinen Mitbrüdern nicht eigens zu versichern."

Vatican (2004) is directly and correctly attributed to Griech-Polelle. "Nor was their [Jews'] persecution condemned by the bishop often hailed as a courageous opponent of the Nazis, the 'lion of Münster' Clemens August von Galen, who denounced, in well-publicized sermons, abuses by the Gestapo and the judicial murders of 'euthanasia,' with no reference to the Holocaust." The sermons were delivered within two months of the invasion of Russia, and not even the most prescient observer could conceive of the slaughter, later to be identified as "Holocaust." As for a contemporary witness, free of the parti-pris above, there is another entry from Victor Klemperer's diary: "Headmaster Voss . . . told us that the Bishop of Münster, Count Galen, had preached publicly against the Gestapo and the killings of the mentally infirm. The bishop had not been arrested on the grounds that 'one does not want to make any martyrs,' in truth, because they had 'not dared to.'" It is not unlikely that Klemperer, a literary scholar, knew of the bishop's motto, *"nec laudibus nec timore,"* "neither for praise nor out of fear." As for how slowly news traveled during wartime from east to west or in this instance, from west to east, the last sermon in Münster, the one on "killings of the mentally infirm," was delivered on July 20; the date of the diary entry by Klemperer in Dresden is November 2.

The fact is that in real life, and not in the feverish imagination of ideologically oriented carpers, it was the bishop's courage in attacking the regime, and thus inviting martyrdom, that brought von Galen to the attention of the nation and ultimately of the world. Moreover, as common sense would dictate, most opponents of the Reich were motivated by a variety of issues, some moral, some religious, some political, some relative to the Jews, some to the aging and the ill, some to the future of Germany, some to the fear of military defeat, some to the mission of the church. The last named was particularly acute for von Galen regarding his own clergy, since in his diocese the ratio of incarcerated priests was far greater than elsewhere in Germany.[24] The Nazi leadership had acknowledged that attacks on the bishop personally could bring rebellion throughout Westphalia, and so it attacked

24. Owen Chadwick draws the following analogy from these statistics, but this time the moral lesson relates to the pope: "If a defending attorney were desirable in a historical subject, the main line of the plea would need to be something like this. Take the two contiguous German dioceses of Bishops Galen and Berning. We revere Galen for his courage and have no use for Berning because of his silence. But many more priests in Galen's diocese ended in concentration camps than those from Berning's. . . . If a higher than Galen behaved like him, how many thousands more would end in concentration camps?" (*The Tablet*, September 25, 1999).

his subordinates. All this, of course, gives the lie to Connelly's vaunt: "Bishop von Galen publicly challenged the regime and was left in peace. From this *we* learn that other German bishops could have risked more."

To argue, as Griech-Polelle does, that von Galen's sermons had little impact ignores their achievement in inspiring scores of others to join the Resistance and in offering to thousands more a living symbol of courage in the face of an inhumane regime. As to "single-issue dissent" and "selective opposition," it is impossible to determine who specifically was engaged in either or both. As indicated above, every opponent of the regime whether in the Resistance or not had his or her own battery of concerns. By this author's standards, journalist William Shirer would have been right when he disdainfully said, "von Möltke had the courage to talk . . . but not to do" — the latter phrase meaning he didn't have the courage to support the assassination of the Führer. In fact, the heroic von Möltke, a student of *The Federalist Papers,* opposed assassination as a likely besmirching of the ideal republic he envisioned after the fall of the Reich — a theme relevant to the Israeli-Palestinian conflict to be examined in the next chapter. To build a new state, even on the blood of a Hitler, would not be an auspicious foundation.[25] Carl Goerdeler's opposition to the assassination plot — according to Joachim Fest in *Plotting Hitler's Death* (1994) — was based "not only on moral principles," but also on fear "that it might lead to civil war."

On the other hand, von Möltke's closest friend and, on the issue of assassination, his most vociferous opponent, Adam von Trott zu Solz, insisted that assassination was a moral obligation. This was also the position of another friend, Dietrich Bonhoeffer, who after much soul searching and reflection — for which he had ample time, having been imprisoned long before the failed von Stauffenberg attempt — also hesitantly embraced the legitimacy of tyrannicide. Eberhard Bethge in his exhaustive life of Bonhoeffer describes the period when both men were awaiting execution in separate prisons, and notes that it was the larger issues of the future that preoccupied them. "Just before his death, Trott zu Solz was asking Bonhoeffer's question"; that question in the words of Trott zu Solz was, "Can our childlike

25. Von Möltke was the victim of his own nobility of spirit. He regarded tyrannicide as staining the new Germany the way slavery had stained the new American republic. In fact, it might well have been a cleansing purge, failing which, the new Germany has been diagnosed — perhaps too stringently, but certainly not without foundation, by W. G. Sebald in *The Natural History of Destruction* (E.T., 2003) — as suffering from "the well-kept secret of the corpses built into the foundation of our state, a secret that bound all Germans together in the postwar years, and indeed still binds them."

Christian faith . . . grow and impress itself upon the entire weight and intensity of our problems today?"[26] Clearly, the reasons for opposition to the regime — like the reasons for any significant and heroic undertaking — were highly selective.

Another Kreisauer, the Jesuit Alfred Delp, who would also be executed, favored the assassination attempt as did Bishop von Preysing of Berlin, who was tireless, but unsuccessful, in trying to persuade the German Bishops Conference to take stronger stands on the abuses of the regime. He disagreed with his close friend von Möltke about the assassination — even though the Condordat explicitly forbade political "interference" by the church. And yet the church was involved since the issues were moral ones, of life and death. Galen had already interfered vigorously in his own way and, as noted earlier, declared himself well-disposed to the goals of the Resistance, though he was hardly opposed to the war against the Soviets. Von Preysing was joined in his approval of the plot against Hitler by Bishop Johannes Dietz of Fulda, Chair of the Bishops Conference, and by Augustinus Rösch, Jesuit Provincial of Bavaria (who after the assassination attempt managed to evade the Gestapo for six months and ultimately survive). Cardinal Michael von Faulhaber, another friend of von Möltke, was on the periphery of the actual planning for the assassination, but was actively making plans for the role of the church in the new state.

Moreover, in von Galen's celebrated "anvil speech" one does not hear the words of what Griech-Polelle haughtily calls a practitioner of "selective opposition"; rather, one hears the words of a man knowing his life is in peril: "And so I say once again: become hard, remain firm, remain steadfast! Like the anvil under the blows of the hammer! It may be that obedience to our God and faithfulness to our conscience may cost me or any of you life, freedom, or home. But better to die than to sin!" In the following tessellation, which selectively focuses mainly on the euthanasia sermon, Griech-Polelle's own single-issue stratagems all converge: the omniscience, the insinuations, the third-person assertions, the omissions, the yes-no dialectic of presenting in one clause what is taken away in the next — all this abuse of scholarship is rationalized and justified, like that of Connelly before her, by privileging anything done in the name of anti-anti-Semitism.

26. Although concern with such a question much preoccupied Bonhoeffer during his long prison term — since the entire issue related to the many failures of all Christian churches during the Hitler era — it would be a mistake to see him as forerunner to such theological fads emerging in the 1960s and 1970s as "religionless religion" and "the death of God."

> What should be pointed out, however, is that these sermons were not a plea for Catholics to use their imaginations and go beyond protecting the mentally ill. . . . What seemed to motivate the bishop to raise his voice to a new level of power and eloquence was not the murder of the incurable but the fear that Catholic institutions were about to be eradicated. . . . Von Galen waited to speak out against euthanasia until numerous public denunciations had been made by Protestant Germans. . . . Von Galen came face-to-face with such a choice [of martyrdom]. . . . he was not the biblical "lone voice crying out in the wilderness." Most studies portray his actions as if they were occurring in isolation. Many studies seem to imply that he had finally gathered enough proof. . . . I would suggest that von Galen and the rest of the Catholic hierarchy carefully chose the time to speak out . . . they waited for Protestants, that is the "true Germans," to risk a confrontation with the government first. . . . Again ignoring how many Jews might be in those camps or cellars, von Galen used Bishop Johann Sproll and Martin Niemöller as examples of suffering innocence. . . . Perhaps a few people in that warm church that day extended von Galen's speech to include Jews . . . [quoting von Galen's conclusion] "therefore as a German, an honorable citizen, a representative of the Christian religion, a Catholic Bishop, I exclaim: 'We demand Justice!'"

The final gloss on that last statement says everything one has to know about the methodology of this author: "It is interesting that he emphasized his Germanness first and his Christianity second."

But the apex of dissembling reaches a new low in the self-contradictory description of the third and last sermon — of which Griech-Polelle says, "In fact, most published versions of von Galen's third sermon do not include its conclusion." Unfortunately, this "in fact" is not a fact regarding any published versions of the sermon, whether print or digitized. Nor is this true even of the copy of the sermon in her book, which she tells the reader was freely available at St. Lambert's Cathedral in Münster "at the time of my visit in 1994." She then proceeds to systematically doctor the very text that anybody can read at the end of her book in the appendix, which is titled "Three Sermons in Dark Times" — a title that is also taken from the copy she acquired in St. Lambert's.

The reason she fabricates the notion that "most public versions of von Galen's third sermon do not include its conclusion" is that she herself in a final culminating effort has concocted a conclusion different from that of the bishop.

Toward the end of the concluding remarks, he refers to his starting point: did Jesus weep only for Israel? This is the bishop's conclusion: "Is the people of Israel the only people whom God has encompassed and protected with a father's care and a mother's love, has drawn to Himself? Is it the only people that would not? The only one that rejected God's truth, that threw off God's law and *so condemned itself to ruin?*" (italics original)

This excerpted paragraph from the body of the book ends there with this manufactured indictment of Jews as responsible for their own plight. But in the complete version (again, reproduced in the appendix), the sermon continues for six more paragraphs to address the failings not of those italicized Jews, but of the Germans in the pews of St. Lambert's.[27]

That explains why immediately following that "condemned to ruin" passage, the next paragraph begins with a surprisingly vehement assault on the bishop — even for this writer: "Open ideological hatred of Jews did not need to be explicitly expressed in a sermon by a member of the Catholic clergy." As a result, rather than reading anything of von Galen's lengthy indictment of his own countrymen, one reads instead Griech-Polelle's summary of the unfortunate implications of supersessionism with references to St. Augustine's anti-Jewishness, to the evils of Jewish rejection of Jesus as the Messiah, and so on, culminating in *her* indictment of von Galen's implicit and concealed "ideological hatred of Jews." This is her non-climactic climax: "Following this line of reasoning [the *adversus Iudaeos* tradition] turning a blind eye to the misfortunes of the Jews would not necessarily make one an indecent person."

Since Griech-Polelle is about to exit the scene an account of the actual impact of the sermons may provide a counterweight to her narrative. They were quoted in leaflets dropped on German cities by the RAF and broadcast by the BBC; they ultimately reached at least twenty million Germans as well as uncountable others through translations into Czech, Dutch, English, French, and Polish. The Gauleiter of nearby Holland attributed the Dutch bishops' opposition to the deportation of Jews to von Galen's sermons in

---

27. "Did Jesus, the omniscient God, also see in that day our German people, our Land of Westphalia, our region of Münster, the Lower Rhineland? Did he weep over us? Over Münster? . . . Did the omniscient Son of God see in that day that in our time he must also pronounce this judgment on us; Ye would not see, your house will be laid waste! . . . That in prayer and sincere penitence we should beg that God's forgiveness and mercy may descend upon us, upon our city, our country, and our beloved German people. . . . O God, make us all know, in this our day, before it is too late, the things which belong to our peace!"

nearby Münster. The White Rose student group — whose five leaders with their professor would be executed — was also inspired by the RAF leaflets, and reprinted hundreds of their own, along with others that both decried the anti-Semitism of the regime and its violation of traditional German Enlightenment values. The much belittled Helmuth von Möltke — with his wife, also a guardian of such values — wrote to her that she should "read the sermons aloud because that brings out their great drive" (*Letters to Freya 1939-1945* [E.T., 1990]).[28] She herself, in a passage I contextualize fully in *First Things,* declared of the Kreisauers: "At the peak of Hitler's triumph after the fall of Poland and France that is when the Circle began. . . . Even though we had no success and even though we were weak, all of us who stood against Hitler kept European humanity alive in Germany." Such a goal, similar to that of the White Rose students, also represents a form of the too facilely condemned "single-issue dissent" — since most people would opine, better a single issue than none at all. Unfortunately, anyone paying homage to the achievement of von Galen can still be posthumously denigrated for contributing to what Griech-Polelle smartly calls "the legend of the Grand Resister."

After such a bombardment of suppositions, insinuations, and mistranslations, one is still left with the question, what is von Galen's place in history? If martyrdom is the single criterion, then clearly the bishop was not a Max Metzger or an Alfred Delp, two executed clergymen, nor a Nikolaus Gross or a Bernhard Letterhaus, two executed laymen, both of whom like the bishop were later beatified.[29] Though ultimately history demands the making of judgments, there is something obscene about people living more than half a century after the most vicious murders known to humankind assigning rank to innocent people from that earlier era — often people about whom we can say, at the least, that they lived bravely and honestly according to their insights into themselves and into the world about them. When the rank is determined by what purports to be micrometrically precise historical methodology, there is something ghoulish about both the process and the foregone conclusion.

28. One can only hope that the recently deceased (January 1, 2010) Freya von Möltke, who had been living for years in the United States, never saw Connelly's *Commonweal* article of 2008, with its nightmarish fantasy about her husband killing innocent people.

29. The two laymen were beatified by John Paul II, the pope whose efforts to raise to the altars so many deserving people earned from Garry Wills the epithet "Stakhanovite." Ironically, the two men *were* former laborers — one was actually a miner — who as union organizers became part of a major Resistance group centered in Cologne at Kettellerhaus, named after Bishop von Galen's granduncle, the great social reformer whose work had influenced Leo XIII — and who was, not surprisingly, also denigrated by Griech-Polelle.

The last paragraph in *Bishop von Galen* begins with authoritative solemnity: "I would not go so far as to say that von Galen was scandalous in his behavior, but I do believe that he lost sight of the larger, more humane questions involved in the brutality of the Nazi regime." Thus after what may be called death by a thousand optatives, von Galen — though condescendingly designated as merely bordering on the scandalous — is reprieved by his benignant prosecutor. However, any non-ideologically motivated reader of her book can go so far as to say that Griech-Polelle *is* scandalous in her behavior, precisely because she has lost sight of the larger, more *human* questions involved in the brutality of the Nazi regime.

What toll did the years of courageous opposition take on the bishop; what toll did the years of facing the likelihood of execution take; what did the years of "preparing for the worst" take? These are questions that would instinctively come to the mind of any normally empathetic human being. That they did not is an indication of the power of ideology — and the ideology of liberal certitude at that — to breed arrogant conviction about the righteousness of one's historical opinions. The bishop died of then unknown causes in April 1946, a little less than a year after the suicide of Adolf Hitler. Had the bishop like his brother been imprisoned in Sachsenhausen, and unlike his brother died there, the protocol of mortmain, history's hidden hand, would have rendered impossible a book such as this. Why is Oberst Graf von Stauffenberg the hero of this historian and not Bischof Graf von Galen? Why is there this insistence on a witnessing "unto death" for heroes and heroines; what is it about the act of dying at the hands of enemies that alone makes a sacrament of praise out of a life's ending?

The final question is raised by an observation made by a committee member at Yad Vashem to Martin Gilbert: "I see the savers as true noble souls of the human race, and when I meet with them I feel somewhat inferior to them. For I know that if I had been in their place I wouldn't have been capable of such deeds" (*The Righteous,* loc. cit.). The larger "more human question," which is not asked by the author of this life of von Galen and by her equally self-assertive admirers, is quite simply, "if I had been in his place would I have been capable of such deeds?"

John Connelly, like Griech-Polelle an emulator of Hochhuth and contemner of long-dead churchmen, has said there is a lesson in the fact that "Bishop von Galen publicly challenged the regime and was left in peace" — though even from Griech-Polelle's rigged narrative one soon learned that "peace" is hardly the appropriate term. Nor is the lesson that somehow the bishop could have diminished Nazi perversity and thus saved lives. Rather, the lesson "we learn [is] that other German bishops could have risked more." (They might even have been so daring as to launch a free speech movement.) But since "we" have seen that this writer also contemns people who risked *everything*, like those two "murderers," von Möltke and Elser, it is not clear whether what any of "us" learn would have had a bearing on diminishing the evil of the regime.

This confusion ends up reducing all of the preceding discussions and disclosures to little more than a subheading in the letter of the nineteen original petitioners. It is not the historical reality of the rampant slaughter in the past that is of primary concern; it is the "symbolic" reality attached to that slaughter in the present — much like the Pius XII of that ubiquitous and obnoxious petition. The crucial issue *now* is not whether anything he could have done was able to halt or even to effectively impair mass murder. That issue is abandoned (too complex, too uncertain, too speculative), only to be replaced by the simpler and more congenial matter of discrediting, and then vilifying him. In that process, in order to be convincing it is imperative that — at least initially — one's own higher moral values be subtly and gently put on display. After one has made one's mark among sympathetic observers — apparently also engaged in Jewish-Catholic relations — one can rev up the rhetoric to the point where one can play the role of scourge of all religious hypocrisy. It is almost as though the monstrosities of people in the Hitler era were perpetrated in order to put on display the moral superiority of people in the present era.

Some of these petitioners apparently embrace the position of Daniel Jonah Goldhagen's *A Moral Reckoning*, which condemned "false Christian martyrs, victims, and heroes of the Holocaust" — certainly a group that from Connelly's and Griech-Polelle's descriptions includes Bishop von Galen. Goldhagen then went on to condemn Pius XII as the man that the church has been "transubstantiating from a culpable offender into a saint" — certainly another position shared by the signatories of the original petition to Benedict XVI. How this viewpoint, no matter its language, can benefit "the future of Jewish-Christian *relations*" is something that remains undisclosed. Add to this dual phenomenon the fact that it is in the name of such "relations" that an entire papal encyclical, the previously encountered *Summi Pontificatus*, is about to be doctored to the point where it allegedly affirms the exact opposite of what it in fact does say — add that in, and one gets a new insight into the fragile nature of this whole "relationship."

First, I will take up the convicted bishop of Münster, and then the doctored encyclical of the culpable offender, Pius XII. At the time of von Galen's beatification, October 9, 2005, there were only minor objections in Germany and none from the Israeli government.[30] The pope, speaking in German, said that von Galen "feared God more than man, and this gave him the courage to say and to do things that many intelligent persons did not do in that period in Germany." The remark addressed a criticism of von Galen — repeated several times in the press before the beatification — by his distant cousin, Bishop von Preysing of Berlin, who had told von Möltke that the bishop of Münster was not an intellectual and "thus had been slow to recognize the nature of the regime." Von Möltke found the bishop's tardy awareness of the regime's ruthlessness to be all the more impressive, since then, "the Holy Ghost has now illuminated and filled him. How much more significant is such a sign than it would be in the case of a highly intelligent man." The irony of a Christian Scientist — as von Möltke had been reared — correcting the bishop of Berlin on the power of the Holy Ghost would not have been lost on von Galen, whose patriotism did initially make it difficult for him to distinguish between the Fatherland and its rulers.

Although there was not the anticipated remonstrance from the Israeli government at the beatification of von Galen, there was the unanticipated approbation of the Anti-Defamation League and its spokesman, the previously introduced Abraham Foxman, who apparently does not share with several of these petitioners their contempt for the bishop. The relevant press release was headed "Vatican-Jewish Relations, ADL Expresses Gratitude to Pope for Beatification of 'The Lion of Muenster.'"

30. Uta Ranke-Heinemann — a one-time student of Benedict XVI and radical debunker of Catholicism as well as of most religious and social orthodoxies — warned readers in *Junge Welt* (November 10) that von Galen had been an anti-Semite and a warmonger. The church historian, Hubert Wolf — whose *Pope and Devil* was cited earlier — in an interview in *Rheinischer Merkur* (September 29) described the bishop as the "prototypical resister," but also cited the question, "Will anyone arise to help us?" which had been presumably addressed to Galen regarding the hopes of Jews, and apparently got no response. (I address this issue in the *First Things* article.) *Der Tagesspiegel* (October 8) and several other journals and websites quoted the dismissive wartime description of Galen by Bishop von Preysing of Berlin, but without quoting the redeeming response from the resistance leader, Count von Möltke — all as cited in the text below. *Die Tageszeiten* (October 7), under the heading "The Blemished Image of the Lion of Münster," noted that members of Pax Christi had raised objections to the beatification on the grounds of the bishop's support for the war against Russia. A major church historian, Victor Conzemius, in *Neue Zürcher Zeitung* (October 7), alluded to von Preysing's criticism of the bishop, and observed that von Galen had never fully realized how corrupt the Nazi government really was. While emphasizing the courage of the bishop in attacking the regime, Conzemius concluded that a beatification was not needed to honor that quality. Lastly, the semi-fascist *Neue Freiheit* (October 11) took the occasion of the beatification to praise von Galen for his patriotism in supporting the war against Russia.

New York, NY, October 12, 2005 The Anti-Defamation League (ADL) expressed gratitude to Pope Benedict XVI over the beatification of World War II–era German Bishop Clemens August von Galen — known as the "Lion of Muenster" — who courageously spoke out publicly against the Nazis' murderous policies.

During an Oct. 9 Vatican ceremony, Pope Benedict hailed the "heroic courage" of von Galen, and described the churchman who condemned anti-Semitism as a model for those in public roles today. The pontiff later praised the bishop for "protecting the Jews," while addressing pilgrims in St. Peter's Square.

In a letter to Pope Benedict, Abraham H. Foxman, ADL National Director and Rabbi Gary Bretton-Granatoor, ADL Interfaith Affairs Director said:

"Cardinal von Galen's life was an example of one who put doing right and good in the eyes of the Lord above political expediency. His brave battle against anti-Semitism and his protection of innocent lives should stand as a lesson for all time, not just to adherents of the Catholic Church, but all peoples and all faith communities."

What makes this laudation all the more interesting is that it was written a few weeks after a copy of Griech-Polelle's book had been delivered to and received by the office of the Anti-Defamation League. (That should suggest another mode of engaging in fruitful and productive Jewish-Catholic relations — and a mode more fruitful than petitions to the pope.)

The issues are interrelated. How does it come about that the Catholics are vocally petitioning for a halt to proceedings for the beatification of Pius XII, while the Israeli ambassador to the Vatican says publicly that such proceedings are "not our concern"? And how does it come about that the staunchest defender of all things Jewish, the head of the Anti-Defamation League, can defend the anti-Semitic and obsessively "single-issue" von Galen, while petition signatories like Connelly and Griech-Polelle have clearly proved the opposite? In both instances it is the Catholic side that is the aggressive proponent, often relying less on scholarly research than on self-generated and pre-determined bias.[31] Admittedly that bias has its re-

---

31. A wise rabbi whom I have quoted earlier and whom I will quote again in the next chapter has said of the temptation to play off one evil with another: "The issues must not be intermingled. If Catholicism has something to say about Jews and anti-Semitism, let them speak the truth. And if we have something to say about the Pope and Catholicism, let us

mote cause in a sense of collective guilt — however warped and anachronistic — for the genuinely horrifying two millennia of church teaching of contempt for Jews. But one evil will not be overcome by another evil, and when the latter is steeped in self-righteousness, in the protection of personal opinion, in the prioritizing of sanctimony, then the defense of what is *mine* becomes the implicitly narcissistic goal of the researcher.

Earlier in the present chapter an axiom of Christian Ethics 101 was introduced into this discussion. Now is perhaps the opportune time for Philology 101; and the axiom is, "When in doubt, etymologize." This is particularly evident in the self-mirroring of the translation of "my opinion" as *meine Meinung*. When reading earlier those quotations from Connelly and Griech-Polelle, too often one got the clear impression that the fact that an assertion was "mine" outweighed the assertion itself, and this explained the appropriateness of characterizing it as "turf-guarding." Since the mythical Narcissus died from his obsession with himself, this entire chapter may be regarded as a lifeline tossed to those deeply immersed ideological liberals whom I have critiqued above, and am about to critique again in the context of the encyclical by that "culpable offender," Pius XII.

Specifically, concerning *Summi Pontificatus*, I have no hesitation about predicting that very few, if any, of the original signatories to the petition to Benedict XVI will agree that there is any kind of racism in the encyclical. The reason for such certitude — and concomitantly the disdainful dismissal of Connelly's doctored text and warped interpretation — is that *much of the encyclical is explicitly and formally a critique of racism and a tribute to the oneness of humankind*. Of course, it violates established literary conventions to italicize that lengthy clause, but it is essential to emphasize that we have to do here with the kind of "scholarship" (at which Kertzer is past master, and Connelly is eager aspirant) that ostensibly prevents someone from seeing what is on the very page being scrutinized — as in that passage where Kertzer simply deleted the reference to the Russian ambassador in order to make the Vatican secretary of state the guilty party.

This is Connelly's original contention:

> The words on "race" I attribute to Pius XII were spoken by him and are not doctored, as anyone who consults the text of *Summi pontificatus* can discern. The sentence's second part does nothing to weaken the surprising

---

speak the truth. Let us not degrade ourselves by trading favors. Good will that has to be bought is not worth the name." Marc Saperstein, ed., *Witness from the Pulpit* (loc. cit.).

call for the church to concern itself with the "orderly evolution of particular forces and tendencies having their origin in the individual character of each race." What in the world did that mean?

I have referred to this text several times, anticipating what I called a "crescendo of manipulation" by Connelly when encountering *Summi Pontificatus*: the quotation that Connelly refers to is in the paragraph numbered 45 in the encyclical. Its proper contextualization — even he would have a hard time denying — is obviously the paragraphs that preceded and that followed that number. Since this is the pope's first encyclical, and also one being delivered in wartime, there are lengthy introductory observations relating to changing conditions in the church and society, to his predecessor, to his own election, and so on, before he approaches his tribute to the unity of humankind. That tribute is initiated as follows (all emphases supplied):

35. The first of these pernicious errors, widespread today, is the forgetfulness of that law of human solidarity and charity which is dictated and imposed **by our common origin and by the equality of rational nature in all men, to whatever people they belong.**

36. In fact, the first page of the Scripture, with magnificent simplicity, tells us how God, as a culmination to His creative work, made man to His Own image and likeness. . . . It shows us besides how **other men took their origin from the first couple, and then goes on, in unsurpassed vividness of language, to recount their division into different groups and their dispersion to various parts of the world.** Even when they abandoned their Creator, God did not cease to regard them as His children, who, according to His merciful plan, should one day be reunited once more in His friendship (cf. Genesis xii.3).

37. **The Apostle of the Gentiles later on makes himself the herald of this truth which associates men as brothers in one great family, when he proclaims to the Greek world that God "hath made of one, all mankind,** to dwell upon the whole face of the earth, determining appointed times, and the limits of their habitation, that they should seek God" (Acts xvii.26, 27).

After those initial declarations, the pope hits his stride in a passage which — if the axiom "repetition is the mother of learning" has any validity

— leaves John Connelly an orphan.[32] And we haven't even come to the contested paragraph 45.

38. A marvelous vision, which makes us see **the human *race* in the unity of one common origin in God** "one God and Father of all, Who is above all, and through all, and in us all" (Ephesians iv.6); **in the unity of nature** which in every man is equally composed of material body and spiritual, immortal soul; **in the unity of the immediate end and mission** in the world; **in the unity of dwelling place, the earth,** of whose resources all men can by natural right avail themselves, to sustain and develop life; **in the unity of the supernatural end**, God Himself, to Whom all should tend; in the unity of means to secure that end.

42. In the light of this unity of all mankind, which exists in law and in fact, individuals do not feel themselves isolated units, like grains of sand, but **united by the very force of their nature and by their internal destiny,** into an organic, harmonious mutual relationship which varies with the changing of time.

43. **And the nations**, despite a difference of development due to diverse conditions of life and of culture, **are not destined to break the unity of the human *race,* but rather to enrich and embellish it** by the sharing of their own peculiar gifts and by that reciprocal interchange of goods which can be possible and efficacious only when a mutual love and a lively sense of charity unite all the sons of the same Father and all those redeemed by the same Divine Blood.

As one approaches paragraph 45, a generous interpretation of Connelly's blunder may come to mind, that is, that he had never actually read the encyclical. Instead, he possibly came across in any of scores of books a snippet from the encyclical that sounded more or less racist — and decided to run with it. What's to fear? After all, it is an implicit datum of ideological liberal thought — *vide,* the implications of the petition to Benedict XVI — that these popes failed to speak out in defense of Jews because they were themselves anti-Jewish. The reason I referred to a "generous interpretation" is be-

---

32. Some readers may be reminded of the comment made by a don after hearing Charles Kingsley's inaugural address as Regius Professor of Modern History at Cambridge: "Alas, who would have thought we should so soon be regretting poor Kingsley."

cause if Connelly had actually read the encyclical containing the quotations above, and he could still say that it contained a "surprising call for the church to concern itself with the 'orderly evolution of particular forces and tendencies having their origin in the individual character of each race . . .'" — if he had read the whole document and still made that statement, he might well find himself excluded from teaching at even the lowliest junior college. Instead, he probably saw only a fragment of the paragraph reproduced below, and then, subsequently learning of that papal proviso, decided to bulldoze his way to righteousness by simply excising the latter — possibly on the assumption that either no one reading *Commonweal* would notice the textual doctoring or, if somebody did notice, they would probably be loyal enough to absolve their liberal fellow-traveler. (As mentioned earlier, all the bloggers at "dotCommonweal," including theologians and church historians, appeared to be enthusiastic over what they were learning from Connelly about the church, about the papacy, about German Catholics — and presumably about East European Catholics as well.)

45. The Church hails with joy and follows with her maternal blessing every method of guidance and care which aims at a wise and orderly evolution of particular forces and tendencies having their origin in the individual character of each race, provided that they are not opposed to the duties incumbent on men from their unity of origin and common destiny.

Looking at that exultant paean in its real context, one has to wonder who could describe it as "a *surprising call for the church to concern itself with*" . . . anything? Yet this is the text that Connelly not only claims he didn't doctor, but now maintains — clambering up on a very high horse — that it left him totally dumbfounded. "What in the world did that mean?" To that question, any randomly chosen Catholic living on planet earth and with middling hermeneutical skills — say, Remedial Reading 101 — would respond. "In light of the previous paragraphs and those to come, it means exactly what it says, that the church hails with joy and follows with her maternal blessing every method of guidance and care which aims at a wise and orderly evolution of particular forces and tendencies having their origin in the individual character of each race."

Far from being a racist declaration that for East Europeans "meant boycotting Jewish businesses" — a singularly nasty interpretation — this is nothing more than what Cardinal Newman meant when he spoke of the

"English-German" element in the church, and lamented its loss at the Reformation. Or, for that matter, this is nothing more than what Connelly meant when he last celebrated the Irish contribution to both church and society on St. Patrick's Day. The mention of Blessed John Henry Newman provides occasion to make note of his response to a friend who had written him about launching a historical journal; the friend was told — more prophetically than anyone could ever anticipate — that it was a good idea, but "unless one doctored all one's facts one would be thought a bad Catholic." Now, it is by doctoring facts that one proves one is a good Catholic.

> 46. She [the Church of Christ] has repeatedly shown in her missionary enterprises that such a principle of action is the guiding star of her universal apostolate. Pioneer research and investigation, involving sacrifice, devotedness and love on the part of her missionaries of every age, have been undertaken **in order to facilitate the deeper appreciative insight into the most varied civilizations and to put their spiritual values to account for a living and vital preaching of the Gospel of Christ**. All that in such usages and customs is not inseparably bound up with religious errors will always be subject to kindly consideration and, when it is found possible, will be sponsored and developed.

> 48. In accordance with these principles of equality, the Church devotes her care to forming cultured native clergy and gradually increasing the number of native Bishops. And in order to give external expression to these, Our intentions, We have chosen the forthcoming Feast of Christ the King to raise to the Episcopal dignity at the Tomb of the Apostles twelve representatives of widely different peoples *and races. . . .* ". . . **Where there is neither Gentile nor Jew, circumcision nor uncircumcision, barbarian nor Scythian, bond nor free. But Christ is all and in all**" (Colossians iii.10, 11).

If ever there were a text that put the lie to papally sponsored Catholic racism, it is the above quotation from St. Paul. It also puts the lie to David I. Kertzer's characteristically sweeping assertion that Pius XII wouldn't deign to use the word "Jew." This is the *first* encyclical of that particular pope. It couldn't come any earlier.

There are almost seventy more paragraphs in the encyclical, covering such things as the role of the hierarchy, ecumenical outreach, the priesthood, efforts for peace, justice among all peoples, the laity, Catholic Action, and so on. One can only be thankful that Connelly when fishing among the snippets didn't come across No. 114, which begins, "And you, white legions of children who are so loved and dear. . . ." There is no saying what blind alley of papal "racism" that might have led him down. However, what one can be sure of is that it wouldn't have led him to treat of Pius XII's vigorous support, even in the early 1940s, for the desegregation of American Catholic institutions — a subject treated with accuracy in John T. McGreevy's *Catholicism and American Freedom* (2003). Interestingly, McGreevy is also among the bloggers at "dotCommonweal" who was enthusiastic about Connelly's article, describing it as "superb." He also offered similar high praise, "terrific," for the earlier and far more detailed "Catholic Racism and Its Opponents." Unfortunately, it is in that more detailed article — as I noted earlier — that Connelly's ambiguous interpretations of the term "race" were initiated.[33]

Near the end of the encyclical — unread by our authority on American English — the pope also addressed some of those boycott-prone East European Catholics. Writing a month after the outbreak of hostilities, he said:

> 106. The blood of countless human beings, even noncombatants, raises a piteous dirge over a nation such as Our dear Poland, which, for its fidelity to the Church, for its services in the defense of Christian civilization, written in indelible characters in the annals of history, has a right to the generous and brotherly sympathy of the whole world.

It is in this larger context that Connelly's affected outrage — "What in the world does that mean?" — can be clearly recognized in all its obsceneness. Concerning the specific answer to that question, and regarding the questioner himself, the final judgment has to be — and here I resort to the aforementioned "American English": He doesn't have a clue.

As to the significance of these rigged texts, it is obvious no one is talking about the Johannine Comma, the Donation of Constantine, the Poems of Ossian, or even Hugh Trevor-Roper's validation of Hitler's "diaries." But one is talking about the manufacture, planned, plotted, and executed, of a bogus religio-political narrative intended to show that three different modern popes made public statements linking them personally to racist anti-

---

33. Among Connelly's other insights in the article is the following bit of *ex silentio* casuistry: "The Holy See, contrary to what is often written, never forbade racist thinking. In 1938 Pope Pius XI issued a set of instructions on the dangers of racism. . . . What is less often noted is that these instructions forbade 'extreme racism' but not recognition of the existence of races or assessments of their relative value." Again, the ambiguity of Connelly's definition and use of the word "race" is in play.

Semitism. One is also talking about a liberal intellectual environment where such a narrative is not immediately questioned and debated, but rather is accepted as a commonplace or truism in the ongoing discourse. In short, one is talking about the triumph of ideological arrogance, an arrogance whose perpetrators believe that *we* are the experts, *we* are the specialists — and, not incidentally, *we* stick together. In religious terms it is almost as though they were saying, we have the "grace of state" to pronounce on these issues. What is lost sight of is that this "we" has no such license; this "we" is only as good as the facts it turns up and the arguments it makes. Thus far, neither those facts nor those arguments have proved to be persuasive, and this may be why some practitioners of this brand of history — I have singled out several — fall back on organizing and publicizing petitions.

The final irony of this larger scenario is that these lockstepping liberals are doing the very things they have accused the Vatican and assorted hierarchs of doing: protecting their own prerogatives and interests rather than those of the larger community; taking care of their own concerns often to the disadvantage of the interests of others; reinterpreting their own well-established rules to favor their shifting views; covering over obvious abuses of long-sanctioned regulations in order to justify their own practices or prejudices. Nor should the latter be read as referring only to incriminating sexual matters among various national episcopates. It must also be read as referring to other kinds of Catholic groups and less blatant offenses, such as — to take an example out of the air — doctoring public statements on the seemingly noble grounds of exposing bad people. It is remarkable how many abuses, whether of word or deed, can be justified by invoking the greater good. As other better-known defenders of Christian and American "values" — appearing in TV newscasts, not in Catholic journals — invariably and repeatedly say, "just looking out for the folks." But even these biased commentators would draw the line at tinkering with papal encyclicals, much less with rewriting them.

Thus it is undeniable that the greatest evil that has been attributed to churchmen, the reduction of the gospel message to a propaganda tool, is precisely what most of the people I critique in this chapter have sought to do. Only in their case the message they are eagerly purveying has been recast to conform to the ruling liberal ideology of Christian guilt (undeniable) at the horrors of the Holocaust (inconceivable), resulting in a self-righteous purge (unforgivable) of anyone predetermined to be less virtuous than they imagine themselves to be.[34]

34. That this is a continuing effort is evident from the review of Susannah Heschel's es-

Following the above lengthy treatment of the background and the views of some signatories to the petition to Pope Benedict XVI, this entire discussion can be brought to a close. While no one doubts the importance of not harming Jewish-Catholic relations, it is unclear how that petition will do anything other than reopen the matter — discussed much earlier — of reciprocal vetoes by the two parties involved. Moreover, rather than dancing around the notion of Pius XII as "symbol" of anti-Semitism, any non-ideological observer would suggest that the petitioners accept their own "challenge" and seek to "separate Pope Pius XII from this legacy." One obvious contribution to that goal, which these petitioners and their Jewish counterparts on the other side of the divide must *ex definitione* accept — otherwise they themselves could be convicted of harming "Jewish-Catholic relations" — would be to examine closely the three documents discovered by William Doino. There is, first, the "Refugee" narrative itself and, second, its supporting testimony by Herman Herskovic, the texts of which are provided integrally in the last chapter. Third, there are excerpts from the previously unknown memoir of the "Refugee" himself — a fascinating story of his life both before and after his papal audience, culminating in his escape from Nazi-controlled Italy to Spain and Portugal, and finally to Palestine. In all, a narrative that will certainly be a major step in putting an end to accusations of anti-Semitism regarding at least one specific modern pope.

---

timable *The Aryan Jesus*, by John Connelly (*Commonweal*, February 26, 2010). After describing various Christian "assumptions about the evils of Jewishness," the reader is told: "Such assumptions made the Holocaust possible." Alas, that too needs to be nuanced. What *might* be said to have made it possible was Zyklon B and/or the offspring of Frau Maria Anna Schicklgruber.

Anti-Semitism and Theological Arrogance

When in *Herder Correspondence* for June 1965 I reviewed Edward Flannery's *The Anguish of the Jews*,[1] several avenues of approach were open for discussing such a book. For example, one might have related it to current politico-moral issues by showing how the methods and styles of anti-Semitism offer a clear parallel with those of anticommunism and segregationism. Thus when Fr. Flannery observed that under Torquemada "elaborate regulations were set forth for detecting Judaizers. A list of thirty-seven clues was published to help ferret them out. . . . Thirty days of grace were given for self denunciation" (p. 138), one might have remarked, how like the days of McCarthyism. Similarly with Fr. Flannery's summation of the goals of Hitler: "Cleanse the country of Jews and there would be jobs for the unemployed, outlets for professional talent, a new world for youth; industrialists would be more secure in their profits, German maidens would be safe, German nationalism would thrive, and Aryan blood would remain uncontaminated" (p. 210) — one may have noted: how like the days of Governor Wallace or Leander Perez. But a discussion of such parallels, however beneficial it might have been, would not have exposed the actual roots of the problem of Christian anti-Semitism, and would perhaps even have left the modern Christian who prides himself on despising McCarthyism and segregation, feeling all the more complacently self-righteous. It was necessary, therefore, to judge Fr. Flannery's book with-

---

1. The background of this annex is provided above. As noted there, it first appeared as an editorial in an issue of *Continuum* on anti-Semitism. The present text was revised very slightly for its publication in *The Range of Commitment: Essays of a Conservative Liberal* (1969). Although, I would now word some of its opinions differently, I am still in substantial agreement with them four decades later. (The gender-exclusive language, unfortunately, has also been retained.)

out any Catholic bias in favor of it as an achievement of good wishes and good intentions. On the assumption that there is no judge like a hanging judge, it was necessary to scrutinize the book as closely and assess it as severely as would any conscientious non-Catholic, as would any Jew.

The *Herder Correspondence* review, because it is a necessary prelude to what follows, is included here.

We have to deal with a history of anti-Semitism by a Catholic priest, and it is this latter element — underlined by the jacket description of the book — which may be presumed to differentiate the present work from other studies of this subject. *The Anguish of the Jews* is conscientiously written, painstakingly researched, and judiciously seeking to avoid extreme judgments; in its overall impact it is an effective critique of anti-Semitism. Nevertheless it must be said that the book does have the tone, the subtly nuanced flavor, of an *apologia*. Although Fr. Flannery could not even remotely be criticized for having written a *plaidoyer*, a simple exoneration of Christian guilt, nevertheless — and perhaps derivative of his own office as Roman Catholic priest — his impeachment of ecclesiastical authorities is grievously attenuated.

While one never has the impression that Fr. Flannery is intentionally slanting his narrative, the cumulative effect remains that of an enervation of the requisite moral severity. Individual assertions taken separately may be unobjectionable, but the total indictment is vague and diffusive. One does not hear in these pages the accents of Lord Acton's Inaugural Address condemning dilution of moral judgment. Lord Acton defined a standard which, in all charity, one feels *The Anguish of the Jews* cannot quite come up to: "If, in our uncertainty, we must often err, it may be sometimes better to risk excess in rigour than in indulgence, for then at least we do no injury by loss of principle. . . . Opinions alter, manners change, creeds rise and fall, but the moral law is written on the tablets of eternity."[2]

Again, it must be emphasized that in no sense is there any debasing of the moral currency in Fr. Flannery's book; but there *is* an excessive balancing of counterweights that in the end serves to erode firm principles. For example, after a particularly vicious screed of St. Hippolytus to the effect that "because Jews killed the Son of their Benefactor," they will always be slaves, Fr. Flannery observes: "No stronger animus than this is displayed in pre-fourth century Christian literature" (p. 38) — as if this were

---

2. *Lectures on Modern History* (London, 1920), p. 27.

not strong and pernicious enough. Similarly, while deploring the anti-Semitic outbursts of St. John Chrysostom, Fr. Flannery also provides an oblique justification by commenting:

> The chief venting of his ire was six sermons delivered in his see of Antioch, where *Jews were numerous and influential* and where, *apparently, some* of his flock were frequenting synagogues and Jewish homes and probably trafficking in Jewish amulets. The saint was not one to meet such a situation with equanimity. *Rigid on principle,* a *born reformer* and a fiery preacher, he threw the whole of his energy and talent into castigating Judaism (p. 47). *(Italics added throughout.)*

Even after the establishment of Christianity as the state religion and when Jews constituted only a very small minority in the empire, Fr. Flannery sees the guilt as equally shared: "Hostilities were brutal and frequent. Blow was met by blow in a scandalous reciprocity of provocation" (p. 56). This exaggeratedly evenhanded justice leads the author to remark of this same period: "That some degree of popular hostility toward Jews existed can be concluded from the attacks on synagogues which, as Marcel Simon has pointed out, could not have been instigated by mere ecclesiastical fiat without a response of anti-Jewish feeling in the populace" (p. 58) — as though such popular sentiment were not itself largely the creation of a long sequence of antecedent ecclesiastical fiats. At the conclusion of this section of the book the reader is told: "But in the final accounting the anti-Semitism of this era was, *as in the case of pagan antiquity, a reaction* against a vibrant and assertive Judaism" (p. 63). Regrettably few of the texts Fr. Flannery cites will bear out this mitigating judgment. There is a comparably naïve prejudice reflected in the assertion that the relatively benevolent and Christian attitude of Theodoric — denominated, "this *Arian* believer" — must be credited in part to Cassiodorus — denominated, "his *Catholic* and well educated secretary" (p. 70): as though Trinitarian orthodoxy had ever been a guarantee of Christian charity.

Again, we are presented with a complex of supposititious reasons to "explain" an act of horror in the book's treatment of the persecution by King Sisebut in Spain: "This monarch, *struggling to free* his territory from the threat of Byzantine imperialism, probably aware of Jewish *'betrayals'* in the East . . . determined to have done with the Jewish problem once and for all" (p. 73). With reference to sixth-century France, Fr. Flannery, after remarking that Jews were "ready on occasion to strike the first blow," finds it "appropriate" to quote "a thorough student of the period" as follows:

"Even the expulsions and other clearly characteristic violence inflicted on Jews by representatives of Christianity lose something of their horror when we discover that Jews, when conditions lent themselves, did not hesitate to have recourse to these measures themselves" (p. 77). In the light of perennial Christian claims to a higher morality than that of other religions, this quotation loses something of its "appropriateness."

With an unintended nod to consensus morality, Fr. Flannery declares of St. Agobard, the author of an incredibly perverse rant against the Jews: ". . . for some he is an ingrained anti-Semite, for others a candid and sincere prelate vindicating the rights of Christians against aggressive and favored Jewry leagued with a philo-Semitic ruler" (p. 83). "Aggressive and favored Jewry" here describes a group of people seeking only to exercise some very restricted rights, and "philo-Semitic" describes a monarch intent on nothing more than treating all his subjects as human beings. Of this whole period of the dark ages, Fr. Flannery observes: "The legislation of both Church and state must, in effect, be seen, above all, [the halting rhetoric betrays the tenuousness of the conclusion] as a *defense* against Jewish proselytism" (p. 87). Moreover, we are told immediately — and irrelevantly — that "heretics still fared worse than" Jews.

Moving to the beginnings of continent-wide slaughter of Jews in the late Middles Ages, the opinion is proffered that some of these massacres "were clearly mob actions, reinforced by religious fanaticism" (p. 93). One fears that "reinforced" is a euphemism for "inspired." The bigoted Vincent Ferrer is also euphemistically characterized as "a miracle worker, an excellent preacher, and totally dedicated to the conversion of the Jews" (p. 134). But such "total dedication" led Jews to think of him as a "scourge": a scourge — Fr. Flannery hastens to remind the reader — "as much" to the enemies of the Jews as to themselves. This tissue of palliating circumstances and suppositions is so unconsciously woven by the author and so subtly enmeshes the reader that neither may appreciate the sad irony of the following statement concerning the background of the persecutions in fifteenth-century Poland: "The Church, *naturally*, was alarmed by the ascendancy of the Jews and the preferential treatment they received from the crown" (p. 156). But as in previous instances, this "preferential treatment" consisted merely in the Jews' being "allowed considerable self-government" and in being accepted "as an integral part of Poland. . . ."

Fr. Flannery concludes his book with some general observations on the entire tragedy of anti-Semitism, and he asserts: "How much more historically plausible it is to see Hitlerian or racist anti-Semitism as the creature of modern laicism, the modern revolt against God, rather than a fruit of Christian teaching" (p. 275). One regrets that it is necessary to add that such an opinion is "historically plausible" only if one reads history as Fr. Flannery unwittingly but persistently writes it.

To the above remarks I would add two additional quotations from that Catholic historian whom Strachey viciously characterized as an "almost hysterical reviler of priestcraft and persecution"[3] — fortunately we now know that the ethic of Bloomsbury would have led us to the exoneration of an Eichmann. The first quotation is again from Acton's Inaugural Address, and simply reinforces the basis for the preceding indictment of Fr. Flannery's book:

> The plea in extenuation of guilt and mitigation of punishment is perpetual. At every step we are met by arguments which go to excuse, to palliate, to confound right and wrong, and reduce the just man to the level of the reprobate. They set up the principle that only a foolish Conservative judges the present with the ideals of the past; that only a foolish Liberal judges the past with the ideas of the present. The mission of that school was to make distant times, and especially the Middle Ages, then most distant of all, intelligible and acceptable to a society issuing from the eighteenth century. There were difficulties in the way; and among others this, that, in the first fervour of the Crusades, the men who took the Cross, after receiving communion, heartily devoted the day to the extermination of Jews. To judge them by a fixed standard, call them sacrilegious fanatics or furious hypocrites, was to yield a gratuitous victory to Voltaire. It became a rule of policy to praise the spirit when you could not defend the deed. So that we have no common code; our moral notions are always fluid; and you must consider the times, the class from which men sprang, the surrounding influences, the masters in their schools, the preachers in their pulpits, the movement they obscurely obeyed, and so on, until responsibility is merged in numbers, and not a culprit is left for execution.[4]

Such, *unwittingly* — as I have stressed over and over in the above remarks — Fr. Flannery has done. But we must bear in mind also the following from Lord Acton: ". . . scientific thought begins with the separation between the idea and its exponent."[5] For nothing is more apparent than that Fr.

---

3. *Eminent Victorians* (New York, 1938), p. 100.
4. *Op. cit.*, p. 24.
5. *Letters of Lord Acton to Mary Gladstone* (London, 1913), p. 164.

Flannery, with the very best of will, with the most noble of intentions, has simply not been able to look upon the Roman Catholic Church's — I emphasize "Church's" — systematic assault on Judaism with the necessary humane detachment and clarity. The reason is that all Roman Catholics, the present writer not excluded, are the products of that unique mindset, cast in the matrix of two millennia of inbred religious paranoia, which can be shattered only by the communal realization that the theology of crusader and conquistador — which, though less noxiously visible, is still our theology — has been a perversion of everything Jesus meant. The shattering of this mindset demands the most deliberate and painstaking therapy aimed at the restoration of an authentic humanism to institutional Catholicism: a humanism, it must be said, which is not sufficiently evident in Vatican II's treatment of non-Christian religions. That twenty centuries of stony sleep "were vexed to nightmare by a rocking cradle"[6] is a truth borne in on all those Christians who shamefully face the fact that the most monstrous crimes in history have been committed either in the name or in the shadow of Jesus of Nazareth.

If there is one lesson that this history teaches it is that the imperialist claims of Roman Catholicism have not brought unity and concord, have not given to men the earthly adumbration of the blessed city of peace. The question must arise in the hearts of Roman Catholics, as it has in the heart of everyone that looks from the outside at their Church, whether any historical reality, any temporal organization, can, without succumbing ultimately to collective derangement, harbor in its communal will and in its official declarations the universalist — not *aspirations,* not *pretensions* but — *demands* that Roman Catholicism has asserted. The attrition by pragma, the corruption by contingency, the erosion by passion, that is, the very karma under which humanity labors, makes the mere assertion of such demands in the name of whatever lofty ideology an affront to man's constitution as a being *in history.* Even as pure theory, then, as pure hypothesis, the following from the Declaration on Religious Freedom may be judged faulty — and this, because in history no pure theory or hypothesis exists:

> The Church is, by the will of Christ, the teacher of the truth. It is her duty to give utterance to, and authoritatively to teach, that Truth which is Christ Himself, and also to declare and confirm by her authority those principles of the moral order which have their origin in human nature it-

6. W. B. Yeats, "The Second Coming."

self. . . . The disciple is bound by a grave obligation toward Christ his Master ever more adequately to understand the truth received from Him, faithfully to proclaim it, and vigorously to defend it. Never — be it understood — having recourse to means that are incompatible with the spirit of the gospel.[7]

It is the very assertion of the claim — be it understood, no matter how gently and benignly enforced — that this historically structured and conditioned body of men can authoritatively teach those principles "which have their origin in human nature itself": it is this very assertion which constitutes a negation of history and of that Incarnation which alone gives history meaning. For if history has one law it is that the full implementing of any absolutist claims necessarily entails "recourse to a means" which is incompatible with them. No contingent means can ever be perfectly compatible with an absolute end.

Enlightened Catholic dogmaticians are perhaps on the way to granting this with regard to Protestantism; and one could imagine some of them arguing in the light of their growing understanding of the temporal that Cardinal Newman would have been right, were he living in the present age, in believing he should have remained an Anglican because it was in Anglicanism that he found himself, that it was in Anglicanism that Providence and history had placed him. And even with regard to the non-Christian religions, Karl Rahner[8] along with H. R. Schlette[9] has underlined their salvific role; J. R. Geiselmann[10] has emphasized the transmission of revelation through the other great world faiths; and Eugene Hillman[11] has reestablished the biblical foundations for envisioning the Church as the sign before the nations and not as the proselytizing agency of conversions. But though the Church is the sign before the nations, it would be very dangerous to say — a danger which the above citation from Vatican II did not successfully skirt — it is the only sign or even the "brightest" sign. To so say would be again to ignore the reality of history, and would ultimately be to succumb once more to the temptation of the Grand Inquisitor and the pogroms that attend *inevitably* his ministry. For a sign is only a sign to those who find it significant, to those who have eyes to see.

---

7. No. 14, in *The Documents of Vatican II* (New York, 1966), pp. 694-95.

8. *Theological Investigations* (Baltimore, 1966), V, chapter six.

9. *Towards a Theology of Religions* (New York, 1966).

10. *The Meaning of Tradition* (New York, 1966).

11. *The Church as Mission* (New York, 1966).

Moreover, the sign which the Church signifies is not a pure sign; it is a sign obscured by its own embodiment. Thus the sign which in fact historical man always is proffered is the sign of an institution, is an institutionalized sign presented to an institutionalized man. One cannot, therefore, say with Père Clérissac that the terms "Church" and "Christ" are simply convertible,[12] any more than one can say that the Church as "the pure sign of Christ" can authoritatively judge what belongs to "human nature itself": neither exists. What does exist is the institutionalized sign and man who has been shaped by his family, his speech, his education, his environment, that is, by all the institutions that play about him and define his history. And this man — there is no other — may find the sign proffered by the Church utterly repugnant. Nor can he be said to be the pathetic victim of "invincible ignorance." That term is meaningless because the truth to which such a man gives himself is the truth to which he has been conformed by Providence and history, and the falsity which he rejects, he does so under those same shaping factors. There exists no other truth or falsity for any man. What Newman said about certain non-British devotional practices may be applied, *mutatis mutandis,* to religious differences: "I venture to say the majority of Catholics in England know nothing of them. They do not colour our body."[13]

All of the above may serve to explain why there is something inherently depressing in such efforts at "Jewish-Christian dialogue" as are represented, for example, by *Torah and Gospel*[14] and *The Star and the Cross:*[15] in the end the votaries of Gospel and Cross, while anxiously and eagerly trying to admire what Torah and Star stand for, remain enmeshed in their own exclusivist notions. In fact, in the light of the commission laid upon them by the Fathers of Vatican II, the Christians in such encounters must regard themselves as working, however gently, subtly, obliquely, for the "conversion" of their — not *perfidious,* we have been taught to say, but — alas, *unbelieving* partners. Yet when one looks at a book such as *Conversion to Judaism*[16] — in many ways not a particularly pleasing book, but probably no more disheartening than scores of Christian handbooks for "convert making" — and reads testimonials of separation from Christianity and Catholicism and acceptance of

---

12. *The Mystery of the Church* (New York, 1937), p. 17. It was a comparable theological naïveté which led Père Clérissac to become an ardent advocate of the Action Française before its condemnation.

13. In Ward, *The Life of John Henry Cardinal Newman* (London, 1912), II, p. 180.

14. New York, 1966.

15. Milwaukee, 1966.

16. New York, 1965.

Judaism, one is not struck by any evidence of ill-will or ignorance. One glimpses only a faith being achieved, as it can only be, through the medium of an institution — even as in the case of conversions to Catholicism. What either faith leads to no man has ever been able to say with certainty. One can only say that it is not faith *in* an institution but *through* it.

Nor can the Christian, with a wink of understanding complicity at his corelegionists, simply declare that here God is writing straight with crooked lines. In the world as we know it, all lines are crooked: and all are converging on one point. This is not to opt for some "higher religion," some syncretist spiritualism à la Friedrich Heiler, because the final convergence will not occur in history. On the contrary, what this is saying is that in concrete reality there is no perfect embodiment of truth; every sign, even as it reveals, obscures. And man himself, a chiaroscuro entity, is obliged to give himself only to that truth with which he feels "at home," to that truth to which he has been conformed.

That is why, with regard now only to the Christian churches, one looks at the ecumenical movement with satisfaction and concern; satisfaction that so many prejudices are being uprooted, and concern that — as with a possible world state — there may be no new frontiers, no institutional embodiments for the Christian dissenter, no, as they used to be called, "free churches." In such a christendom both because of its amalgamated power and because the creative tension between polar viewpoints will have been dissolved, the non-Christian will have all the more to fear. "It is not good to forget over what gulfs the spirit/Of the beauty of humanity, the petal of a lost flower blown seaward by the night wind, floats to its quietness."[17] Which is only to say that since it has been in a "world come of age" and in the dawn of the "noosphere" that the greatest mass murders in history have occurred, it is not good to forget how tenuously does institutionalized man hold on to his sanity and rein in his universalist pretensions. It was those pretensions that Christ spurned when he refused to adore Satan, though all the kingdoms of the earth would have been given to him.

I conclude with one further, and more explicitly Roman Catholic, comment on *The Anguish of the Jews*. Early in his book Fr. Flannery notes that the popular cultus of a saint does not necessarily imply that what the saint represented was officially sanctioned by the Church. Thus the attribution of the title "Saint" or "Blessed" to the alleged victims of medieval ritual murders does not imply that the Church has substantiated "the validity of the murder

---

17. Robinson Jeffers, "Apology for Bad Dreams."

accusation or the historicity of the murders" (p. 100). What it does imply has been brought out in the preceding comments and need not detain us again here. However, the canonization of virulent ant-Semites does raise a theological problem. For example, John Capistrano was responsible for fomenting murderous riots against the Jews, and he presided at a trial of Jews accused of desecrating a host, during which he personally supervised "the torture of some of the accused from whom confessions to this and other ritual crimes were accepted. In all, forty were burned, a rabbi hanged himself, children of the deceased were taken for baptism, and the remainder were banished" (p. 115). John Capistrano was named among the saints not by popular acclamation, but by formal decree, a decree which dogmaticians maintain is one of the ordinary exercises of the charism of *papal infallibility.*

Cardinal Newman, engaged throughout his life in the diaconate of the real, the concrete, the historical, feared the proclamation of the pope's infallibility because it gave so much power to one man.[18] How much more fearsome is that power when it is seen as invested in many men, invested in an institution?

18. Cf. Ward, *op. cit.,* II, p. 380.

CHAPTER 10

Ideals, Institutions, and Reform
— Toward a Conclusion

All of the material in the preceding chapters would be of relatively little importance if it were harnessed only in the cause of putting on display the ways in which the scholarship of a few writers can be used to reach an objective other than the writing of history "as it really was." That last reference is to the oft-cited goal of another student of the papacy, Leopold von Ranke, who also failed to attain his ideal. But von Ranke's work did have the unanticipated benefit of prompting Leo XIII to open the Vatican archives to Ludwig von Pastor and future historians, and thus of achieving results not unlike those which Martin Gilbert in the previous chapter had predicted for the opening of more recent archival deposits.[1] Similarly, there is a significantly beneficial consequence to the preceding examination of the work of David I. Kertzer and others, inasmuch as it can lead to a deeper understanding of the nature of religious institutions as such. In fact, without some kind of practical reformative consequences, much of the previous analysis could be dismissed as merely a purging of mistakes and distortions that happened to mar particular historical narratives, however influential such narratives might have been in some circles.

That the present book is not just intended to set the historical record straight was mentioned in the introduction, was emphasized explicitly in

---

1. It was with regard to the opening of the archives that Leo XIII wrote *Saepenumero considerantes,* the document from which the epigraph at the beginning of this book was excerpted. Now, at the end of this book, it is appropriate to cite his words again: "Rather than an unsubstantiated account there should be comprehensive and complete study; rather than exaggerated declarations there should be thoughtful assertions; rather than wild opinions, there should be factual observations. The first law of history is never dare to lie. The second is never fear to tell the truth."

the first chapter, was referred to several times later,[2] and will be stressed again in this final chapter, which quite necessarily — but also regrettably — is the longest in the entire book. However, I emphasize again that nothing in the present work has been *primarily* about correcting blunders and distortions in this or that particular historical account, regardless of how unexpected or even outrageous they may have been. Nor has it been mainly about refuting serious errors of fact, some of which have been repeated so often they have become stereotypes or popular clichés. For the most part, those mistakes were the surface indicators of a deeper phenomenon having to do with a commitment to reconstructing history for some ideological goal.

Since most of the previous chapters concentrated on David I. Kertzer's work, the initial focus of this chapter will again be on him, specifically on his signature flaw that when putting the papacy into the larger context of European political and social affairs he remained unaware of its necessarily conservative socio-religious structure. This unawareness engendered a perspective in which the controversial or seemingly incomprehensible deeds of those who ruled the church were almost invariably attributed to personal moral failings.[3] While this lent a dramatic note to the narrative, it also resulted in history "as it really wasn't," since the interpretation of personality, if not the mind reading of persons, became the key to understanding past events. For one last instance of this triumph of the therapeutic over historic realities, there is the following account of Pope Clement XIV — who as Cardinal Ganganelli played a posthumous role in the ritual murder trial in Kiev. When this pope loosened restrictions on Jews and his successor reinstated them, Kertzer's explanation is that the latter pope, in this case, Pius VI, was "angered by his predecessor's benign attitude toward the Jews." But there is nothing in Kertzer's narrative to validate that interpretation. All

---

2. "It was the accumulation of these tactics joined to the flood of errors indicated [earlier] that finally led to my decision to examine more closely the entire book. But the tactics and the errors were simply the external indicators of a more profound flaw which appeared to be rooted in some kind of ideological fixation on the papacy" (p. 20, above).

3. As with previous chapters, in the background of this one is Peter Berger's observation about institutions carrying within them "a principle of inertia, perhaps founded ultimately on the hard rock of human stupidity." To that I had added, ". . . and perhaps founded penultimately on the hard rock of human stability." In this final chapter, I would suggest adding another principle — an ancient and more comprehensive one, *omne agens agit propter finem:* "every agent acts on account of [its] goal," meaning that each institution seeks to fulfill its own relatively unique institutional purpose, and everything else — its administrators, its membership, its regulations — is subordinated to that end.

that is known is that Pius restored the regulations that Pope Ganganelli had abrogated.[4]

As exemplified in Kertzer's treatment of the papacy from 1846 to World War II, personal traits, usually exposed by the author's imagined ability to discern the thought processes of the protagonists, were what motivated each individual pope's allegedly anti-Semitic acts or statements. The entire indictment of Pius IX was based on the pathology of an evil man personally avenging himself against the despised Jews — a despisal based on such phantasms as "satanic synagogues" adherence to "sects," and identity as "dogs." This led to Kertzer's conviction that every untoward event that happened to Pio Nono — exile to Gaeta, loss of the Papal States, and loss of Rome — was attributable to the Jews, though Kertzer provided very little historical evidence for this attribution. What was provided is some commonsense evidence that a pope who had embraced liberalism, but found himself driven from his own city and subsequently imprisoned in it by the forces of liberalism, not surprisingly came to abhor that particular ideology.

Under Leo XIII, the scapegoating of Jews was the mission of the Catholic press, which the pope secretly manipulated. Less often did one get the mind reading that accompanied Pius IX's alleged misdeeds, but occasionally the reader did hear such things as, "This time, with God's help, thought the Pope, the same would happen again." It doesn't matter what "the same" is; this author could read minds. And occasionally the reader heard about Leo and his secretary of state thinking that some villain "could be valuable, very valuable,"[5] thus echoing Pio Nono's sinister monologue on how "it was tempting, very tempting" to treat Jews viciously. That latter non-existent declaration, it is worth remembering, concluded with a uniquely racist epithet: "Vilified for centuries, *the Jew* could, if properly conjured up, be used to discredit the forces that had sought to create a modern, secular state." Unlike the historian as "Oprah" in the previous chapter, this is the historian as "Karnac the Magnificent" — as Kertzer waves the sealed envelope in the air and reveals its contents.

---

4. The mention of Ganganelli in the present context evokes the religious principle defined at the beginning of chapter 7. "When institutional survival preoccupies church leaders . . . it often eclipses Gospel teachings such as those set forth in the Sermon on the Mount and the Magnificat — teachings which clearly animated Ganganelli" (pp. 146-47, above). Mere physical survival — as notoriously exemplified by several Renaissance popes — is by definition a contradiction of the ideal goals defined above.

5. This was said of an influential priest, Stanislaw Stojalowski, who ended up "rousing the Catholic peasants against the Jews."

Moreover, in all these instances the popes' motives had little to do with such genuinely historical factors as ancient religious teachings originally formulated to separate a tiny community of breakaway Jews from its parent body. Nor were those motives related to a badly misunderstood story of a Roman crucifixion; nor even, finally, to the carefully prescribed duties of the head of that former tiny community — now evolved into a worldwide organization — to preserve intact all those time-worn teachings that had become formally established doctrines of the church. Rather than recognize these motives, traits, and duties as expressions of the essentially conservative nature of religious institutions, the concerns of the popes were reduced to their personal antagonism toward Jews, an antagonism impelled by hatred, and making use of crafty deceptions. Even Pius XI, although already tainted by Kertzer's manufactured "antipathy," had to be further manipulated into believing in pestilential hordes of Mongolian Jews intent on contaminating good Italian Catholics.

As for Pius XII, Kertzer's personal ideological fixation, along with his need to assert the originality of his own historical project, demanded that this pope be treated not as evil, but merely as negligible. Unlike the turf-guarding in the previous chapter that led to the systematic denigration of Pacelli, Kertzer's brand of self-preservation led to the exact opposite conclusion: "The debate over what Pius XII might have done during the Holocaust is a distraction." Regarding "ideological fixation," the following excerpt from chapter 3 described Kertzer's opinions even before he had begun his book:

> In the February 7, 1998, *New York Times*, shortly after a Vatican announcement that the secret archives of the Inquisition were being opened to scholars, David I. Kertzer in an op-ed piece wrote: "We can learn much from the newly opened archives. The explanation of what made the Holocaust possible is to be found in no small part in the files of the Inquisition. . . ." Since the archives had been closed to Kertzer, and he had never seen the files, the fact that he knew this explanation was to be found in them suggested what it is the purpose of this chapter to determine — either scholarly prescience or unscholarly prejudice.

Given that it was the latter which prevailed, it is no surprise that even if Kertzer had had access to what I described in the first chapter as "one of the most significant papal utterances not only of the twentieth century but of the second millennium of the history of the church" (referring to the story of "Refugee"), one can be certain that because of such prejudice it would never have surfaced in the pages of *The Popes Against the Jews* — even as it did not surface in the writing of any of the Catholic historians mentioned in the previous chapters.

As to why all that took place regarding Kertzer's book, the answer became obvious as the author told his story: this was the only way the people who ruled the church could be villainized, the only way they could be made personally engaged in their unholy war. It bears repetition, Kertzer's thesis would collapse if a given pope's actions were attributable to fidelity to the religious principles of which he was the guardian and spokesman, or to the conviction that Catholicism was the true faith, or to the belief that the Scriptures warranted this or that practice. Such things may be mentioned as elements in the incidental background of the papacy, but it is the resentment or the animus or the innate duplicity of each individual pope that is the real engine of his actions. Only then can he be demeaned as criminal. All this took place, in spite of Kertzer's preemptive assertion at the beginning of *The Popes Against the Jews* that "this is not a book about the battle of good against evil."

The one element of truth in the latter statement is that it is indeed about a battle, but a far more subtle kind of battle than Kertzer ever envisioned. It is a battle, on the one hand, between what I have been calling the religious institution's essentially conservative nature — which has an invaluable role in preserving its foundational principles — and, on the other hand, the new insights, new challenges, and new opportunities presented by a providential history as the institution moves into succeeding eras. That such a history *is* providential explains why the church's future can be discerned by appraising "the signs of the times" (Matt. 16:3), while its past is preserved by "holding fast to what is good" (1 Thess. 5:21). Those two scriptural phrases also illuminate the dialectical relationship between the temptation by rulers to cling with excessive rigidity to the past, and the temptation by the ruled to embrace with excessive enthusiasm the future. This in turn is but an aspect of the more all-embracing and overriding dialectic at play in the relationship between the institution and the individual.[6]

---

6. The newly beatified Cardinal Newman in the last chapter of the *Apologia* treats this relationship in terms of "Authority and Private Judgment." "Every exercise of Infallibility is brought out in act by an intense and varied operation of Reason, both as its ally and as its opponent, and provokes again when it has done its work, a reaction of Reason against it; and, as in a civil polity the State exists and endures by means of the rivalry and collision, the encroachments and defeats of its constituent parts, so in like manner Catholic Christendom is no simple exhibition of religious absolutism, but presents a continuous picture of Author-

Since the focus of Kertzer's book has been almost entirely on the failings of the institutional church, I will in this last chapter view the latter in the light of two other contemporary institutions that also have moral values, traditional roots, and present-day socio-political implications — as well as failings relative to each of those entities. The first of these institutions is of relatively recent origin, and is embodied in the government of the United States. The second is even older than the church itself, Judaism as a faith and a people, which for present purposes can be represented by modern Jewry's most important institutionalized expression, the State of Israel. What follows will provide a brief, moderately conjectural, and avowedly sketchy survey of those two institutions as they may both interact and offer some critical parallels with institutionalized Catholicism in its relations with the larger world. The goal is not only to shed some light on the church, but reciprocally to view those other two largely political institutions in its reflected light.

The first goal of this survey is to determine how any institution founded on noble principles — and few institutions survive that are founded on ignoble ones — can cope with the old heritage that it is partially abandoning as well as with the new phenomena, political, social, and religious, which by their very nature as novel appear to threaten the stability of institutional well-being. The second goal is to determine how such an institution can reconcile past and future, old and new, without losing sight of or abandoning its foundational principles. As to its original heritage, the church, which regarded itself as a rebel movement in relation to the synagogue, gradually began to discredit its parent body, but not to the point of rejecting it entirely, as the heretic Marcion had advocated. Rather, it built upon the teachings of the parent, thus absorbing and fulfilling the latter's doctrine while also ultimately affirming, as at Vatican II, the validity of the more ancient engendering vision. The intellectual collision between those two principles represents "a hard saying," but this is not the first time that mature institutions, whether religious or secular, have had to learn to live with their inner contradictions. For the religious institution, there is at least the foundational promise: *solvitur in excelsis*. Christians learn to live amidst a world of conflicting values where often evil flourishes, knowing that they have not here a lasting city but seek the one that is to come. During this entire process of building on Judaism, the church more or less as a necessary tactic of survival

---

ity and Private Judgment alternately advancing and retreating as the ebb and flow of the tide." Newman on private judgment, i.e., "conscience," will be cited more fully later in this chapter.

also began to shore up the bastions separating it from the novel threatening forces in the surrounding pagan culture.[7]

Unfortunately, the consequence of this preoccupation with past and future, Judaism and paganism, was that the Christian community, and particularly its rulers, became almost entirely focused on those two *relatively* peripheral matters rather than on those at its core — the latter being, in fact, the very principles that led to the creation of the institution in the first place.[8] It is thus not difficult to see how over the decades and then over the centuries, those principles would often come to be paid mere lip service by many Christians, the exceptions being a few determined figures for whom the kernel of their faith, the Beatitudes, was more important than the shell, institutional survival. On the other hand, as the great seventeenth-century reformer St. Francis de Sales said, "it is the shell that preserves the kernel." It is only by recalling and then returning to such core values, usually through the efforts of farsighted reformers, that not only the church but also the parallel "institutions" to be discussed in this chapter — the U.S. government and Judaism as represented by the state of Israel — manage to survive with their essential missions relatively intact.

For the church those core values and foundational principles are also embodied in the Sermon on the Mount's blessings on those who not only "hunger and thirst after justice" but who also "suffer persecution for justice's sake." For the United States those values and principles are based on "the laws of nature and of nature's God," and specify "that all men are created equal" and endowed with "unalienable rights." For the state of Israel, those values and principles as set forth in its own Declaration of Independence are "freedom, justice, and peace as envisaged by the prophets of Israel," and the guarantee of "complete equality of social and political rights . . . irrespective of religion, race, or sex" — the latter is a principle that was put to the test from the very beginning of the nation.

Since the history of the church is so chronologically enormous by contrast to the history of the other two relatively "new" institutions, and since

---

7. See Robert L. Wilken, *The Christians as the Romans Saw Them* (1984), a work that among other insights shows the adaptability and utility of Roman paganism at a time when it was being challenged by its two alien rivals. (Wilken appears to be only partially convinced of the fate of Julian the Apostate — at least as envisioned by the poet Swinburne: "Thou hast conquered, O pale Galilean; the world has grown grey from thy breath.")

8. Again, I cite the following from chapter 7: "When institutional survival preoccupies church leaders . . . it often eclipses Gospel teachings such as those set forth in the Sermon on the Mount" (p. 147, above).

all the previous discussion was focused on "the Vatican's role in modern anti-Semitism," this chapter starts with the final event in *The Popes Against the Jews,* and traces it back to its earliest sources in the first millennium of what is now called the common era. The reader will recall Kertzer's last chapter designating the Vatican as the antechamber to the Holocaust, and his explicit conclusion that the papacy — already "crucial" to the rise of modern racist anti-Semitism — bore the burden of guilt for the deportation and murder of a thousand Roman Jews, a guilt that by extrapolation made it not merely a bystander but virtually a participant in the deportation and murder of the six million. The implicit thesis was that without the church, there would have been no genocide; or, in the ironic language of Marc Saperstein's previously cited review of Kertzer, "no *Civiltà cattolica,* no Holocaust" — a thesis that is not only historically untenable but one that also plays havoc with the essential distinction between sufficient and necessary causality. The unfortunate outcome of Kertzer's view is that the victims of the Nazi death machine were not just collateral damage in the papal "unholy war," they were its targets.

As the preceding chapters of this book have acknowledged, Christianity was undeniably the seed bed in which modern racist anti-Semitism grew and flourished. In that sense the "war" had already begun in the second century with an interpretation of stories in the Gospels identifying the Jews as Christ-killers, and, on the Jewish side, with an interpretation of Jesus as the leader of a threatening heretical sect.[9] In the first two centuries of the Common Era when both Torah and Gospel were more or less equally contemned by the governing authorities, the antagonism between the two groups, however vigorous in reciprocal denunciations, was relatively unimportant to society at large. What was more important to that larger world was the relationship of Judaism and its spawn, Christianity, to the prevailing religion of the empire. In the second and third centuries, Christianity by adhering to its foundational message of the Beatitudes began its expansion particularly among women, the poor, and the enslaved, until it became such a presence in society that finally in the fourth century the church's beliefs were embraced by the ruling class with the conversion of Constantine — an event that still remains historically inexplicable. One unfortunate consequence of this embrace was that it allowed leading

9. What follows is so abridged that to describe it as approximating history "as it really was" would be akin to describing Griech-Polelle's *Bishop von Galen* as written "with authority not only in history but also in theology," and as knowledgeable about "the inner workings of the Church."

churchmen to broaden and intensify their accusations against the Jews and Judaism until such accusations became a new way of thinking and a new genre of writing — known to history as *adversus Iudaeos*.[10]

The central theme of the latter was that the Jews as a people and a nation were to be penalized for the death of Jesus and for misreading their own Scripture. As punishment they had been dispersed throughout the world where their only mission was to bear witness to the triumph of Christianity. It was on the latter ground alone that their existence, if not their equality, could be tolerated. The "Jew as witness" was a notion that survived with varying practical consequences, though inevitably negative for Jews, from the time of St. John Chrysostom, through that of St. Augustine, and on into the twentieth century — as noted in the preceding chapter, up to and including theologians like Dietrich Bonhoeffer.[11] This tradition led to active and

10. The pioneering and still indispensable study is Rosemary Ruether's *Faith and Fratricide: The Theological Roots of Anti-Semitism,* which I published in 1974. That latter seemingly redundant clause is significant because over the next two decades we would be at loggerheads regarding the Israeli-Palestinian conflict. This disagreement was given its fullest expression in the first issue of the second series of *Continuum* (Autumn 1990), titled "Anti-Semitism, Middle East, Feminism." In addition to several generally sympathetic treatments of the Israeli position (including a lengthy editorial), the issue contained a symposium on *The Wrath of Jonah: The Crisis of Religious Nationalism in the Israeli-Palestinian Conflict* (1989) by Rosemary Ruether and Herman J. Ruether with nine critiques of the book. In the next issue I published, as a simple matter of comity, Rosemary Ruether's letter in which she accused her critics of participating in "the ongoing ethnocide of the Palestinian people," an observation to which I also replied. That was over two decades ago, and by the early years of the present decade it was becoming clear that she had been nearer to the correct moral position than had I or her other critics.

As previously noted, all issues of *Continuum* can be accessed on the web at http://search.Ebscohost.com. As a matter of the historical record, this is owed to the manager for acquisitions at the American Theological Library Association, whose persistence overcame the opposition to the digitization by the St. Xavier University administration: President Judith Dwyer; Vice President Francis S. Tebbe, OFM, and Mark A. Vargas, Library Director, who in the name of St. Xavier University claimed ownership of the journal, although each issue clearly stated, "© Copyright Justus George Lawler."

11. For St. Augustine, see Paula Fredriksen, *Augustine and the Jews: A Christian Defense of Jews and Judaism* (2008). For Bonhoeffer, see Stephen R. Haynes, *The Bonhoeffer Phenomenon: Portraits of a Protestant Saint* (2004). I reintroduce Bonhoeffer only because of his unquestionably noble character, his heroic life, and his theologically advanced vision. Yet even he could not shed the traditional theological view of Jews as the witness people. Such fidelity to tradition is another aspect of the essentially conservative nature of institutionalized religion — a conservatism that regarding the Jews would be modified only by the horrors of the Holocaust.

increasing persecution of Jews, so that by the first millennium, particularly at the time of the Crusades, it had resulted in several mass killings. The only thing that can be retrieved from this tradition — which Paula Fredriksen cites as a faintly redemptive consequence — is that when Crusades were being preached and Jews were being threatened with murder, there was some safety to be found in the assertion of churchmen like St. Bernard that "a far better triumph for the Church [is] to convince and convert the Jews than to put them to the sword."

Nor does the presence of a counter-adversarial tradition within Judaism itself provide any justification. That tradition, represented by the Babylonian Talmud of the seventh century, made its way gradually into Europe after the Second Crusade. According to its latest chronicler, Peter Schafer (*Jesus in the Talmud*, 2009), its parody of New Testament stories "ridiculed Jesus' birth from a virgin, as maintained by the Gospels of Matthew and Luke, and they [the rabbis of Babylonia] contest fervently the claim that Jesus is the Messiah and the Son of God." Schafer went on to discuss the aggressiveness of these Talmudic scholars who, rather than denying the story of the crucifixion with its proclamation of Jewish guilt as Christ-killers, instead embraced it wholeheartedly. "Yes, they maintain, we accept responsibility for it, but there is no reason to feel ashamed because we rightfully executed a blasphemer and idolater."[12] One consequence of this was to provide more ammunition to promoters of Jew hatred in the centuries to come when the Talmud was viewed by Catholics as a manual for the practice of sorcery. Ironically, that accusation doubled back on itself, since in the Talmud Jesus was put to death for the crime of magic. In both instances each rival confessional body was losing sight of its foundational principles and getting drawn into major conflicts over relatively minor matters. Unfortunately for the older body, the culmination of hatred against it led in the year 1242 to a mass burning of thousands of "Talmudic" books in Paris — funeral pyres that would be repeated in sixteenth-century Venice and Rome, and which presaged those of the Nazis centuries later.

The above is not a particularly uplifting note on which to end this brief sketch of "Catholic-Jewish relations" around the end of the first millennium of the common era, a period encompassing much of what used to be called "the Dark Ages." But even that expression gave rise to what *Popes and Politics* called "cautious optimism" — at least regarding Catholicism:

12. This was the Talmudic tradition that was perversely, and unsuccessfully, introduced into the testimony at the ritual murder trial of Mendel Beilis described in chapter 6.

Any reading of history, even by the most bigoted anti-Catholic or anti-Romanist, makes clear that the state of the present church is purer than the church at the end of the Dark Ages, purer than during the Babylonian Captivity, purer than during the high Renaissance, purer than during the reign of Pius IX. And even the most prejudiced historian would have to say that the evils embodied in the church have been less apparent as each new age dawned, so that what would have been tolerated during the reign of Leo X would have been abominated during the reign of Pius IX, and what was tolerated during the reign of Pius IX was in fact abominated by John XXIII.

Concerning the last named pope, he is both a hero and an exception. But the reform of Catholicism from Leo XIII on is an exception; its reform from the Council of Trent on is an exception; its reform from the Council of Constance on is an exception; its reform from Hildebrand on is an exception. Ultimately, the Incarnation is an exception, history is an exception. Spirit emerging out of the primordial planetary mass is an exception.

As for that pejorative term, "Dark Ages," at least it augured a transition to what has come to be called "the Enlightenment," a cultural illumination that was preceded by the conflicts of the Reformation and the subsequent wars of religion that engendered in the eighteenth century such burgeoning political-social tenets as the separation of church and state, the decrees of toleration for other religions, and the primacy of individual conscience, partially rooted in Luther's doctrine of private judgment. These novel trends found their political expression in the American Revolution, the Kosciusziko Uprising, and the French Revolution, followed by the Napoleonic reforms with which David I. Kertzer's *The Popes Against the Jews* had begun. All of these revolutions and uprisings represented also a slow and gradual alleviation of social, cultural, and religious prejudices against Jews.

And just as it was "a few popes and many saints" in that earlier dark period who preserved the message of the Sermon on the Mount, it was the founders of new religious orders and institutes dedicated to teaching, to nursing, and to sheltering the poor in the seventeenth and eighteenth centuries who represented the Beatitudes in action, and who prepared the way for the doctrines of social justice enunciated first by Leo XIII, and then commemorated and amplified by all his successors from Pius XI on. Similarly, those same sainted founders, preeminently Francis de Sales and Jeanne-Françoise de Chantal, fostered the cultivation of the interior life and mystical experience along with the denigration of rationalism — the latter abetted by cul-

tural romanticism — which in the event planted the seeds for that enlarge-
ment of the scope of Catholic thought known as Modernism.[13] The latter
much maligned movement, or rather *"Tendenz,"* was at the root of much of
the theology of the second Vatican Council, which — in addition to formally
and definitively moving Christian thought from an *adversus Iudaeos* orientation to one that was definitively *pro Iudaeis* — also brought the institutional
church into line with much of the Enlightenment tradition. That tradition,
particularly in its Anglophone expression, had also been shaped by those
same Judeo-Christian biblical values that affirmed the unique importance of
the human person, including persons not of one's own family or tribe.[14]

But before looking at the decrees of Vatican II, their anticipation by
popes who have been specifically demeaned by Kertzer — as well as by the
historians named in the previous chapter — must be briefly considered. An
appropriate context for that consideration is one of the break-through documents of the twentieth century, the "Universal Declaration of Human
Rights" made by the newly created United Nations in the same year, 1948,
that the state of Israel was established. The Declaration reflected the language of Pius XII's 1941 Pentecost address, invoking "the inviolable rights of
man," and was specifically singled out for praise in 1963 by John XXIII's encyclical *Pacem in Terris:*

> In the most solemn form, the dignity of a human person is acknowledged
> to all human beings; and as a consequence there is proclaimed, as a funda-
> mental right, the right of every man freely to investigate the truth and to
> follow the norms of moral good and justice, and also the right to a life
> worthy of man's dignity.

Even more immediately relevant in the present context is the fact that the
ancestral text for both popes' affirmation of human rights was Leo XIII's
1891 encyclical, *Rerum Novarum,* a document that explicitly addressed the

---

13. On this specific theme in the growing mass of literature on Modernism, see *Modernists & Mystics* (2009), edited by the previously cited C. J. T. Talar.

14. The term "Anglophone" is intended to modulate this reference to the Enlightenment tradition. The latter, as mentioned in chapter 2, was often tainted by the kind of anti-
Semitism described by Arthur Hertzberg in *The French Enlightenment and the Jews* (1990).
On the other hand, though certainly to a lesser degree, the Anglophone tradition itself was
often tainted by the kind of anti-Christian mentality displayed by Edward Gibbon in *The
Decline and Fall of the Roman Empire,* and by Thomas Hobbes in *Leviathan,* where the papacy was defined as "the ghost of the deceased Roman Empire."

rights of workers. Through *Rerum Novarum* — in the words of Pius XI's fortieth-anniversary commemoration of it — Leo XIII "taught the whole human family to strike out upon new paths to solve the social crisis." (Leo happens also to be the pope who in Kertzer's narrative plotted with his secretary of state to have Jews persecuted for ritual murder, while Pius XI was the pope who had fostered exterminationist priests in Poland.)

When Vatican II set forth on those new paths, it was primarily in two decrees, *Dignitatis Humanae* on religious liberty, and *Nostra Aetate* on the corollary teaching against racial, religious, and gender discrimination. Concerning the first document, the same popes whom Kertzer denigrated are again encountered. Peter Hebblethwaite, in his previously cited *Paul VI: The First Modern Pope,* tells of a private meeting between the pope and the American theologian John Courtney Murray, the architect of *Dignitatis Humanae.* When Murray spelled out the papal sources of the proposed decree, he mentioned the pope whose efforts, according to Kertzer, were "crucial to the rise of modern racist anti-Semitism," and the pope who, also according to Kertzer, was "eager to repair relations with Hitler":

> The roots of the doctrine are in Leo XIII — in his doctrine on the two orders of human life, and in his emphasis on the freedom of the Church as the cardinal principle governing the relations of the Church to the temporal order. The more proximate roots are in Pius XII, in his doctrine on the human person as subject and goal of the whole social order by which he [Pius] transcended the more ethical doctrine of Leo XIII, derived from Aristotle ultimately, on the society-state. The line of development is clear.[15]

The heritage of those two disdained popes was even more evident in *Nostra Aetate,* where the marriage of Enlightenment rights and Judeo-Christian personalism was solemnized and blessed — as the italics below highlight in the official (though gender-laden) language of the document:

> Furthermore, in her rejection of every persecution against any man, the Church, mindful of the patrimony she shares with the Jews and moved not by political reasons but by *the Gospel's spiritual love,* decries hatred, persecutions, displays of anti-Semitism, directed against Jews at any time and by anyone. We cannot truly call on God, the Father of all, if we refuse

---

15. *Paul VI: The First Modern Pope* (1993).

to treat in a brotherly way any man, created as he is in the image of God. Man's relation to God the Father and his relation to men his brothers are so linked together that Scripture says: "He who does not love does not know God" (1 John 4:8). . . .

No foundation therefore remains for any theory or practice that leads to discrimination between man and man or people and people, so far as their human dignity and the rights flowing from it are concerned. The Church reproves, as foreign to the mind of Christ, any discrimination or harassment of them because of their race, color, *condition of life,* or religion [*stirpis vel coloris, condicionis vel religionis causa factam*].

"Condition of life," which I have here italicized, relates not only to social and economic status but also to what a post-conciliar world would call "sexual orientation" — although, ironically, that world would exclude Catholics. Thus *Nostra Aetate,* with its parallel emphasis on "rights," can be invoked not only as a revolutionary document on the two-millennial prejudice against Jews, but also as such a document regarding the even more ancient prejudice against homosexuals — particularly as the latter was conceived and expressed in the Hebrew Bible, and as it is now ecclesiastically enforced, particularly in the United States, by a Catholic hierarchy blind not merely to human rights, not merely to gay rights, but blind also to the all-encompassing document *Gaudium et Spes.* (This regnant myopia will be examined presently.)

Overlooked in the United Nations' eloquent declaration of a truly catholic commonality are historical facts that are still part of the living memory of people throughout the world. Here I turn again to the pope originally described with patent contempt by Kertzer as the man who wouldn't deign to use the word "Jew" even though, as noted in the previous chapter, it appeared in his first encyclical. I am referring, of course, to that "symbolic" anti-Semite, Pius XII, who through an unprecedented accident of history — as well as the misplaced guilt of many Catholic academics — has for more than half a century carried the entire burden of the *adversus Iudaeos* heritage. That accident, it should now go without saying, was Rolf Hochhuth's play, *The Deputy,* a work that was best denominated not by the English translation of the German title *Der Stellvertreter,* but by the French *Le Vicaire,* making more explicit the reference, first, to the pope's traditional title, "Vicar of Christ," and, second, to his designation as *vicarious* bearer of the sins of the Holocaust — with the untraditional title, "Scapegoat."

Among the historical facts to which I earlier referred are, first, that the council convened by John XXIII had been originally conceived by his predecessor who in 1948 had actually established five preparatory commissions and consulted scores of bishops — to no avail, since it was too soon after the upheaval of war. Not only was it Pius who had made Roncalli a cardinal, but it was he who had also appointed the overwhelming majority of the Council's delegates.[16] Second, there is the fact, foreshadowed in the quotation above from John Courtney Murray, that Pius XII was himself the most quoted authority in the Council's declarations. The third entails another paradox in that the credibility attached to Hochhuth's ill-wrought plot — a pope by the mere nature of his office successfully opposing a murderous regime and saving millions of lives — stemmed from the growing awareness of the worldwide influence and prestige of the church, displayed particularly (as rhetorical paradox became historical irony) in the closing years of that same pope's reign.[17]

I have previously quoted in these pages the judgment of John Lukacs that no pope in the modern era had been so esteemed and admired, both in and out of the Catholic world, as in the last decade of his reign was Pius XII — now by a whim of fate, plus the resentment of disgruntled Catholics and the anguish of perplexed Jews, viewed as a collaborator with Hitler.[18] Fortunately, the fact that preparations for the Council were begun four years before the *hallucination publicitaire* engendered by *The Deputy* meant that the Hochhuth phenomenon had no impact on its most important decrees, those on religious freedom and anti-Semitism — regardless of how damaging that phenomenon was to the subsequent reputation of the pope.[19] Though Hochhuth's plot was clumsy, his timing was unerring. The Eichmann trial and execution (1961-62) had brought the Holocaust back to the attention of

16. As for the significance of Pope Pacelli's appointments, one need only imagine the membership of a council convened any time in the past two decades. For a brief summary of the other matters, see Francis J. Weber, "Pope Pius XII and the Vatican Council," *The American Benedictine Review* (September 1970). For a firsthand and first-rate treatment of the similarities of the two popes, see the previously cited Kenneth L. Woodward, *Making Saints,* "The Blending of Two Pontificates."

17. That prestige and influence also came to a concerted public climax — front-page headlines in the major newspapers of the West — with the opening of the Council (October 11, 1962), an event that occurred four months before the opening of the play, thus making even more creditable to its viewers and (more important) to its reviewers the prestige, power, and authority of the papacy. Certainly, the leader of an institution with such worldwide influence could have put a stop to — or at least diminished — the mass murder of Jews.

18. John Lukacs, "The Roots of the Dilemma," *Continuum* (Summer 1964).

19. In the posthumously published two volumes and 1,200 pages of Yves Congar's *Mon Journal du Concile* (2002), there is a passing mention of Hochhuth in one sentence.

a world grown increasingly baffled by the sheer incomprehensibility of the genocide. Furthermore, the failure of leaders like Winston Churchill and Franklin Roosevelt — who unlike the pope wielded power beyond that of mere speech — was eclipsed by their stature as heroic victors in the war. Lastly, the superstitious aura attached to the age-old biblical scapegoat as well as to its modern post-Holocaust instantiation made almost predetermined the selection of the vicar of Christ as the figure who must be "bruised for the iniquities" of a shattered humankind. Etymologically, as we have seen, the meaning of the word "vicar" is one who vicariously acts for others.

That such a bruising is not a burden to be lightly borne is apparent from this vignette from Primo Levi's 1985 novel, *If not Now, When?* I cite that novel here both because it has echoes of the story of "Refugee" — shortly to be told in its entirety — and because it prepares for Levi himself to be regarded as an institutional "reformer" of Israel later in this chapter. The broader subject of the novel is a band of Jewish Partisans in Belarus, much like the group around the Bielski brothers in Poland — immortalized in the 1993 book *Defiance,* by Nechama Tec (in the preceding chapter paired with Gordon Zahn) — who evaded both Russians and Germans in an effort to save their fellow Jews. The band is joined by Mendel, the novel's protagonist, who with a few other escapees is trying to make his way through the war-torn countryside to reach Italy, and from there embark for Palestine — a journey if not a destination similar to that of Levi himself after being liberated by sheer good fortune from Auschwitz. (And a journey and a destination similar to that of "Refugee.") Here Mendel, who later will be seen as a harbinger of Israel's relationship to the Palestinians, considers his destiny:

> Once, on Yom Kippur, the Day of Atonement, the Jews used to take a goat, the priest would press his hands on its head, list all the sins committed by the people, and impose them on the animal: he and he alone was guilty. Then, laden with sins he hadn't committed, the goat was sent into the desert. This is how the gentiles think, too; they also have a lamb that takes away the sins of the world. But not I, I don't believe that. If I've sinned, I bear the burden of my sins, but only those, and have more than enough. I don't bear the sins of anybody else.

Since that lamb referred originally to Jesus, it is not surprising that Hochhuth, a lapsed Lutheran, would have identified the "deputy" or "vicar" of Jesus as the man who failed to embrace his own sacrifice for the betterment of humankind.

As for the council, what it did manage to achieve, particularly by *Nostra Aetate,* was to guarantee that the hatred that stemmed from the ancient effort to differentiate the young Jesus community from its parent body — begetting that long-lived and baleful *adversus Iudaeos* tradition — could no longer find a theological sanction in Catholic thought, word, or deed. As previously noted, in that long process of differentiation, elements extrinsic to the mission of Jesus gained the ascendency. The adherents of the parent body were attacked, villainized, and finally demonized, while the self-designated protectors of that mission, the popes, more and more viewed such attacks as merely incidental to the well-being of the larger institution. In effect, those popes were affirming that their paramount object was to protect the institutional church at all costs, even if that meant subordinating some of its fundamental principles to that hoped-for survival. Regardless of the price that must be paid, *to save the church* became the overriding goal.

It is difficult to see how one can shed light on an institution as unique and as ancient as the church by drawing a comparison with any other present-day institution, much less with one that is totally secular and of relatively recent origin. But that is precisely the parallel that emerges from the words that echo the brief italicized phrase above — words by the man who would be the preeminent head of that institution, and, moreover, who has been regarded as the most noble-minded of all its leaders, Abraham Lincoln. In a now famous letter to Horace Greeley, Lincoln wrote:

> My paramount object in this struggle is to *save the Union,* and is not either to save or destroy slavery. If I could *save the Union* without freeing any slaves, I would do it, and if I could save it by freeing all the slaves I would do it; and if I could save it by freeing some and leaving others alone I would also do that. (italics supplied)

This sounds as brutally calloused as did the words of the churchmen who engaged in the polemical slanders integral to the *adversus Iudaeos* tradition. The statement is particularly shocking when one recalls that the third option, "saving some and leaving others alone," is exactly what Lincoln adopted. In the Emancipation Proclamation, thousands of slaves in non-Confederate areas were deliberately excluded, and were in effect knowingly condemned by this unquestionably humane leader to continue in a state of chattel.[20]

---

20. "All this occurred in regions where the Union government was in control. Unpunished were such crimes — in fact such deeds were not even recognized as criminal — as the

Defenders of Lincoln parse the letter to Greeley with all the diligence biblical exegetes devote to explicating "texts of terror," including not only those in the Christian Testament that gave birth to the religious anti-Jewish tradition, but also those in the Hebrew Testament that gave birth to the religious pro-slavery tradition. The major difference is that Lincoln was writing a century and a half ago about people living in North America, while the biblical texts relate to times and peoples lost in the shadows of antiquity. The Bible obviously raises issues beyond the scope of the present discussion, but what is significant here is that no matter how much ingenuity is brought to bear on Lincoln's words, they cannot obliterate the fact that this most justly admired of leaders was less concerned with the fate of millions of inhumanely treated people than with the preservation of a relatively novel political system, much as the churchmen described above were indifferent to Jewish suffering because they believed it helped to "save" the all-important ecclesiastical institution. Lastly, and to be examined here shortly, there are the heirs of those suffering Jews, some of whom are unquestionably in positions of authority in Israel, and who are now striving to reconcile the politics, culture, and realities of the Middle East with the biblical claims to a Promised Land. For obvious reasons, this latter is the most difficult subject of all, since unlike Christian anti-Semitism or American slavery — the essential elements of which relate primarily to events of the past — the issues relative to Palestine come up against present-day concrete realities having to do with the fate of millions of living people.

But first the Lincoln parallel must be pursued more thoroughly, particularly because the popular view of the president is that he emphatically believed that all people "are created equal" and should therefore live in a state of equality with one another.[21] Strangely, and certainly unfortunately, the consensus of non-ideologically motivated Lincoln scholars says otherwise. Here it is voiced by Eric Foner who, after noting that Lincoln's personal feelings were of opposition to slavery as such, observed that he "did not share the abolitionist conviction that the moral issue of slavery overrode all others. Lincoln, as he explained to his Kentucky friend Joshua Speed, was

---

continuing dissolution of slave families, the selling of slave children, the unpunished rape of slave women, and on and on." See "Proclamation v. Reprisal" in *Popes and Politics* where the Lincoln parallel is introduced.

21. Such is the riddle (or the muddle) of Lincoln scholarship that there are two recent books that take clearly opposing positions regarding his attitude to slavery. Richard Striner's *Father Abraham: Lincoln's Relentless Struggle to End Slavery* (2006), and Michael Lind's *What Lincoln Believed: The Values and Convictions of America's Greatest President* (2005).

willing to 'crucify [his] feelings' out of 'loyalty to the Constitution and the Union.'" Foner also noted that Lincoln maintained he had never been in favor "of qualifying them [Negroes] to hold office, nor to intermarry with white people."[22]

Some broader questions raised in the context of such views are, first, whether institutions other than civil polities — for example, the church — would be allowed the exemption from the "opinions of mankind" these utterances reflect; and, second, whether there were people in Lincoln's time who accused the "Great Emancipator" of being an antiblack racist, as a host of writers have brought the accusation of anti-Semitic racism against the "Holy Father" — more specifically, all those waffling scholars who accuse him of being a symbolic anti-Semite. One of the more damaging indicators of racism on the part of Lincoln — damaging, particularly in the present context of this political-religious parallel between the two institutions — was that he accepted the notion that deportation and colonization could be a way to resolve the dilemma of slavery.

Just as Pius XII allegedly rationalized his silence in the name of a religious higher good, so did Lincoln and his supporters, not allegedly but factually, rationalize their views on the deportation of black slaves to distant work camps. Garry Wills views Lincoln's adoption of the colonization project as due to the influence of Henry Clay. But regardless of source or influence, the language and even more the all-justifying rationale were clearly religious — although religious in a way that might well have embarrassed a Scholastic casuist or a Spanish inquisitor:

> Lincoln singled out Clay's promotion of the colonization of freed blacks as his greatest contribution to political thought. It was what excused the fact that Clay still held slaves — he was only holding them until they could be sent out of the country. Clay said that freed blacks would carry back to Africa the Christianity and civilization they had acquired here. Lincoln quotes with admiration Clay's words: "May it not be one of the great designs of the Ruler of the universe (whose ways are often inscrutable by shortsighted mortals) thus to transform an original crime, into a

22. "Our Lincoln," *The Nation,* January 26, 2009. One distinguished American historian, James M. McPherson, writing about another distinguished historian, George M. Fredrickson, observes that the latter "rightly maintained that Lincoln always considered perpetuation of the Union more important than the abolition of slavery." "The Historian Who Saw Through America," *The New York Review of Books,* December 4, 2008.

signal blessing to that most unfortunate portion of the globe." Lincoln fervently endorsed this dream.[23]

The fruits of this self-vindicating dream have been on display for over a century — up to the very present — in the history of the country that is ironically still called Liberia. One may also note that all this is rationalized as done for the well-being of the victims. It is probably unknown whether Madagascar was another of the venues envisioned for future North American black "colonists," as it would be envisioned in the next century for the Jews of Germany.

Another "institutional" parallel is that Lincoln did not believe full citizenship should be extended to all blacks, particularly as this related to voting rights. Rather, the latter would be reserved for a few reliable and pliable former slaves — an arrangement not entirely unlike the exceptions to Italy's racial laws that the Holy See sought for baptized Jews. The anti-Semitic prejudice was influenced mainly by teachings in the New Testament, the anti-Negro prejudice mainly by those in the Old. As to the overall historical record, one would be hard pressed to decide which Scripture, the Jewish or the Christian, has had a more devastating — as well as, *pari passu*, a more beneficial — consequence for humankind.

Since this entire chapter, and much of this entire book, has been based on what since Plutarch have been called parallel lives, it is worth noting here that while the argument that Lincoln was tainted by the anti-Negro racism of the period is made by almost all historians, the argument from the "silence" of Pius XII to the conclusion that he was an anti-Semite is based on unalloyed ideological prejudice — most emphatically, though not exclusively, displayed by John Cornwell. As for Lincoln, the near unanimity is based on a record of public statements that are incontrovertible and that, in sum, reflect a willingness to sacrifice the freedom of slaves in non-Confederate territory for the survival of a national polity that had been in existence for less than a century. It is also to be noted that Lincoln's utter certitude about the necessity of his program for slaves represented the kind of mentality that is ordinarily identified with religious faith, possibly even with the kind of blind faith allegedly exemplified by Pius XII. Even more damaging is the president's invocation of religious imagery to express his dubious

---

23. "Lincoln's Black History," *The New York Review of Books*, June 11, 2009. Wills is summarizing and quoting material from *Lincoln on Race and Slavery*, edited and with an introduction by Henry Louis Gates Jr. and co-edited by Donald Yacovone (2009).

vision: he would "crucify his feelings" out of loyalty to the Union and would colonize Africa in the name of "Christianity and civilization."

Lastly, there are the present-day reputations of the president and the pope. The latter, who had been the object of adulation when alive, was almost universally disdained if not contemned through the influence of Hochhuth's dramaturgical depiction, a depiction that is now widely recognized as not merely inaccurate but as a caricature. It was not Hochhuth's Schillerian artistry that won acclaim for what he touted as his "Christian drama," it was two decades of frustration among researchers and the populace in general at having in effect traversed the byways of academic scholarship and journalistic speculation, only to end up back once more in the same blind alley of uncertainty about the "how" of the genocide, about how it could even have been allowed to happen. The professors, the reporters, and the public eagerly applauded a drama in which beefy red-faced prelates — *ganz rund, ganz rot* — were rendering obeisance to the ticker-tape preoccupied supreme pontiff who was so obviously bored with hearing about all those mass murders in the East.

Similarly, with the American president, whose ever-growing image as the Great Emancipator was drastically smirched by depictions of him as every white bigot's favorite president. This transformation is described in Merrill D. Peterson's *Lincoln in American Memory* (1995), where the most dramatically persuasive presentation of Lincoln was owed to one Thomas Dixon, a KKK clergyman, whose best-selling books in the first two decades of the twentieth century advocated total segregation of the races, and/or the deportation of blacks. All of this occurred in the name, and often in the words, of the assassinated leader. Peterson also notes that the celebrated film director D. W. Griffith "saw eye to eye with Dixon. He, too, loved Lincoln and hated the Negro." The consequence was Griffith's adaptation of Dixon's *The Clansman* for the screen in 1915, resulting in the film *The Birth of a Nation,* which broke all records for attendance by movie viewers — not entirely unlike the record-breaking attendance at the first performances of Hochhuth's drama. In 1998, *The Birth of a Nation* was adjudged by the American Film Institute to be one of the hundred "top films" of all time. The film version of Hochhuth's play, directed by Costa Gavras and titled *Amen,* came out in 2002 — unfortunately for piophobes, too late to make the cut. For reasons on which one can only speculate, the reputation of the pope as an anti-Semite — which he provably was not — is now an *idée fixe,* at least in the Anglophone world, while the reputation of Lincoln as a less than enthusiastic liberator of slaves — which he clearly was — has had little impact on his gleaming image in the nation or in the world at large.

The first lesson of these institutional parallels is that the fate of such leaders is less significant than the fate of what they led. The second lesson, and the one described in the previous treatment of Jews and Christians, is that such a fate depends primarily on reliance on the foundational principles of the institution, whether civil or religious, as the surest guide not merely to surmounting the apparent inadequacies of individual leaders but also to re-forming and revivifying the institutions themselves. The flowering of church reform that burst forth at Vatican II was the result of seeds planted originally by the primordial texts of Christianity, particularly in the Gospels, and more particularly in the Sermon on the Mount. It is not surprising that the most far-reaching document of the Council, *Gaudium et Spes,* began by invoking that Sermon. "The joys and hopes, the grief and anguish of the people of our time, especially of those who are poor or afflicted, are the joys and hopes, the grief and anguish of the followers of Christ as well."

Here, it must again be emphasized that among "the afflicted," the most contemned are those whose sexual orientation now separates them from the hierarchical leaders of the "followers of Christ."[24] Moreover, it is those same leaders who by ceaseless rebuffs and condemnations have themselves become the cause of grief and anguish. To convert such leaders, one shouldn't have to invoke the truism that these disdained followers have their counterparts in every species known to science; nor should one have to invoke the additional truism that they have their counterparts within the human species among saints as well as among popes and bishops. Rather, to convert those leaders it should be enough that they truly embrace the message of the Beatitudes. Instead, what the world witnessed was, first, an episcopate that over a period of nearly three decades couldn't get its house in order to treat the scandal of the sexual abuse of minors efficiently and honestly,[25] and, sec-

24. This is the hierarchy referred to earlier as "blind not merely to human rights, not merely to gay rights, but blind also to the all-encompassing document, *Gaudium et Spes.*"

As a first step in healing this regnant myopia, these leaders might attend to the goals and the achievement of such lay Catholic organizations as Call to Action, DignityUSA, Fortunate Families, and New Ways Ministry. As will be shown presently, this would not be the first time in history when the "church teaching" was enlightened and, in fact, saved from serious error by the "church taught."

25. Among the rare exceptions to that indictment is Joseph P. Chinnici, not a bishop but the head of the West Coast province of the Franciscans when the crisis broke. His story of confronting the abuse by combining the traditions of his religious order with Christian

ond, an episcopate that now appears to be trying to obscure that failure by its vehemence in denouncing everything that pertains to homosexuality — as though there were any correlation between it and clerical molestation.

As I write, *The New York Times* (February 15, 2011) has an editorial titled, "More Shame," where among other things one may read:

> The Roman Catholic hierarchy in this country has promised accountability and justice for children sexually abused by priests. A new inquiry has found that nearly a decade after the scandal engulfed the American church children are still in peril and some leaders are still stonewalling investigations.
>
> A grand jury report released Feb. 10 accused three priests and a teacher in the Philadelphia Archdiocese of raping two young boys in the 1990s. It also accused a senior church official of knowingly endangering thousands of children by shielding accused priests for years. . . . Monsignor Lynn was secretary of the clergy under retired Cardinal Anthony Bevilacqua, responsible for investigating abuse allegations from 1992 to 2004. Instead, according to the grand jury, he shuffled credibly accused priests among unsuspecting parishes, putting "literally thousands of children at risk of sexual abuse."

The editorial went on to mention that "at least three dozen accused priests remain in active ministry," and it quoted a "blistering grand jury report in 2005 [exposing] the abuse of hundreds of children by more than 60 archdiocesan priests."

So, what will the response to this "new" information be? Certainly, it is fairly predictable that it will not differ much from the response when "the scandal engulfed the American church" a decade or so earlier. What it did then was look for a scapegoat, and the discoverer of such a sacrificial victim was the aforementioned Cardinal — and his emulators.

> In the last several weeks, one American cardinal, Anthony Bevilacqua of Philadelphia, said that homosexuals are not suited for the priesthood, even if they have never committed a homosexual act. Pope John Paul II's press secretary, Joaquin Navarro-Valls, was quoted as saying that not only

---

compassion and candor is told in *When Values Collide: The Catholic Church, Sexual Abuse and the Challenges of Leadership* (2010). It is a narrative that should be mandatory reading at annual meetings of the United States Conference of Catholic Bishops.

should homosexuals not be ordained, but that the church should consider removing homosexuals who have already been ordained. The Most Rev. Wilton D. Gregory, bishop of Belleville, Ill., president of the U.S. Conference of Catholic Bishops, spoke of "an ongoing struggle to make sure that the Catholic priesthood is not dominated by homosexual men." And Archbishop Julian Herranz, head of the Pontifical Council for the Interpretation of Legislative Texts, described pedophilia as a "concrete form of homosexuality." Cardinal James Stafford, the former archbishop of Denver who is now assigned to the Vatican as president of the Pontifical Council for the Laity said it was a misnomer to call the U.S. church's crisis a pedophilia scandal. "I think it's more of an acting out homosexually," he said.[26]

The mean-spiritedness of this representative sample of views remains a scandal that redounds to the dishonor of the entire American church. For even those bishops who might deviate from the official line, rather than speaking in their own voices, have also become zealous regarding these kinds of decisions by their Roman masters. As for the latter, their own views are tainted by primitive patriarchal biblical taboos regarding gender and sexuality — and here I would recommend to the reader a return to the treatment of "collective derangement" in the annex to the previous chapter.[27] However, since that also refers primarily to the domain of religion and the supernatural, what is even more to be recommended before invoking that domain is serious reflection on "the natural" as such, particularly as it has been defined by the Enlightenment tradition that proclaimed as self-evident that everyone is endowed by the Creator with an inalienable right to the pursuit of happiness. That being acknowledged, it is clear that what everyone is also

26. Larry B. Stammer, "Gay Priests Say It's Harder Now to Tell the Truth," *Los Angeles Times,* May 22, 2002.

27. The original context for the quoted phrase was the tradition of anti-Semitism founded on the Patristic *adversus Iudaeos* writings. The rejection of the teaching at the postwar Vatican Council was preceded by the events that are central to the present chapter, i.e., the public affirmation by Pius XII of the worthiness of Jews and Judaism in the economy of salvation. As shall be seen, that is a *theological* development which can only be eclipsed — because it relates not to one people but to all peoples — by the church's inevitable affirmation in the twenty-first century of the worthiness of lesbian, gay, bisexual, and transgender people in the economy of human existence. Where the wartime pope said in effect, "be proud of your Jewishness," one is justified in affirming that another pope will say, "be proud of your sexual orientation." Here it is appropriate to quote Chesterton's *Heretics:* "Exactly at the instant when hope ceases to be reasonable it begins to be useful."

endowed with by that same Creator is their sexual orientation. Where else than from the Creator could it have come?

Returning to the domain of religion, what illustrates how basic Gospel principles have become deformed is the fact that in contemporary America it is the Catholic bishops and some Protestant ones as well, along with chief clerks and other religious leaders, who are fostering prejudice against ordinary people seeking simply to exercise their endowed natural rights. It is as though the *anima naturaliter Christiana* were attempting to smother the *anima naturaliter humana* — a distinction to be examined later in this chapter — or as though grace did not presuppose nature but subverted it. However, it would be a serious mistake to attribute this malevolence exclusively to members of various church hierarchies. For those hierarchs have been joined in opposition to the homosexual community by the leaders of fundamentalist religious and political groups of every persuasion from right-wing TV broadcasters — whether Bible ranters or news retailers — to second-amendment cranks, border-watchers, "birthers," and advocates of anti-Shari'ah legislation.[28]

In short, the Christian leaders — who putatively trace their mandate directly back to the gospel of love and the Beatitudes — have now allied themselves with the nation's social and moral dregs in a campaign against fellow citizens who are simply living in accord with their endowed human rights and faculties. Fortunately, in contrast to the bishops, there is the ordinary clergy, the ordained priests and ministers in the rectories and parsonages, who do know better, and who have borne witness by publicly defending those same fellow citizens. Such dedicated priests and ministers see no reason why they shouldn't engage in what used to be called "cure of souls" among members of the LGBT community, even though this runs counter to the decrees being handed down from above.

The existence of this fairly widespread and dedicated effort among "curates" is what, by contrast, made the career of the convert-priest, the late Richard Neuhaus, so unfortunately atypical. His anti-gay rants against "fashionable sins" (*First Things*, November, 2007) became so vehement that any non-biased reader — which I originally was, having published several of his books — had to conclude that their only historical parallels in language

28. In the earlier context of Philadelphia, there is no indication that the latest appointee as archbishop, Charles Chaput, will display any more enlightened a view of homosexuality than his predecessors. This is the prelate who believes homosexual unions are contrary to the gospel, and who therefore supported the dismissal of children from a parish school because they had been raised by a lesbian couple.

and motivation were the anti-Semitic tirades of the Jewish Karl Marx. One could not avoid the impression of an element of self-loathing lurking in the suave and polished polemics of Neuhaus. As to the use of the word "fashionable," it probably related to his own personal *ressentiment* at the whole in-your-face and gender-bending flamboyance of the gay community that was forever *en robe de parade* before the eyes of its straight antagonists.[29] In any case, and regardless of motivation, the views of Neuhaus stood in sharp contrast with those held by the kinds of dedicated priests referred to above. One of these priests, Gerard Thomas, has written earnestly and sincerely of the awesome sense of the presence of God he experienced when finally reconciling his sexual orientation with his faith, and bringing both of them into line with his vocation as a priest.[30]

As for other extremist views held by Neuhaus, he had also claimed that "50 or 60 percent of children reared by homosexuals turn out to be homosexual or bisexual," and that "the incidence of sexual abuse of children in such settings is many times the norm" (http://www.firstthings.com/onthesquare/2006/03/rjn-31606). Both claims can be disproved by consulting the Gay and Lesbian Alliance Against Defamation (GLAAD) or the Gay Journalists Association (NLGJA); but they were explicitly refuted by Andrew Sullivan on his blog, "The Daily Dish" (March 24, 2006), where he traced Neuhaus's statistics to an already provably rigged study by Pat Robertson's Regent University. Reliance on the latter represented another aspect of Neuhaus's unusual religio-political apostolate, his outreach to the Evangelical fringe mentioned earlier under the heading "fundamentalist religious and political groups."

A comparably conflicted situation prevailed in the Church of England when, in the aftermath of the consecration of an openly gay man by the Episcopal Church in the United States, the 1998 Lambeth Conference pub-

---

29. One meeting with Neuhaus is lodged in my memory. After a dinner at a restaurant of his choice — what I suppose could have been called "a fashionable eatery" — I and my publishing colleague, Werner Mark Linz, were trying to flag a cab while our guests, Peter Berger and Neuhaus, were getting into the latter's car, a large two-door yellow Chrysler. The only words by anyone that stay in my mind from that entire evening were his, when I mentioned something trite to the effect of "nice car," or "good-looking car." The response was, "Yeah, it goes over big with the parishioners." The condescending tone and air of being on display both startled me since he was then the Lutheran pastor of a predominantly African-American parish.

30. "A Gay Priest Speaks Out: The Vatican, Homosexuals & Holy Orders," *Commonweal*, January 28, 2005.

lished a Report adopting a semi-Catholic position condemning homosexuality. The Oxford theologian Andrew Linzey, previously cited in chapter 4, criticized the report and observed that it "presumes a model of church in which the people are connected with God only through their highest liturgical officer." He went on to add: "It is, in fact, a papal model, even if the Report proposes, in effect, a council of popes as distinct from a single one": his conclusion was that "the classic Anglican preference is for none at all." As to the contentious issue of homosexuality, he made the following carefully nuanced observation when drawing a comparison between Nazi hatred for Jews and Nazi homophobia:

> If today theologians declared, in all seriousness, that Jewish practices were "perverted," "deformed" or "handicapped," their utterances would receive universal condemnation — and rightly so. But, nowadays, bishops can typify homosexual behavior as "objectively disordered" or "intrinsically evil," without even attracting the mildest of censure. It is as though Christians have at least woken up to the fact that their thinking about Jews helped lead them to the death camps, but cannot quite grasp that Christian thinking also helped lead gays to the same destination.[31]

---

31. "Introduction," *Gays and the Future of Anglicanism*, ed. Andrew Linzey and Richard Kirker (2005).

That Vatican lawmakers are at least *somewhat* aware of the larger world is evident from this report by John Allen, "Ecumenical Manners Can't Blunt the Pro-Life Message, Pope Says" (*NCR Today*, January 24, 2011):

> Noting that since 2009 the Catholic bishops of Germany and leaders of the Evangelical Lutheran Church have had a biblical dialogue commission on "God and Human Dignity," Benedict expressed the hope that "no new confessional differences" will erupt in the pro-life questions.
>
> That dialogue has at times been contentious, given that many Lutheran churches in Germany accept openly gay clergy and view homosexuality as morally acceptable, and some also bless same-sex unions. Benedict's warning that ecumenical good manners cannot blunt the church's pro-life message comes at a time when disagreements over gay rights and gender roles are already producing new fault lines in Christianity, perhaps especially with the Anglican communion.

In that larger context of ecumenical *manners* — not of the thrice-mentioned pro-life offenses — cf. Justus George Lawler, "Rome and the Holy Offices of Protestant Churches," *Theology Today*, April 2010, which explicitly refers to the pioneering work of Andrew Linzey in animal ethics. One lesson of the latter is that the "compassion on the multitudes" of Jesus extends to all sentient creatures. On the "pro-life message" as such, cf. Justus George Lawler, "Phantom Heresies," *Commonweal*, April 24, 2009.

It is against the background of what appears an almost international campaign, as well as against the background of the child-abuse scandal in the American Catholic church, that the issue of homosexuality has reached critical mass in today's religious world. Although everybody concerned is aware of the more or less official condemnation, it is nevertheless useful to look at the "defining" Catholic document itself. The following is from the *Catechism of the Catholic Church* (2357), and it echoes the language cited by Andrew Linzey in the excerpt above. "Basing itself on Sacred Scripture, which presents homosexual acts as acts of grave depravity, tradition has always declared that homosexual acts are intrinsically disordered." But if the authors of the Catechism are going to have its twenty-first-century reader take seriously Sacred Scripture's pre-eminent (as well as pre-scientific) story of depravity, that of Lot and Sodom, they are also going to have such a reader take seriously the story of its being "prevented" by having one's daughters play the whore — since according to the Bible that is what occurred.[32] So too with what "tradition has always declared." Since, in fact, what it has declared of homosexual acts is, of necessity, contaminated by the hoary prejudices and slanders perpetrated by the descendants of the wandering tribes of the Mediterranean Basin during the Common Era.

To invoke Scripture and tradition regarding the "grave depravity" of homosexual acts is not unlike the Catechism's invocation of tradition and church teaching to maintain that "masturbation is an intrinsically and gravely disordered action" (2352). The truth of the matter is that neither of these things has any connection with religion as such, save that to the primitive mind any variation from the socially sanctioned, particularly anything relative to the mysterious sexual drive — the poet's *eros turannos* — was under the supervision of the priests. At the dawn of the third millennium, for these catechists to ascribe "grave depravity" or "grave disorder" to either or both of these categories is simply to engage in an exercise in anachronism. In fact, the heading for this subject in the Catechism could be "Hippocrates Meets Hypocrisy" — since its authors are putting on public display the imbalance in the four humors that is so obviously afflicting them. The harsh reality is that this kind of "theology" represents fundamentalism run wild.

32. That they engage in incest and ultimately become the primordial ancestors of the Moabites and the Ammonites is explained by biblical scholar John L. McKenzie: "to a more primitive people the daughters of Lot could be heroines who against all hope found a way to fulfill their destiny as women." This genteel accommodation to womanhood is from his *Dictionary of the Bible* (1964).

What's next could well be a world created in seven days, and an economic system built on the unlimited exploitation of labor.[33]

Furthermore, "basing itself on Sacred Scripture," as the Catechism says, has also been the foundation for much of the denigration of women in the Christian tradition. Bernard Häring, probably the most creative and influential moral theologian of the twentieth century, expressed the fear that "male opponents of the ordination of women are still bedeviled by the old-time deeply rooted fear of women's 'impurity.'"[34] What he called the "burden of the past" was largely owed to the twelfth chapter of Leviticus, which begins as follows:

> The Lord said to Moses, "Say to the people of Israel, If a woman conceives, and bears a male child, then she shall be unclean seven days; as at the time of her menstruation, she shall be unclean. . . . Then she shall continue for thirty-three days in the blood of her purifying; she shall not touch any hallowed thing, nor come into the sanctuary, until the days of her purifying are completed. But if she bears a female child, then she shall be unclean two weeks, as in her menstruation; and she shall continue in the blood of her purifying for sixty-six days. And when the days of her purifying are completed, whether for a son or for a daughter, she shall bring to the priest at the door of the tent of meeting a lamb a year old for a burnt offering, and a young pigeon or a turtledove for a sin offering."

Not only is the woman impure and thus forbidden to contaminate the holy things that only men are entitled to handle, but if she bears a female child she is doubly impure. This the Lord makes clear when addressing Moses with the mathematical precision of a merchant haggling with a customer in the local marketplace: males = one week, and thirty-three days; females = two weeks, and sixty-six days. (It would be embarrassing to point to the common roots in folk etymology of bazaar and bizarre.)

This part of the last chapter of the present book is being written in Feb-

33. All twenty-first-century Catholics, in fact, all twenty-first-century Christians, should breathe a sigh of relief (and maybe the Catholics will also make a novena of thanks) that providentially Leo XIII had an inborn sense of social justice, and that Pius XII had the good judgment to have as his personal confessor Augustin Bea, the open-minded rector of the Biblical Institute, who strongly influenced the pope's *Divino Afflante Spiritu*.

34. Bernard Häring, *My Hope for the Church: Critical Encouragement for the Twenty First Century* (1999). This edition of the book has an Introduction by Charles E. Curran, who not only studied with Häring but has inherited his mantle as well.

ruary 2011, a month whose second day celebrates the feast variously called "the Presentation of our Lord" or "the Purification of the Blessed Virgin Mary," or (later, and more neutrally), "Candlemas Day." The feast commemorates the truly touching story that occurs at the center of the second chapter of Luke's Gospel, and which takes as its point of departure the Leviticus passage above. Referring to Jesus and his mother, the Gospel says: "Now when the days of her purification according to the law of Moses were completed, they brought [Jesus] to Jerusalem to present him to the Lord." Here Simeon, the man who would not die until he had seen "the Lord Christ," is led by the Spirit to the temple, "and when the parents brought in the child Jesus . . . [Simeon] took him up in his arms" and uttered the prophecy that is now known as the canticle "Nunc dimittis." This is not quite matched by the prophetess Anna, who goes unquoted, but who "gave thanks to the Lord and spoke of him to all those who looked for redemption in Jerusalem."

While one may think, "at last, three cheers for supersessionism," it still must be pointed out that both scriptural passages simply accept as a matter of fact the assumption of a female stigma attached to anything sexual. That such an assumption underlies a narrative as moving as that in the Gospel of Luke only further reenforces the tradition of woman as defiling and inferior, and of female sexuality as polluted and polluting. Regardless of how ridiculous it may be in the twenty-first century to even enunciate such assertions — but no more ridiculous than the equally antiquated notions regarding homosexuality and masturbation — it remains undeniable that Bernard Häring was correct in believing they have been a major factor in the denigration of women, and more specifically in the papal decision that they are intrinsically unworthy of ordination.

The absurdity of those positions is particularly evidenced not only by the remarkable achievement of the American Episcopal Church regarding women in the highest offices of the worldwide Anglican Communion, but also by a phenomenon unique to American Catholicism. This is the ever-increasing number of women trained in theology, and more particularly trained in Bernard Häring's own discipline of theological ethics. Although less relevant to rulership and priestcraft, while simply eclipsing the controversy over ordination altogether, this unique achievement confronts directly the primitive "fear of women's 'impurity,'" by plainly exposing it as a sign of male insecurity. Such an achievement also confronts the father-knows-best role when it comes to all matters relative to what are euphemistically called "cultural issues," but in plain English are mainly related to Leviticus-like notions of women, sexuality, and reproduction.[35] It would be a display of partisanship to name the twenty or so most prominent female theologians who have brought to bear on these issues arguments that at least thus far have gone unanswered by the official male guardians of Catholic orthodoxy. That these theologians and their fellow scholars will be remembered by posterity once the remnants of the present extremism have been swept away is something that is historically inevitable. I will mention only one such scholar, Margaret Farley, a Mercy nun whose *Just Love: A Framework for Christian Sexual Ethics* won the Grawemeyer Award in Religion in 2007. That hers has been a theological concern that is not merely of academic import is apparent from the fact that she also co-directed the All-Africa Conference, "Sister to Sister," a project designed to empower African women to cope with the AIDS pandemic. The growing influence of women on such issues is what offers hope that the cause of women's ordination will not be seen as merely symbolic, but as a reality to be attained.[36] Moreover, the reversal of the kind of misdirected zeal that led to the "fear" of women is already on the horizon.

Within the Catholic heritage there is a redeeming factor that helps to rein in warped zealotry and to balance it with reality. This factor is implicit in the term "dialectical relationship" — previously introduced at the very beginning of this chapter — and it explains another earlier quotation from Cardinal Newman: "Catholic Christendom is no simple exhibition of religious absolutism, but presents a continuous picture of Authority and Private Judgment alternately advancing and retreating as the ebb and flow of the

---

35. I don't want to turn this chapter into a chronicle, but the mention of those three issues brought to mind a special section of the *National Catholic Reporter* (January 7, 2011), titled in 62-point type simply, "PRO-LIFE." Underneath that large text was a half-page color photo of some informally dressed men apparently leading a larger group of people. A couple of children can be seen in the foreground, and of the three men at the head of the march, the ones on the right and left wear the Roman collar, while the leader in the center wears a black shirt with sleeves rolled up and the words "CHOOSE LIFE" printed across the chest. A woman can be glimpsed in the background of the photo.

Accompanying this special *NCR* section was a full-color glossy folder titled, "Just in time for Sanctity of Human Life Sunday!" — which, if nothing else, provided its own insight into the world of Catholic superstitionism, with pictures of gimcracks galore. These were not the Philomena cords or scapulars of yesteryear, but rather such things as plastic "fetal models," "precious feet in gold electroplate," "preborn spiritual adoption bracelets," "precious feet lapel pins," "first-trimester models in white or brown," and assorted bumper stickers of the same genre. Here the bizarre and the bazaar truly merge.

36. Only among American Catholics would one refer to "the growing influence of women on *such* issues," because it would obviously expose the absurdity of the situation if one were to refer to "the growing influence of women on women's issues."

tide. . . .'" There have already been two instances of this intersection of authority and private judgment: the child-abuse scandal and homosexual rights. In both of these the judgment of the episcopate was found to be grievously flawed. Not only did the bishops ignore or conceal the wounds inflicted on the most vulnerable members of their flocks, but they crassly sought to exploit the mob-like prejudice against homosexuals to divert attention from their cover-up.

The third instance where authority and private judgment have collided was referred to earlier in the context of "Leviticus-like notions of women, sexuality, and reproduction" — the phrase that introduced footnote 35 on the abortion crusade.[37] This was a crusade in which, it can be noted in passing, Richard Neuhaus was a major figure — and which was also led mainly by the bishops. Unfortunately, along with hundreds of thousands of sincere and dedicated people, like the campaign the bishops led against homosexuals, this crusade has also enlisted the support of what were described earlier as "fundamentalist religious and political groups of every persuasion from right-wing TV broadcasters — whether Bible ranters or news retailers — to second-amendment cranks, border-watchers, 'birthers,' and advocates of anti-Shari'ah legislation."

Nevertheless, if the anti-abortion crusade does prove to be a worthy cause, possibly it will elevate the moral and intellectual horizons of all its advocates. The issue does not have to do with whether abortion is intrinsically either good or evil; it has to do with whether it is necessary — as in certain clearly defined circumstances it surely is. The criteria set forth by the Supreme Court, while necessarily broad-gauge and controversial, do seem as realistic as it may be possible to get for a nation of three hundred million people. Inevitably, abuses will occur, but as an ancient maxim said, "abuse

37. On reexamining that photograph I became convinced that its appearance in the *National Catholic Reporter* was an exercise in the semi-ironic on the part of the editors. *NCR* has been quoted with considerable deference several times in this book because it largely speaks from the perspective of the laity (the *Ecclesia docta*) and less so from that of the episcopate (the *Ecclesia docens*). Not that the laity is not engaged in the anti-abortion movement; it is, but with less vigor and certainly less obsessiveness than the episcopate. That there was a touch of irony in that photo is also suggested by another "special section" of *NCR*, Charles Curran's perceptive article, "A Critique from Within the Church" (November 26, 2010), correcting some overreaching views on abortion by the episcopate. Cardinal Newman — to be cited in detail presently — deployed the "church teaching/church taught" distinction when he said that the divinity of Jesus in the early church was preserved "far more" by lay people than by the hierarchy. His stark conclusion was simply that *"the body of the episcopate was unfaithful to its commission, while the body of the laity was faithful to its baptism."*

does not take away use." In any case it makes more sense to err on the side of the woman's decision than on the side of various outsiders' opinions, including child abuse–tolerant American bishops.[38] What remains a cause of concern, however, is the vehemence of the crusaders themselves and, more particularly, of those who are male. One wonders if the dominant presence of the latter may not represent as much an anti-woman crusade as an anti-abortion one — or whether in fact the latter was not invented in order to validate the former, much as the ban on capital punishment was, if not reinvented, then certainly resurrected, in order to validate the ban on abortion. Certainly the chilling lack of empathy for women who must face the intrinsically agonizing decision to put an end to the child they are carrying bespeaks the male trait of contempt and fear displayed in the Leviticus text and in Pope John Paul's *Inter Insigniores* condemning women's ordination. Both texts reflect an indifference to the all-embracing compassion "upon the multitudes" displayed by Jesus.

As to Cardinal Newman's "authority and private judgment," insofar as these concern the institution and the individual, the linchpin of the relationship — that is, of the negotiating process between the two previously mentioned entities, the church teaching and the church taught — is the sacredness of individual conscience. This is Newman in his "Letter to the Duke of Norfolk":

38. In *Popes and Politics* the issue of abortion was considered in the chapter titled, "The Rhetoric of Stigmatization," and in the context of the declaration of the doctrine of the Immaculate Conception — which is also the setting for the relevant texts by Cardinal Newman to be examined presently. This is an excerpt from a footnote in that chapter which had as its purpose to indicate that the tradition does not support many present-day views:

> Moreover, though the tradition of forbidding baptism of the fetus is well known, another and perhaps more significant tradition — since it relates to holy orders — seems to be less well known. For over seven hundred years from Innocent III to Benedict XV, that is from roughly the thirteenth to the twentieth century, penitential practice was based on the tradition of what was varyingly called the "ensoulment," "animation," "quickening" of the fetus *as subsequent* to embryonic life. A candidate for the priesthood who *concurred in* an abortion could still be ordained if his involvement took place before "ensoulment," the latter defined by some canonists as one hundred and sixteen days after bodily conception *(conceptio seminis carnis),* by others forty days for a male and sixty for a female — already so slow-witted *she* could never be ordained anyway. This was the law and the practice until 1917, and even a possible interpretation until the revision of canon law under John Paul II. (original italics)

The passage following the dash was intended to be a feminist-friendly irony, pertinent still to the advocacy of women's ordination by Father Häring and many others.

Conscience is not a long-sighted selfishness, nor a desire to be consistent with oneself; but it is a messenger from Him, who, both in nature and in grace, speaks to us behind a veil, and teaches and rules us by His representatives. *Conscience is the aboriginal Vicar of Christ,* a prophet in its information, a monarch in its peremptoriness, a priest in its blessings and anathemas, and, even though the eternal priesthood throughout the Church could cease to be, in it the sacerdotal principle would remain and would have a sway. (italics supplied)

This daring notion was a retort to the former (and again to be) British Prime Minister, who had publicly asserted that submission to the Vicar of Christ made Catholics unworthy citizens. It was also a notion that defined conscience vis-à-vis religion as a *human* trait transcending even "the eternal priesthood throughout the Church," and thus even if the latter ceased to exist conscience would continue to be invoked. The section in the letter titled "Conscience" ends, rather famously, as follows: "Certainly, if I am obliged to bring religion into after-dinner toasts (which indeed does not seem quite the thing), I shall drink — to the Pope, if you please, — still, to Conscience first, and to the Pope afterwards."[39]

Notwithstanding its seeming boldness, the clause *"Conscience is the aboriginal Vicar of Christ"* was endorsed by that generally enlightened pontiff, Paul VI, who was himself a staunch promoter of the cause of Newman's canonization, a cause that had been first initiated by Father Stephen Dessain, superior of the Oratory in Birmingham where Newman spent most of his Catholic years.[40] Unfortunately, it is not necessary to emphasize again that

39. This over-discussed and seemingly odd imagery of toasts is less peculiar when viewed in light of the following section in the letter, titled "The Encyclical of 1864," which begins: "When I was young the State had a conscience, and the Chief Justice of the day pronounced, not as a point of obsolete law, but as an energetic, living truth, that Christianity was the law of the land. And by Christianity was meant pretty much what Bentham calls Church-of-Englandism, its cry being the dinner toast, 'Church and king.'" (www.newmanreader.org/works/anglicans/. . ./section5.html).

40. The pope's endorsement is made in "Letter to the Bishop of Luxembourg, Msgr. Léon Lommel, concerning the thought of Cardinal John-Henry Newman" (May 17, 1970), www.Vatican.Va.

In 1958-59 I spent a semester at the Oratory and still recall a conversation with Father Dessain — for whose hospitality I expressed my appreciation in the Foreword to *Popes and Politics* — in which I suggested (wrongly) that Newman's cause would go nowhere because of his statement on conscience as the aboriginal vicar of Christ. To say this in the wake of the

the one shadow on this pope's nobility of spirit was his handling of the contraception issue. "Handling" is the operative term, since the resultant document, *Humanae Vitae,* in addition to failing the test of being "an ordinance of reason," has been put to the test of reception by the great mass of the faithful and has simply been found wanting.

In this precise context, Bernard Häring, himself, as we have seen, one of the greatest moral theologians of the twentieth century, cited one of its greatest dogmatic theologians on the efforts by the Congregation for the Doctrine of the Faith, and presumably John Paul II, to claim infallibility for *Inter Insigniores.*

> In this area, one can rely on thorough studies of Yves Congar, the great theologian whom Pope John Paul II himself made a cardinal. This is the carefully articulated theory of "reception." According to Congar and the many theologians who cite him, a papal teaching can count as definitive and infallible only insofar as it finds a "reception," that is, free assent, in the entire Church. If it finds no such assent, then the pope has most likely not "received" the sense of the faithful on the question.

Häring then quoted Congar's citation of the first Vatican Council's *Pastor Aeternus,* "the most important text in this regard."

> The popes of Rome, in accord with the time and circumstances, have defined what must be firmly believed in agreement with Holy Scripture and apostolic traditions. But they have done so only after determining this through ecumenical councils or investigating the conviction of the Church dispersed all over the earth, for example through particular synods and other means made possible by divine Providence.

Häring concluded by observing that "despite the pope's undeniable intention of proclaiming an infallible doctrine, no such thing took place."

Perhaps, at this point, some statistics will help ground the larger issues regarding the reception of *Humanae Vitae.* Although in advanced societies economic well-being and enlightened governmental support are major fac-

---

lobbying for infallibility by the actual Vicar of Christ seemed to me something that would never be forgotten or forgiven in Rome.

For a detailed narrative of the process leading to the beatification of Newman in 2010, the previously cited *Making Saints* by Kenneth L. Woodward is invaluable.

tors in affecting the birth rate, it is noteworthy that there is little significant difference in those rates relative to countries that are predominantly Catholic or non-Catholic. Second, and more significant, is the fact that among the most dramatic drops in the birth rate during the period from 1999 to 2009 were in the nation of which the pope is the Primate, Italy, and in the nation that is the Holy Father's Fatherland, Germany. Additionally, the runner-up to those two nations was Catholic Portugal. Such statistics indicate that for great numbers of the faithful contraception has indeed very much to do with Catholics and Catholicism.[41]

The data above lend a note of the surreal to the international carnival of speculation that emerged from Benedict XVI's mention of contraception in his interviews published as *Light of the World* in November 2010. Almost totally ignored by the media were such things as his stand in favor of global warming (clarifying his less positive view in December 2007) and his new overtures to Judaism and Jews (clarifying his earlier imagery of "elder brother"). Instead, the subject of contraception ran rampant in newspapers, magazines, and particularly in blogs — in all of which it was the object of the most elaborate commentary, analysis, condemnation, speculation, and so on. Any mythic visitor from another planet would certainly have been dumbfounded to discover that what the bearer of such weighty titles as "Patriarch of the West," "heir of St. Peter," and "Vicar of Christ" was actually talking about was . . . *condoms*. (On the web, the terms "Benedict XVI" and "condoms" at that time elicited from 150,000 to nearly a quarter of a million hits.)

As for the specific failure of Paul VI in *Humanae Vitae*, it was the result of the pope's *not* relying enough on Newman, particularly on his remarks (originally related to the proclamation of the doctrine of the Immaculate Conception) called "On Consulting the Faithful in Matters of Doctrine," which appeared in a publication he briefly edited, and which was explicitly focused on the role of the laity. Newman's first and still indispensable biographer, Wilfrid Ward, provides the context:

> There remained one number of the *Rambler* to appear before his retirement from the position of editor. His thoughts were dwelling at this time on the short-sightedness and the unwisdom of ignoring the important functions often performed by the faithful laity in the history of the Church. It is possible that this feeling helped to determine the subject of

41. For these statistics see http://www.guardian.co.uk/news/datablog/2010/may/19/.

the article which he contributed to the number — an article which had unforeseen results. It was entitled 'On consulting the Faithful in matters of Doctrine,' and was written in justification and explanation of some words he had used in the previous number in connection with a question already raised by Mr. Nasmyth Stokes as to its being desirable that the Bishops should consult the opinion of the laity in taking decisions of importance in which they were specially concerned.[42]

The following are the particular issues Newman raised and with which Paul VI certainly was familiar — though he systematically ignored their implications in drafting his encyclical. "First, whether it can, with doctrinal correctness, be said that an *appeal* to the faithful is one of the preliminaries of a definition of doctrine; and secondly, granting that the faithful are taken into account, whether they can correctly be said to be *consulted*" (original italics). The latter issue, which Newman took up first, is of major significance in setting the stage for a teaching that, unlike the Marian doctrine itself, directly affected almost the entire body of the faithful, i.e., the exercise of human sexuality and the concomitant exercise of human life (*humanae vitae*).

In concluding his argument Newman drew on his own book, *The Arians of the Fourth Century,* written in 1833, more than a decade before he was received into the Catholic communion — but amended with explanatory notes in his later years. This is his conclusion:

> the Nicene dogma was maintained during the greater part of the 4th century, not by the unswerving firmness of the Holy See, Councils, or Bishops, but by the consensus of the faithful [*"consensus fidelium"*]. On the one hand, then, I say, that there was a temporary suspense of the functions of the Church teaching [*"Ecclesia docens"*]. The body of Bishops failed in the confession of the faith. (http://www.newmanreader.org/works/rambler/consulting.html)

If this can be said of a doctrinal heresy that Newman himself had proved almost corrupted the entire hierarchy of the church — "the Holy See," the "Bishops" — while it was the lay people who stood firm, what can be said of moral regulations concerning sexuality in general, which are mandated by the present-day members of that same ruling body, but which in effect dis-

---

42. Wilfrid Ward, *The Life of John Henry Cardinal Newman* (1912), vol. I, chap. 17.

franchise not only married people, but also people of any differing sexual orientation? The growing *consensus fidelium* regarding both contraception and homosexual rights is totally opposed to what is being proclaimed by contemporary spokesmen for the *ecclesia docens*. Today's "body of Bishops" and today's "Holy See" may in effect be said to have engaged in fostering a kind of ethical heresy — not entirely unlike the doctrinal heresy of their Arian predecessors — by their repeated condemnations of contraception and homosexuality. At the least, they are certainly putting on display what Newman called "short-sightedness" and "unwisdom." As regards the cause of Newman's canonization and the papacy, Wilfrid Ward noted that after the article "On Consulting . . ." appeared, this was the reaction: "Although Rome did not take official action in the matter, the Holy Father was reported to be pained; and the rumours of the hour proved to have had the effect of shaking the public confidence in Newman." Fortunately, a later pope would take official action, and it would be to raise Newman to the altars.

Finally, there is a much more recent declaration that certainly does coincide with Newman's prescription. The following is by a future pope, John Paul I, who also happened to be treating of ancient heresies and contemporary issues — in this instance, issues that also relate to the matters regarding reproduction considered above:

> For me, this is the most serious theological question that has ever been dealt with by the church. In the age of Arius and Nestorius, the issue was the two natures of Christ, and these were serious questions, but they were understood only at the very top of the church, among theologians and bishops. The simple people understood nothing of these things and said, "I adore Jesus Christ, the Lord who has redeemed me," and that was it, there was no danger. Here, on the other hand, it's a question that no longer regards solely the leadership of the church, but the entire church, all the young families, the young Christian families. It is a truly central point that they are still studying.[43]

43. The source of the quotation is a lengthy article (*National Catholic Reporter*, September 5, 2003) by John Allen, the indefatigable researcher already cited several times in these pages. The pertinent section of the article began as follows: "Last week I carried an interview with Fr. Diego Lorenzi, the private secretary of Pope John Paul I, on the 25th anniversary of the pope's election. . . . A few readers wrote to ask if it was true that prior to becoming pope, Cardinal Albino Luciani had expressed a positive view of birth control. In short, the answer is yes."

Particularly important is the fact that while the future pope got the issue of the ancient heresy exactly wrong, his reading of the modern issue regarding sexuality is exactly right — thus proving himself to have been an ideal pope for the new era of the church. And, as just mentioned, it was Blessed John Henry Newman who showed that the voice of the faithful must not only be heard but must also be taken into account. In this context, it is also of interest that the future Pope John Paul I wrote his doctoral dissertation at the Gregorian University on the origin of human life in the works of Antonio Rosmini. It seems not unlikely, particularly given the insights above, that future research on such a document might shed some light on the present-day assertion that an embryo *ex definitione* should be treated as a human person.

This notion appears to be explicitly endorsed by the second Pope John Paul in *Evangelium Vitae,* though possibly with some fudging, since his is actually a reiteration of this earlier declaration: "Nothing and no one can in any way permit the killing of an innocent human being, whether a fetus or an embryo, an infant or an adult, an old person, or one suffering from an incurable disease, or a person who is dying." This is rightly referenced to the Congregation for the Doctrine of the Faith, "Declaration on Euthanasia" (May 5, 1980), though it still leaves unclear how one can even refer to an *innocent* embryo, particularly since the definition of "human being" is not exactly coterminous with that of "human person." Even in traditional philosophy — going back to Boethius — personhood added to "human being" the notion of reasoning; similarly, while "human being" pertained simply to existence as such, "human person" added to that concept the element of relationality.[44]

---

44. Until the identity of the two can be affirmed, observations such as the following on the CDF's *Dignitas Personae* must be taken *cum aliquanto salis* — with a large dose of salt. The writer is mainly seeking to resolve what he calls "the destructive divide between 'moral-status conservatives' and 'social-justice liberals.'" The hyphenated adjectives are a superfluous distraction. The resolution takes this form: "For example, the church should draw a clear analogy between its defense of embryos exploited in biomedical research and its defense of workers exploited during the Industrial Revolution. Of course, such an analogy is not itself an argument, but it does make the church's underlying argument about human dignity appear more coherent and compelling." Charles Camosy, "Right Tune, Wrong Words," *Commonweal*, June 5, 2009. The excessive hedging here ("clear analogy," "appear more") obscures the root fact that any analogy still leaves the two entities, embryos and workers, "simply different" and only "in a certain sense" (*secundum quid*) the same.

Nevertheless, the writer does have John Paul II on his side, since in his "Letter to all my Brothers in the Episcopate regarding the 'Gospel of Life'" (May 19, 1991), the pope said the following — in that self-congratulatory tone that made him so lovable to his admirers:

Lastly, moving out of the world of speculation and into the world of historical reality, there is certainly some significance to be attached to the fact that the first Pope John Paul in one of his earliest public acts chose to praise the parents of an *in vitro* baby, even though they had implicitly violated the encyclical of his own esteemed predecessor, Paul VI's *Humanae Vitae*. What is one to conclude from this mélange of personal opinion and this medley of official texts? At the least, that *all* expressions of absolute certitude — including this one — are to be respectfully adjudicated in the court of conscience before being embraced wholeheartedly, whether by the lay individual or by what Newman would call "the theological school."

*   *   *

This final chapter has come a considerable distance from the conciliar texts that initiated this discussion, with their declaration that "the joys and hopes, the grief and anguish of the people of our time, especially of those who are poor or afflicted, are the joys and hopes, the grief and anguish of the followers of Christ as well." That latter passage began this treatment concerning reliance on the foundational principles of the Gospel to reform and revivify the contemporary church. Similarly, the flowering of civil rights under the aegis of Martin Luther King Jr. was the result of seeds that had been planted in the foundational texts of the American Republic, particularly the Declaration of Independence. And just as the earlier examination of the Lincoln

---

In that same letter, written shortly after the celebration of the centenary of the Encyclical *Rerum Novarum,* I drew everyone's attention to this striking analogy: "Just as a century ago it was the working classes which were oppressed in their fundamental rights, and the Church very courageously came to their defense by proclaiming the sacrosanct rights of the worker as a person, so now, when another category of persons is being oppressed in the fundamental right to life, the Church feels in duty bound to speak out with the same courage on behalf of those who have no voice. Hers is always the evangelical cry in defense of the world's poor, those who are threatened and despised and whose human rights are violated."

However, this may not resolve the matter of whether an embryo can be classified as "among the world's poor" or as "another category of persons" whose human rights are so violated that the Church must raise *her* voice, as though *she* too were another such category of person — possibly with all the rights that term implies. In short, the issue is whether much of this entire treatment of embryos is constructed on the figure of speech, personification, by which humanness is more or less arbitrarily attributed to a given entity. Professional rhetoricians would call this trope of the pope "prosopopoeia" — and *ex definitione* not a manifestation of the charism of infallibility.

heritage cast new light on the similarities of the institutionalized North American polity and the institutionalized ecclesiastical order, so too further light can be shed on the latter by examining it in relation to the institutionalized expression — specifically mentioned earlier — of "Judaism as a faith and a people," embodied in our time by the conflict-ridden state of Israel.[45]

But this is not going to segue immediately into that political body, since there is an intermediating national entity, Poland, which first requires consideration. That requirement is based on the fact that Poland in terms of its "ecclesiastical order" is viewed as the most Catholic country in all of Europe, while it is also viewed — by Kertzer, among others, when treating of a future pope there — as being the most anti-Semitic. This was the entire point of the self-satisfaction, not to say snideness, of John Connelly's willful distortion of Pius XII's reference to "the individual character of each race" as fostering anti-Semitism among "East European Catholics." But this consideration of Poland is intrinsically important regarding institutionalized religion and institutionalized polities in general, and it will be seen shortly as having a more precise application regarding Israel and the burgeoning Palestinian state.

I begin with an observation by a previously introduced writer, the Auschwitz-haunted Primo Levi. He is here describing the murder by Christian Phalangists of Palestinian women and children in the refugee camps of Sabra and Shatila in southern Lebanon — a mass murder that took place in 1982 while Israeli forces stood passively by. What is telling about Levi's remarks is that rather than draw on a multitude of examples of other preventable killings of blameless people, he selected an incident that had occurred while he was himself a Nazi prisoner, and about which he learned only from reading postwar accounts — hence the intensification of the experience by his use of the term "vividly" below.

> The slaughter in those two camps brought vividly back to me the Russians in Warsaw in August 1944. They stopped and waited at the Vistula while the Nazis exterminated all the Polish partisans of the uprising. . . . Israel, just like the Russians in 1944, could have intervened and had the force to stop the gangs who were carrying out the massacre of those people, but

45. There is also a tangential connection between Lincoln and Israel. Allis Radosh and Ronald Radosh in *A Safe Haven: Harry S. Truman and the Founding of Israel* (2009) have noted that President Truman, when under pressure by American Jews to officially recognize the State of Israel, compared himself, good-naturedly, to Lincoln being urged by abolitionists to free the slaves.

they did not. . . . That slaughter is not Israel's style. The situation must have got out of hand. And then again, maybe someone deliberately held back, wasting time before intervening to defend those women and children . . . what more can I say?[46]

What can be said, at least as an initial response, is that this vivid recollection indicates how an empathetic sense of commonly shared humanity can transcend ethnic loyalties, as the Jews in Lebanon like the Russians in Poland are condemned for playing the role of bystanders at the murder of the innocent.

A more encompassing insight that can be drawn from Levi's Polish imagery is that although nobly conceived institutions, whether religious or political, must rely on their foundational principles for self-reformation, those principles themselves are based on an a priori awareness of a commonly shared transcendent humanity. That common element is what the third-century Church Father Tertullian referred to when he made his much cited observation, referred to earlier, *anima naturaliter christiana,* that is, the soul is Christian in its very nature. But by this must be meant not "Christian" in any sectarian sense, but Christian in the sense of humankind in its most fundamental aspirations. What Tertullian meant is also what another churchman, Thomas Aquinas, a thousand years later, affirmed in the maxim that *gratia presupponit naturam,* that is, the supernatural order of divine gifts and insights that makes humanity reach beyond its limitations is built on the natural order that constitutes human being itself. The supernatural is the complement of the natural. The saying *anima naturaliter Christiana* is thus akin to saying, *anima naturaliter humana.*[47] That people

---

46. "If This is a State," in Marco Belpoliti and Robert Gordon, eds., *The Voice of Memory: Interviews, 1961-1987* (2000). The original interviewer, Gad Lerner, began by observing: "Only once in the course of the tormented and passionate relationship with Israel did Primo Levi decide to speak out . . . during the invasion of Lebanon." But in fact he had spoken out proleptically through the ambiguous figure of Mendel in *If not Now, When?* as Israel itself would become the scapegoat nation for what the Palestinians call Nakba, *their* "holocaust." Another parallel, however seemingly tenuous, is the scapegoating of the pope for the six million, explicitly made in the wake of writers like Hochhuth, and the scapegoating of the Poles — explicitly made in the wake of writers like Kertzer — as the allegedly papal-endorsed anti-Semites who were engaged in pogroms.

47. This visionary conception has been identified in the Catholic world with the "immanentism" of Maurice Blondel which — as noted briefly in chapter 5 — was approved by Pius XII at the instigation of the future Pope Paul VI, then Monsignor G. B. Montini, and later was publicly defended by Pope John Paul II. This is a theme that will also be developed in *Historians Against History.*

are related to ultimate ("super") spiritual values presupposes the existence of a receptive natural order in humankind. It is that "natural order" to which Primo Levi was being faithful in his seemingly harsh judgment on Israel when he heard of the massacred victims. It was a judgment not unlike that of the poet Denise Levertov, who even-handedly but passionately wrote:

> In Lebanon
> so-called Jews have permitted
> so-called Christians
> to wreak pogrom ("thunder of devastation")
> on helpless folk (of a tribe
> anciently kin to their own, and now
> concentrated in camps . . .)[48]

In further response to Levi's question in the prose excerpt above, "what more can I say?" at least so far as this comparative analysis of institutional structures goes, what can be said is that for the shocking condition of Jews under the supervision of the popes, spelled out in detail in the first chapters of Kertzer's book, there is the similarly appalling status of Palestinians in the "territories," not to mention, in neighboring countries where they have been locked into refugee camps under conditions that are comparable to those in the ghettos of the Papal States. Obviously, none of this in any way justifies the abuses by either party, the old church or the new state; nor is this some kind of *tu quoque* response. But while giving pause to people who share views such as those of Kertzer, it does again indicate the importance of taking into account the nature of institutions, their benefits and their liabilities, before attributing every appalling act done in the name of religion to the evil will of evil men. The paradoxical fact is that the benefits — constituting a permanent embodiment of foundational ideals — are also the pitfalls, since that very embodiment, while assuring survival and continuity, also brings with it the concretizing and stultifying of the initial creative impulses. This was largely the point of beginning this chapter as well as this entire book with Peter Berger's remark, "Institutions carry within them a principle of inertia, perhaps founded ultimately on the hard rock of human stupidity" —

---

48. "Perhaps no Poem . . . ," in *Making Peace* (2006). At the end of this chapter and of this book, I will cite a poem on what remains the all-eclipsing, all-encompassing evil in the history *of* history.

which was immediately amended to, "and perhaps founded penultimately on the hard rock of human stability."

Before returning to Israel, Poland, and "the burgeoning Palestinian state," it should first be emphasized again that for the church, such stability is based on "the Gospel's spiritual love" as expressed primarily in the Sermon on the Mount, and it is the interplay of that ancient foundational teaching and modern contemporary structures that must be ceaselessly engaged by the larger body and by the individual as they both relate to the traditions of the past in the present moment of history.

Nevertheless, for anyone who celebrated the two-thousand-year end of the dispersion of the Jewish people and their return to their biblical home, the treatment of the Palestinians is a terrible blot on the government of Israel; even as the peculiar institution of slavery along with its post-emancipation detritus of violent racism has stained permanently "the land of liberty"; and, lastly, even as the undeniable pogroms perpetrated by peasants and rationalized by Polish ecclesiastics are blots on church and state in Poland.[49] As for the failures of "the Holy See" — the spurning of its own tradition of condemning ritual murder; its implicit propping up of anti-Jewish sentiment; and the inadequate supervision of Vatican entities like the Inquisition and *Civiltà cattolica* — not even the heartfelt expressions of repentance by Pope John Paul II have proved to be satisfactory. Fortunately, or some would say providentially, it also remains true that such blots, stains, and failures do not remove from these institutions the resuscitating power of their foundational principles, which remain not only the basis for their survival but also for their self-reformation and renewal. In mid-twentieth-century Catholic circles such a return to foundational principles was called *ressourcement,* and its many exemplifications set the stage for

---

49. That Poland would come to the mind of Primo Levi in the context of the Palestinians and Jews in the Promised Land suggests that even the allegedly most anti-Semitic nation in Europe also has its roots in what can be described as a kind of messianic aspiration, if not of messianic victimhood — espoused particularly by the nineteenth-century Romantic poet Adam Mickiewicz.

Jan T. Gross, first encountered in chapter 5, and now exploring the theme of Poland as "the Christ of Nations," has described the inability of Poles at Jedwabne "to recognize a fellow victim, not in some faraway land but in the neighbor living right across the street." Gross then asked: "Have they not, by this failure, betrayed their own destiny?" Gross will put in a more formal appearance presently, but in response to his question, it can be said that such language is too definitive; just as it would be too definitive to speak of Israel's betrayal of its destiny at Sabra and Shatila. Jan T. Gross, "A Tangled Web," in Istvan Deák, Jan T. Gross, and Tony Judt, eds., *The Politics of Retribution in Europe* (2000).

Vatican II, while continuing its reformative program even into the twenty-first century.

One such foundational principle is about to be validated in the context of Primo Levi's broaching Soviet indifference to the Nazi annihilation of the Polish army to illustrate his shock at the massacres at Sabra and Shatila. The latter will broaden out the present treatment to encompass another conflicted site of religious and political renewal, and will also return this discussion to the original issue of "the popes against the Jews." Comparable to Sabra and Shatila — at least in terms of horror, if not of numbers killed — are the two most widely discussed pogroms of wartime Poland, Jedwabne during the war, and Kielce a year after it.[50] And just as Sabra and Shatila served to indict the entire Israeli polity, it was a contention of Jan T. Gross, the chronicler of the pogroms, that they were representative of Poles in general. As briefly discussed in chapter 5, Gross maintained that the murders in Kielce "could have happened anywhere in Poland and at any time during this period." A consequence of that careless judgment was that Deborah Lipstadt, courtroom victor over the odious David Irving, publicly stated, "the next time I hear someone say the Poles were as bad as the Germans, I will probably still challenge that charge — after all the damage wrought by the Germans cannot be compared to what the Poles did — but my challenge will be far less forceful. I may even keep silent" (*Publishers Weekly,* May 29, 2005).

Those kinds of exaggerations helped revivify an old conflict between the two peoples, each of which to a greater or lesser degree defined itself as fated to what was earlier called "messianic victimhood." An aspect of the latter was treated briefly and under a different name in chapter 7 in its post–World War I instantiation, and I described it in more detail in its post–World War II phase in the previous chapter when referring to "The Other Warsaw Uprising."[51] An examination of this additional example of the conflict between foundational ideals and contemporary applications will also provide a different but analogous perspective on the interrelationship of religious principles and political realities, particularly as they relate to Israelis and Palestinians. Certainly, it can be said that to emphasize the savage acts of less than two hundred Kielce citizens to the point where such acts color the en-

50. They are described, respectively, by the aforementioned Jan T. Gross, in *Neighbors: The Destruction of the Jewish Community in Jedwabne* (2001); *Fear: Anti-Semitism in Poland after Auschwitz* (2006).

51. *Commonweal,* September 24, 2004; the article's subtitle is "Why the World Has Forgotten."

tire body of Poles is as regrettable as identifying all Jews with the violent territorial acquisitions — also agonized over by Levi, who specifically mentioned Gaza and the West Bank — in the institutionalized state of Israel.[52]

Gross noted that Polish Jews were the "core and bulk of the ruling elite" in Israel, but seemed oblivious to the attendant irony that this elite was responsible for assaults on fellow dwellers in Palestine as murderous as anything conceived by wartime or postwar Polish mobs. This does not mean that "Poland has slain its thousands, Israel its tens of thousands," since there were scores of separate pogroms in Poland's history that cumulatively *might* outweigh the killing of the innocent in Palestine from 1948 on. Nor, in turn, does this exonerate the latter killings since any numerical account obscures the real point at issue here, an issue that has to do with the dangers in selective indictments of entire social or ethnic groups for the acts of a segment, large or small, of its members.

However, that does not mean numbers have no importance. In *The Neighbors Respond: The Controversy over the Jedwabne Massacre in Poland* (2004), Thomasz Szarota, a Polish historian of the Nazi occupation, was rightly less generous regarding Gross's account. "Proportions are important here. For the resident of Melbourne or New York, the name of Jedwabne may mean almost as much today as Auschwitz, Treblinka, or Majdanek." He then described an interview by two American journalists who wanted to discuss Jedwabne, but who had apparently never heard of Babi Yar. He told them, "in the course of two days 33,000 people were murdered there." The journalists exclaimed, "What? Where?" Szarota explained: "the Germans murdered 33,000 Jews in Babi Yar." They answered: "Germans?" "Who cares?" Like John Connelly, they were only interested in crimes against Jews carried out by East Europeans.

In an effort to oppose the kind of selective indictments mentioned above, Israel Gutman — historian and advisor at Yad Vashem as well as a

---

52. In footnote 10, I described as briefly as possible the severe disagreement with Rosemary Ruether on the status of the Palestinians in Israel, and my subsequent tardy realization that she was largely right and I and her other critics were largely wrong. As noted, the title of the issue of *Continuum* where this disagreement was aired was "Anti-Semitism, Middle East, and Feminism." Although the articles on feminism had nothing to do with the Middle East, I have in retrospect wondered whether there was a nexus. Ruether at the time was certainly among the three or four most important Catholic feminists, and I have been struck by the fact that within the relatively narrow precincts of present-day American Catholicism the most discerning critic of Israel vis-à-vis the Palestinians has been another feminist, Margaret O'Brien Steinfels, a former editor of *Commonweal.*

survivor of the Warsaw ghetto and of the death camps — wrote in a balanced but nevertheless critical introduction to Gross's *Neighbors:*

> the notion that the Poles are an anti-Semitic people — an idea that has made some inroads among us — ought to be rejected. Poland had more Righteous Among the Nations who rescued Jews, than any other country. . . . Many of them paid for their actions with their lives. The circumstances in Poland were such that only about 1 percent of Jews were rescued by Poles, but the act of rescue in such an era serves as a ray of light and hope that sustains faith in man in benighted times.[53]

As to the role of the institutional church in Poland, that ray of light and hope certainly seemed to be flickering at the time of the pogrom in Kielce, when only one bishop out of more than a dozen spoke out against killings that had been instigated by rumors of a kidnapping by the Jews, that is, rumors of a ritual murder. As noted in chapter 5, the future primate, Stefan Wyszyński, actually brought up the 1913 ritual murder trial of Mendel Beilis in Kiev — the occasion of Kertzer's most slanderous effort to implicate a pope in the libel — and asserted that "the matter of blood was not definitively settled." But it has now been settled, mainly by a reconsideration of the import of the foundational Gospel texts as understood by Wyszyński's protégé, John Paul II, in his admirable fulfillment of the mandate of *Nostra Aetate.*

Moreover, the achievement of the Council led to a sense of "shared responsibility" for the Holocaust among a new generation of Poles. "One can share the responsibility for the crime without taking part in it," said the Polish literary critic Jan Blonski in "The Poor Poles Look at the Ghetto." That widely published 1987 statement effected a *crise de conscience,* and challenged the Polish nation to rethink its past. The title alludes to Czeslaw Milosz's "A Poor Christian Looks at the Ghetto," which ends with its persona expressing fear that he too will be "counted among the helpers of death."[54] According to Blonski, this fear, which "warps and disfigures" Polish thinking, can be over-

---

53. "Do the Poor Poles Really Look at the Ghetto?" in *The Neighbors Respond,* ed. Antony Polonsky and Janna B. Michlic (2004).

From Nechama Tec's *When Light Pierced the Darkness: Christian Rescue of Jews in Nazi-Occupied Poland* (1987) to *They Were Just People: Stories of Rescue in Poland During the Holocaust* by Bill Tammeus and Jacques Cukierkorn (2009), the literature is vast and deeply affecting.

54. The English translation of this poem appears in Milosz's *Selected Poems,* which Continuum published in 1973.

come by emulating Pope John Paul II's speech at the synagogue of Rome, and by living in the spirit of the conciliar documents "written at the time of Pope John XXIII." That speech and those documents made one thing clear:

> Christians of the past and the church itself were wrong. They had no reason to consider Jews as a "damned nation," a nation responsible for the death of Jesus Christ. . . . The new church documents do not attempt to exonerate the past; they do not argue over extenuating circumstances. They speak clearly about the failures to fulfill the duties of brotherhood and compassion. The rest is left to history.[55]

Unfortunately, one of the drawbacks of the latter is that it is also left to historians, who — as the previous nine chapters attest — too often fail to record many of the acts of brotherhood and compassion that those documents extol.

I have referred more than once to just such a document, called "Refugee," as "the most significant papal utterance relative to Jews not only of the pre–Vatican II twentieth century, but of the second millennium of the church." The original context of that seemingly inflated observation, in chapter one above, was Kertzer's reference to Pius XII as the man whose contempt for Jews was so great that he wouldn't refer to them by name — though, as noted in the previous chapter, he used that disdained name in his first encyclical, *Summi Pontificatus*. At the beginning of the present chapter, I also suggested that given Kertzer's performance as a chronicler of Jewish-Christian relations, even if he had had access to this "Refugee" text, it would not have appeared in print under his name. Nor have either his reviewers or the Catholics who share his view discussed or even mentioned it. The peculiarity of this situation is that many of them are researchers, scholars, editors, and writers who are publicly, vocally, and sometimes self-servingly preoccupied with issues in Jewish-Christian relations, and thus — any outside observer would assume — are diligently on the lookout for relevant material.[56]

---

55. It may be noted that this is the same brotherhood and compassion that was described above in terms of Primo Levi's "empathetic sense of commonly shared humanity" that transcends ethnic loyalties, and which was then described in terms of the seeming tautology, *anima naturaliter humana*.

56. "Refugee" was discovered by the researcher and bibliographer William Doino, and appeared first on the website of "Inside the Vatican" (October 25, 2006) with links to *The Palestine Post*, where it had originally appeared during the war. It was picked up by less than forty online journals and blogs around the world, and by two wire services, Catholic News Agency

It may also be noted that venues favored by conservative Catholics like *First Things* and the Catholic League have at least commented on an abridged story of "Refugee."

Possibly if a "Refugee" article had been titled "The Real Secret History of Pius XII" it would have resonated among those liberal reviewers of *Hitler's Pope* who, while usually critical of the book, nevertheless went on to praise it for at least daring to open up the entire matter of Pacelli's allegedly aberrant behavior and anti-Semitic conduct. Characteristic of the latter — in what may be a new form of the *"sic et non,"* or "yes, but" trope — is the following from an otherwise critical review in *The National Catholic Reporter* (November 19, 1999).

> Despite its condemnatory tone, Cornwell's book is an honest challenge to the church, to history and Christians. Canonization will not cleanse Pius XII's reputation. Only Pius XII himself could have done it. The pope had 13 years between the end of World War II and his death to explain himself. He had a duty as head of the Roman Catholic church to do that. Do it in some detail, even if it was not to be released until after his death. . . . He didn't.

These sentiments were voiced by Arthur Jones, a veteran editor and reviewer. Unfortunately, in his attempt to be even-handed, Jones goes to the opposite extreme. Cornwell's book may present a challenge to the church, to history and Christians, but the last adjective that could be said to modify that challenge is "honest." Cornwell's book is not a work where the occasional error occurs unintentionally — what was defined in chapter 9 as an "honest mistake"; rather, such "errors" directly support the overall thesis of the book, and must be characterized as simply and intentionally dishonest. In short the "yes, but" trope dictates something along these lines: "Yes, Pacelli did some good things, and it is certainly a terrible thing to call him 'Hitler's pope,' but he did do the horrific XYZ" — even though it is not clear whether XYZ actually relate to events and deeds that are historically validated — "and so it is necessary that he. . . ." Here criticism drifts off into self-redemptive non sequiturs, usually about the misfortune

---

("Archival Document Reveals Pope Pius XII's Support for Jewish People") and the international Zenit News agency ("'Be Proud to Be a Jew!' Pius XII Told Visitor in '41"). Still, as of late 2010, the entry "Palestine Post" "April 28, 1944" "refugee" generated only two hundred results. None of these were from what might be called either "liberal" or "mainstream" sites.

of efforts at canonizing the wartime pope — a tired and tiring topic scrutinized fully in the previous chapter. Similarly, *The Popes Against the Jews* — a book that can be recognized now as scarred by errors that in no way pass the test of honest mistakes — originally met with relatively unabated praise. It is true, of course, that the latter was occasionally tempered by some mild reservation — after all, these *are* academics habituated to complexity — to the effect that while from time to time Kertzer might overreach or overreact, in the main he too, like Cornwell, had written a book deserving of commendation.

The following excerpt reproduces a footnote in chapter 3 that contained a sample of reviews of *The Popes Against the Jews* by various writers, both Christian and Jewish (p. 52, n. 5, above). Those judgments can now be evaluated in terms of the previous nine chapters as well as in light of the "Refugee" story to follow.

> The reviewers who provide the glowing comments — beginning with the Christians — are a combination of genteel irenicists and kindly reformists. *Eugene Fisher:* "remarkable," "gone through archives," "lively and compelling." *Jack Miles:* "with meticulous documentation tells a sickening story . . . an iron to burn scars in the mind." *John Pawlikowski:* "substantive volume based on sound scholarship . . . serious work that deserves significant attention," "a basically accurate picture." The most fulsome praise was by *Kevin Madigan,* who described Kertzer as a "national treasure" and his book as a "masterpiece." Among the Jewish commentators the following are also representative: *Michael Marrus:* "well documented," "rests solidly upon materials from the Holy See's own archives," "showers us with evidence." *A. James Rudin:* "Those who challenge his disturbing conclusions will have to match Mr. Kertzer's scholarship, research and command of the Italian language." *Robert S. Wistrich:* "a powerful and incisive analysis . . . solid documentation and clear exposition." *Richard Bernstein:* "Important . . . Fascinating . . . [A] riveting piece of historical detective work."

The commendation by Rabbi Rudin is particularly noteworthy since there are few errors that are as flagrant as Kertzer's assaults on "the Italian language."

But all of these commentators, the Christian as well as the Jewish, will surely find new light in the document reproduced below, and to which I referred in the first chapter as the pope's "affirmation of Jews as such." That earlier reference bears repeating here:

"As such" is significant, since it will become evident in the body of this book that Jews, when they weren't being viciously persecuted, were tolerated because they were the "witness people" to the triumph of Christianity, or because they were the protected wards of the papacy, or because of a common Scripture — or because of some other reason extraneous to their sheer reality as human beings. To that long tradition of humiliation, the statement of Pius XII says: "Not so!" For the first time in more than a thousand years (and probably much longer), a pope spoke *of* and *to* Jews as fellow children of God — and this occurred well before the revolutionary reforms of Vatican II.

As several times noted, the document at issue appeared originally in *The Palestine Post* (April 28, 1944); it was titled "A Papal Audience in Wartime"; it was attributed to "Refugee"; and it was accompanied by an editorial note saying, "The author of this article arrived in this country in the refugee ship Nyassa." A present-day reader will also notice that its style is somewhat self-consciously "literary."

It is on a sunny Wednesday morning in the autumn of 1941. An up-to-date Roman bus takes me from the center of the Eternal City to the Vatican. In the pocket of my dark suit I have a permit to enter the Palace of Vatican City for an audience with His Holiness Pope Pius XII.

As the bus crosses the Tiber, I can see the complex of Hadrian's Tomb. A moment later we arrive at the huge square in front of St. Peter's.

The *portal di bronzo,* leading to the Governmental Palace, is guarded by foot soldiers, who look like the lansquenets of some centuries ago. They are the Swiss Guards, and their multicolored uniforms and polished halberds and swords seem to be taken from a museum. An officer with a big moustache gives me the pass permit, the Guards take up their halberds and salute while I enter the Palace and mount a staircase. On the second floor a footman, in tight velvet trousers, shows me into a vestibule, where about 80 people are waiting. Among them are many German soldiers, in field uniform, their caps in their hands. For about an hour I stand around or pace the parquet floor among those warriors of Herr Hitler — probably on their way to Benghazi and Tripoli, anxious not to miss the chance of taking a papal blessing with them for further heroic deeds.

After some time we are led into another hall, its walls are decorated with oil paintings, antique engravings and maps. We then pass through a corridor into another anti-chamber, and, finally we stand before huge double doors ornamented with gold.

One of the Papal under-secretaries appears and gives us instructions about what to say to His Holiness and how to behave. Then one after the other, we are allowed to enter the richly furnished hall, where the Pope receives visitors.

I am the last one to enter, after the German soldiers. The Pope, sitting in a throne-like armchair, dressed in magnificent vestments, resembles some wise doctor, a good friend. His eyes shine in a friendly way through gold-rimmed glasses as each petitioner kneels to kiss the ring on the thin fingers of the Father's right hand.

The Pope speaks to everybody — asking the soldiers in fluent German from which part of the Reich they come and whether they have a special wish. And he speaks so naturally and so simply that one cannot but feel his benevolent influence. Afterwards the Holy Father gives his benediction and hands over the petitions to his retinue: cardinals, bishops and other high dignitaries of Mother Church, officials of the Vatican Government, secretaries and diplomats. They stand respectfully in the background behind the audience chair, dressed in richly colored garments of mediaeval style.

At last it is my turn. I step forward, feeling very uneasy and shy. Then I kneel down on a velvet cushion, bow over the Papal hand, and breathe a kiss on the ring.

Then I look up and address him, stammering some Italian phrases.

But the Pope interrupts me; — "My son, you can speak your own language with me; you are German, too, aren't you?" —

— "No, your Holiness, I was only born in Germany. But I am not a German any longer — I am a Jew" —

— "So you are a Jew, what can I do for you? Tell me, my son!" —

I begin to explain why I have come. I report about the shipwrecked Jewish refugees, saved by Italian warships in the Aegean Sea and now starving in a prisoner of war camp on one of the islands. The Pope listens carefully to my explanations of how to help these poor people either by taking them to Palestine or by bringing them back to Italy to avoid epidemics and further starvation. Then Pius XII says:

— "You have done well to come to me and tell me this. I have heard about it before. Come back tomorrow with a written report and give it to the Secretary of State who is dealing with the question. But now for you, my son. You are a young Jew. I know what that means and I hope you will always be proud to be a Jew!" And the Pope raises his voice that everybody in the hall can hear it clearly, "My son, whether you are worthier than others only the Lord knows, but believe me, you are at least as worthy as every other human being that lives on our earth! And now, my Jewish friend, go with the protection of the Lord, and never forget, you must always be proud to be a Jew!" —

After having pronounced these words in his pleasant voice, the Pope lifts his hands to give the usual benediction. But he stops, smiles and his wonderful fingers only touch my head. Then he lifts me from my kneeling position. . . .

I join the others by the wall, not caring for the expression on their faces. Have they heard it too?

Now the Holy Father, Pope Pius XII, rises from his chair, spreads out his hands over us and speaks the general benediction. I bow my head.

Afterwards, after leaving the Palace, I walk alone across the piazza before St. Peters, back to the Tiber embankment. I sit down on a bench looking at the Eternal City, at Rome, her ruins and palaces, at the Capital on which the sun shines brightly from a Roman sky.

In the Sermon on the Mount, Jesus said, "Blessed are you when people insult you and persecute you." The pope said to the refugee, "You are a young Jew. *I know what that means,*" and then gave him his personal blessing, "go with the protection of the Lord, and never forget, you must always be proud to be a Jew!"[57]

57. There is a similar though far less significant instance in which a Jewish chaplain, Harold Saperstein — father of the Marc Saperstein cited earlier in these pages — at a postwar audience was moved by the pope's civility when he saw the Star of David insignia rather than a cross on the chaplain's uniform, and so did not present his hand to be kissed. Saperstein then visited with Roman Jews who volunteered the information that they owed their lives to the pope's intervention. Of course, this narrative was pre-Hochhuth — the lens through which all Holocaust events are now viewed.

But when *The Deputy* appeared Rabbi Saperstein gave a series of sermons to his congregation, one of which, after acknowledging the pope's silence, began as follows: "But there is another side to the picture to which Hochhuth did not do justice. This is what Pius XII did do, a story that another playwright might have made another play in which the Pope is the hero. Yes Hochhuth refers to the fact that the pope instructed the Church to help the Jews, that Jews were taken into Catholic institutions, that the Vatican paid out money to redeem Jews. But he passes this off as if it were a piddling detail compared with the duty to speak out" (Harold Saperstein, *Witness from the Pulpit* [2001]).

Now comes, again, David I. Kertzer, writing in his introduction about *his* father's

As noted earlier, in the previous thousand years, no pope would make a public statement on the Jews that wasn't indebted to the teaching of contempt, and that didn't explicitly or implicitly humiliate them as the homeless people who in the economy of salvation existed only to bear witness to Christianity as the true religion. No pope would make a statement negating that position until the above unrehearsed response to the plight of a Jew — fittingly called "Refugee" — was made in the autumn of 1941 by the now defamed Pius XII. This was a revolutionary clarion, made long before the actual revolution — the latter now known to history as Vatican II.

However, as also noted earlier, it is less than understandable why the response of liberal Catholics to the "Refugee" statement would be so negative. It was treated by editors, writers, commentators, and academicians of the left as at worst fake or, at best, inconsequential — and here I speak as someone who intentionally from 2007 on brought the matter to the attention of precisely such people. How inconsequential? Certainly as inconsequential as all those eulogies at Pacelli's death by Israeli politicians — eulogies that are cited by piophiles as proof of Jewish appreciation of Pacelli. In short, and unbelievable as it seemed to me at the time, this text so detailed and appearing in so utterly a neutral a venue (*The Palestine Post,* predecessor of *The Jerusalem Post*), was on its way to being viewed as merely another pawn in those previously mentioned "Pius wars." The document, which to this committed liberal appeared self-validating, was greeted on the left as a not-so-clever fabrication by their antagonists on the right. Or as one observer worded it: "My gut instinct is that because something appeared in a newspaper doesn't make it a fact." Another comment was, "Many Jews said all sorts of nice things about Pius and for all sorts of different reasons." One partisan of the left said that the information was unreliable because the person proffering it, William Doino, was himself "too partisan." A similar response went as follows: "I think the story's provenance is dubious (a proud Jew kneeling before the pope?)" — the latter also indicating that this critic wasn't a particularly close reader.

It was the unreflecting tone of these opinions, some expressed by journalists, that betrayed their thoughtless arrogance. None of them asked them-

---

award of a Vatican medallion honoring his service in Jewish-Catholic relations. He also mentions "the bronze star he [the father] had been awarded for his service as an army chaplain in Italy." It is difficult to avoid the suspicion that Rabbi Kertzer may also have been received graciously by Pius XII, albeit in the antechamber to the Holocaust, and may even have heard of the pope's intervention for the Roman Jews.

selves why the wartime editors of *The Palestine Post* would have published this apparently bogus story. Were those editors less professional than their American counterparts?[58] They had nothing to gain by exalting the pope. This was not like Ben-Gurion or Golda Meir praising him after the war in order to get Vatican approval for what was happening in Palestine. These self-satisfied observers, who simply rejected *tout court* the mere possibility that the "Refugee" tale might be authentic, in fact represented what is now being called "the commentariat" — editors, researchers, writers, "public intellectuals," and the like — but for this reader they only brought to mind Victor Klemperer on the academics of Nazi Germany, Julien Benda on those of France, as well as my own description of ideological liberals in the previous chapter.

Similar reactions to *The Palestine Post* article — occurring over a period of several years — were so hard to believe that in need of a combination of relief and answers I actually returned to those theories of interpretation mentioned in chapter 1 in the context of *Truth and Method* by Hans-Georg Gadamer, the granddaddy of what came to be known as *Rezeptionstheorie*. This term was now established academic parlance for how to respond to a previously unknown body of writing — which certainly the "Refugee" narrative was. After renewing my acquaintance with the tangled web of what its practitioners refer to possessively as "theory," I began to muse on whether these ideological liberals themselves may not have been blindsided by Wolfgang Iser, Hans Robert Jauss, and the other grand Teutons looming on

---

58. The seeming exception was *Commonweal*, which published a one-page article under my name, "The Audience" (*November 5, 2010*). The irony of the date is that in the Anglophone world this is Guy Fawkes Day, honoring the failure of an earlier pope to engage in tyrannicide. Since the editors had blocked the article for nearly a year (several anti-"Refugee" quotes are theirs), they had no wish to honor Pius XII's disengagement from genocide. A file of e-mails made clear their view that the article was fake and its author delusional — even though I had published two articles critical of the pope in their magazine. (Cf. page 252.) Ironies multiplied when the editor wrote: "I don't like getting in the middle of another nasty exchange between you and one of my prized writers," referring to John Connelly, but not to his provably delusional assertions. (These were also the editors who had made room for a Richard Neuhaus eulogy, honoring Bush's chaplain general in the Iraq war.) Just before the purged article went to press, the final bit of *delectatio morosa* played out: "I'm getting questions about your 'three independent' sources who confirm the story about the papal audience. I'm going to take your word on this, but please make sure you're right." The moral here is that the Catholic editors, like the historians and theologians fawning over Kertzer, will embrace ideology if it is decked out as a "noble liberal cause." And in today's world few things are more noble or more liberal than demeaning Pius XII.

the "cognitive horizon" — the latter, another term adopted as exclusively theirs. However, not even the most whimsical reflections fading off into the acerbic could dissipate the shock that out of sheer ideology, a plain and relatively simple text was being spurned by presumably well-educated, religiously concerned, and — this is the supreme irony — professedly *liberal* people.

Fortunately, the words in a poem by a scholar and a clergyman came to mind (as similarly helpful words by Robert Browning were described in this book's introduction): "Riddle who list, for me, and pull for Prime" — meaning, let whoever is so inclined spin their complicated verbal webs; what counts is attention to plain, straightforward matters of fact.[59] And nothing was more plain and straightforward than the origins, the background, the context, and the content of "Refugee" — particularly since its discoverer, William Doino, had also tracked down several third-party witnesses to the narrative. Just as Rabbi Saperstein in New York rejected the portrait of the anti-Semitic pope in *The Deputy,* so too another American, this time in Ohio, also contradicted the well-established viewpoint of Rolf Hochhuth.

The following testimonial appeared in the weekly *L'Osservatore della Domenica* (June 26, 1964) under the title "I Owe My Life to the Pope."

> My name is Herman Herskovic and I am forty three years old. My parents were Jews and we were living in Czechoslovakia. During the last war it was necessary to leave the country in order to escape the Nazi persecution. Today I live in Cleveland. . . . But I would never have been in America had it not been for Pius XII. I have read that Hochhuth in his "The Vicar" accused Pope Pacelli of indifference to the fate of millions of Jews. This accusation immediately struck me as deeply unfair to a person who had done so much for others. So I said to myself, "If Pius XII were alive he would be able to defend himself. Since he is not, I at least can tell how the pope saved my life, and how he saved several hundred of my fellow Jews."

The testimonial went on to explain how in 1940 the writer and a group of Czech Jews, mainly members of a Zionist youth organization, made plans to

---

59. The writer is George Herbert, the poem is "Jordan I": and there is paragraph after paragraph of appreciation and explication in *Celestial Pantomime: Poetic Structures of Transcendence* (enlarged edition, 1994).

flee to Palestine. On June 15, five hundred "men, women, and children" embarked from Bratislava on a ship formerly used for hauling cattle.

> The plan was to follow the course of the Danube to the Black Sea and there transfer to a larger ship. It was estimated that the journey would take four days. Four months later we were still on the same ship, sleeping on the deck, starving, without water, and with no radio. Arriving finally at the mouth of the Danube, we had a nasty surprise. The ship we were to have taken had left. . . . Pointing the bow of the old tramp steamer south we put our trust in the Lord *(affidammo l'anima al Signore).* These were terrifying days. The boat was like a box of matches. Everyone had to stay exactly where they were. If ten people moved at the same time, the ship would have capsized.

At last they managed to reach Istanbul. But they were refused permission to enter the harbor because the British insisted to their Turkish allies that some passengers would try to find their way to British Mandated Palestine. After entering the Aegean, the boiler burst, and they drifted for several days until the ship foundered on an isolated island. After eleven days of near starvation, an Italian warship discovered them and took them to a prison camp on the isle of Rhodes (Rodi).[60] At this point in the testimonial, "Refugee" puts in an appearance.

60. Meanwhile another ship, *The Schoenbrunn*, with eight hundred German Jews aboard had left Vienna, and one of the refugees later reported:

> As we arrived we saw a black ship with a strange big wheel on its side standing in the middle of the Danube, exactly where the border between Romania and Bulgaria runs. . . . The leaders of our transport, together with the Jewish communities, succeeded in bribing the Romanians to supply food and some of their essential needs. . . . When they entered the Mediterranean they got into many troubles. The old ship was not suitable for these conditions and ran aground. . . . They swam to a deserted island, prepared a 'rope' made of sheets, and pulled the ship, so they were able to take some belongings and the rest of their food. . . . After 13 days of suffering, being very short of food, Italian pilots spotted them. . . .

Herman Rothman, *Hitler's Will* (2009). What is extraordinary about the narrator of the above is that she saw her husband on the side-wheeler and was ultimately reunited with him.

The fate of the Czech Jews and the German Jews differed drastically from that of the eight hundred Romanian Jews two years later whose ship *The Struma* had to be towed into the harbor at Istanbul because of engine failure. After weeks of negotiations, which resulted in a few passengers with visas journeying overland to Palestine, the British again prevailed on their Turkish allies. The ship was towed out into the Black Sea and abandoned. After a

The father of one of our companions obtained freedom for his son and permission for him to go to Switzerland. On his journey north the young man arrived in Rome and was received in audience by Pius XII. He told the pope what had happened and also informed him of the presence of German troops in Rodi. Pius XII listened attentively and promised to inform the Italian government immediately. Two weeks later we were transferred to a safe concentration camp in Calabria.

The Allied landing in Sicily renewed our concerns. We feared we would be slaughtered [*massacrassero*] by the retreating German army. It was then the Church intervened to save us again. The chaplain of the "lager" persuaded the guards to let us escape before the arrival of the SS. For three days we were hidden in a forest. And when we were able to return to the camp, it was already under the control of Allied soldiers.

The writer then told how he and other able-bodied men in his group joined a Czech brigade fighting with the British "until the liberation of Europe," after which he immigrated to the United States. Nearing the end of his testimony, he went on to say that notwithstanding everything the Germans had done, he didn't feel any excessive resentment toward them "because I think the majority of them were misled. But I know for sure that many people in many places did not help the Jews." He then returned to the original issue raised by Hochhuth's *The Vicar*. "Nor is it right to accuse Pius XII of something that was not under his control. Personally, I owe him much, and I thought it well worth the telling. HERMAN HERSKOVIC., Cleveland, Ohio."

In light of this confirmation of the narrative by "Refugee," one has to wonder whether comfortable liberal Catholics can continue to rely on their "gut instinct" in maintaining this tale is fabricated; that is, whether they can continue to respond to it by observing that "the story's provenance is dubious," or that "many Jews said all sorts of nice things about Pius." After that original discovery, William Doino began to dig deeper — "dig" being one of Kertzer's favorite terms for his manufactured methodology — and discovered the name of the "old tramp steamer": the *Pentcho*. Then he discovered the entire story of its voyage and the fate of its passengers in *Odyssey*, a richly illustrated book published by Simon & Schuster in 1984, and written by the

---

few days adrift there was an explosion causing the ship to sink with all its crew and passengers, a total of 768 people. Later it was determined that it was another ally, the Russians, who were responsible, since it was a Soviet torpedo that caused the explosion.

journalist and BBC reporter John Bierman. This discovery, among other things, provided the name of "Refugee," Heinz Wisla, along with a brief account of his papal audience. Third, and most important, was Doino's discovery of the complete text of an unpublished memoir by Wisla himself — who in the event had emigrated from Israel and taken up residence in the United States, where he adopted the name Howard Heinz Wisla. The complete story of these remarkable findings has been told by William Doino himself, and therefore I abridge considerably the remainder of the tale.

The memoir, "Long Journey Home," provides further information on all the incidents mentioned by Herskovic, as well as those known only to the writer himself. The latter include a brief mention of his birth and early life in Germany; his subsequent horrifying imprisonment as a young man in Sachsenhausen; his deliverance through the manipulations of his father, a decorated veteran of the Great War; and his flight to Slovakia, followed by the disastrous voyage that ended up with him and the other Jews on the Isle of Rhodes. That takes up eight chapters of the memoir. Chapter 9, "Roman Experience and the Pope," is in its essentials identical with the account in *The Palestine Post*, though the author provides information about the priest in Rome (a Father Weller) who made contact with the Vatican to arrange for the audience. The remaining five chapters — a remarkable adventure in its own right — describe Wisla's efforts to avoid being picked up by various police and military agencies in Italy and Spain, until in 1944 he managed, with the considerable assistance of local as well as of American Jewish agencies, to escape from Portugal and travel on to Israel.

The last chapter, titled "Homeward Bound," begins as follows: "On January 23 [1944] I board the 'Nyassa'" — the ship that was mentioned by the editors of *The Palestine Post* when they noted of "A Papal Audience in Wartime" that "the author of this article arrived in this country in the refugee ship Nyassa." The writer continues:

> At 4 PM a siren sounds. The "Nyassa" leaves Lisbon, steaming down the Tajo [Tagus] River. . . . Then south along the Portuguese shore. The sea is smooth like a mirror.
>
> I decide to compose a letter which I will send to the family of Wilfrid Israel to whom I owe this trip "home" to Palestine.

Wilfrid Israel was the wealthy German-Jewish businessman and humanitarian who since the rise of Hitler had devoted his life to helping large groups of Jewish children find refuge in England via what was called the

Kindertransport. During the war itself he arranged the escape of scores of Jews from Nazi-dominated Europe, usually through Spain and Portugal. "Refugee" became a close friend, and had visited with Israel immediately before his death on June 1, 1943, when his flight to London was shot down by German aircraft. In a note dated "Fall 1943," in Wisla's memoir he speculated that "German fighters attack the plane in the belief that Winston Churchill returns on it from Africa." The letter that Wisla was composing on the *Nyassa* finally ended up being included in the memoir under the heading "Postscript." It is a detailed tribute to the writer's friend as well as a remembrance of their last visit in Lisbon. It also has a faint echo of the words of the pope to "Refugee" — who in the memoir is writing about a promise made earlier with Wilfrid Israel — that they would both "try and understand our people and to always be proud of being a Jew."

In closing this phase of the final chapter, I should emphasize that the reason for citing the whole of the "Refugee" document is twofold. The first is that it is particularly important in the context of the historical sketch that opened this chapter, beginning with Christianity's conflicted origins and going through the hate-filled *adversus Iudaeos* tradition. That sketch then continued with the murderous Crusades, and concluded with the modern era. At the dawn of that era, and lest that dismal history of contempt become blurred in the memory, there is a declaration by a predecessor pope to Pius XII who is here in the process of explaining why he is driving Jews out of most of his domain. The following excerpt is from the Bull (*Hebraeorum gens*, 1569) by the subsequently canonized Pius V, previously encountered in chapter 4.[61]

> Their godlessness has assumed such forms that, for the salvation of our own people, it becomes necessary to prevent their disease. Besides usury, through which Jews everywhere have sucked dry the property of impoverished Christians, they are accomplices of thieves and robbers; and the most damaging aspect of the matter is that they lure the unsuspecting through magical incantations, superstition, and witchcraft. . . . On account of these and other serious matters, and because of the gravity of their crimes which increase day to day more and more, We order that,

61. Probably the best thing that can be said about Pius V is that he inspired G. K. Chesterton to write "Lepanto," not only one of the great historical narratives in English verse, but also a foot-stomping and rafter-rattling work, superior even to Vachel Lindsay's "General William Booth Enters into Heaven."

within 90 days, all Jews in our entire earthly realm of justice — in all towns, districts, and places — must depart these regions.

Note that this, too, is done for the greater good, "the salvation of our own people."

It took nearly five hundred years for Pius XII's blessing to obliterate Pius V's curse. The contrast is stark. The young man petitioning the pope was addressed as "my son," and was then told: "And now, my Jewish friend, go with the protection of the Lord, and never forget, you must always be proud to be a Jew!" It is difficult to imagine that those petition-signing scholars in the previous chapter who are "eagerly awaiting" the opening of "numerous archives" will discover a stronger and more irrefutable proof that Pius XII — unlike his canonized predecessor — was neither a real nor a "symbolic" anti-Semite. Will the above narrative change their minds? To cite David I. Kertzer, "I'm not holding my breath." Concerning the matter of sainthood, Pius XII is the pontiff of whom it was previously said by those same "Catholics who have worked on Holocaust issues," and who defined themselves as "part of the current struggle over possible beatification" (John Pawlikowski), that "we are strongly opposed . . . to even [his] elevation to 'venerable' status." That would certainly seem to cover every base, as well as much that is literally base, though perhaps if "venerable" is unacceptable it would still be possible to refer to this pontiff as "servant of the servants of God," since that last category would include the petitioners who are certainly putting into their service Pius XII.

I had mentioned that the reason for emphasizing the "Refugee" story was twofold. The second element of that reason was that the story is propaedeutic to the last and possibly the most pressing current issue regarding the relationship between institutionalized religion and institutionalized polities. That issue, adumbrated earlier, explicitly concerns the Palestinians and the state of Israel, the latter embodying its own parallels with the institutional church. Such parallels begin with the one between the Gospel texts privileging Christians and the biblical texts relating to the Chosen People. For the seat of the papacy in Rome, based on the tradition of St. Peter's death in that place, there is the ancient Jewish home in the Middle East, based on the tradition of the Promised Land. For the "Donation of Constantine," which purportedly gave much of Italy to the popes, there is the Balfour Declaration, which was the political rationale for establishing Israel in much of Palestine. Lastly, for the papal construal of Gospel texts to favor its position of preeminence, there is the invocation of the biblical prophets in the Israeli Declaration of Independence.

On a less positive note, for the appalling abuse of Jews, which the popes tolerated or enforced, there is the still ongoing abuse of Palestinians by Israeli officials and citizens, the latter often being made up of those who profess to be most orthodox in their religious beliefs. For the anti-Semitic Catholic clerics that Kertzer introduced (with considerable gusto), there are the rabbis, in some cases highly placed in their communities, calling down on the natives of Palestine the biblical curses against its ancient inhabitants.[62] For the ghettos into which the Jews were driven by papal regulations, there is the expulsion of Palestinians — most appallingly in the early years of Israel's independence — through acts of organized violence that were subsequently denied or papered over.

The witness to the latter by the previously cited Arthur Hertzberg is one of a host of such declarations. His testimony, however, is for many people particularly persuasive, since as a young man his enthusiasm over the establishment of the Jewish state led him in the following year to journey to Palestine — only to discover "the appalling fact" that "Israel's victory had cost six thousand dead." (And that — it must be acknowledged — is a modest figure.)

> Everyone knew that the official story — that some seven hundred thousand Arabs had left their homes during the war because they had been promised by their leaders that they would come back in triumph after the Jews were pushed into the sea — was simply not true. . . . The official narrative soon became, and remained, that Israel never expelled the Arabs: they did this to themselves. This account was challenged forty years later, in the 1980s, by revisionist historians. . . . I have no doubt that the revisionists are telling the truth because I was there in the summer of 1949. . . . Those who had just won Israel's War of Independence were being lionized and lionizing themselves as "new Jews." Israel's victory was being interpreted everywhere as the "answer" to the Holocaust.[63]

---

62. In a conversation between two committed peacemakers, the Buddhist monk Thich Nhat Hanh and the Jesuit Daniel Berrigan, the latter said of a recent visit to Israel, "The religious people we met were very closed in their suppositions about the state, in obedience to the state, and in their attitude toward violence." "As far as he could tell the traditional religious language of Judaism had been pretty much co-opted by the state." Robert H. King, *Thomas Merton and Thich Nhat Hanh: Engaged Spirituality in an Age of Globalization* (2002).

63. Arthur Herzberg, *A Jew in America: My Life and a People's Struggle for Identity* (2002).

The revisionists to whom Hertzberg referred have since become known as "new historians" because they sought to rewrite the official narrative ("old history") about the founding fathers who embraced the United Nations partition agreement, and respected Palestinian rights while struggling against the forces of neighboring Arab countries. In that sense, these historians may be loosely compared to the advocates of abolition in the nineteenth-century United States, or to the advocates of *ressourcement* and reform in the twentieth-century church.

David Ben-Gurion, certainly one of the fathers of the nation, was criticized by Tom Segev for anticipating and justifying as early as 1930 the expulsion of Palestinians because "revolutionary times" called for revolutionary deeds (*One Palestine, Complete,* 2001). Ben-Gurion was also a target in Segev's *The Seventh Million: The Israelis and the Holocaust* (1993) for his relative indifference to the plight of Jews during the Holocaust, an indifference that also allegedly tainted other founders.[64] But while there was little that Ben-Gurion, Golda Meir, or Yitzak Rabin could have done for the Jews of Europe, there was an absence of a sense of statecraft about some of their decisions, particularly those that showed little awareness of the consequences of the expulsion of the Palestinians from their own homes and land. Notwithstanding Israel's Declaration of Independence, the expulsion implied that the new society would be founded on acts of violence against an innocent native population. In fact, in the 1948 war itself, the Israelis, although professing to follow to the letter the terms spelled out by the United Nations, intentionally occupied land designated for the Palestinians, thus initiating the first of several breaches of international law that were to characterize Israeli policy over the years.

The experience of the American republic, where all three prime ministers had spent considerable time, might have been instructive. There is, for instance, the now relatively forgotten, but well-recorded and extremely cruel expulsion of indigenous peoples from their traditional lands — an act of cruelty symbolized by the expression "trail of tears." Two decades before the Civil War, nearly fifty thousand Native Americans were driven from their tribal homes in the South. Closer to present-day reality is the fact that the

---

64. In *Popes and Politics,* the new history and its targets were briefly introduced in the context of the ongoing wave of criticism of Pacelli in such books as *Papal Sin* and *Hitler's Pope.* The overall conclusion of *Popes and Politics* was that there was probably little that either leader, Pacelli or Ben-Gurion, could have done to disrupt or prevent the Nazi murders. That, of course, is a conclusion that flies in the face of the views of the scholar-petitioners who wrote to Benedict XVI.

land consigned to Native Americans *now* suggests what the future fate of Palestinians — possibly those today confined to Gaza — might well be like:

> Native American reservations have historically had some of the highest poverty statistics. Characteristics of reservations have included high unemployment rates, school dropouts, welfare dependency, sanitation inadequacies, and alcoholism. This is not surprising, as the reservation is a window in which Native Americans can see what freedom epitomizes for those outside, while solemnly acknowledging the limitations of the reservation in failing to provide that same equity for the people inside. (www.goinside.com/02/1/repairs.html)

What Israel has confronted, almost from its very origins, is the likelihood of a permanently destructive war between Jews and Palestinians. And while no one doubts that it is futile to impose post-factum standards on people from an earlier period of history, nevertheless for those who in 1948 greeted the creation of the state of Israel as literally a world-redemptive event, the animosity of the declarations by some of its founders foreshadowed the dark future that has in fact come into being. To these foundational failings, one might contrast the Enlightenment heritage in the studies known as the *Federalist Papers* by the American creators of the Constitution. Perhaps a better model would be the members of the German Resistance, specifically the Kreisau Circle under Helmuth von Möltke, who — as noted in the previous chapter — originally opposed the assassination of Hitler not only on the pragmatic grounds that it was almost certain to fail or at best cause a civil war, but also on the more farsighted ground that the new German state would then be founded on the unrestrained shedding of blood.

However, there was one policy of Israel's founding fathers that even today may constitute an important precedent regarding relations between Jews and Palestinians. This was the refusal by both Ben-Gurion and Golda Meir to embrace any kind of alignment with the racist government of South Africa — notwithstanding the efforts by the latter's publicly Christian government to forge such a relationship. Here the lesson of the American experience of the Jewish founders appears to have illuminated their statecraft, since all of them had witnessed the degradation of African Americans and its attendant social upheavals in the United States. Moreover, the rejection by these Jewish leaders of Afrikaner overtures was formally and publicly based on the militant segregation laws of the country. As a consequence, while Israel allied itself with several newly liberated African nations, it continued its ban on relations with the bigoted white government of South Africa into the 1970s.[65]

Unfortunately, the heritage of the founders was so completely ignored that by the end of the century not only were close relations with South Africa firmly in place, but segregation of Palestinians had been embraced in all but name by every succeeding government. This made the official expressions of outrage over Jimmy Carter's book, *Palestine Peace, Not Apartheid* (2006), appear even more hypocritical. There are several passages in *The Unspoken Alliance* defending Carter's book and its choice of terms, but few are as balanced as that of Shulamit Aloni, a former minister of education, in an article titled "Yes, There is Apartheid in Israel," where one may note the even-handed criticism of American Jewry and the "Israelophile community":

> The U.S. Jewish establishment's onslaught on former President Jimmy Carter is based on him daring to tell the truth which is known to all: through its army, the government of Israel practices a brutal form of apartheid in the territory it occupies. . . . Jimmy Carter does not need me to defend his reputation that has been sullied by Israelophile community officials. . . . The trouble is that their love of Israel distorts their judgment and blinds them from seeing what's in front of them. Israel is an occupying power that for 40 years has been oppressing an indigenous people, which is entitled to a sovereign and independent existence while living in peace with us.

In light of these various political and diplomatic phenomena, rather than the example of von Möltke and the Kreisau Circle mentioned above, a more relevant and representative model would have been Nelson Mandela, who persisted in his efforts to pursue independence for South Africa through nonviolent means. Fortuitously, therein may lie something of a key or at least a sliver of hope for the resolution of the Israeli-Palestinian conflict, since Mandela shortly after his release from prison in 1990 had told representatives of the American Anti-Defamation League that he recognized Is-

---

65. The history of this relationship from the foundation of the State of Israel and into the twenty-first century is narrated in Sasha Polakow-Suransky, *The Unspoken Alliance: Israel's Secret Relationship with Apartheid South Africa* (2010). This careful study treats of the close bonds between Israel and South Africa particularly after the 1967 war — relations that both symbolized and set the tone for the ongoing and ever accelerating crisis of Israel and the Palestinian Authority up to the present time.

rael's right to exist while, however, he also praised Yasser Arafat, who had supported Mandela when he was a prisoner. In the event, it was during Mandela's visit to Israel in 1999 — described by the *New York Times* (October 20, 1999) as "a trip intended to heal old wounds" — that he publicly supported "Arab recognition of its [Israel's] right to existence within secure boundaries."

Of course, Mandela also asserted the need for Israel to give up claims to Gaza and the West Bank, a concession that Primo Levi would have seconded. That Mandela may prove a lasting exemplar is evident from the fact that he strongly influenced the leaders of the now resolved conflict in Northern Ireland between Catholics and Protestants, a conflict that certainly appeared as intractable as anything in the Middle East. The two leading antagonists in Northern Ireland, Ian Paisley, who became first minister, and Martin McGuinness, who became deputy first minister, have frequently attested to the influence of Mandela on their negotiations.[66] Those negotiations, in turn, were facilitated by the former majority leader of the U.S. Senate, George Mitchell, who — as these disputes also come full circle — had been the mediator of the Arab-Israeli conflict.

But in the period immediately after Israel's foundation, it was the shedding of blood that became characteristic of the struggle between Jews and Palestinians, admittedly because of acts of violence committed primarily by militant Zionists before and after independence, but also, and undeniably, because of the invasion of the new nation by the combined armies of predominantly Arab neighboring countries. The almost inevitable consequence of such a foredoomed relationship was that after the 1967 war, the new Israeli state would become the political scapegoat of the Middle East, and more particularly in the last two decades, the scapegoat of the Western world.[67]

66. This is the second appearance of Ian Paisley in these pages. The first was his criticism of the beatification of Pius IX in chapter 4 when, among several other things, he said: "The controversy over Pius IX follows the uproar over the beatification of his namesake, Pius XII, the notorious 'Hitler's Pope.'" This was in September 2000, when negotiations in Northern Ireland were going smoothly, notwithstanding the fact that Paisley's co-negotiator's full name was Martin *Pacelli* McGuinness — an expression of the esteem in which the wartime pontiff was held in Ireland.

67. In the early nineteenth century, Lord Byron referred to Rome, once the seat of a vast empire ruling over millions, as "the Niobe of nations," a reference to the Greek mythic figure who boasted so proudly of her many children that they were all killed by rival gods. It now appears that Israel might well become the Hagar of the Middle East — after the biblical slave girl and "surrogate" mother of Abraham's child, Ishmael, both of whom were expelled from the household and left forlorn in the desert.

The latter may be symbolized by Primo Levi's "Mendel," and may be represented more explicitly by Levi's comparison of the annihilation of Poles in Warsaw with the previously mentioned slaughter of women and children in Lebanon — a dismal augur for a state founded as the expression of the world's repentance for complicity in the slaughter of the Holocaust.

In light of that history, the question now is whether Israel Gutman's "ray of light and hope that sustains faith in man in benighted times," which has shone on the two-millennium Christian church and the century-and-a-half American republic, will now illuminate the decades-old Israeli state. For, just as it was the return to the foundational teaching of the gospel that inspired the words and deeds of the two reforming popes cited above, and a similar return to the foundational teaching of the Declaration of Independence that all people "are created equal" that motivated the antislavery movement, so too it may be a return to the foundational teaching of one of the first legal codes in human history, "love your neighbor as yourself" (Lev. 19:18), which will inspire the still very young nation in the Middle East to take long overdue steps toward resolving its Palestinian dilemma.[68]

That mention of all three "parallel" institutions points up the fundamental issue regarding the interplay of religion and politics. This, in turn, can be broached in terms of two scenarios — both relative to the troubled relationship of Christianity and Judaism — which although not identical are isomorphic. If institutions, as Emerson said, are the shadows of their founders, both synagogue and church must acknowledge with Moses that they do not see the full reality of their hope (Exodus 33), and with St. Paul that they glimpse it only through a blurred reflection (1 Corinthians 13). Given those biblical truisms, Christians can reject the fundamentalist notion of Jewish guilt for shedding the blood of Jesus, while also emphasizing his prayer of forgiveness; and Jews can reject the fundamentalist notion of Palestine as exclusively their promised land, while also finding in that place a home and

---

68. In the previously cited *Thomas Merton and Thich Nhat Hanh: Engaged Spirituality in an Age of Globalization,* there is a report of a conversation in Sri Lanka between Thich Nhat Hanh and a rabbi from Israel. The latter asked Nhat Hanh what he would do if it "came down to a choice between peace in Vietnam and the survival of Buddhism. When he replied that he would choose peace, the rabbi was shocked." Nhat Hanh explained, "Buddhism is in your heart. Even if you don't have any temple or any monks, you can still be a Buddhist in your heart and life." While not embracing that as a solution to Israel's Palestinian dilemma, it is perhaps an arrow pointing in the right direction. First must come peace, then everything else. On the side of the rabbi, however, it must be said that Buddhism is hardly a religious vision founded on an age-old quest for a promised land.

hearth. And both communities can perhaps acknowledge with Primo Levi that "there is a thread of racism" running through their Scriptures that has to be interwoven into the larger tapestry of the biblical pursuit of peace being wed to justice.

A presentiment of that resolution is the fact that the one branch of the Israeli government that thus far offers some hope of constitutionally redeeming the past and guaranteeing the future is the Supreme Court, a body that by definition must live by the law of Leviticus cited above. Aharon Barak, president of the court from 1995 to 2006, and his successor, Dorit Beinisch, one of five women members of the court, have both publicly addressed the issue of Palestinian rights. While it would take an entire chapter to begin to summarize their work, even a cursory scrutiny will show that the amount and quality of material disclosed give some cause for hope. I will proffer only two instances, the first of which, by sheer happenstance, brings together Palestinians and Israelis as well as Catholics. It is described in an address to an American audience by Beinisch on the scope and procedures of the court.

> In the Bethlehem case, decided in May 2002 (Judgment: "Regarding the Church of the Nativity"), the Court looked at the conditions of the people — wanted terrorists and fighting men, civilians and priests — barricaded in the Church of the Nativity. The petitioners asked that medical teams be allowed to enter the compound to bring food and medicine to those inside. The petition was filed when negotiations were being conducted between the Israeli Government and the Palestinian Authority to find a solution to the situation. We said that the court does not participate in or direct the negotiations. Nonetheless, we examined the claims concerning the position of the people who were suffering a shortage of food and medicine because of the terrorist activities. We concluded that the army would fulfill its legal responsibilities by allowing unarmed civilians to leave the compound, receive extra food and medicine, and then return to the compound.

Given the lethal militance of both parties in the early years of the Second Intifada, this decision borders on the Solomonic. (In the event, it was the Vatican that raised objections to the government of Israel regarding an alleged violation of church property rights.)

The second instance, also from Justice Beinisch, relates to the expanded mission of the court and provides further reason for hope in the future:

Questions arising from Israel's security situation have prompted our Court to adopt doctrinal controls that restrict the military's ability to infringe on personal rights by simply reciting the mantra of "national security." . . . According to these principles, our Court considers petitions concerning the detention conditions of thousands of persons recently detained on suspicion of terrorism. Almost every day the judges of the Supreme Court consider petitions for injunctions against the use of improper interrogation methods, the demolition of houses, or other measures taken in the name of security.[69]

It is worthy of note that David Kretzmer in *The Occupation of Justice: The Supreme Court of Israel and the Occupied Territories* (2002), while being — as his title indicates — less sanguine, in the overall confirms Dorit Beinisch's viewpoint. On the other hand, there is the more critical report, "Israel's Supreme Court: Conservative or Liberal?" by Marwan Dalal.[70] Obviously, this is not the place nor is the present writer the person to even broach the resolution of such differences; but it is important to commend the pursuit of every possible avenue that might lead to the end of a conflict that on the political and military fronts has proven mutually destructive. Given the assault on Gaza in 2009-10, which resulted in the imposition of sanctions that virtually turned it into a vast prison camp, merely to advocate resort to the Supreme Court may sound naively pollyannaish. But to counter the crackpot realism (a term coined for nuclear-war advocates in the 1960s) of Israel's initiating a divide and conquer policy by separating Gaza from the West Bank — and thus transforming the already precarious two-state solution into an impossible three-state one — it is necessary to invoke the idealism of all the resources in Judaism's rich tradition of Halakhah, a body of regulations that has always implicitly gone beyond the rigid observation of legal minutiae. Such reliance means a heightened role for the Supreme Court as well as fidelity to the principles of the nation's founders as necessary steps toward a tradition-sanctioned resolution of these conflicts — since it is only by a return to its foundational principles that the words of the ancient prayer will be fulfilled: "justice and peace shall kiss" (Ps. 85:10).[71]

69. "The Role of the Supreme Court of Israel in Times of Emergency," www.jewish federations.org/content_display.html?ArticleID=65284.

70. www.thejerusalemfund.org/ht/a/GeneratePdfAction/url/. . ./Transcripts.pdf.

71. From Uri Avnery, a member of the Knesset, comes a more recent and more pessimistic assessment of the rule of law. "Today, the production of irresponsible laws, most of them racist and anti-democratic, is booming. The only remaining obstacle to their progress

But more than the invocation of the most lofty prayers or the citation of the highest legal decisions will be required to heal the wounds of both parties in the twenty-first century. The conflict has been exacerbated on the one side by Israeli religious extremists and political hawks, and on the other by Palestinian intermural struggles between Fatah and Hamas. The following description now expresses the prevalent mood.

> Careful analysis of official positions shows that neither side is ready yet to make the concessions that would be acceptable to the other. Israel is not yet ready to give total independence to the Palestinians, the Arabs will accept nothing less. More concessions will have to be made on both sides. Otherwise . . . they are on a collision course that will leave an aftermath of disillusion and bitterness and a hopelessness that can lead to tragic conclusions.

That this was written *in 1977* by the previously cited Rabbi Harold Saperstein — whose views I have come to value — is an irony that is too obvious to labor, since in the intervening period of time, and certainly in the last decade, those tragic conclusions have become a harsh reality.

And although Israel can point to the outrageous conduct of Hamas, its own policies during the last decade have been a consistent and systematic affront to the advocates of a peace agreement with the Palestinians. The hundreds of thousands of outside observers who have persistently over the last two decades cut the Israeli government reams of slack because Israel represented the world's effort at recompense for the Holocaust — those observers appear to be gradually changing their minds. The most recent indication of that is the following from the American and European bishops who constitute the Holy Land Co-ordination group. On January 13, 2011, they published a report on their three-day annual visit titled "A Pledge of Prayer, A Call for Pilgrimage and A Commitment to Pursue a Just Peace."

> We have also been made aware of the suffering of those people whose marriages are put under enormous strain by the demands of "security" and religious differences, by individuals and communities whose land

---

is the Supreme Court. In the absence of a written constitution, it has the power to annul laws that violate democracy and human rights. But the Supreme Court, under assault from rightists, intervenes only in the most extreme cases." Uri Avnery, "In the Knesset," *London Review of Books,* August 5, 2010.

and property has been damaged or taken from them, including by the route and construction of the wall, and by the people whose lives are made so difficult by the situation where they live in Gaza. (http://www.catholic-jew.org.ukPress-Releases-20)

This mild critique is now often embraced even by the more guilt-ridden observers, the Christian believers who have frankly acknowledged that their tradition was the seed bed of the hatred that ultimately led to the mass murder of six million Jews. Without in any way ceasing to repent for the Christian roots of anti-Semitism, those believers no longer are willing to give Israel carte blanche in the Middle East to do what it wants to the Palestinian remnant.[72] Moreover, that viewpoint is shared by hundreds of thousands of Israeli citizens on the political left. Lastly, in terms of what was earlier referred to as "the relatively narrow precincts of American Catholicism," it can be stated plainly — here at the end of this chapter and the end of this book — that two decades ago the severe critics of Israeli policy toward the Palestinians were more discerning, more perceptive, more politically insightful, and probably more truly Christian in their views and beliefs than were their liberal antagonists, including the present writer.

But just as those same liberal Catholics have come to embrace a wartime pope's saying "be proud of your Jewishness," they will also embrace, as in note 27 above, a present-day pope's saying "be proud of your sexual orientation." And thus such Catholics will now embrace the requirement (and here we leap to the only explicitly political opinion in the present book) that after

---

72. The group of Christians that appears hesitant to share this viewpoint is the membership of religious organizations dedicated to the previously examined "Jewish-Christian relations." Members of these groups — as already pointed out — along with an understandable preoccupation with the anti-Jewish consequences of their religious affiliation, are sometimes also passionate defenders of all things Israeli. Since their numbers are small, this has little bearing on the practical order of affairs in the Middle East, but it does have a bearing on the religion they profess. It can lead to the jettisoning of its foundational principles in the name of — almost the bane of this book — "supersessionism," and out of a misplaced sense of guilt it can also lead to the distortion of historical research in order to convict various past Christian leaders of evil intentions, speech, and deeds. That allusion is to Pius XII, a pontiff who is beginning to assume the aura of the greatest pope in the four hundred years since Clement XIV. The latter's *gran rifiuto* — suppression of the Society of Jesus — is comparable to Pope Pacelli's own suppression of some of the greatest theologians of his time. Weighed against that is the achievement, also mentioned earlier, of his having appointed the overwhelming majority of the delegates to the reforming council, Vatican II — including those same theologians.

the beginning of Barack Obama's second term, just as a cold-war president said, "Tear down this wall, Mr. Gorbachev," so also a newly reelected president will say, "Tear down this wall, Mr. Netanyahu." Not only will these formerly vigorous liberal defenders of all things Israeli make this a requirement; they will make it the *sine qua non* of their support.[73]

These are the aspirations and convictions that still nourish the belief that the words of Psalm 85 can be fulfilled: "justice and peace shall kiss." And if justice is truly wedded to peace, as all people of good will ardently pray, then it will render impossible that the following verses from the beginning of Psalm 79 will ever again preoccupy the memories of Jews haunted by the Holocaust or burden the consciences of Christians tainted by the teaching of contempt:

> O God, the nations have come into your inheritance;
>> they have defiled your holy temple,
>> they have laid Jerusalem in ruins.
> They have given the corpses of your servants to the birds of the air
>> for food,
>> the flesh of your faithful to the wild animals of the earth.
> They have poured out their blood like water
>> all around about Jerusalem,
>> and there was no one to bury them.

With that threnody from three millennia ago, this book comes to an end — signaled by a twentieth-century poet, Nelly Sachs, whose own threnody, "O the Chimneys," is now her most widely known poem. But regarding the race against time — those "long overdue steps" mentioned earlier — she has a more apposite poem that begins: "Why the black answer of hate to your existence, Israel?" The reference here is not to the state but to the Jewish people who speak through such historic documents as the psalms cited above.

---

73. The assumption is that a pragmatic leader like President Obama knows he would lose the pro-Israel vote and probably the election if he pressed for such essential reforms as reversal of recent settlements in the Occupied Territories and a negotiated return to the 1967 borders. With that overriding threat, he has no reason to resolve the Jewish-Palestinian impasse until his new term begins. Then the commonsense goals for peace in the Middle East of such an organization as J Street can be realized, and in fact become the signature achievement of the Obama administration and presidency. This is also the final tribute to the rabbinical line of Saperstein, since among the leaders of J Street is Rabbi David Saperstein. For a courageous declaration of comparable goals, see also "A Man, a Plan," by David Remnick (*The New Yorker*, March 21, 2011).

In ten short stanzas, the poem traces the fate of this people, which in the course of its existence has always been so seemingly out of joint with place and time and history, but which has always risen through fidelity to its holy book from apparent defeat to renewed vitality.

> Why the black answer of hate
> to your existence, Israel?
>
> You stranger
> from a star one farther away
> than the others.
>
> Sold to this earth
> that loneliness might be passed on.
>
> Your origin entangled in weeds —
> your stars bartered
> for all that belongs to moths and worms,
> and yet: fetched away from dreamfilled sandy shores of time
> like moonwater into the distance.
>
> In the others' choir
> you always sang
> one note lower
> or one note higher.

The second half introduces the omens of the Holocaust, the apparent last destiny of these chosen people who for more than four millennia have appeared somewhat dissonant in the ambience of the surrounding culture. "In the *others'* choir you always sang one note lower or one note higher."

> You flung yourself into the blood of the evening sun
> like one pain seeking the other.
> Long is your shadow
> and it has become late for you
> Israel!
>
> How far your way from the blessing
> along the aeon of tears

to the bend of the road
where you turned to ashes.

And your enemy with the smoke
of your burned body
engraved your mortal abandonment
on the brow of heaven!

O such a death!
When all helping angels
with bleeding wings
hung tattered
in the barbed wire of time!

Why the black answer of hate
to your existence, Israel?[74]

And there the poem ends, as this people — from whom, Christians must still believe, salvation comes — manages to survive its ultimate ordeal and to return to its ancient land, all as a sign of its divinely mandated mission. But that this sign is clearly a sacred one explains why the self-administered spoliation of its own long-promised home, as well as the political ruination of its neighbors' home, is incompatible not only with Israel's nature but with Judaism's role as spiritual custodian of Western humanism. That Israel will be "ever reformed" *(semper reformanda)* as was the Christian church; that it will hear "the mystic chords of memory," as did the American republic; that it will come "into its inheritance" as did its Davidic ancestors — that is the promise of history for it, as it is also the promise for all institutions that renew their life by ceaselessly returning to their noblest foundational ideals.

---

74. *O The Chimneys: Selected Poems, including the Verse Play, Eli* (1967). This translation is by a former colleague, Michael Roloff; the other translators of the poems in this remarkably well edited and translated work are Michael Hamburger, Christopher Holme, and Ruth and Matthew Mead.

Acknowledgments

David I. Kertzer began *his* list of acknowledgments by thanking the Vatican for making available its "treasure trove of documents to allow researchers to dig into the Church's history," even though his "own project was not one that all in the Vatican were enthusiastic about." While Kertzer's own book is not exactly a Staffordshire hoard, I too have enjoyed digging into it, even though he may not be enthusiastic about what I have dug up, particularly in the lower strata of the cache.

But, then, after I had assembled my own list of people to be acknowledged, and had reached a number well over a hundred, I decided to skip the omnium gatherum protocol altogether and, instead, to mention only a few indispensable names. As I had in *Popes and Politics,* I began with my own Shadrach, Meshach, and Abednego — who are still managing to survive "the fiery furnace of contemporary American life" — although the musical setting of that trio is not high on their list of favorites.

First, I must mention William B. Eerdmans, my publisher, who has shown that what couldn't be achieved in New York or London or San Francisco — an independent, genuinely ecumenical, and quality-oriented religious house — could be achieved in (of all places) Grand Rapids. He has also assembled a team that has proved to be close to nonpareil, a team that is best represented by my patently overworked but patiently understanding editor, Jennifer Hoffman. In that same broad arena of publishing, I must take this opportunity to also extol — however tardily — the comparably outstanding team created by Werner Mark Linz and led by Ulla Schnell in the aftermath of the demise of Herder and Herder, when Linz was engaged in an ecumenical publishing program whose public motto was, in fact, "a commitment to excellence." The consequences over half a century of that decision have rightly won him the plaudits of everyone associated with Continuum and its various offshoots, whether it be in the work of Evander Lomke and of Gene Gollogly, or of several others too numerous to mention.

More recently, there is Jamie Manson, who was thanked in *Popes and Politics* as deserving "a plurality of *kudoi*" for her contribution to that book, and who is now doubly deserving for her contribution to this one. Then there are the early supporters of the project, including Eve C. Zyzik at U of C, Santa Cruz, who analyzed Pio Nono's address to the women of Rome long before it became notoriously misread by others. Also reading the text in its early phases was Ronald J. Rychlak, whose legal defense of Pius XII I admire, knowing he may not embrace my views on the present American episcopate. Then, I must mention the best meditation guide this side of Thich Nhat Hahn, the Yogini, Pam O'Brien. Brenda de Geer has kept my accounts on the straight and narrow, and *pari passu* myself as well. Pam Kirk — who initiated my relationship with the apostle of animal rights, Andrew Linzey — our authority on Sor Juana Ines de la Cruz, and her husband, Ed Rappaport, brought further confirmation to the story of Pius XII's audience with "Refugee," the story that is the climax of this book. Most recently, personal thanks are owed to Rich Toepfer, who opened a window of memories, closed for over sixty years, on St. Mel's High School in Chicago. Since working on his first book, Francis Schüssler Fiorenza has displayed a vast range of theological knowledge, without being a theological know-it-all. And lastly, Thomas ("Tom") Niforatos, who transformed a Galleon into a Carolingian argosy.

To everybody mentioned here or lauded in the text, I say, "Toughly I hope ye may thole." To myself, I say, as I did in the epigraph to *The Range of Commitment:* "Tomorrow to fresh fields and pastures new" — as I return to my first love, not the criticism of ideologues, but the criticism of literature *tout court.*

Index

Index

Index

Index